Upon My Husband's Death

STUDIES IN MEDIEVAL AND EARLY MODERN CIVILIZATION
Marvin B. Becker, General Editor

Charity and Children in Renaissance Florence:
The Ospedale degli Innocenti, 1410–1536
  Philip Gavitt

Humanism in Crisis: The Decline of the French Renaissance
  Philippe Desan, editor

Upon My Husband's Death: Widows in the Literature
and Histories of Medieval Europe
  Louise Mirrer, editor

Upon My Husband's Death

*Widows in the Literature and Histories
of Medieval Europe*

Edited by
LOUISE MIRRER

Ann Arbor

THE UNIVERSITY OF MICHIGAN PRESS

Copyright © by the University of Michigan 1992
All rights reserved
Published in the United States of America by
The University of Michigan Press
Manufactured in the United States of America

1995   1994   1993   1992   4   3   2   1

Library of Congress Cataloging-in-Publication Data

Upon my husband's death : widows in the literature and histories of
medieval Europe / edited by Louise Mirrer.
    p.   cm. — (Studies in medieval and early modern civilization)
Includes bibliographical references and index.
ISBN 0-472-10257-5
    1. Widowhood—Europe—History. 2. Widows—Europe—Social
conditions. 3. Women—History—Middle Ages, 500–1500. 4. Women in
literature—History. I. Mirrer, Louise. II. Series.
HQ1058.E97U66   1992
305.48'9654—dc20   91-39974
                                                              CIP

A la muerte de mi marido,
poca cera y mucho pabilo.

(*Upon my husband's death,
little wax and a lot of wick.*)

—Medieval Castilian Proverb

Acknowledgments

This volume is the result of a collaborative effort, and I would like to thank, first of all, the contributors for their unfailing assistance and support. In particular, I would like to express my gratitude to Barbara Hanawalt, who so willingly helped with the various aspects of this project and who provided many thoughtful comments and suggestions. I am grateful also to Thelma Fenster, who directed my attention to the work of Liliane Dulac.

Scholars other than the collaborators also cooperated in the making of this volume. John Boswell, Edward Peters, and Susan Mosher Stuard were all kind enough to identify potential contributors of essays in history; Robert Halle tracked down some obscure references for me in the British Museum Library and at the Cambridge Group for the History of Population and Social Structure; Lía Schwartz Lerner suggested I look at Castilian proverbs; and David Halle generously extended support and encouragement throughout. I am thankful to all of them for their help.

I would like to dedicate my own work on this volume to my grandmother, Kate Friedelbaum, a woman, widowed young, who continues to this day to provide a model of female strength and scholarship for her daughters, granddaughters, and great-granddaughters.

Funds from the National Endowment for the Humanities and from the Fordham University Research Council enabled me to bring this project to completion. For this support, I am truly grateful.

Contents

Introduction

Louise Mirrer

La mula buena, komo la biuda, gorda y andariega.
[*The good mule, like the widow, fat and fond of roving.*]

Antes biuda que casada.
[*Better to be a widow than a married woman.*]

—Combet 1971, 435–36

Widowhood was an ambiguous state in medieval culture. On the one hand, it was regarded as a stage in a woman's life that endowed her with the potential for a special grace. Widows could devote themselves to God in a way they could not as married women. Freed from carnal cares, they could almost approach virgins in holy status. Widows were also vulnerable, needing and deserving the special protection of the Church and of knights. They could be seen, too, as courageous examples, carrying on the work of husbands, rearing children against odds, and discretely pursuing correct political ends. So valued might society find their contributions that they were permitted by law to work independently in agriculture, business, crafts, and administration.

On the other hand, widowhood was regarded as a state that freed women to act on the wanton, whorish, and unprincipled tendencies ascribed to women in general by medieval misogynist writers. Widows would be sexually voracious once deprived of their husbands' company in bed. They would be loose women, like prostitutes. And, left to their own devices in the marketplace or on the farm, they would squander their husbands' fortune and their sons' inheritance. Young, beautiful widows were seen as a snare for the devil. Although the Church and moral advisers generally counseled widows not to remarry—Jerome termed widowhood the "second rank" (after lifelong virginity) of purity [*secundum punicitiae gradum*] (*Epistula* 22.15)—they encouraged attractive young widows to repeat their nuptial vows.

At the heart of many of the ambiguities of medieval widowhood was the perception—if not the reality—that widows had more options than either married or single women. Popular medieval portrayals of widows drew on this perception in their descriptions of the festal bearing of women upon their husbands' death and the delight these women took in their emancipation from the bonds of marriage. Learned texts, too, often centered around the relative "liberation" widowhood offered to women,[1] depicting widows as independently integrated into the fabric of medieval life in ways that wives were not. (Even the poor widow in Chaucer's *Nun's Priest's Tale* is represented this way, busily laboring as a dairywoman on a manor farm.)

Legal and historical documents of the period suggest that, indeed, widows did, in important ways, have more options than either single or married women. In these documents are descriptions of what women actually did as widows in medieval society, as well as examples of peasant, bourgeoise, and noble widows who independently chose their own partners when they decided to remarry and administered wealth and property on their own.

Yet any understanding of medieval widows as "liberated" must be tempered by the larger picture of medieval society, where women, irrespective of their marital status, faced restrictions based on their sex, and where the association of widowhood with poverty could be expressed in a byword, as in the common expression, "the widow's *mite*." That medieval widowhood might represent liberation—and, consequently, a "golden age"[2]—for women is also challenged by a more nuanced assessment of literary images, for, in texts that were composed almost exclusively by men, the portrayal of widows taking pleasure in, and prospering from, their husbands' death surely responded to the gender ideologies of an antifeminist society.

The contributions to this volume address both the larger picture of widows in medieval society and the complicated issue of widows' representation in medieval literature. They also look at how real widows of different social classes functioned in the medieval world and at how these women operated within such key intellectual structures as canon law. Posing such provocative and challenging questions as, "To what extent did medieval widows—but not other women—have opportunities to enjoy public authority?"; "Why were legal issues concerning widows so common during the medieval period?"; "What were the consequences of widows' litigation?"; "How were the theories of academic canonists regarding widows implemented during the Middle Ages?"; "How was a literary text's emphasis on a woman's marital status likely to have been interpreted by a contemporary audience?"; and "In what respect can medieval literary works be said to have made manifest the historical evidence for widows' participation in the public sphere?"; the essays provide a rich and stimulating discussion of women on their own in medieval Europe.

The widows examined in this volume come from such diverse texts as the Castilian *Libro de Buen Amor* and *Romance de Fonte Frida;* the Catalan chivalresque novel of *Curial e Güelfa;* the French *fabliau, Livre des Trois Vertus, Yvain,* and *Widow of Ephesus* tale; the Italian *Del Reggimento e Costumi di Donna;* and the records of church and secular courts, private correspondence, rabbinical *responsa,* and histories of medieval England, France, Italy, Germany, and Spain. They are peasants, nobles, merchants, and scholars; and they are the creations of writers of fiction as well as flesh-and-blood women whose stories come to life through legal, historical, and personal documents.

With the wide range of situations the widows in this volume represent, it is remarkable that so many of the essays find the same themes, concerns, and attitudes reflected in the geographically and culturally diverse works and documents that they treat. The essays suggest that these commonalities, at least in part, have to do with the fact that medieval widows had some access to power, prestige, and authority in the public sphere because they were not confined, in the role of *wife,* to the private domain. But the essays point out, too, that such similarities as existed among different widows' conditions were intimately related to the fact that widows' access to the public sphere was limited during the Middle Ages, that it nearly always fell short of direct participation in the workings of politics and the holding of public office.

Indeed, only three of the widows discussed in this volume approached the pinnacle of medieval society's power structures; the two widowed queens and the mistress of a deceased king whom Clara Estow describes in her essay on widows in late medieval Castilian historical literature. Estow shows that these women (Leonor de Guzmán, María de Portugal, and Catalina of Lancaster) enjoyed sanctioned authority in the public sphere for a time, exercising the full extent of royal power and assuming personae independent from their husbands. Yet in reality, only one of the widows Estow discusses legitimately determined policy and controlled expenditures in the Kingdom of Castile. This was Catalina, the widow of Enrique III, who had been designated coregent in her husband's will.

Some of the women Cheryl Tallan examines in her essay on Jewish widows also managed, to a degree, to command the attention of the public domain, though they did not assume personae independent from their husbands. These women took over the leadership positions of their late husbands, who had been prominent rabbis in Spain and in France, and gave advice to followers on matters similar to those on which their husbands had ruled.

Filling a husband's occupational position did much to enhance the public stature of medieval widows. This strategy, as well as other, similar strategies, which included engaging in trade, renting and selling land, and lending money, is at the heart of many medieval widows' assumption of positions of importance and influence in the public sphere. But it could also be a crucial strategy that they employed to secure their continued maintenance. Barbara Hanawalt's and Judith Bennett's essays on medieval English widows make this clear. Both argue that it was in assuming the economic functions of their dead husbands and in asserting control over their dower or inheritance that many medieval widows succeeded in making a definite impact on society.

While Hanawalt's essay focuses on urban widows and Bennett's on rural widows, both essays describe women who responded to the responsibilities of widowhood with vigor, actively participating in the economic and social structures of their communities and defending their financial interests. Both essays also direct attention to another recurring theme in the discussion of medieval widowhood, that is, widows' involvement in disputes and cases argued before medieval courts of law. Bennett notes that widows took an active part in the salient legal issues of householders in the medieval English countryside, accepting responsibility for the actions of dependents and pledging for them, but she also describes widows' implication in a darker side of litigation—that is, formal conflict with family over the disposition of land provided for them by their deceased husbands.

Hanawalt's study, which uses the London plea rolls and wills of the fourteenth and fifteenth centuries, focuses particular attention on the legal problems of seeking to recover property from family and tenants. The women she discusses, largely widows of comfortable London craftsmen or wealthy merchants, had to sue to receive their full *dower*—that is, the property settled on them by their husbands at the time of their espousal. Hanawalt's essay demonstrates widows' access to the law courts in the medieval urban English setting. Indeed, her study is facilitated by the voluminous court materials that chronicle the progress of these widows' myriad litigations.

Evidence of widows' active participation in the medieval law courts is found throughout Europe, with dower disputes predominating. Because these cases could touch on issues fundamental to medieval economic and social organization—control over such valuable properties as mines and the formulation of rules of succession and inheritance—their resolutions often had far-reaching applications in the world of politics, law, and finance. Thus, while women were not highly visible participants in the power politics of the Middle Ages in general, they did sometimes, through their presence in the courts as widows or through their control of their dower, play a key role.

Harry Miskimin's essay takes up the issue of widows' standing before the law courts of France and their use of it. Miskimin studies fifteenth-century appellate case law as recorded in the *Registre du Parlement* in Paris and relates how medieval French widows brought or argued cases before the highest French court—in the expectation of a favorable result. He finds that one of the most important consequences of a major class of litigation involving widows had to do with currency. His case studies exhibit the manner in which a widow's dower rights could conflict with currency legislation and interfere with the effort to develop a true legal tender currency. Furthermore, widows used their standing before the courts to establish their economic and inheritance rights.

Miskimin's essay discusses, too, the participation of French widows in decisions that defined the relationship between secular and ecclesiastical courts. Since widows generally enjoyed special protection under canon law, their privileged position undercut civil court decisions and raised some serious questions about the power of canonical judges and their limitations. Thus widows were permitted, for example, to apply to the Church to overrule the decisions of civil authorities.

The Church, of course, also had a long-standing moral obligation to protect widows, for Church fathers attached great importance to continent widowhood and special legal protections enhanced the Church's ability to support widows in upholding the doctrinal ideal of chastity.

James Brundage's essay addresses the objectives and procedures for, and the implications of, Church intervention in cases concerning widows. He discusses the Church's particular obligation toward widows as detailed in works produced during the mature phase of the development of canon law—that is, from 1140, when Gratian's *Concordia discordantium canonum* appeared. Widows, subsumed under the larger category of *miserabiles personae* [disadvantaged persons], were a special target of Church policies concerning poor relief and could appeal to Church courts for intervention when secular judges failed to do justice to them.

Was every disadvantaged widow entitled to the protection of canonical courts? Brundage's essay shows that the particular criteria that qualified widows for Church protection had to do with the type of hardship they had suffered as well as their social standing and economic resources. In this he makes clear the real hardships that medieval widows faced—whether financial, social, or physical—and the concrete basis for their *miserabiles* status.

If the Church carved out a special niche for widows in medieval society, so, too, did the widows themselves. Tallan studied widows such as Licoricia, a well-known Jewish businesswoman in medieval Winchester whose clients included the clergy of the local cathedral. Hanawalt describes English urban widows such as Emma, widow of William Hatfeld, who carried on her husband's chandler business as *femme sole*. Bennett demonstrates that a rural Englishwoman such as widow Alice Avice purchased and sold land on her own. Miskimin's essay points to widows like the former wife of Raoul Goatre, a Frenchwoman, who won the right to control and draw iron from a mine.

Moving to aristocratic women, Linda Mitchell's essay looks at three generations of Mortimer widows. These Welsh noblewomen appointed bailiffs to oversee property, managed households, raised younger children, arranged marriages, controlled wardships, transacted business, paid debts, and performed service for property held in fee. Mitchell argues that, while the theorists of feudal and common law did not spell out the dowager's place in the social and political milieus, the daily activities of noble widows in Wales made transparent the important role of these women in the public sphere. While noble widows could not participate in many male activities, such as sitting on royal councils or being appointed as sheriffs, widows' baronial duties and their activities as landlords were nevertheless comparable to those of their male peers.

Joel Rosenthal's essay assesses the lives of widows of English peers whose husbands died violently as a result of dynastic struggles and the

War of the Roses. Rosenthal found that the lives of such peeresses could be shattered by politicomilitary widowhood, for they were placed under the peculiar burden of their dead husbands' sentences. These widows paid fines, forfeited honors, and lost their estates. Rosenthal writes, for example, of Anne Fitzhugh, widow of Francis, lord Lovel, whose dismal circumstances as a war widow aroused pity from even the hard-hearted and tight-fisted Henry VII. Even war widows who did not suffer great economic loss experienced great hardship, for they were socially tainted and disgraced as a consequence of the circumstances that surrounded their husbands' death. The experiences of these peeresses leads Rosenthal to speculate that perhaps aristocratic widows may have, in some respects, been more constrained than less-prosperous widows in other social classes.

Ann Crabb discusses a Florentine widow who similarly endured economic and social hardships because of the circumstances that surrounded her husband's death. Alessandra Macinghi Strozzi's husband, a fifteenth-century Florentine political figure, died in exile. For Alessandra, widowhood brought disaster as well as empowerment. The special conditions of her widowhood forced her into the role of agent and representative of the family, a role normally unavailable to patrician women. Crabb speaks, in her essay, of Alessandra's independence during her widowhood—her guardianship and financial support of her five children, her control over her finances, and her political efforts. But she writes also of Alessandra's loneliness and longing for what she had lost through her political widowhood.

Through Alessandra Macinghi Strozzi's letters, Crabb is able dramatically to reconstruct her story. Alessandra's letters relate, among other things, how she worked to end the political exile of her sons, how she negotiated their return, how she found them wives, and how she suffered emotionally and economically because of her political widowhood.

Similarly, we know of Christine de Pizan's hardships as a widow through words written in her own hand. In response to the financial exigencies of widowhood, she turned to writing and thereby became one of the best known of medieval widows. Christine, who married at fifteen and was widowed at twenty-five, turned to professional writing in order to support her three children and her mother. Her work specifically addresses the problems surrounding widowhood, which ranged from the challenge of maintaining a modest demeanor to the difficulties of hiring trustworthy servants.

Liliane Dulac's contribution to this volume, appearing in English for the first time in a translation by Thelma Fenster, studies Christine's advice to widows in the *Livre des Trois Vertus*. Dulac shows how Christine's work put rhetoric to the service of a moral and political pedagogy whose principles guided literate women of every rank. She discusses the tenderness and emotion of Christine's autobiographical pages, but highlights the rigor and severity of the ideal Christine proposed for widows.

The material obstacles for widows described in Hanawalt's, Bennett's, Miskimin's, Brundage's, and Mitchell's essays find echoes in Christine's work. Christine spoke of threats to the sovereign widow's dower and goods, of dissension between barons, of attacks from enemies, of internal revolts, of extortion, and of the theft of taxes by farmers. She drew attention to the assaults by *felons* [traitors] against goods and of lawsuits that widows of lower stations suffered. She placed in relief, too, the difficulties that the customs of the time entailed for women and women's multiple inferiorities in the social world.

Francesco da Barberino, writing about a century earlier than Christine, also gave advice to widows. Dulac's essay compares the Italian writer's *Del Reggimento e Costumi di Donna* to Christine's *Trois Vertus*. While the two works in many respects differ, their shared definition of the social category "widowhood" is central to both an understanding of medieval widowhood and of didactic, particularly moral, discourse directed toward women.

Dulac's essay underscores the ambivalent views medieval society had of widows. On the one hand the status was endowed with dignity, allowing widows into spheres not ordinarily open to women. On the other hand, in theological, didactic, and vernacular literature, widows were chastised and even ridiculed when they moved out of the typical spheres of women's activity.

That widows were frequently projected onto the pages of medieval literary works no doubt had much to do with medieval writers' fascination with ambiguity and their recognition that the widow was, par excellence, an ambiguous human sign. A woman neither chaste nor married who might claim special protection from Church and secular institutions alike but who might also act on her own, the widow was often portrayed as both needful of safeguards against men and as a formidable enemy of men. While, for example, Church authorities made special efforts to defend the widow, they also lamented her tendency toward incontinence and sometimes attempted to control her behavior by limiting some of her legal capacities.

In popular as well as in learned texts, the ambiguities of widowhood were drawn on to emphasize the frightening excess to which widows might potentially enjoy their independence. They were portrayed, for example, as requiring constant reminders of the virtues of continence, for their liberation from male control was dangerously played out in their overindulgence of sexual desire (widows were proverbially pictured on the lookout for a new sexual partner as soon as their husbands were buried—"Llorar poko i buskar otro" [cry a little and look for another (man)], to cite one example from the Castilian tradition [Combet 1971, 435–36]).

The sexual excess to which medieval widows were supposedly enticed as a result of their "liberation" from male control is at the heart of Heather Arden's essay on grief, widowhood, and women's sexuality in medieval French literature. Arden looks at three versions of the *Widow of Ephesus* fable, two *fabliaux* about newly bereaved widows, and Chrétien de Troye's *Yvain*. She finds that widows in medieval French literature were portrayed among the most lecherous of women; fear of pregnancy afforded the only brake on their wanton behavior and was a chief reason for their remarriage.

Why should widows have been pictured this way? Arden argues that the texts operated within the matrix of sanctions and affirmations of a misogynist society. Depicting widows as weeping uncontrollably upon their husbands' death, then immediately, or almost immediately, satisfying their enormous sexual appetites with new men, they presented incontrovertible evidence of women's variability and untrustworthiness. The texts that Arden studied revealed medieval men's attitudes toward, and fears of, women's extramarital sexuality. For, above all, the texts addressed husbands' fantasies about their wives' infidelity. In showing how difficult it was for women to practice sexual restraint and how even the Church's admonishments were useless in inhibiting their propensity for sexual adventurism, the texts Arden studied cautioned men to keep their wives constantly in tow.

Since women could most freely act out their wanton sexuality when their husbands were not around to control them, it comes as no surprise that the texts Arden studied used widows, rather than wives, to convey their warning. Literary examples graphically pictured what widows would do—cut the head, break the teeth, cut the side, even castrate the body of their dead husbands—if they believed they could thus better appease their animal-like lust. Widows were indeed a perfect vehicle for describing the conduct of women out of men's control.

The question of widows' remarriage was another point that raised the ambiguities of widowhood. Canon law recommended against remarriage and widows who remarried before the end of a stipulated waiting period might be subject to ecclesiastical penalties.[3] Law codes that granted the widow broad civil rights might also see her as a threat to society, capable of deceiving—even murdering—her husband. The medieval Castilian *Siete Partidas,* for example, suggested that permission for a widow's immediate remarriage might provide her the motivation to do away with her husband.[4] On the other hand, remarriage served to put these newly single women once again under male control and seemed to channel their sexuality into legitimate unions.

The ambiguities of widows' remarriage provided medieval male authors with a special opportunity to make a point about the ambivalence of human signs. Juan Ruiz, the Archpriest of Hita, recognized this in the *Libro de Buen Amor,* a fourteenth-century Castilian text whose focus on the ambiguity and complexity of the human sign was its sine qua non. In the longest episode of the work, the widow, Doña Endrina (Lady Sloe Plum), is pursued by, and ultimately married to, the secular alter ego of the work's first-person clerical protagonist, Don Melón de la Huerta (Sir Melon of the Garden).

Louise Vasvari's essay focuses on the *Doña Endrina* episode of the *Libro de Buen Amor.* She sets the work in the context of popular and literary traditions concerning the widow that prevailed during the Middle Ages, pointing out that, in general, the ambiguous social category "widowhood" fared badly in medieval European literature. Like Arden, Vasvari locates the reasons for the appearance of widows in so many antifeminist texts and for widows' almost exclusively negative portrayal in men's fear of women's sexual excess, which the imagined uncontrollability of the vidual sexual appetite made patent. Yet, Vasvari points out that one genre in which widows did tend to be favorably treated was the stylized debate over the relative advantages and disadvantages of sexual relations with women of various conditions.

Vasvari notes that the comparative accessibility and sexual ardor of virgins, wives, widows, and nuns was a popular question in medieval texts, related to such other love debates as the advantages, for a woman, of taking a cleric versus a chevalier as a lover. She argues that, in the

Doña Endrina episode, the widow's representation drew on such debates, particularly as formulated in the surrounding popular oral culture and in the erotic literary tradition of the medieval Latin *comedia* and vernacular genres. Doña Endrina, Vasvari says, embodied the image of widow-as-*fembra plaçentera*—that is, that category of pleasing woman whose reputation had made her even more so because she offered men a slightly fairer chance of success.

While Vasvari's essay, like Arden's, shows that widows might typically be depicted as faithless and as having an overdeveloped sexual appetite, her attempt to untangle the intricate tissue of threads out of which the medieval literary image of widows might, in fact, have been constructed leads her to an understanding of the *Doña Endrina* episode as primarily reflective of popular oral and literary traditions rather than of the moral or didactic intent of the text's author.

Philip Gericke, who writes on the medieval Spanish *Romance de Fonte Frida,* also underscores the role of tradition in the work he studied. He notes that *Fonte Frida,* a classic ballad that treats the ideal of a conjugal fidelity so powerful that it transcends the death of a spouse, drew on symbols and motifs dating from pre-Christian antiquity. He shows how the protagonist of the work, a turtledove—an animal that early-on represented the monogamous spouse but later came to symbolize chaste widowhood—corresponded to a Christian feminine ethos and therefore reflected a universal medieval ideal for women.

Did the ballad also have a direct, immediate, or specific reference to widowhood in the medieval Spanish context? Gericke believes that, while it might be tempting to argue that it did, in fact, *Fonte Frida*'s exaltation of chaste widowhood expressed an ideal that probably bore no relationship at all to contemporary reality or to the values of a particular people.

In his essay, Gericke notes that some ballads did, indeed, reflect events of immediate relevance (e.g., political disputes) as well as the values and concerns of the people among whom the texts circulated. And, although Gericke detects no specific reference to a uniquely Hispanic ethos in *Fonte Frida,* he nevertheless maps out the different motivations that might have led to this kind of a reference in other texts. Montserrat Piera's and Donna Rogers' contribution takes up this problem of relating literary images to the attitudes of a particular people in a particular historical, cultural, and economic context.

Piera and Rogers studied the fifteenth-century Catalan chivalresque novel of *Curial e Güelfa,* an anonymous work that made manifest the perquisites of widowhood for a woman of high social standing. Their essay suggests, among other things, that certain patterns of medieval Catalan society might have motivated some of the elements included in the text, for the story focuses attention on such details as the will made by its protagonist's husband on his deathbed. In this will, Güelfa, a young noblewoman, is specifically decreed by her husband Lady of Milan—and all that entailed—*whether or not she remarried*. In analyzing *Curial e Güelfa*, Piera and Rogers looked at studies of wills made in Barcelona from 1350 to 1410, letters from fifteenth-century Catalan widows, and a doctrinal treatise of the late fourteenth century. They found that, while *Curial e Güelfa* specifically recorded the widow's inheritance as *not* conditional upon her future nuptial activities, almost all Catalan wills of the period did, in fact, impose conditions. They also found clear-cut arguments for the widow's chastity in doctrinal writing. Thus, they note, *Curial e Güelfa* departed from Catalan custom and doctrinal ideals in its treatment of widowhood. As an explanation, Piera and Rogers suggest that the text might actually have been arguing for widows' remarriage. For in *Curial e Güelfa*, not only is the widow specifically *not* discouraged from remarrying, but she is portrayed as using her fortune and the social standing she has acquired as a result of her dead husband's will to transform a young man of humble birth into a suitable marriage partner for herself. Indeed, the widow's successful accomplishment of this goal is what gives the text its happy ending.

Piera and Rogers term *Curial e Güelfa* a novel of transition between the medieval and early modern periods. Is it possible to understand the text as ushering in a new, early modern, way of thinking about widowhood? Piera and Rogers make no sweeping claims, but their essay does demonstrate the significance of Güelfa's husband's will in its explicit rejection of conditions that would have inhibited her remarriage. They also point to Güelfa's description in the text as having "everything save a husband," and the dependence of the work's happy resolution on the widow finding a new husband.

It is difficult to make generalizations about any change in widows' status during the Middle Ages that apply to all countries and classes. There is, however, much evidence to suggest a change in attitude toward widows during the early modern period.

In many parts of early modern Europe laws specifically singled out the widow for regulation, significantly modifying her authority and rights.[5] The gild ordinances of sixteenth- and seventeenth-century Germany, for example, limited the rights of widows to carry on their husband's shop after his death (Wiesner 1986, 194–95). Earlier gild ordinances made no mention at all of widows, who were free to continue operating the shop—indeed to run it on their own—after their husbands died (Wiesner 1986, 194–95).[6] In France, the 1560 edict of King Francis II reacted to the independence of widows and their ability to manage their own finances by placing limits on the gifts that a widow with children could give a second husband in marriage (Diefendorf 1982, 379). Whereas such kinds of restrictions regarding freedom to dispose of properties had earlier applied equally to men and women, now the changes were aimed strictly and solely at widows (389, 394). In Florence, a 1415 statute replaced usufructuary rights with alimentary rights, thus readjusting rules affecting female inheritance to stress women's dependence on support coming from property controlled by a man (Kuehn 1987, 16). In Nordic countries, the Reformation's message that marriage was the highest and most desirable state for women eliminated the widow's special spiritual space in religion (Jacobsen 1989, 56–67). The change in custom in Cheltenham in 1625 deprived the widow of her right to the whole of her husband's tenement and, consequently, of her ability to shape her family's destiny (Paget 1982, 173).

In early modern European literature, the image of the proverbially "merry" widow competed with an image of the widow as sadly alienated from her society. Widows, in many works of the period, were portrayed as bereft not only of husbands, but of beauty, wealth, and friends. These texts made clear that it was in marriage that women might flourish, not widowhood. The Elizabethan poem *An Olde Womans Tale in hir Solitarie Cell*[7] is but one salient example of this attitude. The poem relates the experience of a man who, walking deep in the wood, stumbles upon an old widow living in her solitary cell of a forest cave. The widow, described as "sickly, pale, and melancholic," explains to her visitor how she first "snared" her husband, then married him, flourishing at his side "in wealth, beauty, and many other things" for twenty years. Her "woe," she declares, only began when she was forty and her husband died, leaving her with three children. The woman complains to the adventurer that her husband did not think about her well-being as a widow when he wrote his will—according, she adds, to the "vile custom" of

England, which discouraged men from considering their wives' future. Thus forgotten by her husband and her society, she retreats to a cave in the wood, where she remains invisible to all but the chance adventurer.

An Olde Womans Tale in hir Solitarie Cell is not the only early modern European text in which widows are depicted as alienated from friends, family, and society. Other writings of the period provide many similar examples. Interestingly—and suggestively—it is this early modern image of the sadly alienated widow that has often prevailed in European literature to the present day. The modern writer, Federico García Lorca, for example, always portrays widowhood—the most common fate of his female characters—as a time of intense isolation and frustration.[8]

Do the early modern restrictions placed on widows and such literary images as implied that widows were alienated from their societies suggest a revival of the notion that medieval widowhood was a time of relative "liberation" for women—a "golden age"? The essays in this volume, which point to a special niche for widows in medieval society, do seem to suggest that the early modern period might, indeed, have marked a deterioration in widows' status. Yet this hardly means that medieval widows were all merry. In their careful analyses of widowhood in medieval societies, intellectual structures, and literary images, the essays in this volume paint a much more balanced picture of medieval widowhood. They show that, while there may have been a significant number of options for widows during the Middle Ages, not all widows could take advantage of them. And they make clear that widows almost never were allowed to participate directly in the workings of medieval politics or economics. Moreover, the essays point out that, while widows' merriment upon the death of their husbands may have been commonplace in medieval literary texts, this image was probably not generated by the life stories of any real medieval widows, but instead by the traditions, ideals, and attitudes of an antifeminist society.

This volume does not pretend to cover the literature and histories of all of medieval Europe. Those wishing to pursue the topic further, in other locations and texts, are directed to the extensive bibliographies at the end of each essay.

This volume does not cover, either, the lives of medieval Europe's most downtrodden widows. Indeed, almost all of the widows studied here were "better off" than other medieval women precisely because they had the freedom to spend their wealth as they saw fit. Yet, while it would be important to study those medieval women whose widowhood exacerbated their already dire financial straits, these widows are sparsely—if at all—described in the documents of the period. It is thus impossible to study them properly.

Finally, the essays in this volume do not speculate about how or why the position of widows might have changed in the early modern period. Only further study of this topic will provide a locus for understanding the problem. Indeed, it is hoped that this question—as well as others posed but not answered in these essays —will make interesting points of departure for future work in the field.

NOTES

I would like to thank Barbara Hanawalt for reading two drafts of this essay. Her comments and suggestions came from such far-flung locations as Minnesota and Berlin, and I truly appreciate all of her generous assistance. Any errors of fact or of style that remain were made by me and in spite of her. Translations of the epigraph proverbs are mine.

1. For a modern critical assessment of the widow's relative "liberation," see Franklin 1986.

2. In her Introduction to *Women and Work in Preindustrial Europe,* Hanawalt notes that a search for an "El Dorado" has characterized a number of investigations into the condition of medieval women (1986, xiv). In the context of her study of preindustrial women's work, she finds little evidence to support this quest. Hanawalt does make the point that, in widowhood, a woman could have real opportunities as *femme sole.* But she adds that the widow's capacity to carry on alone varied greatly with local custom and the pressures of the marriage market (xi).

3. The manuscript version of Brundage's "Widows as Disadvantaged Persons in Medieval Canon Law" (1–3) discusses this. Brundage notes that social policy might also inhibit a widow's remarriage and that civil penalties might be imposed on her when she failed to observe the one-year waiting period. Brundage cites the following sources: Michael M. Sheehan, "The Influence of Canon Law on the Property Rights of Married women in England," *Medieval Studies* 25 (1963): 109–24; Philippe de Beaumanoir, *Coutumes de Beauvaisis* 13.442, 456, ed. A. Salmon, 2 vols. (Paris: A. e J. Picard, 1899–1900; repr. 1970), 1:211, 219; Thomas Izvicki, "'Ista questio est antiqua': Two consilia on Widows' Rights," *Bulletin of Medieval Canon Law* 8 (1978): 47– 50; *Las siete partidas del rey don*

Alfonso el Sabio, cotejadas con varios codices antiguos por la Real Academia de la Historia 4.12.3, 3 vols. (Madrid: Imprenta real, 1807; repr. 1972), 3:83; *Le livre au roi,* 30 and *Assises des bourgeois,* 166–67; *Recueil des historiens des croisades,* Lois, 2 vols. (Paris: Imprimérie royale, 1841–43), 1:626–27 and 2:113–14; Sue Sheridan Walker, "Widow and Ward: The Feudal Law of Child Custody in Medieval England," in *Women in Medieval Society,* ed. Susan Mosher Stuard (Philadelphia: University of Pennsylvania Press, 1976), 159– 72, and Walker, "Free Consent and Marriage of Feudal Wards in Medieval England," *Journal of Medieval History* 8 (1982): 123–34; and James Brundage, "Marriage Law in the Latin Kingdom of Jerusalem," in *Outremer: Studies in the History of the Crusading Kingdom of Jerusalem Presented to Joshua Prawer,* ed. B. Z. Kedar, H. E. Mayer, and R. C. Samil (Jerusalem: Yad Izhak Ben-Zvi Institute, 1982), 270–71.

4. See Sponsler 1982, 129, for further discussion.

5. See Howell 1986 for discussion. The Netherlands appears to have been an exception to this trend. See Wyntjes 1982, but note her remark on how widows' rights changed when New Amsterdam became New York (404).

6. Wiesner (1986, 194) notes that "limitations on the rights of widows are the most common and widespread of all restrictions [on women in textile occupations]."

7. I came across the manuscript of this little-known poem in the British Museum Library. While there is a newer edition of the text with commentary (see An Olde Womans Tale), there is, to date, no discussion of the interesting image the poem presents of the widow.

8. See Burton 1983 for further discussion.

BIBLIOGRAPHY

An Olde Womans Tale. *The Lamentation of Troy for the Death of Hector whereunto is annexed An Olde Womans Tale in hir Solitarie Cell,* by I. O. (1594) now first attributed to Sir John Ogle (1569–1640). Ed. Elkin Calhoun Wilson. Chicago: Institute of Elizabethan Studies, 1959.

Bennett, Judith. *Women in the Medieval English Countryside.* New York: Oxford University Press, 1987.

Bornstein, Diane. *The Lady in the Tower: Medieval Courtesy Literature for Women.* Hamden, Conn.: Shoe String Press, 1983.

Brundage, James. *Widows as Disadvantaged Persons in Medieval Canon Law.* Manuscript.

Burton, Julianne. "The Greatest Punishment: Female and Male in Lorca's Tragedies." In *Women in Hispanic Literature: Icons and Fallen Idols,* ed. Beth Miller, 259–79. Berkeley: University of California Press, 1983.

Combet, Louis. *Recherches sur le "Refranero" Castillan*. Paris: Société de l'Edition "Les Belles Lettres," 1971.

Diefendorf, Barbara B. "Widowhood and Remarriage in Sixteenth-Century Paris." *Journal of Family History* 7 (1982): 379–95.

Erler, Mary, and Maryanne Kowaleski. "Introduction." In *Women and Power in the Middle Ages,* ed. Mary Erler and Maryanne Kowaleski, 1–18. Athens: University of Georgia Press, 1988.

Ferguson, Margaret W., Maureen Quilligan, and Nancy J. Vickers, eds. *Rewriting the Renaissance: The Discourses of Sexual Difference in Early Modern Europe*. Chicago: University of Chicago Press, 1986.

Franklin, Peter. "Peasant Widows' 'Liberation' and Remarriage Before the Black Death." *Economic History Review* 39 (May, 1986): 186–204.

Goldberg, Harriet. "Two Parallel Medieval Commonplaces: Antifeminism and Antisemitism in the Hispanic Literary Tradition." In *Aspects of Jewish Culture in the Middle Ages,* ed. Paul Szarmach, 85–119. Albany: SUNY Press, 1979.

Hanawalt, Barbara, ed. *Women and Work in Preindustrial Europe*. Bloomington: Indiana University Press, 1986.

Howell, Martha C. *Women, Production, and Patriarchy in Late Medieval Cities*. Chicago: University of Chicago Press, 1986.

Jacobsen, Grethe. "Nordic Women and the Reformation." In *Women in Reformation and Counterreformation Europe,* ed. Sherrin Marshall, 47–67. Bloomington: Indiana University Press, 1989.

Kuehn, Thomas. "Some Ambiguities of Female Inheritance Ideology in the Renaissance." *Continuity and Change* 2 (May, 1987): 11–36.

McNamara, JoAnn, and Suzanne Wemple. "The Power of Women through the Family in Medieval Europe, 500–1100." In Erler and Kowaleski, 1988, 83–101.

Paget, Mary. "A Study of Manorial Custom Before 1625." *Local Historian* 15 (August, 1982): 166–73.

Power, Eileen. *Medieval Women,* ed. M. M. Postan. Cambridge: Cambridge University Press, 1975.

Roelker, Nancy Lyman. "Papers from the 1981 Berkshire Conference: Widowhood and Rational Domesticity: Modes of Independence for Women in Early Modern Europe." *Journal of Family History* 7 (1982): 376–78.

Sponsler, Lucy A. "The Status of Married Women Under the Legal System of Spain." *Journal of Legal History* 3, no. 2 (1982): 125–52.

Wiesner, Merry E. "Spinsters and Seamstresses: Women in Cloth and Clothing Production." In Ferguson, Quilligan, and Vickers 1986, 191–205.

Wyntjes, Sherrin Marshall. "Survivors and Status: Widowhood and Family in the Early Modern Netherlands." *Journal of Family History* 7 (1982): 396–405.

Part 1
Lower- and Middle-Class Widows

Chapter 1

The Widow's Mite: Provisions for Medieval London Widows

Barbara A. Hanawalt

One of the recurrent themes of medieval prescriptive literature was the need to guard and preserve the provisions made for widows. The theme appeared in knight's vows, in sermons, and in literature. Those who deprived widows of their "mite" were singled out for condemnation from the pulpit, in chivalric stories, and in courts. The very special quality of the widow's "mite" was a popular theme in the Middle Ages. Among others, Langland referred to the superior holiness of the poor widow who gave her two mites (roughly 1/24*d.*), which was her sole support, compared to others who gave only a part of their abundant wealth. He was, of course, calling upon the poignant parable recorded in the gospels of Luke and Mark.[1] The emotional connection between the widow's defenselessness and her poverty were a constant theme in medieval culture. Historians know that, when a society repeatedly re-issues decrees and moral injunctions, it is because the problem continues to be an irritant, and so it was for the recovery of the widow's portion. Thus we find the king confirming that widow women of London are "freely absolved from all kinds of tallages, redemptions, and all kinds of contributions" because he is unwilling to infringe on their liberties and customs "but rather being willing to protect them and their liberties." He further ordered the city officials not to molest widows so that he will hear "no more clamour thereupon."[2]

The source of the widow's "mite" was usually her dower, or the property settled on her by her husband at the time of her espousal. The property would be for her use during her lifetime if she survived her husband; but she held it from her husband's heirs and could not alienate it. The widows that I will be investigating in this essay are seeking control over considerably more than a "mite" or two. They are, for the most part, widows of comfortable London craftsmen or wealthy merchants. Although not the stereotypical poor widow of medieval literature or even disadvantaged in the London law courts, the widows studied here did have to sue to receive their full dower from other parties who had a claim to it.

Because the widow's "mite" was so materially important to the widow, her former husband's heirs, and perhaps her new husband, the resultant disputes have given historians abundant information on the provisions that men made for their wives and the success of the wives in securing their continued means of living at the death of their husbands. Looking at fourteenth- and fifteenth-century London Husting Court rolls involving common pleas and wills, I will investigate the types of property left to women along with other provisions such as tools of a craft, charge over the property and persons of children born in wedlock, personal effects, and access to rooms and a hearth. I will also look at the struggles that some of these women had with family and others to keep their dower and suggest ways in which they used their dower.

London's multiple court systems supply ample evidence for the provisions and problems of London's widows. The mayor and aldermen held three courts, two of which involved the interests of widows directly. The Husting Court of Deeds and Wills recorded deeds of land transfers and those wills of Londoners who held real property within the city and were bequeathing it to other parties. It was not imperative to record wills involving property, but it was a wise precaution. When a man arranged for property to dower his wife or for additional bequests to her and his heirs, his executors were prudent if they enrolled the will with the Husting Court. The other court relating to widows that the mayor and aldermen conducted, the Husting Court of Common Pleas, dealt with the writs initiated by widows who felt that they had not received their full dower. The Husting courts mentioned in this study should not be confused with the royal court of Common Pleas held at Westminster. In addition to these two major sources, I have used other sets of wills for the diocese of London generated from ecclesiastical offices, petitions found in the Early Chancery Proceedings (fifteenth century) in the Public Record Office, and the London Consistory Court Rolls. Widows were ubiquitous in London, as they were in all European urban centers. The relatively late age of marriage for men and early age of marriage for women in European cities meant that many women experienced widowhood. The first concern of the bereaved widow was her life right to a portion of her former husband's estate; it would be her livelihood and perhaps her key to a future marriage.

London courts have a major advantage over the royal courts as a source for the study of widows and their access to their dower. The records of the Husting Court of Common Pleas are continuous from the late thirteenth into the fifteenth century. The population of London widows was large enough to provide an adequate statistical sample, but small enough that it was possible to follow the widows through a number of court sessions. Being limited to one locality meant that, in doing the research, the cases could be followed through to either conclusion or to disappearance from the record. The evidence presented here, therefore, represents a first comprehensive view of the ways widows pursued dower rights in London courts and of their success in doing so. In addition, this essay is the first to make use of the voluminous material in the Husting Court of Common Pleas. While not all questions can be answered in this preliminary study based on a sample of the available data, the evidence should provide an overview and point the way to more detailed studies of the fascinating topic of dower and the provisions made for widows in London.

Provisions for Widows

London widows enjoyed comfortable provision under the City's law.

> Wives, on the death of their husbands, by the custom of the city shall have their free bench. That is to say, that after the death of her husband the wife shall have of the tenement in the said city, whereof her husband died seised in fee, and in which tenement the said husband and wife dwelt together at the time of the husband's death, the hall, the principal private chamber, and the cellar wholly, and her use of the kitchen, stable, privy, and curtilage in common with the other necessaries appurtenant thereto, for the term of her life. And when she marries again, she shall lose the free bench and her dower therein, saving to her her dower of the other tenements as the law requires.[3]

London custom gave widows a third of the husband's estate for life if the marriage had produced children. In this case, a third would go to the children and the other third, after paying debts, for the good of the

testator's soul or as he directed. If the marriage had not produced children, the widow was entitled to half the estate for life. These benefits
went to the widow even if no written instrument preserved the dower
arrangement. At a minimum, London law put the dower as the "widow's
chamber," which included a portion of the husband's tenement that was
their dwelling: the hall, principal chamber, and cellar along with use of
kitchen, stable, garden, and privy. Alice, widow of John de Harwe, applied to the city for exactly those things when her husband died intestate
and the mayor awarded them.[4] The dower, as mentioned in the quotation above, did not depend on "pure widowhood" (the widow remaining
unmarried), but continued into subsequent marriages. While a remarried
widow lost free bench (the hearth and appurtenances in the principal
residence), she did not lose other dower property.[5]

As an alternative to simply letting the law take its course, the husband
could contract a specific dower at the time of their marriage or make
arrangements in a will.[6] By whatever arrangement, well-endowed widows were choice marriage partners. As a corollary, the long-lived widow
who monopolized a third of the property was a problem to her children,
for she hindered their full inheritance, or to her previous husband's
family, because she tied up their patrimony until she died.

When property was involved on both sides of the marriage, a prenup-
tial contract was common. The marriage contract consisted of an agreement on the groom's part to arrange for real property or rents to devolve
on his wife and children of their marriage if he died first (dower) and on
the bride's part to provide household goods and money toward founding
the new household (dowry or marriage portion).[7] The wife, therefore,
contributed capital to the new marriage partnership and in return she
could expect property or rents if she outlived her husband. A late
fifteenth-century petition appearing in the Early Chancery Proceedings
lays out the terms of such an agreement. John Scarlet of London, a
goldsmith, married Alice, daughter of the widow, Alice Harrys of St.
Albans. They agreed that after the espousals he would make "a yount
[jointure]" of certain tenements lying in the parish of St. Austin in London. In exchange for the jointure "by way of dowry [*sic*] [dower]" Alice,
the mother, would give him 20 li. in marks. She failed to do so and he
petitioned the Chancellor for redress.[8]

After the parties agreed to the contract and celebrated the marriage,
they came together at the parish church door [*ad ostium ecclesiae*] and
announced the terms before witnesses.[9] When widows protested that

they had not received their dower, they referred to the ceremony at the church door as proof of their claim. The marital contract had both advantages and disadvantages. The husband had to be seised (have legal possession) of the property at the time of espousal and jointure. As we shall see, the most common reason for disputed dower was the claim that the husband was not seised of the property at that time. The arrangement had the advantage of guaranteeing a living for the widow regardless of how the family fortunes fared over the course of the marriage, although sometimes she had to relinquish even this agreement.

Husbands could also make arrangements for their widows by a last will and testament. A will, like a marriage contract, gave the husband an opportunity to designate which property would form the dower of his surviving wife. From the widow's point of view, a will had the advantage of recognizing the accumulation of wealth during the marriage rather than simply that property that the husband held at the time of marriage. The flexibility of the will also meant that the husband could make more generous provisions beyond the dower. If the husband died intestate, his widow would still receive a third of the property.[10] The risk, of course, was that the family could experience more misfortune than fortune, and the widow would be left destitute because of debts. One imagines that a young couple marrying on the advice and counsel of family and friends would have both a marriage contract and an agreement about provisions in a will. In the Middle Ages, marriage was fundamentally a property agreement, whatever else it might be.

In the London Husting Court wills, 1,743 out of 3,300 nonclerical men's wills contained provisions for widows. Of the ninety-three men leaving wills in which they specifically mention dower, it was only part of the bequest they made to their wives. In addition to the dower, they left their wives other property as well. The husband might give his wife a choice of taking either the dower or the provisions of the will. Husbands making wills followed the London custom, with 86 percent leaving their wives real property along with various goods. The property might be lands, tenements and rents, shops, gardens, taverns and breweries, wharves, or land in the country. Only 13 percent left goods and money alone, and 1 percent set up an annuity for their widows. People registered wills in the Husting Court when they had real property to record (the court also recorded deeds) so that these wills represent the upper end of the social scale.

The wills recorded in the Archdeaconry Court are less detailed but contain more wills of the ordinary craftsmen of London.[11] Of the 116 men who made provisions for their widows, only 18 percent mention real property while 65 percent simply refer to the residue of their estate. Seventeen percent specify the dower, usually adding to it with specific sums of money or a portion of the residue.

In making their wills, an act that usually occurred as they realized that their end was approaching, 86 percent of the husbands who had a wife still living made her chief executor. The 17 percent who did not may have had wives either too young or too old to be trusted to carry out the legal and financial work of a probate. Thus, the partnership that established the marriage with a contract for dower and dowry carried on through the end of the husband's life.

The evidence of the wills suggests that husbands were, on the whole, generous to their wives in providing for their widowhood. Most gave the property without strings attached. In some instances, the widow was to share with surviving children, but in only 3 percent of the cases in the Husting Court did the husband specify that the widow was not to remarry. In 1403, a skinner left his business and apprentices to his wife along with her dower with the specification that she continue the business or marry someone in the trade within three years.[12] Some husbands tried to make their wives heirs to real property, but the court always objected, stating that the widow could only have a life interest in it.[13]

Contested Dower

Whatever the husband might intend, a portion of the widows found that other parties who had an interest in the property disputed their dower right. In London, the Husting Court of Common Pleas was the usual route for a widow to pursue her claim. London law spelled out the form of both the writ and the action.

> In Writ of Dower [*Unde nihil habet*] tenants shall have three summonses and after those one essoin. They shall have the View and after the View one essoin. Tenants shall have the View although they entered through the husband of the demandant, and also notwithstanding that the husband died seised. Tenants may vouch to warranty, and after each appearance may be essoined; and all the other process shall be made as in Writ of Right in Husting of Pleas of Land. And if the demandant recovers dower against the tenant by default made or by

judgement of law on such Writ of Dower, and the said female de-
mandant alleges in a Court of Record that her husband died seised,
then the Mayor shall command the Sheriffs, by precept, to have summoned an Inquest of the venue where the tenements are, against the
next Hustings of Common Pleas; for enquiry if the husband died
seised, and as to the value of the tenements and the damages. And if
she recovers upon Inquisition, enquiry shall be made as to the damages by the same Inquest.[14]

Complicated wording to be sure, but the widows understood well what
the process entailed.

The chief contenders for the widow's mite were people ("tenants" by
the legal formulation above)[15] who claimed title to the land, buildings,
shops, taverns, wharves, and so on to which the widow had a claim
through dower. When she started the proceedings to gain control over
her dower, the stalling process began. The tenants were summoned three
times and allowed an essoin (an excuse not to attend court) the fourth
time. In practice, this formula was almost always followed. Since the
court met every two weeks with several vacation periods, the process
automatically extended for two months. During this time, the litigants
might have resolved the dispute out of court or one of the parties might
have died (neither of these events was necessarily mentioned in the court
rolls). The tenants then had a view to look at the claim to the property
and after that they were allowed one more essoin. This would add another month. They could have a view even if the claim to the property
through the husband was clear. If the matter was in dispute, they could
call to warrant heirs or other parties with relevant information. It could
take months for the correct people to testify, for they might be in outly-
ing counties and have to wait until a circuit justice could interview them.
But it might also be that the husband was not seised of the land when
he endowed his bride at the church door. If her claim proved true, if the
tenants failed to appear to pursue their case (defaulted), or if they accepted her claim, then the widow recovered her property and could also
sue for damages.

The dower cases sampled in this study span more than a century
(1301–1433).[16] During that time the number of cases coming into court
declined sharply, but procedure remained remarkably constant. The
samples are for a six-year period taken roughly every twenty years (inter-
ruptions in records and regnal years determined the years sampled in

some cases). Reconstituting the cases meant following the widows through their initiation of the case to either the point at which the case dropped from the record or it was resolved. In doing a sample, some of the cases were not followed through to completion and some appeared in their final stages. In all, the sample includes 299 cases, 186 of which reached some sort of resolution and 113 of which dropped out of the record. The sample permitted a thorough investigation for the length of time cases lasted, use of attorneys, success rate for widows, remarriage of widows, and a variety of other information about the circumstances that led to success or failure of the widow's case.

As Table 1.1 indicates, a widow could expect a fairly lengthy procedure in court. While the total number of cases decreased over the span of time under study, the average length of time that they took did not. The decrease in cases can be partially explained by a decreased population after the plague of 1348 and its subsequent visitations and also by a decrease in the popularity of the Hustings Court of Common Pleas. Unfortunately, we have no source that would tell us the percentage of distressed widows forced to sue for their dower before the mayor in Common Pleas. The wills do not represent the total population by any means, and other sources do not indicate mortality. If London had a population of about 40,000 to 60,000 in 1300 (a conservative estimate) then 96 widows over a five year period would be a rather small proportion that contested their dower.

Widows initiated the first phase of the proceedings by procuring the writ of *Unde nihil habet* and presenting it in the mayor's court of Common Pleas. The process was mechanical up until the view or the warranty and few widows employed attorneys until that stage. In 1301–6, 55 percent of the widows used attorneys while only 34 percent of the defen-

TABLE 1.1.   Average Length of Time for Dower Disputes (in months)

Period	Number of Cases	Mean No. of Months Elapsed	Mode	Longest Case
1301–6	96	13.0	11.0	63.0
1327–32	68	11.0	11.0	45.0
1348–53	42	11.5	6.0	44.5
1374-79	30	11.0	7.0	42.0
1400–1405	11	12.0	10.0	23.0
1427–33	6	9.5	9.5	28.5

dants did. By 1327–32, the same percentage of widows were using attorneys, but 71 percent of the defendants did. In the immediate postplague years (1348–53), only 26 percent of the widows had attorneys, compared to 21 percent of the defendants. The number increased again by 1374–79, with 48 percent of the widows represented and 14 percent of the defendants. By 1400–1405, 75 percent of the widows had attorneys and 19 percent of the defendants did. In general, therefore, widows were more likely to use attorneys than defendants.[17]

The use of an attorney did not force the cases into lengthy battles. The average length of time using an attorney was similar to the overall average. Furthermore, the hiring of an attorney did not increase the chances of winning the case. For the most part, written records, the warranty of heirs, or reliable witnesses were decisive. The attorneys must have been used for court appearances during the waiting periods and for searching and copying records.

One might assume that a widow suing alone would feel the need of an attorney to represent her, either because she could not afford the time to appear in court, would need the legal expertise, or would lack the literacy or experience in an essentially male world to carry her case through court on her own. The evidence does not bear out these assumptions. It is true that, in 1301–6, 61 percent of those widows who remained unmarried finally hired an attorney and only 39 percent of those who remarried did so. But by 1327–32, 56 percent of the widows, compared to 55 percent of those who had remarried, hired attorneys, and by 1348–53 the balance shifts with 19 percent of the widows represented by attorneys and 38 percent of those who remarried. The balance remains similar through the rest of the century, for in 1374–79, 36 percent of the unmarried widows have an attorney and 56 percent of the remarried do. In the fifteenth century, the number of cases overall becomes very small, but in the majority of cases both the widows and those who remarried used attorneys. Among defendants, the proportion of widows who used attorneys is under a quarter. One may conclude, therefore, that unmarried widows had some preference for using attorneys to represent them in the first half of the century but that, as lawyers became more professionalized during the latter part of the fourteenth century, the choice of using expensive counsel fell more to the new husbands trying to gain control over the life interests of the widows they had married.

For the most part, the widows faced as defendants men (two-thirds to three-fourths of the defendants) or couples (49 percent in 1301–6 but dropping to about 15 percent thereafter) who were tenants of the property their husbands had promised in dower. Because they might have been dowered with a number of different properties, they often had a number of concurrent cases, but the mode was for the widow to have one defendant against whom she prosecuted. In 1301–6 the average number of defendants was 2.5. Throughout the century-and-a-half, the number of defendants remains about the same.[18]

Based on the royal Court of Common Pleas, the general assumption has been that the husband's brother or a son will be the most likely to gain by defrauding the widow of her dower. In London, however, throughout the fourteenth century, only about 10 percent of the cases involved someone related to the widow; usually a son or the husband's brother.[19] But the third most likely kinship relation was a sister-in-law, either married to the husband's brother or a sister of the husband. These disputes were over the way that the initial patrimony was divided. When the children of a family entered into a marriage contract, the father distributed property to them, giving dowry to daughters and property that sons could use to dower their wives. Such arrangements, as seen in wills and wardship cases, stated that if one child died before the others and there were no children of the sibling's marriage who could inherit the property, then it would revert to the surviving son(s) or, failing a son, to a surviving sister. Since the unhealthy living conditions of London meant that direct male heirs frequently died, sisters-in-law often pursued claims to land rights, either for themselves or for their heirs.

The disputed dower followed the same pattern as bequests made in wills. For the most part, widows sought rights over real property (about 90 percent or more of the cases) and only occasionally over money alone or in addition. The most common dower was one messuage that would have given them a home and probably a yard area as well. Such a dower would fit with the description I gave earlier. Shops, gardens, and wharves might be added to the benefits accruing to the widow. Some of the dowers were sizable indeed, with ten shops and four solars or twenty messuages along with shops, cellars, and solars or sixteen messuages and twenty-four shops. Even if the dower were only 20s. or a third of 44s., it is easy to see that a widow was a very desirable marriage partner and a new husband would willingly hire an attorney to get the life use of her dower.

Once the case came into court, a number of actions were possible. As I have mentioned, the parties could settle out of court or the widow died so that no resolution appeared in court. During the fourteenth century, 56 to 83 percent of the cases reached resolution.[20] But in the samples taken from the fifteenth century, only a third of the cases came to resolution.

If the parties pursued the suit in court, the various stages set forth in the *Liber Albus* came into play. Views of the property or scrutiny of deeds and wills enrolled in the Hustings court were common. But the defendants might also call to warrant the person who granted the property to them or someone who could uphold the grant (usually the grantor's heir). In other words, if they argued that the widow's husband had granted them the property before he died, they would call upon his heir to confirm the grant. Since the parties called to warrant were usually heirs to the property, they were sons, brothers, or other kin of the widow's former husband. In about three-quarters of the contested cases, the defendants called one or more parties to warrant. The parties Sibilla, widow of Roger Loveday, sued, called to warrant his son by a former marriage who vouched that his father was not seised of the property on November 4, 1302, when Sibilla married Roger Loveday.[21]

Other actions might be removal of the plea to another court (usually to the king's court under a writ of *melius*), the delay of the case through a love day, or a renewal of the plea in a new writ by the widow. In the first case, the widow might have property outside London that would make it easier for her to take her case to the king's court or she might perceive that she stood a better chance there. The parties might decide to delay the court case either because the parties were too ill or busy to pursue the matter, were out of the country, or were trying to arrange an agreement. In London, a delay could be procured through a "love day"; a term very different from that which appears in the manorial courts where it applied to a concord. In London, it was clearly a delay and the cases were taken up again where they left off after the agreed recess of proceedings. When the widow failed to pursue her writ or withdrew it, she might have given up her claim, but she might also have remarried and had to take out a writ with her new name and that of her new husband or she might have cited the names of the defendants incorrectly or named the wrong property. Whenever one of these more complicated legal actions occurred, both the defendant and the widow were likely to employ the help of an attorney.

The defendants had a variety of arguments that they used to dispute the widow's right to dower. The most common one was that the husband was not seised at the time of the marriage. In those fourteenth-century London Common Pleas cases that specified the grounds for the defense, 38 (1301–6) to 69 percent (1348–53)[22] argued that the contract the husband made at the church door was not valid because, at the time of the espousals, he was not legally seised of the land. When Matilda, widow of Thomas de Lincoln, complained that she had been given one tenement for life and that Adam Pykemann, fishmonger, retained it, he was able to prove that Thomas was not seised at the time of the marriage. Likewise Agnes, widow of Gilbert Trippe, found that the jury would not support her claim because her husband did not have legal possession and could not have endowed her at the time of her marriage.[23]

Although this sad commentary on the honesty of husbands was the most common objection cited by the defendants, in other cases they claimed that the widow renounced her dower. Agnes, widow of William le Marschal, lost her claim against John de Langton, clerk. He used a variety of arguments, first saying that she had remarried Francisco de Villers and therefore lost her rights. This argument apparently was not clear enough, so he appealed to William le Marschal's will. In it, Agnes was to relinquish her right to a messuage in exchange for 10*s.* 1*d.* per year for her life. John was able to prove that she and her coheirs had consigned the property to him. Johanna, widow of Simon Corp, won her case against a couple who claimed that she had agreed to accept goods in lieu of dower. She successfully argued that the goods were in the capital tenement and the will did not exclude her right to the tenement, which she would have automatically under London customary law. She was able to point to the clear statement in the will that she would have the real property and one-half of the household goods in lieu of dower.[24]

The widow sometimes cited the wrong property in her suit, and then either had to drop the case or begin again.[25] Other technicalities that her adversaries cited were defective writs. For instance, Emma, widow of Robert Burdeyn, brought a writ against William de Thorntoft. He claimed that he held the land with his brother, Hugh, who was not mentioned in the original writ. The widow, therefore, had to start the process again with both William and Hugh mentioned in the writ.[26]

In a few cases, the defendants claimed that the marriage was not valid and, therefore, the widow had no claim to the property. Maria, the widow of Simon le Bole, sued both Simon atte Gate, butcher, and John de Stafford, cordwainer, for her dower. Simon used the argument that her husband was never seised of the land, but John said that Maria had relinquished her claim to one-third of 13s. 4d. eight and a half years before when she committed adultery with John de Thorp in the parish of Saint Nicholas of the Shambles. She did not deny the adultery, but claimed that she was reconciled with Simon before he died. She did not win.[27]

Widows were not always innocent victims of husbands' deceits or tenants' rapaciousness. The widow, and sometimes her new husband, contrived to make a claim to property that the widow had legally alienated. John del Mauntes, Johanna his wife, and Simon de Merworth were able to produce a charter with the seal of Alinora, widow of Adam Russel, that clearly showed that she had alienated the property to them. Alinora and her attorney could not deny that it was her seal.[28]

The rights of the husband to devise (sell) the property assigned to the wife as dower was a thorny problem in borough law. Some boroughs would only allow it in extreme poverty and if all other property had been sold, but others gave the husband the right to sell.[29] In London, the enrollment of the land transaction in Husting waived the widow's dower right. When a husband and wife alienated property, the final concord meant that the wife had voluntarily renounced her right and title. The court examined her, separated from her husband, in private. If she voluntarily renounced title, she could not make a claim later for dower.[30] Thus, when the parties could produce evidence of the woman's signature or seal, she would lose the case. But some tenants had to pay twice for their property if they did not have a clear record. First, they paid the husband and wife for the property and, after his death, they had to secure title again from the widow for her dower. Widows (and their new husbands) could make a good profit if they knew that no written instrument recorded the earlier property transfer. Since pressing a claim was not expensive, they risked little in trying to dispute the title.

Of the cases that came to a resolution of some sort, the widows had moderate success; 53 percent of them recovered all or part of their dower. As shown in table 1.2, they could win their cases in a number of ways.

The most common way to win was through the default of the defendant. If the defendant did not essoin or have a love day to delay proceedings, then the mayor instructed the sheriff to take a third of the property into his hands. If the defendant continued to default, the widow recovered her dower. For instance, Matilda, widow of Robert de Worsted, mercer, claimed property from Randulph de Branghinge of London and Robert de Dodgard and Elena, his wife. They did not come and the land was taken into the hands of the city. After two more sessions of the court to which they were summoned, they still did not come and Matilda regained her dower.[31]

The second most common resolution in favor of the widow was for the defendants to voluntarily surrender the dower to her. For instance, Cecilia de Morton, sister-in-law to Lenota, widow of Richard de Morton, claimed that she had received the shop from her father, but in the end she surrendered one-third of it to her brother's widow. Richard, son of Robert Moteun, surrendered dower to his stepmother and her new husband and the guardian of a minor son surrendered the property to his widowed mother. Many of the voluntary surrenders were among kin.[32]

Rather than an outright surrender, the parties might reach a concord. Emma, widow of Godefried de Essex, agreed with Richard de Refham that out of the 100 li. in question she would get 43s. 6d. In another case, the defendant was non compos mentis and his attorney agreed to an out of court settlement.[33]

In 47 percent of the cases, the widow did not recover her dower for a variety of reasons or she chose to pursue the matter out of court or in another court. In fifty-four of the cases she either finally did not present a writ or she retracted her writ before the case came to trial (see table 1.3). In another nine cases she simply defaulted and did not come to the court. In these cases of default or deficiency in regard to the writ, we cannot know if the widow tried legal action again or if she gave up. She lost in twenty-four cases. Of the cases that came to a resolution, therefore, widows lost outright in only 13 percent of them and won in 53

TABLE 1.2. Widows Recovering All or Part of Dower

Period	Wins Suit	Voluntary Surrender	Concord	Default of Defendant	Total N^a
1301–6	7	5	4	10	66
1327–32	7	8	4	14	53
1348–53	3	4	1	11	34
1374–79	2	4	1	9	27
1400–1405	0	3	0	1	4
1427–33	0	0	0	1	2
Total	19	24	10	46	186

[a]N = total number of cases for which there is a resolution.

percent. If legal action did not guarantee the dower, at least the odds were worth the relatively small fee for pursuing the case.

Family were far from being the worst adversaries that a widow faced when she took her case to court; the widow won in 72 percent of the cases where a kinship relation is mentioned. In a dower dispute with another widow who had not remarried, she won in only 42 percent of the cases. The clergy were the most difficult of the identifiable adversary groups; the widows won in only 25 percent of the cases in which their adversary was a member of the clergy. Clergy probably had more sense of written evidence or knew the terms of wills better than other adversaries.

The Widow's Use of Her Mite

Once the widow had secured her dower, with or without a legal battle, she entered that unique phase of a woman's life when she was not under the legal guardianship (*mund*) of either her father or her husband. Widows had more legal freedom of action than any other women. Age, wealth, and personal preference determined their decisions about what to do with their newfound freedom and their dower.

Widows made attractive wives because they retained their dower rights for life and might have some property of their own as well, either land from kin or that entered into jointly with their husbands during marriage. Thus, widows with wealth found themselves under pressure from friends, family, and suitors to remarry. Even if part of the dower was in dispute, the chances of winning were slightly better than 50 percent, so that a new husband might expect to enjoy the economic fruits of marrying a widow. Dower cases were initiated fairly quickly after the

TABLE 1.3. Widows Not Recovering Dower

Period	Loses Suit	Does Not Present Writ	Defaults	Retracts Writ	Total N^a
1301–6	13	17	2	8	66
1327–32	4	11	0	5	53
1348–53	5	1	7	2	34
1374–79	1	10	0	0	27
1400–1405	0	0	0	0	4
1427–33	1	0	0	0	2
Total	24	39	9	15	186

^aN = total number of cases in which a resolution was reached.

death of the husband and the probate of the will, as can be observed in comparing wills with the initiation of dower cases. In this short time, roughly one-third of the widows had remarried and brought the case with their new husband. The proportion who remarried increased to half following the Black Death in 1348–49 but dropped again in the fifteenth century. Sometimes the widow had already started the case and then procured a new writ in the name of her new husband and herself. These were widows with property, sometimes very substantial, for their cases appear in the court of Common Pleas and involve real estate and rents for the most part.

Another source of information about widows remarrying are the letter books that record the awarding of guardianship over orphaned children of London citizens. Again, the surviving widows were women of property for the most part and they had children who also had property that a new husband might hope to manage until the child reached the age of twenty-one. Between 1309 and 1458, about two-thirds of the widows mentioned with minor children had remarried in the brief interval between their husband's death and the registration of their orphaned children and their goods with the mayor and chamberlain of the city. Again, the demographically troubled years of the late fourteenth and early fifteenth century saw an upswing in remarriages.

Neither of these figures may be taken as a reliable indicator of the overall rate of remarriage. Because they record marital status usually within a year of the husband's death, they deal only with the wealthier segment of London's widows, and in both record series the widows are select groups (those with minor children and those with disputed dowers). All these latter conditions might have been some hindrance to remarriage. The overall remarriage rate was certainly higher.

Individual cases show something of the demand for the well-situated widow. Richard Rous of Cornwall, who stood to lose dower, complained that his widowed daughter-in-law was abducted and married while she was in the governance and rule of her uncle in London. Margaret Wodevyld of London said that her brother-in-law was trying to marry her off to someone from the countryside and that this bumpkin had promised him and a friend 100s. for a horse if he would bring about the marriage. She wanted no part of it and the brother-in-law had her arrested and put in prison. The whole marriage market is laid out in another case when Nicholas Boylle, a draper of London, said that he ran into John Walsale in Lombard Street who told him that he knew of a widow who was worth more than 200 marks and that he would take a commission of 20 li. if he succeeded in arranging the marriage. Nicholas says that the woman wanted to know if Nicholas had the good will of his father and wanted assurances in front of his father that he would leave all his goods and livelihood to her and his son. He delivered jewels to her as part of his courtship. But, in the end, she married someone else. John wanted the 20 li., but Nicholas refused because no marriage resulted.[34]

For widows, remarriage could be a source of security, particularly if their dower included a business or if they were left with small children. In addition, marriage could be highly lucrative for the widow as well as her new husband. Thomasine Bonaventure was born to poor parents in Cornwall about 1450. While she was tending the sheep one day, Thomas Bumsby, a London mercer who traded in Cornwall, saw her and was struck by her beauty and good manners. He asked her to come to London as his servant. Her parents consented after he produced witnesses as to his character and contracted to endow her if he died. The young woman might well have been mistress as well as servant to him. In any case, his wife died several years later and he married Thomasine. He died two years later and, as they had no children, she got half of his estate. As a wealthy and beautiful young widow, she had many suitors and finally married Henry Galle. When he died she was about thirty and again without children so that she got half of Galle's estate as jointure. She then married John Percival, a merchant tailor and, later, mayor of London. When he died in 1507, she was so wealthy that she fell victim to one of Henry VII's money-raising schemes. He pardoned her for a trumped up offense in exchange for a payment of 1,000 li.[35]

Widows who did not remarry could carry on their own businesses as *femme sole* and trade freely in the city. Those who inherited their husband's trade could continue to run his shop, hire apprentices and servants, and market the products. Studies of the sixteenth century, however, indicate that only 3 to 5 percent of guild membership included widows acting alone.[36] Guilds encouraged widows to remarry guild brothers in order to keep the tools of the trade and shops within the guild, a significant pressure that had implications for the social structure of London. When occupation is given for first and second husbands in the wardship cases, women did tend to marry into allied trades if not into the same one. In addition to working in a former husband's trade, the widows continued to work in a variety of trades and service positions, including victualing, inn keeping, silkmaking, embroidery, dressmaking, and so on, that they may have pursued when their husbands were still alive.[37] One woman successfully supported her four children as a dressmaker and was able to give them 20 li. to be divided among them when she died.[38]

Independent business ventures did not always go smoothly. Apprentices did not necessarily respond well to working for a woman. Roger, son of Richard Grosse of Thame, was an apprentice of Emma, widow of William Hatfeld, a chandler. She finally had to have him committed to Newgate "for being rebellious, refusing to serve her, and unwilling to be punished by her as was fitting and proper he should be."[39] Other widows found themselves taken advantage of in debt cases. For instance, Isabel Donton claimed that Richard Weste, a sergeant of London, had put a false seal on an obligation for her to pay 40s.[40]

For the widow who remained single, keeping an honest reputation was also somewhat of a problem. Jane Burton, widow of London, claimed that she was of good name and fame but that evil disposed people of malice and evil will and without cause brought her before the ward moot accusing her of having a house of misrule. They had her put into prison and were forcing her to leave her house. Another widow claimed that, in a dispute over rent, her opponent brought a charge in the ward moot of Faringdon Without calling her a "common woman." She said that they came while she was at high mass at St. Brides and right after the Passion they pulled her out of her pew and took her off to prison. She indignantly argued that she had been "a pure maiden and wife in the same parish for fourteen years." Both women took their case to Chancery.[41]

As in the contested dower cases, the widows were not always victims of those seeking their posessions. Some widows were aggressive about keeping more than their share of the former husband's property. John Cope, son and heir of Adam Cope, and Ivo, son and heir of Ivo de Fulham, both took their mothers to court to regain their inheritance.[42]

For the most part, our records have shown us widows who were left land and tenements or, at the minimum, a place by the hearth and a chamber. But some widows were left to fend for themselves in living arrangements. Petronilla Rothirford, a widow, complained that she had been lodging in the house of Thomasine Berkeley and paying her for meat and drink. Because of the misrule of the house she wanted to leave, but Thomasine sued her twice for 40s. and lost. Now, out of malice, she brought a trespass suit and imprisoned the widow.[43] For other widows, their portion was so small that they surely ended their lives as beggars. When John Essex, a pauper, died in 1394 he left 18*d.* for his soul and ringing of church bells and the rest of his estate to his wife, Margaret, and his daughter. Out of this, she was to pay off his debts.[44]

At the end of their lives, widows made wills that distributed their worldly possessions. The range of their wealth and comfort was large. Maud Penne, who died in 1394, was the widow of a skinner. She left large bequests to the Skinner's guild, hospitals, and the poor. She had maintained her husband's trade and left the shop, tools, contents, houses, and apprentices to a kinsman (perhaps a nephew) and his wife. She then settled her personal effects on a variety of friends, godchildren (40*d.* each), servants, nieces, and her brother. She was obviously a woman living in comfortable surroundings with ample silver plate to brighten her rooms and endow her circle of friends and kinsmen. Servants lightened her load of household tasks and apprentices shared her work, learning their trade from her. In contrast, when Widow Skarlet died in the same year, she was described as a pauper who could leave only 12*d.* for her soul and the residue to her son.[45] If she had a circle of friends, her "mite" was not large enough to include them.

The widows of fourteenth- and fifteenth-century London had legal provisions that allowed for a generous division of property in their favor. The dower could be established in a precontract, be part of her husband's will, or accrue to the widow by custom of the city. The provision that the widow could take her dower with her into a new marriage had important social consequences for the structure of London society. Unlike Florence, where the husband's family kept the young widow from remarrying so that they could continue to control her dowry and dower,[46] London widows could exercise considerable control over whether or not they remarried and whom they married. Thus, the control of patrilineal lines was not as strong. Instead of vertical structures of male family identity predominating, the horizontal ones of guild and craft became important in London. Widows remarried frequently and underwent some pressure to select husbands from within the trade of the former spouse. While disputes over dower arose, the widows, either acting alone, with attorneys, or with a new husband, enjoyed a fair degree of success in the courts.

The overall picture of the widow and her "mite" in medieval London leaves the impression that widows enjoyed considerable freedom in their new status. In fact, given the substantial amounts of property they controlled for their lifetime, they had a definite impact on the social structure of London that differentiated it from continental equivalents. Further study of dower as a social determinate will be of great importance for our understanding of societies in which the portion for the widow can have a major impact on inheritance. I make no claim, however, that all London widows were merry, or happily remarried, or materially well off. The amount of the dower would determine how physically comfortable their lives would be. Not all could enjoy the luxury of ordering a jewel in the form of a bee, wrought in gold and set with rubies, as did Etheldrede Bolsore.[47]

NOTES

I am very grateful to Sue Sheridan Walker, Janet Loengard, and Caroline M. Barron for reading this essay and aiding me with their superior knowledge of dower law and practice. Caroline Barron also kindly let me have a copy of her article, "The 'Golden Age' of Women in Medieval London" (*Reading Medieval Studies* 15 [1989]: 35–59) prior to its publication. In spite of the very good help I have received on the intricate legal distinctions, I have certainly made some mistakes for which my learned mentors are not to blame. My goal has been to make the material clear to general readers and I hope I have not offended the specialists in the process. Support for the archival research undertaken in the Corporation of London Archives was made possible through a fellowship from the John Simon Guggenheim Foundation and a grant from University of Minnesota.

1. Luke 21:2: "And he saw also a certain poor widow casting in there two mites. And he said, Of a truth I say unto you that this poor widow hast cast in more than they all." Mark 12:42 adds: "For all they did cast in of their abundance, but she of her want did cast in that she had, even all her living."

2. *Calendar of Letter Books Preserved among the Archives of the Corporation of the City of London: Letter Book C,* ed. Reginald Sharp (London, 1901), 36–37; Charter of Henry III to the Widows of London (1268).

3. *Borough Custom,* ed. Mary Bateson, Selden Society no. 21 (London, 1906), 2:126.

4. *Calendar of Wills Proved and Enrolled in the Court of Husting, London, A.D. 1258–A.D. 1688,* pt. 1, ed. Reginald R. Sharpe (London, 1903), xl (hereafter referred to as *Husting Wills*); *Calendar of Letter Books Preserved among the Archives of the Corporation of the City of London: Letter Book E,* ed. Reginald Sharpe (London, 1903), 33.

5. *Husting Wills* xxxiii, xxxix. Sharpe observes that London was more liberal in its dower than common law because it did not observe the "widow's quarentine," which allowed the widow only forty days to remain in the capital messuage (xli). He read Bracton to mean that, in London, the widow's dower and free bench were interchangeable terms, but Ricart's formulation makes the distinction clear. See also Anthony J. Camp, *Wills and Their Whereabouts* (London, 1974), xi.

6. Janet S. Loengard, " 'Of the Gift of Her Husband': English Dower and Its Consequences in the Year 1200," in *Women of the Medieval World*, ed. Julius Kirshner and Suzanne F. Wemple (Oxford, 1985), 220, and subsequent discussion in which she proposes the contract as in some ways equivalent to a nominated dower. The exact terms applying to arrangement of dower are complicated because modern equivalents do not completely capture medieval meaning. Loengard's article is extremely valuable for the early history of dower.

7. Camp, *Wills and Their Whereabouts*, xiii. A married woman could not make a will without her husband's consent and a husband could revoke consent even after her death if it was done before probate. To get around these problems, women relied on marriage contracts and women's wills sometimes mention these.

8. Public Record Office: Early Chancery Proceedings C1/108/113 (hereafter referred to as C1 with the reference number). Dating of these cases is approximate, because dates are seldom given. The Chancelor's term is the closest one can get to dating these petitions. In this case, the possible dates are 1486–93. People who took their cases to Chancery had to show that they could not use the regular courts of common law. The petitions, therefore, are unusually detailed "hard luck" stories of people trying to show that they have no other recourse. In this case, the agreement appeared to be an oral one that did not work. Not all the stories could be "the truth and nothing but the truth" but they did have to have plausibility in order to receive any attention at all in Chancery. The researcher has no way of knowing how many of the petitions the Chancellor heard and settled.

9. *Husting Wills*, xli.

10. C1/64/596. Johanne, late wife of Thomas Swayne, got her third from the Bishop of London when her husband died intestate (mid-fifteenth century).

11. Guildhall Library: Archdeacon's Court, MS 9051/1 and 9051/2 (hereafter referred to as Archdeacon's Court and ms. number). The wills start in 1393 but are largely fifteenth century. The Archdeacon's Court and the Consistory Court of London recorded wills in addition to the Husting Court. These two ecclesiastical courts were more concerned with provisions for the soul of the deceased. It is often the case that people had two wills; one for the Husting Court and another for the ecclesiastical court. The Church also made efforts to extend the testamentary privilege to the poor and more ordinary people.

12. Archdeacon's Court 9051/1, 105v.

13. See, for instance, the will of Adam de Forsham, who left a legacy in fee but she agreed to hold it according to the law and custom of the city for her life (*Calendar of Wills in Husting Court*, 1:292 [1321]; see also, 1:128 [1296], 1:216 [1310–11], 1:237 [1312–13], 1:455 [1340], and other cases throughout the rolls).

14. Henry Thomas Riley, *Liber Albus: The White Book of the City of London compiled 1419 by John Carpenter and Richard Whitington* (London: Richard Griffin Co., 1861), 165–66.

15. To the modern reader, the word *tenant* may be confusing. It is not a simple renter, but rather someone to whom the husband had granted the land. As we shall see, it is not necessarily a relative, but rather someone to whom the husband had sold or deeded the property.

16. Corporation of London Archives: Husting Court of Common Pleas (hereafter referred to as CP and archive number). Again, these rolls are not to be confused with the Common Pleas rolls in the Public Record Office, which deal with the country as a whole.

17. There is not a study of the development of the legal profession in medieval London, but it is apparent that, by the second half of the fourteenth century, a profession was developing. The same names reappear as attorneys rather than the earlier practice of using friends to stand in for the people bringing the case or defending it.

18. The averages for the periods are: 1301–6, 2.50; 1327–32, 2.03; 1348–53, 1.70; 1374–79, 2.20; 1400–1405, 2.60; 1427–33, 1.70.

19. In reading the Husting Court of Common Pleas cases, I looked up the wills in Husting Court of the various parties. The defendants were not executors of other people mentioned in the wills. The figure of 10 percent, therefore, is based on a more complete search than simply surname or relationship mentioned in the common pleas rolls.

20. In 1301–6, 51 cases (44 percent) dropped out and 66 cases (56 percent) reached resolution; in 1327–32, 24 cases (31 percent) dropped out and 53 cases (69 percent) were resolved; in 1348–53, 17 cases (33 percent) dropped out and 34 (67 percent) reached resolution; in 1374–79, 5 cases (16 percent) dropped out and 27 cases (84 percent) reached resolution; in 1400–1405, 12 cases (75 percent) dropped out and 4 cases (33 percent) were resolved; in 1427–33, 4 cases (67 percent) dropped out and 2 cases (33 percent) were resolved. Obviously, by the fifteenth century, there were too few cases to be statistically significant.

21. CP28, ms 2-16; CP29, ms 1-12.

22. In 1327–32, 65 percent; 1374–79, 50 percent; 1400–1405, 100 percent; and likewise in 1427–33.

23. CP55, ms 3-19; see also CP27, ms 4, CP53, ms 7-20, CP54, ms 1-8.

24. In 1301–6, 6 cases (21 percent); 1327–32, 3 cases (23 percent); 1348–53,

2 cases (12 percent); 1374–79, 1 case (10 percent). These arguments are not used in the fifteenth century (CP53, ms 15–24; CP54, ms 1; CP54, ms 3–15).

25. In 1301–6, 5 cases (17 percent); 1327–32, 3 cases (23 percent); 1348–53, 1 case (0.06 percent); 1374–79, 1 case (10 percent).

26. CP52, ms 5-12; CP53, ms 1-14. Thomas de Pakyngho and Christina, former wife of John de Braghwyng, had to start their case again because they spelled the defendant's name wrong—it was Edelena not Elena. See CP74, ms 18; CP74, ms 2-18; CP77, ms 1-3.

27. CP52, ms 12-14; CP53, 1-19; CP54, ms 2-4. Alice, widow of Elias de Braghyngge, lost to Agnes, widow of John Russell, when she admitted that Agnes was right that she had lived in adultery the whole of Elias's life. She, too, claimed to have been reconciled with her husband before he died (CP75, ms 10; CP76, ms 9-13). Katherine, widow of John Arnald, was accused of adultery with Peter of Nealdon, chaplain. The jury said that she was never reconciled (CP30, ms 8-17; CP31, ms 1-15). Loengard cites Glanville's injunction that the widow loses her dower because of her own "shameful act" (" 'Of the Gift of Her Husband,' " 207).

28. In 1301–6, 6 cases (21 percent); 1327–32, 5 cases (38 percent); 1348–53, 1 case (0.06 percent); 1374–79, 3 cases (30 percent). CP55, ms 15-19; CP56, ms 1-16. For other cases, see CP52, ms 1-11. Emma, widow of Godefred de Essex, had quit claimed the tenement and did not deny it when confronted.

29. Bateson, *Borough Custom*, ci–cii.

30. G. H. Martin, "The Registration of Deeds of Title in the Medieval Borough," in *The Study of Medieval Records: Essays in Honour of Kathleen Major*, ed. D. A. Bullough and R. L. Storey (Oxford, 1971), 153–56.

31. CP52, ms 4-15; CP53, ms 2. For another example, see CP28, ms 16.

32. CP27, ms 15; CP28, ms 2-15; CP51, ms 3-8; CP101, ms 1-6.

33. CP51, ms 12; CP53, ms 11-21; CP54, ms 2. Another widow agreed to relinquish the one-half provision of the will in return for one-third (CP54, ms 8-12; CP55, ms 1-19).

34. C1/158/35; C1/66/389; C1/43/65.

35. Charles M. Clode, *The Early History of the Guild of Merchant Tailors*, pt. 2 (London, 1888), 11-13, 20-21.

36. Maryanne Kowaleski and Judith M. Bennett, "Crafts, Gilds, and Women in the Middle Ages: Fifty Years After Marian K. Dale," *Signs* 14 (1989): 478–79. They cite studies by Mary Prior, "Women and the Urban Economy: Oxford, 1500–1700," in *Women in English Society* (London, 1985), 93–117; and Steve Rappaport, *Worlds within Worlds: Structures of Life in Sixteenth-Century London* (Cambridge, 1989).

37. A. Abraham, "Women Traders in Medieval London," *Economic Journal* 26 (1916): 276–85; Marian K. Dale, "The London Silkwomen of the Fifteenth Century," *Economic History Review* lst ser., 4 (1933): 324–35; Eileen Power,

Medieval Women (Cambridge, 1975); Kay E. Lacey, "Women and Work in Fourteenth- and Fifteenth-Century London," in *Women and Work in Preindustrial England,* ed. Lindsey Charles and Lorna Duffin (London, 1985), 24–82.

38. Guildhall Library: Consistory Court Wills, 9051/1.

39. A. H. Thomas, *Calendar of Plea and Memoranda Rolls Preserved among the Archives of the Corporation of the City of London at Guildhall* (Cambridge, 1929), 2:128.

40. C1/7/263; C1/7/283. See also *Calendar of Plea and Memoranda Rolls* 2:128.

41. C1/123/6; C1/61/189.

42. *Calendar of Plea and Memoranda Rolls,* 2:213–15.

43. C1/64/1130.

44. Archdeacon's Court, 9051/1, 18v.

45. Archdeacon's Court, 9051/1, 5v, 6v.

46. Christiane Klapisch-Zuber, *Women, Family, and Ritual in Renaissance Italy,* trans. Lydia G. Cochrane (Chicago, 1985). See particularly "The 'Cruel Mother': Maternity, Widowhood, and Dowry in Florence in the Fourteenth and Fifteenth Centuries," 117–31.

47. C1/66/445.

BIBLIOGRAPHY

Abraham, A. "Women Traders in Medieval London." *Economic Journal* 26, no. 2 (1916): 276–85.

Barron, Caroline M. "The 'Golden Age' of Women in Medieval London." *Reading Medieval Studies* 15 (1989): 35–59.

Borough Custom. Vol. 2, ed. Mary Bateson, Selden Society no. 21. London, 1906.

Camp, Anthony. *Wills and Their Whereabouts.* London, 1974.

Clode, Charles M. *The Early History of the Guild of Merchant Tailors,* pt. 2. London, 1888.

Dale, Marian K. "The London Silkwomen of the Fifteenth Century." *Economic History Review,* 1st ser. 4 (1933): 324–35.

Guildhall Library. Consistory Court Wills.

Klapisch-Zuber, Christiane. *Women, Family, and Ritual in Renaissance Italy.* Trans. Lydia G. Cochrane. Chicago: University of Chicago Press, 1985.

Kowaleski, Maryanne, and Judith M. Bennett. "Crafts, Gilds, and Women in the Middle Ages: Fifty Years After Marian K. Dale." *Signs* 14, no. 2 (1989): 474–88.

Lacey, Kay E. "Women and Work in Fourteenth- and Fifteenth-Century London." In *Women and Work in Preindustrial England,* ed. Lindsey Charles and Lorna Duffin. London: Croom Helm, 1985.

Loengard, Janet S. " 'Of the Gift of Her Husband': English Dower and Its Consequences in the Year 1200." In *Women of the Medieval World*, ed. Julius Kirshner and Suzanne F. Wemple. Oxford: B. Blackwell, 1985.

Martin, G. H. "The Registration of Deeds of Title in the Medieval Borough." In *The Study of Medieval Records: Essays in Honour of Kathleen Major*, ed. D. A. Bullough and R. L. Storey. Oxford: Oxford University Press, 1971.

Power, Eileen. *Medieval Women*. Cambridge: B. Blackwell, 1978.

Riley, Henry Thomas. *Liber Albus: The White Book of The City of London compiled 1419 by John Carpenter and Richard Whitington*. London: Richard Griffin Co., 1861.

Sharpe, Reginald, ed. *Calendar of Wills Proved and Enrolled in the Court of Husting, London, A.D. 1258–A.D. 1688*. Part 1. London, 1889.

———. *Calendar of Letter Books Preserved among the Archives of the Corporation of the City of London: Letter Book C*. London, 1901.

———. *Calendar of Letter Books Preserved among the Archives of the Corporation of the City of London: Letter Book E*. London, 1903.

Thomas, A. H. *Calendar of Plea and Memoranda Rolls Preserved among the Archives of the Corporation of the City of London at Guildhall*. 6 vols. Cambridge: Cambridge University Press, 1929.

Chapter 2

How Typical Was Alessandra Macinghi Strozzi of Fifteenth-Century Florentine Widows?

Ann Morton Crabb

Alessandra Macinghi Strozzi, a member of Florence's patrician ruling class, was widowed in June, 1435. Her husband, Matteo Strozzi, a merchant and humanist scholar, died of plague in Pesaro, where he had recently been exiled as a political opponent of the Medici. Three of the couple's children died of plague along with their father, and Alessandra took the four who survived back to Florence. A fifth child was born a few months later. Alessandra was twenty-nine; she spent the remainder of her life as a widowed mother, dying in her early sixties.[1]

Considerable evidence remains about Alessandra in the collection of Strozzi letters and papers in the Archivio di stato in Florence, including seventy-three letters she wrote in her own hand and had sent to her sons while they worked abroad as merchants. There is also a nineteenth-century Italian edition of Alessandra's letters, with selections from relatives' correspondence.[2]

Whether Alessandra was typical of Florentine widows of the fifteenth century—particularly those of the propertied classes[3]—is a question of interest to historians of women. There are few fifteenth-century widows who left such a rich array of letters filled, as Alessandra's are, with political and social commentary. A comparison of Alessandra with other widows described in the didactic writings of the time and alluded to in Catasto tax returns, wills, and other papers in the Archivio di stato, as well as in modern studies, suggests that, while Alessandra's position may have been stronger in some respects than that of other fifteenth-century Florentine widows, she was neither extraordinary nor remarkable.

No letters remain from the early years of Alessandra's widowhood, and the few surviving documents, while outlining her practical circumstances, reveal nothing about her personal characteristics. By the time her letters begin in 1447, she was forty and feeling old and in uncertain health. We never learn what she looked like, although it can be assumed that, if she described her daughter as "thin like her father," she was not thin.

While Alessandra's letters tell many things about her attitudes and activities, they do have their limits. Written to her sons about important family concerns and not as a chronicle of everyday happenings, they rarely allow a glimpse of their author as a person with pleasures and interests separate from her sons. They also understate the role played by other women in her life. Furthermore, the letters show Alessandra as she preferred to portray herself: a mother struggling against odds to do the best for her children—the kind of widowed mother admired by moralists and preachers. Nonetheless, all evidence indicates that the self-image Alessandra presented, although incomplete, reflected the important realities of her life.[4]

Alessandra was more than ordinarily intelligent and competent, but not to the degree that she seemed anomalous. Like most patrician women, she had learned, in her childhood, to read, write, and keep accounts. She was also like other women in the limits on her learning. She felt uncomfortable doing complex accounts or composing formal letters. She was also unaffected by the literary and artistic trends of the Renaissance, and never mentioned her husband's humanist accomplishments. In fifteenth-century Italy, only a few women from aristocratic or professional families were highly educated devotees of arts and letters.[5]

Alessandra, the daughter, widow, and mother of merchants, was thoroughly imbued with a merchant mentality. Alessandra prided herself on guarding against useless expenditure, and also tried to earn a small profit when she could. For example, in the 1450s, at a time when she could afford to keep few decorative objects, she wrote, "Let me tell you about two paintings on cloth that I have, one of the Three Wisemen offering gold to our Lord . . . ; the other of a peacock. . . . To me they seem beautiful. . . . If I find someone to sell them to at a good price, I shall sell them both."[6] Her letters regularly interweave concern for "profit" with concern for "honor," concern for family affection, and sometimes concern for beauty, a combination characteristic of other Florentines, as well.

Alessandra had deep religious beliefs, and took vows in a lay religious order in 1465. Her faith helped her face the many deaths, exiles, and other troubles she suffered. On almost every page of her letters, she expressed opinions like, "There is no hope in this world that does not turn sour; one can have hope only in God," and "When your plans fail, believe it is for the best; because every time God does not give you what you wish, He does it . . . for the best" (AMS *Lettere* 438, 507, 493–494). Nonetheless, she had a lively interest in people and events around her, and was worldly and cynical in her judgments, adding spice and individuality to her letters.

Alessandra's conviction that God did not intend life to be happy or fair contributed to her support of the established order. She, like most people, did not question the unequal distribution of wealth among rich and poor; the traditional division of labor between men and women; or women's low place in the hierarchy of power. She also accepted the patriarchal and patrilineal family in which she spent her life and made furthering its interests one of her principal concerns.[7]

Alessandra had more independence for a longer time than most women; however, a substantial minority had as much. She spent years as a widow, but one in four Florentine women were widows, largely because husbands were, on average, twelve years older than wives. Most were widowed after their children were grown, but about a sixth lived with minor children. Alessandra never remarried and never came under the authority of a second husband, but in this she was like about two-thirds of women widowed in their twenties, and nine-tenths widowed at thirty or older. Florentines preferred very young brides, and it was teenage widows who most often married again. Good wives were discouraged from remarrying out of loyalty to their husbands' memories and because a chaste and religious life was considered best. Good mothers were discouraged from remarrying for their children's sake. When a woman remarried and joined another patrilineal family, her children rarely lived with her and never fell under her guardianship; the children also lost her dowry, which she took to her new husband, and the dowry normally made up a substantial part of their inheritance.[8]

Alessandra headed her household, as did about a third of widows. The other two-thirds lived under the protection of male relatives, since Florentines valued the patrilocal extended household of father and/or mother, adult sons, their wives and children, and the occasional widowed sister. When Alessandra married, she moved in with her husband's parents and brother, as well as her husband. This created, until her in-laws' early deaths, a household of more than one nuclear unit, as in about a fifth of propertied city households and households of rural peasants. After Matteo died, Alessandra was like other widows in having the legal right to support by her family of birth or, since she had children, by her family of marriage. But she was also similar to about ninety-five percent of them in not taking up that right. Her husband had no suitable surviving relatives in an age of plague, and she herself had been orphaned young. Her one full brother, Zanobi, needed help rather than gave it, and she had quarreled with her stepmother, half siblings, and uncles. Alessandra was unusual in living separately from her sons in the many years they were abroad: over half of widows, rich and poor, lived with adult sons, a high proportion considering that many widows had no surviving sons (only about five percent lived with adult daughters). During her years alone, Alessandra eagerly awaited her sons' marriages and return to Florence, so that she, too, could live with her sons, their wives, and children.[9]

Although Alessandra was head of the household, she received advice, assistance, and companionship from many relatives, because Florentine patricians emphasized kinship solidarity outside the household as well as in it. Patrilineal ties had particular importance, and patricians clustered together in family neighborhoods: Alessandra's ties with the Strozzi were strengthened by the years she lived among more than thirty Strozzi households. She had intimates in her family of birth, as well, although fewer than some widows, and she depended greatly on her sons-in-law, Marco Parenti and Giovanni Bonsi. She was on casual visiting terms with a large number of people linked to her by more distant kinship ties, providing her with useful contacts.[10]

Alessandra's financial position in her husband's surviving will, written several years before his death, was like that of about half of all widows. She could reclaim her dowry or (in order to discourage her from taking the dowry from her children) she could receive support for herself and a servant in the family home—as long as she remained a widow, lived with her children, and did not ask for her dowry. If she chose to live apart from her children, but remained an "honest widow" and did not ask for her dowry, she was left usufruct of a farm. Smaller numbers of widows were left legacies ranging from their dowries alone, to money or property, to sole usufruct of their husband's patrimony. Widows were almost never universal heirs of their husbands' estates in a system that kept dotal and patrimonial property separate.[11]

Alessandra was like about seven-tenths of widows in that she was named in her husband's will as guardian of her children as long as she remained a widow. (The other three-tenths were passed over in favor of male relatives or friends, the occasional female relative, or the government office of wards of state.) Widows became guardians only when specifically chosen by their husbands, although nonguardians continued to live with and care for their children, while lacking financial authority over them. Matteo left Alessandra the deciding vote in a group guardianship, the common position for female guardians. About a tenth of widows were in a stronger position than she because their husbands named them sole guardian.[12]

Matteo's exile and early death gave Alessandra more authority than expected at the time he wrote his will, and more than many, but not all, other widows. She began gaining financial experience after the exile, when she stayed behind for a time to settle the family affairs. However, women often managed the family while husbands were away from home as international merchants, officeholders in the Florentine territories, or political exiles. After Matteo died, Alessandra became owner of much of his property, in spite of Florentine inheritance customs. Her husband's assets had been eaten up by the taxes that were levied on an enemy of the regime, and his children and heirs were left with nothing but debts. Alessandra, however, was able to rescue two houses in Florence (including the family home), a villa and several farms in the Tuscan countryside, and shares in the Florentine funded debt, by taking them as the equivalent of her large dowry of 1,600 florins, which she was owed no matter what her husband's debts. Her children, without paternal assets, were more than usually dependent on their mother until they could earn money. However, nearly a third of widows with minor children lived on dowries in a city where bankruptcy and tax default were frequent.[13]

Alessandra was one of the richest widows in Florence but, like other widows, she lived mainly on a fixed income and had difficulty bringing up her children at the patrician level.[14] Her efforts to preserve her money and manage her lands involved her in legal contracts: free of a husband's control, she still needed a *mundualdo,* or male facilitator, but this could be a formality; Alessandra sometimes had a stranger provided by the court as *mundualdo,* who had no influence on her intentions.[15]

Alessandra took part in business in a small way. She could not join a merchant guild or be an active partner in a merchant company, but she invested capital as a passive partner in relatives' companies and occasionally sold cloth and yarn that her son bought cheaply for her in

Naples to acquaintances in Florence.[16] She was also unable to avoid the government tax authorities. She complained with some exaggeration, "I have done nothing else for the last six months but go first to this office, then to that one," before coming to an agreement about tax payments. Elsewhere she wrote, "The high taxes upset me ... because, if I wish to pay, I must use capital; if I do not pay, I have all sorts of bother; and no matter what I do, I am in a bad way" (AMS *Lettere* 7, 160; ASF S3 249: 75).

Alessandra made *mezzadria,* or sharecropping, contracts with peasants who tilled her lands. Male relatives often traveled out into the countryside to deal with peasants for her, but she went herself when she was staying at a villa nearby. She improved the farms when she could afford it, writing, for example:

> I have hired a worker at Pazzolatico, who will begin by February.... Because the farm is in disorder and the weather has been bad, I have made the effort to provide him with an ox ... ; the farm needs it and will repay the expenditure. If ... [it] had been improved in the past, it would have given greater return.[17]

When Alessandra sold lands, she made the decision herself, once responding to her son's inquiries about a sale, "Let us not discuss it any more for now; leave it to me and I will notify you." Her sons, as her heirs, had to cosign sale agreements, but so did a man's heirs. When she became involved in a lawsuit over land, she appeared before the court to argue the case; her adversaries summoned her son, too, for giving her advice they disapproved of, something they would have been less likely to do with a man.[18]

Alessandra's main interest in life was her children, as was expected of widows with children. She oversaw their educations, insisting that her sons practice writing and accounting skills before they embarked on merchant careers. She chose husbands for her daughters in 1447 and 1450, consulting relatives but making the decisions herself. She did not have to find her sons jobs, because their father's first cousins took them into their merchant banking companies overseas, but she encouraged them to succeed, telling them they had to rescue the family fortunes and that her happiness depended on their hard work.[19]

Alessandra's authority over her children was less than that of a father who, by law and custom, had the almost unlimited power of the Roman *patria potestas.*[20] She used love more than discipline in molding them into people she could admire. Her love, although intense, had a selfish side, but it was an effective lever in getting them to behave as she wanted. There was no sign in her family of the distant relationships and lack of emotional commitment some writers believe characterized the premodern European family. Conservative fifteenth-century Italian moralists recommended severity and remoteness to fathers, but not to mothers, and humanists recommended them to neither.[21]

Alessandra's letters, written to her sons Filippo, Lorenzo, and Matteo, tell us much more about her feelings for them than for her daughters, Caterina and Alessandra. They also suggest that, although she loved her daughters, she set greater value on her sons. This has to be treated with caution, since she wrote to please her sons. Nonetheless, statements like, "I have no other good in this world but you my three sons," cannot be dismissed.[22]

Preferring sons to daughters was widespread and acceptable in fifteenth-century Florence. Daughters soon married into other patrilineal families, creating a barrier, even among people who saw each other often. For example, when Filippo Strozzi presented his sister Caterina with a large quantity of fine cloth, Alessandra wrote, "It seems too much . . . to give to Marco, who can afford to pay."[23] However, Alessandra (like many, but not all, people at high social levels) gave greater emphasis to the patrilineal principle than did some Florentines, and thus she may have treated her sons and daughters less equally than some. In a group of 100 wills of propertied men and women, about half the testators made daughters, granddaughters, sisters, mothers, and other females substitute heirs after sons, while Alessandra, like the other half, chose male relatives as substitute heirs.

The Strozzi letters show Alessandra sharing authority with her hardworking and responsible eldest son, Filippo, by the time he was in his midteens; once he was an adult, she rarely contradicted him directly.[24] The letters also show her reprimanding her second son, Lorenzo (four years younger than Filippo). Although Lorenzo later reformed, in his youth he chased women, gambled, and took money from the cash box of his cousin's company in Bruges. Alessandra appealed to his sense of obligation to her: "Of all the troubles I have, yours affect me most." She did not know why he followed his desires, knowing first that it displeased God, which was most important, and then that it displeased her. If he had just begun, she would still be hopeful, but he had been behaving badly for years; he had only been tolerated out of love for her and, if he did not change his ways soon, her pleas would no longer do him any good. "Do not throw aside my criticisms, which are offered with love and tears. I pray God to dispose you to do what I desire."[25]

Alessandra was ambitious for her sons, but there were limits to her ambition. Florence was a competitive society, in which men strove for honor and profit in the public arena, but Alessandra's goals (when not religious) were home centered, as women's were supposed to be. She wanted her sons to have wealth and other patrician characteristics as a background for a happy and honorable family life. Great fame did not interest her, although, as it happened, her son Filippo became one of the richest and most famous Florentines of the later fifteenth century.[26]

Most of all, Alessandra wanted her sons near her, and one of her greatest sorrows was that, in a Florence governed by their father's enemies, the Medici, it was best for them to begin their careers abroad. She had to be persuaded over several years to send her youngest child, Matteo, to join his brother Filippo in Niccolò Strozzi's company in Naples. Filippo had already suggested she send Matteo at age ten; when he was twelve, she wrote, "He is small and still needs my care. . . . Matteo went to Marco's villa recently and stayed there six days . . . ; I did not think I could live until he returned." When Matteo was thirteen, she grudgingly agreed he should leave: "I will not consider my consolation, but your welfare; I have always done this and so I will do until the end." It seemed hard, when she thought how she had been left while still young to raise five small children, with Matteo, the youngest, as yet unborn; and how she raised Matteo thinking that he would not part from her except in death, especially since her other sons were already outside Florence. A few months later, she wrote, "I have so much sorrow at losing this last one. . . . He looks so much like his father; he has changed into a handsome, grown-up lad in the time he was at villa." Soon afterwards, Matteo departed for Naples, and Alessandra's son-in-law Marco described her as comforting herself "not with the spirit of a woman, but of a man," telling herself of the good that would come of it.[27]

Alessandra directed her sons toward becoming successful, God-fearing, family-loving merchants. She gave weight to her wishes by providing them with their first capital, gradually selling off her farms and lending them the proceeds to invest and keep the profits. Although she considered her money to belong ultimately to her sons, she insisted they avoid risky ventures and that they repay her on time. At first, she had the eldest, Filippo, invest on behalf of all the brothers and share profits with them. As they grew older, she expected each to invest on his own until they could form a company together. She contributed to the fraternal solidarity Florentines valued by acting as mediator among her sons, writing to Matteo in 1458: "I see that you never had your part from Filippo. I told him that he has not treated you fairly and that he must provide you with it as soon as he can so that you have no cause to complain either of me or him."[28]

A few months later, one of Alessandra's worst nightmares came to pass. Matteo died in Naples of a fever at the age of twenty-three. In a letter to Filippo signed, "your poor Mother," Alessandra wrote that she was trying to accept that God, who had given her Matteo, had taken him back. However, she deeply wished she had been in Naples "to see and touch my sweet son while he was alive. I would have been comforted, and could have given comfort to him and to you." She felt great pain in her heart, but it helped her to know that Filippo had been there and had done everything possible to keep Matteo alive, which meant that his death had been God's will. At least Matteo had been given time to confess his sins and take the sacrament. Now she worried that Filippo's health would fail under the strain: "I beg you resign yourself to what happened, out of love for me, and look after yourself, putting business aside a little.... Remember that I set more store on your person than your possessions.... I grieve, my son, that I am not near you, where I could lift the burden of the many things you must do" (AMS *Lettere*, 178–81).

Matteo's death provided further evidence of life's uncertainty, and Alessandra and Filippo decided the remaining brothers should go into business together as soon as possible. Lorenzo agreed to leave Bruges, where he was by then doing well in Jacopo Strozzi's company, and join Filippo in Naples, but he seemed in no hurry to do it. Alessandra wrote to Jacopo: "I beg you ... that if you see he does not plan to make this move, out of love for me tell him I do not wish him to disobey." Although a mother's authority was less than a father's, children, even when adults, were supposed to obey both parents. Jacopo's death delayed Lorenzo's departure, but Lorenzo recognized his obligation.

My dearest mother, in good faith, if this matter of Jacopo had not happened, I would have mounted my horse this May as you command me. I would have gone there to obey you, and because I want to as much as either of you. . . . Therefore, I beg you affectionately to excuse me for not obeying you. . . . Be satisfied . . . that my excuse is legitimate and honest.[29]

Alessandra thought it her job to unite her sons, as she told Jacopo, "so I can be content in the little time I have left to live; moreover, if I die, I want them to be adjusted to each other in such a way that they will not quarrel, but be good brothers who live in peace. It is up to me to do it, and get them together while I live." A few years later, after the brothers established a partnership in Naples, Alessandra commented to Filippo, "You say that you and Lorenzo are in good accord, which pleases me greatly: profit and honor will come from it. I am glad that you do it mainly for my happiness" (AMS *Lettere*, 234 and 396).

The brothers could not start a business in Florence. In 1458, the Medici government extended the ban against the exiles of 1434 for twenty-five years and broadened it to cover male descendants of exiles. For a time, Alessandra seriously considered moving abroad to be with her sons; then, as Cosimo de' Medici weakened with age, hope of the Strozzi brothers coming home to Florence grew. Alessandra and her relatives turned their attention to ending the exile, and carefully watched political developments in order to take advantage of them.[30]

Alessandra was as acute an observer of the political scene as her male relatives; she also participated in politics as her sons' representative. Florence's formal government was a male monopoly, but, in practice, much of the city's political life went on outside its established institutions and was tied to the patrician social world. Most patrician women would have kept abreast of events because of the close connections between politics and social status and politics and new taxes. A few patrician women, like Alessandra, could act if their families needed them. Alessandra would have liked to have seen the restoration of Florence's traditional government, controlled by an elite group of citizens of near equal power, not by one family—the Medici. But she worked for her sons' return, no matter what the form of government—the approved approach for a woman and also the practical one for her, as well as for her sons, as long as the Medici remained in power.[31]

Alessandra received the good news of Cosimo de' Medici's death in August, 1464, while staying in the country to escape the plague. She told her sons she had not yet heard who would be in charge or how the exiles would be affected, but she was sure citizens were discussing new ideas about the government of the country. If there had been the smallest hint of any developments,

> I would not have been kept away [from Florence] by twenty a day dying of the plague. . . . Do not doubt that when I hear anything at all, I will approach the right people; nor will I neglect to use relatives or friends, either because of lack of money or lack of will. No effort will be spared; however, first we must wait for some moves to be made and for some indication of the opinions of those who govern. (AMS *Lettere* 323–24)

During the next couple of years, while politics became a battle for supremacy between Cosimo de' Medici's son, Piero, and other powerful citizens, Alessandra and her relatives worked to persuade the opposing factions to repeal the exile. Alessandra sometimes sounded as if she thought arranging her sons' return should fall entirely on her, although her son-in-law Marco had as important a role in negotiations as she did. In one place, she wrote, "Because I have not been feeling well for some time . . . and have gone out very little, I have been conferring about every-thing with Giovanni and Marco," and when she sent her sons long letters of advice about how they should proceed, she wrote, "I think" and "I decided."[32]

Nor did she hesitate to insist on her opinions. In the winter of 1464, Filippo planned a trip to Florence on the King of Naples' business, for which, as an exile, he needed a safe conduct. While his relatives arranged the safe conduct, they mentioned the repeal of the exile and received encouraging replies. When it was decided in Naples that Lorenzo should replace Filippo, Alessandra warned her sons that she would stop delivery of letters asking for the change, since she feared the new plan would harm "the larger and more important request for the smaller one." How-ever, she did not carry out her threats because, by the time the letters arrived, she had been persuaded that the principal citizens accepted the change (AMS *Lettere*, 359).

As Lorenzo approached Florence, Alessandra decided his safe conduct was too limited to prevent an enemy from having him arrested as a rebel for entering the city while an exile; he should stay outside unless the safe conduct was made more secure. The principal citizens told her not to worry, because they thought it adequate but, "I did not wish to put your person at risk on the basis of words alone. . . . They did not risk anything but words, while I risked flesh and blood."[33] Lorenzo eventually gained safe passage as far as the city gate, and Alessandra spent several days with him outside the gate. After he left, she commented that his visit made her realize more strongly than ever that she must live with her sons in what remained of her life, even if it meant moving abroad; she had felt so alive while he was there, and she was like a dead person now that he was gone.

In May, 1465, all the important citizens, including Piero de' Medici, seemed willing to sponsor the Strozzi brothers' return, and Alessandra's expectations rose: "I am like a sick person who is comforted when the doctor says, 'You are not going to die from this illness, but will be better in a few days.'... Although he still feels sick, the words...make him hope that he will get better, and sometimes he does and sometimes he does not." Then, an electoral reform movement inimical to Medici control, and also to the civic peace needed for ending exile, erupted in the summer and fall of 1465, before anything had been done for the Strozzi. Alessandra wrote bitterly about the principal citizens: "He who does not work at the right time will not have a good harvest. He who is at the right time and yet waits, misses his chance."[34]

Describing conditions in early 1466, Alessandra demonstrated the modesty she sometimes felt as a woman living apart from the world.

> The people are very discontented and, furthermore, there is no one capable of doing anything.... Things are going in such a way that it seems to me, although I do not know much...that no one would open even a shop in this city until they know what is going to happen. There are people here who think there will be a great change and soon, so we must wait and see awhile. But you know better than I what we should do, as do those who advise you.[35]

A few days later, she explained why calm had been restored, writing from a mother's point of view:

> The reason was that the principal citizens have made up their quarrels.... I have to laugh at them: One day they wish to exile one another and the next day they make peace; they are like little boys. It is difficult to write about things, as they change their minds every day, swirling like leaves in the wind.[36]

New trouble broke out, lasting for several months. Piero de' Medici triumphed in September, 1466, exiling his opponents, but lifting the exile of Alessandra's sons, who had played a cautious game, remaining friendly with both sides and committing themselves to neither until the outcome was clear.

With the end of exile, Alessandra attained one of her most heartfelt goals. Another major goal was arranging marriages for her sons, which she had been longing to do for years. In 1450, when Filippo was twenty-two, she told him, "I want to give you a wife because you are now old enough to know how to govern a family. It would bring me consolation, because I have none except the hope I have in you and the others." Fifteen years later, when her sons were thirty-seven and thirty-three years old, respectively, and still unmarried, she wrote, "I wish to see you married, as I have said other times, so that when I die, I will know that you are set on the course all mothers want . . . and so your children will enjoy what you have earned with so much fatigue and effort" (AMS *Lettere* 100, 547–48).

Filippo finally agreed to marry in 1465, and Alessandra and her son-in-law, Marco Parenti, asked around Florence about possible brides. The new daughter-in-law would live with Alessandra, and Alessandra was determined that she be attractive. She wrote about some girls who did not appeal to her: "As for me, I would not wish to see those sad creatures in front of me. There would be little contentment in seeing them around the house."[37] The choice soon narrowed to a daughter of Francesco Tanagli, age seventeen, and to Fiammetta Adimari, age fourteen. Families immediately involved in delicate marriage negotiations avoided meeting until a contract was signed, and people went to considerable lengths to gather information indirectly, with men specializing in finding out about grooms, even gaining access to their tax returns, and women specializing in finding out about brides. Alessandra asked friends, relatives, and neighbors about the girls' characters and accomplishments; she stationed herself in a house across the street from where one lived, so she could observe her from there; and she attended masses they were reputed to attend. After sitting next to the Tanagli daughter during mass, she hinted at the uncomfortable position in which the young women found herself: "I could not see her face well, as it seemed to me she noticed me looking at her, and after the first moment never turned toward me. Then she rushed out like the wind."[38]

Alessandra became convinced that Filippo should marry the Tanagli daughter: "I have looked at this merchandise so closely and have such good information about her that I do not think any other possibility . . . would be half as good." In a letter showing she thought the match nearly settled, she discussed gifts for the bride, revealing the Florentine desire to keep up with other Florentines, while also getting good value for money.

> I will be proud to see her beautiful and furnished with beautiful things. I do not want her to be less well provided with jewels than others are. . . . If we do not decorate her clothing with pearls, we will have to do it with other ornaments, which cost enough, and the money would be thrown away. (AMS *Lettere*, 470 and 466–68)

When the match with the Tanagli foundered, Alessandra spent more than one sleepless night worrying about it: "I have had the idea . . . for the past two months that God does not wish to give me this consolation because of my sins. I have put myself in His hands." They turned their attention to the other girl, Fiammetta Adimari. Alessandra agreed with Filippo that, at fourteen years old, Fiammetta was "a little green" for him, but "if they wish to give her, I would not refuse her." For a time, they thought she had been betrothed to someone else, and Alessandra lamented: "Perhaps it is not for the best that I have the consolation of a beautiful girl during my lifetime" (AMS *Lettere*, 510, 569, 495).

Alessandra's despair over failed marriage arrangements and her emphasis on the bride's appearance need to be explained. To her, a daughter-in-law was much more than the wife of her son; Filippo's marriage would allow her to embark on the existence she had been waiting for, to achieve the culmination of a mother's wishes, and to find the only remaining pleasure she expected. She would finally live in a large household, which included a successful and loving son, an attractive and good-tempered daughter-in-law, and, she hoped, intelligent and attractive grandchildren.

Fiammetta's betrothal proved a false alarm, and soon after Filippo returned to Florence, he and Fiammetta married. Filippo became head of the household, and Alessandra settled down to enjoy her young daughter-in-law, whom she loved but dominated, and three grandchildren born before she died. Her second son, Lorenzo, also married shortly before she died, but he and his wife lived in Naples, where Lorenzo managed the Strozzi's Neapolitan business.[39]

By the time her sons married, Alessandra Macinghi Strozzi had spent most of her life in a position stronger than that of many widows, but not so strong that she seemed atypical to those around her. She had more than average financial and other control over her children when they were young, but a good number of widows had as much. Her authority was prolonged by her sons' need for a representative in Florence during their residence abroad; however, that was not uncommon in a city where men often spent long periods away from home. Alessandra's efforts to end her sons' exile involved her in politics more than most widows, but she was not unique in that either. She was doubtless more assertive and efficient than many widows, but she used those qualities to further goals well approved for a woman of Renaissance Florence.

Alessandra's letters show her as wholeheartedly accepting the patrilineal and patriarchal system. This set psychological limits on her actions, in addition to the constricting legal limits on women in politics, business, and the family. Perhaps in everyday life she was somewhat less preoccupied with carrying out her sons' goals than the letters indicate. There are hints in them that she had female friends and interests, although she rarely mentions them. Nonetheless, the self-image she projected in the letters was doubtless the one on which she preferred to model her behavior, and it was one that increased her authority within the boundaries available to her.

Outside the church, a woman's best path to influence lay in becoming a trusted representative, agent, adviser, and mediator among male kin. Since men and women alike considered this a praiseworthy calling, Alessandra personified the admirable Florentine woman in the eyes of her own and also later times, making her more archetypical than typical, the main reason we know about her today: her son Filippo, feeling great affection and respect for her and attributing to her some of his success, carefully preserved her letters; seventeenth-century Strozzi genealogists were impressed and did the same; and the nineteenth-century editor of her letters, Cesare Guasti, held her up as a corrective example to the "modern" women of his time. Guasti wrote,

Every day women are further emancipating themselves, and loosening the bonds that supported their weakness and veiled their modesty. [However], I give [this volume] to the keeping of ... women who prefer a loving heart to pedantic erudition, and the joys and sorrows of family life to self advertisement. (AMS *Lettere,* viii–ix)

ABBREVIATIONS

ASF	Archivio di stato di Firenze
ASF Dipl.	Archivio diplomatico, Archivio di stato di Firenze
ASF Not.	Notarile antecosmiano, Archivio di stato di Firenze
ASF S	Carte strozziane, Archivio di stato di Firenze
AMS *Lettere*	*Lettere di una gentildonna del secolo XV ai figliuoli esuli,* ed. Cesare Guasti (Florence, 1877)
AMS Libro	Alessandra Macinghi Strozzi's account book, ASF S5: 15.
Stat. Flor.	*Statuti Populi et Comunis Florentiae, MCCCCXV,* ed. Michaelem Klutch (Friburg, 1777–83)

NOTES

1. On Matteo's exile, death, the months after he died, and the ages of Alessandra and her children, see ASF Otto di guardia, 224; ASF S5 12:23, 39; Pampaloni 1963, 29–33; ASF S5 1250; AMS *Lettere,* 127; ASF Catasto 76: 135; 612: no. 387; 816: no. 357; AMS Libro, 100. On Matteo Strozzi, see also Vespasiano 1963, 245–46; Kent 1978; Bec 1967; and AMS *Lettere,* "Introduction."

2. See AMS *Lettere.* There is another edition, *Letter ai Figliuli* (ed. R. Carabba [Florence, 1914]), much less useful than Guasti's because it lacks notes and selections from relatives' letters.

3. I emphasize propertied widows because they are more comparable to Alessandra Strozzi than poor widows, especially when considering literacy or political contacts. However, preliminary evidence indicates that rates of guardianship and remarriage, relationships with children, and even household structure were not too different among widows at different levels of wealth—something to investigate further at a later time. For the purposes of this essay, I have considered widows to be "propertied" if they had incomes over the modest sum of 20 florins in the Catasto of 1442—as did slightly fewer than four out of ten widows in ASF Catasto, vols. 612 and 613. I chose this sum because widows with surnames rarely fell below it, and surnames were a sign of patrician or near patrician status. See nn. 8 and 14 for my use of the Catasto of 1442.

4. For evidence about Alessandra's appearance and health, see ASF S3 249: 75; AMS *Lettere,* 33, 39, 60. For works indicating how widowed mothers and mothers whose husbands were away were supposed to behave, see Sant'Antonino 1859, no. 10; San Bernadino 1934–40, 1:XII; Fra Giovanni Dominici 1927; Fra Girolamo Savonarola 1952; Velluti 1914, 85, 105, 119; Vespasiano 1963, 439–62; Vespasiano 1843, 512–33.

5. On Alessandra's learning and the limits on it, see AMS *Lettere,* especially

160 and 182–83; AMS Libro. For account books kept by other fifteenth-century Florentine women, see ASF S3 LXXXII: 188; S3 LXXXVIII: 28; S4 72, 73; S5: 54, 56, 60, 61, 1747; ASF Conventi Soppressi, Inv. 142, vols. 71–78. In the early sixteenth century, historian Francesco Guicciardini praised the skill of account keeping in a female relative (1936). On women's role in humanist learning in fifteenth-century Italy, see King and Rabil 1983; Labalme 1980.

6. AMS Lettere, 230–31; see also 276 and n. 16.

7. For evidence of her matter-of-fact acceptance of inequalities in wealth and status, see AMS Lettere, 360, 438, 525–26 On the different roles of men and women, see her different expectations for her son Matteo and her daughters in her letters of 1447–51. On her attitude about the family, see below.

8. On the marriage ages of men and women and the proportion of widows, see Herlihy and Klapisch-Zuber 1985, 205, 216, 221. My estimate of the proportion of widows living with minor children is based on numbers in gonfalone Drago, Santo Spirito quarter, in the Catasto of 1442, vols. 612 and 613. I used that year and gonfalone because Alessandra Strozzi, a widow with minor children, was living there at the time. For the rate of remarriage of widows, see Klapisch-Zuber 1980, 117–31. On attitudes to remarriage, see Sant'Antonino 1859, no. 10; Savonarola 1952, 42–54; San Bernardino 1934–40, 1:IV, 129–36; Vespasiano 1963, 460; Morelli 1956, 202–3, 214–18; Rucellai 1960, 118; and Klapisch-Zuber 1980. For the dowry law, see Stat. Flor. I, 2: LXI, LCIII, LXLV.

9. For Alessandra's household arrangements, see ASF S5 12: 1, 27; ASF Catasto 76: 138; 612: 92–95; 620: 403; 654: 174; 671: I, 147; 816: 188. Figures for the household arrangements of other widows are based on ASF Catasto 1442, vols. 312 and 313. For the Florentine law of tornata di casa, see Stat. Flor. II: CXXX, LXI. On the high number of patrilocal extended households in Florence by European standards, see Kent 1977, 21–62; Herlihy and Klapisch-Zuber 1985, 280–336; Laslett 1983. For Alessandra's relations with her own family, see, especially, AMS Lettere, 104–5, 125–26, 204–5, 220, 224–25; AMS Libro, XVII, 18, 27, 86–87, LXXXXI.

10. On kinship ties outside the household, see Kent 1978; Weissman 1982, chap. 1; Kuehn 1982; and Cohn 1980. On the kin in Alessandra's life, see Crabb 1981, especially 203–13, 240–65, 273–83.

11. For copies of Matteo's will, see ASF S5 12: 25 and S5 1250. Statements about the inheritance position of other widows are based on a sample of thirty-nine wills found in ASF Not. 8525 and 1800, in which husbands with surviving wives made provisions for guardianship of children.

12. On Alessandra's position, see ASF S5 12: 25, and S5 1250.

13. For Alessandra and her children's financial position, see ASF Catasto: 612, no. 398; 620, I: no. 173. For Alessandra staying behind after Matteo's exile, see ASF S5 12: 29. On other women staying behind to manage the family affairs,

see Vespasiano 1963 and 1843; Dominici 1927; del Lungo 1906, 242–77; Velluti 1914, 119; Foster 1985, 108–24, 643–67; Origo 1962, 87. On the proportion of families living on dowry property, see, for the Strozzi, Crabb 1981, 49; for others, see ASF Catasto, vols. 612 and 613.

14. In the Catasto of 1442, Alessandra was the wealthiest widow holding her property in her own name in Drago, Santo Spirito quarter; Leon Rosso, Santa Maria Novella quarter; and Vaio, San Giovanni quarter; and only four households in Drago, Santo Spirito containing widows but listed in men's names declared higher incomes (ASF Catasto, vols. 612, 613, 620, and 628). Since, in the Catasto of 1442, people declared income from property but not from salaries or business profits, this catasto has limited usefulness as a measure of men's wealth, and, thus, for households including widows but listed in men's names; however, it is a reasonable indicator of the wealth of widows declaring in their own names, because widows' incomes were likely to be mostly from property. On the legal status of widows, see *Stat. Flor.* I, 2: IX, XXII, CXII, CXX, and I, 3: CVII; Calisse 1928, 57 and 519ff.

15. For Alessandra's accepting *mundualdi* provided by the court, see AMS Libro, 88, 93.

16. For women's low level of participation in the economy, see Herlihy and Klapisch-Zuber 1985, 124; and Brown 1986. For their occasional membership in guilds, although not in merchant guilds, see ASF *Arti dei rigattieri, linaioli e sarti* 10; Park 1987, 71–72. On Alessandra's investments and her trading in cloth, see ASF S3 249: 75, 83; AMS *Lettere*, 71; AMS Libro, 158, 168. On other women's investments, buying, and selling, see ASF S3 249: 83; S5 54: 52, 86, 100, 169, 201; Foster 1985, 653–55.

17. AMS *Lettere*, 525. On her managing the farms, see also ASF Catasto 816, nos. 188, 358; AMS Libro, LXXXI–LXXXII. On others acting as her agents, see AMS Libro, 7, 11, 15, 34, XXV, 81.

18. AMS *Lettere*, 224. For the lawsuit in which she and Filippo appeared before the Signoria, the highest executive council, acting in its capacity as court, see AMS Libro, LXXXXI, 92. For another widow who presented petitions and argued cases before a court, see Foster 1985, 666–67. For Alessandra's controlling sales of her lands while her sons signed as guarantors, see AMS *Lettere*, 224; AMS Libro, 90, 91. For the Florentine law on land sales, see *Stat. Flor.* II: CIX. Similarly, Alessandra signed as guarantor for the receipt of her sons' wives' dowries (AMS Libro, 100).

19. On choosing husbands for her daughters, see AMS *Lettere*, 4-5, 70, 101-2, 120-21; ASF S3 145: 24, 26. On her teaching, see AMS *Lettere*, 6, 33–34; ASF S3 131: 29, 32; S3 249: 75, 79, 83. On her encouraging her sons to succeed, see AMS *Lettere*, 8–9, 68; ASF S3 249: 75.

20. On a father's power, see *Stat. Flor.*, II: CX; Kent 1977, especially 55–60, 71–72; 83–84, Kuehn 1982.

21. For the view that premodern European families lacked love and intimacy, see Ariès 1961; Stone 1977; Shorter 1975; de Mause 1974. For the opinions of fifteenth-century Italian didactic writers, see Alberti 1969, 88–89; Sant'Antonino 1859, 125; San Bernardino 1934–40, 185–86; Dominici 1927, 155–61; Rucellai 1960, 36.

22. AMS *Lettere*, 60; see also AMS *Lettere*, 100; ASF S3 249: 75.

23. AMS *Lettere*, 280. On the general preference for boys, see AMS *Lettere*, 507, 596, 599; ASF S3 178: 6; S3 249: 250. For Alessandra's wills, see ASF Not. 8525, 40; AMS *Lettere*, 317–21. Estimates of inheritance patterns for sons and daughters in fathers' and mothers' wills are based on an analysis of wills in ASF Not. 8525 and 1800.

24. For Filippo's giving Alessandra advice in 1445, see ASF S3 180: 50. On her going out of her way to agree with him, see for example, AMS *Lettere*, 454.

25. AMS *Lettere*, 128–29. For Lorenzo's misbehavior, see ASF S3 131: 73, 74; S3 249: 83, 71.

26. For a good discussion of Florence's competitiveness, see Weissman 1982, 26–35. On Filippo Strozzi's success, see Strozzi 1851; Goldthwaite 1968 and 1973.

27. For the quotations in this paragraph, see ASF S3 249: 75; AMS *Lettere*, 45–46, 60–61, 77. See also ASF S3 131: 29; AMS *Lettere*, 6, 47–48. For her sons' need to work abroad because of political conditions and because of the large tax debt inherited from their father, for which they were liable at age sixteen, see AMS *Lettere*, 6; ASF S3 131: 29.

28. AMS *Lettere*, 136. On the money Alessandra sent her sons and her attitude to sharing money with them, see AMS *Lettere*, 128, 136, 170, 312; Biblioteca nazionale di Firenze, II, IV, 197: 50; ASF S3 131: 29; S3 249: 97, 103; AMS Libro, 27, XXVII; ASF S5 1250. For another widowed mother who acted as mediator in dividing money among her sons, see Panzano 1889, 160.

29. AMS *Lettere*, 234, 243. On Matteo's death, see AMS *Lettere*, 177–211. On Filippo and Alessandra's attitudes toward the brothers working together, see AMS *Lettere*, 207–8, 212–13, 225, 230, 233–34, 238. On Lorenzo's doing well in Jacopo's company, see ASF S3 249: 112, 137; S3 131: 81.

30. For the ban of exile, see ASF Otto di Guardia e Balìa 224, 85v–86r. Information about Alessandra's political activities is found mainly in AMS *Lettere* for 1464–65, the most extensive part of her correspondence. For accounts of political events in Florence in 1458–66, see Rubinstein 1978, especially 129–73; Phillips 1987, 3–19, 97–149, 169–214. For Alessandra's plans to leave Florence, see ASF S3 131: 81; AMS *Lettere*, XXXIII–IV, 143–44, 164–66, 199–200, 212–13, 230, 234, 393–94.

31. On informal politics supplementing formal politics, see Kent 1978, especially 11–30; Brucker 1969, 137–60. On the connection between politics and taxes, see AMS *Lettere* 7, 564. For other women involved in political activities

because of male relatives' exiles, see Vespasiano 1963, 461, and 1843, 448. Guicciardini mentions that women in his family had a good knowledge of affairs of state (1936, 31). For Alessandra's political stance, see her support of the reform movement of the fall and winter, 1465–66 (AMS *Lettere,* 503, 519–20), but also her desire to cultivate the Medici's favor, if useful (AMS *Lettere,* 255–66, 579).

32. AMS *Lettere,* 332; also 368–69, 373–79.

33. AMS *Lettere,* 366; also 363–64, 373–74, 381–84.

34. AMS *Lettere,* 406, 534. The idea expressed in the latter quotation is close to what Edgar Wind (1958) suggested was a typically Renaissance idea, "ripeness is all."

35. AMS *Lettere,* 566–67. For the electoral reform movement, see Rubinstein 1978; Phillips 1987.

36. AMS *Lettere,* 567–68. For the repeal of exile, see ASF Balie, 30, 20v–22v.

37. AMS *Lettere,* 467, also 447–49.

38. AMS *Lettere,* 463–64. On Alessandra's investigations, see AMS *Lettere,* 445, 458–59, 463–65, 469–71. When Alessandra's son-in-law, Marco Parenti, was looking for husbands for his daughters, he tried to gain access to Catasto returns of potential grooms (ASF S3 249: 300). See also Marco in ASF S3 178: 11; Alberti 1969, 115.

39. For Filippo and Lorenzo's marriages, see ASF S5 22: 22; AMS Libro, 100. For Alessandra's relations with her daughter-in-law Fiammetta and grand-children, see AMS *Lettere,* 583–93, 598–600, 603–6.

BIBLIOGRAPHY

Alberti, Leon Battista. *The Family in Renaissance Florence.* Trans. Renée Neu Watkins. Columbia, S.C.: University of South Carolina Press, 1969.

Ariès, Philippe. *Centuries of Childhood: A Social History of Family Life.* Trans. Robert Baldick. New York: Vintage Books, 1961.

Bec, Christian. *Les marchands écrivains à Florence, 1375–1434.* Paris: Mouton, 1967.

Brown, Judith C. "A Woman's Place Was in the Home: Women's Work in Renaissance Tuscany." In *Rewriting the Renaissance: The Discourses of Sexual Differences in Early Modern Europe,* ed. Margaret W. Ferguson, Maureen Quilligan, and Nancy J. Vickers, 206–24. Chicago: University of Chicago Press, 1986.

Brucker, Gene. *Renaissance Florence.* New York: Wiley, 1969.

Calisse, Carlo. *A History of Italian Law.* Trans. Layton B. Register. Boston: Little, Brown, 1928.

Cohn, Samuel Kline. *The Laboring Classes in Renaissance Florence.* New York: Academic Press, 1980.

Crabb, Ann. "A Patrician Family in Renaissance Florence: The Family Relations of Alessandra Macinghi Strozzi and Her Sons, 1440–1491." Ph.D. diss., Washington University, (St. Louis, Mo.), 1981.

del Lungo, Isidoro, ed. *La donna fiorentina del buon tempo antico.* Florence: P. Bemporad, 1906.

De Mause, Lloyd, ed. *The History of Childhood.* New York: Psychohistory Press, 1974.

Dominici, Fra Giovanni. *Regola di governo di cura familiare.* Ed. P. Bargellini. Florence: A. Garina, 1860.

Foster, Susan Kerr. "The Alberti of Florence." Ph.D. diss., Cornell University, 1985.

Goldthwaite, Richard. *Private Wealth in Renaissance Florence: A Study of Four Families.* Princeton: Princeton University Press, 1968.

———. "The Building of the Strozzi Palace: The Construction Industry in Renaissance Florence." *Studies in Medieval and Renaissance History* 10 (1973): 97–194.

Guicciardini, Francesco. "Libro di Ricordi." *Scritti autobiografici e rari.* Ed. Roberto Palmarocchi. Bari: G. Laterrza, 1936.

Herlihy, David, and Christiane Klapisch-Zuber. *Tuscans and Their Families: A Study of the Florentine Catasto of 1427.* New Haven: Yale University Press, 1985.

Kent, Dale. *The Rise of the Medici: Faction in Florence, 1426–1434.* Oxford: Oxford University Press, 1978.

Kent, F. W. *Household and Lineage in Renaissance Florence: The Family Life of the Capponi, Ginori, and Rucellai.* Princeton: Princeton University Press, 1977.

King, Margaret L., and Albert Rabil, Jr. *Her Immaculate Hand: Selected Works by and about the Women Humanists of Quattrocento Italy.* Binghamton, N.Y.: Medieval and Renaissance Texts and Studies, 1983.

Klapisch-Zuber, Christiane. "'The Cruel Mother': Maternity, Widowhood, and Dowry in Florence in the Fourteenth and Fifteenth Centuries." In *Woman, Family, and Ritual in Renaissance Italy,* 134–62. Chicago: University of Chicago Press, 1980.

Kuehn, Thomas. *Emancipation in Late Medieval Florence.* New Brunswick, N.J.: Rutgers University Press, 1982.

Labalme, P.H. *Beyond Their Sex: Learned Women of the European Past.* New York: New York University Press, 1980.

Laslett, Peter. "Family and Household as Work Group and Kin Group: Areas of Traditional Europe Compared." In *Family Forms in Historic Europe,* ed. Richard Wall, 513–63. Cambridge: Cambridge University Press, 1983.

Morelli, Giovanni. *Ricordi.* Ed. V. Branca. Florence: F. LeMonnier, 1956.

Origo, Iris. *The World of San Bernardino.* New York: Harcourt, Brace and World, 1962.

Pampaloni, Guido. *Palazzo Strozzi*. Rome: Instituto nazionale delle assiacrazioni, 1963.

Panzano, Luca di Matteo. "Un fiorentino del secolo XV e le sue ricordanze domestiche, 1406–1461." *Archivio Storico Italiano,* 5th ser., 4 (1889): 145–73.

Park, Catherine. *Doctors and Medicine in Renaissance Florence*. Princeton: Princeton University Press, 1987.

Phillips, Mark. *The Memoir of Marco Parenti: A Life in Medici Florence*. Princeton: Princeton University Press, 1987.

Rubinstein, Nicolai. *The Government of Florence under the Medici*. Oxford: Oxford University Press, 1978.

Rucellai, Giovanni. *Zibaldone*. Ed. Alessandro Perosa. London: Warburg Institute, 1960.

San Bernardino da Siena. *Le prediche volgari*. Ed. Ciro Cannorozzi. Pistoia: A. Pacinotti, 1934–40.

Sant'Antonino da Firenze. *Lettere*. Florence: Tipografia Barbera, Bianchi, 1859.

Savonarola, Fra Girolamo. "Il libro della vita viduale." *Prediche e scritti*. Ed. Mario Ferrara. Florence: Olschki, 1952.

Shorter, Edward. *The Making of the Modern Family*. New York: Basic Books, 1975.

"Statuti ed ordimenti dell'ufficio dei pupilli ed adulti nel periodo della Reppubblica fiorentina, 1388–1434." *Archivio storico italiano* (1954): 522–51; (1956): 92–111; (1957): 87–104.

Statuti Populi et Comunis Florentiae, MCCCCXV. Ed. Michaelem Klutch. Friburg: 1777–83.

Stone, Lawrence. *The Family, Sex and Marriage in England, 1500–1800*. New York: Harper and Row, 1977.

Strozzi, Alessandra Macinghi. *Lettere di una gentidonna del secolo XV ai figliuali esuli*. Ed. Cesare Guasti. Florence: Sansoni, 1877.

Strozzi, Lorenzo di Filippo. *Vita di Filippo Strozzi il Vecchio*. Ed. Giuseppe Bini and Pietro Bigazzi. Florence, 1851.

Velluti, Messer Donato. *Cronaca domestica*. Ed. I. del Lungo and G. Volpi. Florence: G.C. Sansoni, 1914.

Vespasiano. "Life of Matteo Strozzi." In *Renaissance Princes, Popes, and Prelates: The Vespasiano Memoirs*. Trans W. George and E. Walters, 245–46. New York: Harper Torchbooks, 1963.

———. "Life of Alessandra de Bardi." In *Renaissance Princes*, 439–62.

———. "Notizie d'alcune illustri donne." *Archivio storico italiano* 1st ser., 4 (1843): 512–33.

Weissman, Ronald. *Ritual Brotherhood in Renaissance Florence*. New York: Academic Press, 1982.

Wind, Edgar. *Pagan Mysteries of the Renaissance*. London: Faber and Faber, 1958.

Chapter 3

Widows in the Medieval English Countryside

Judith M. Bennett

In the judgment of many historians, few medieval women were as fortunate as peasant widows. Doris Mary Stenton has argued that, in general, peasant women were "relatively in a stronger position" compared to women of higher social rank, and that this relative advantage was particularly marked among widows. Rodney Hilton has suggested that the powerful dowagers of the late medieval aristocracy might have only achieved their power "in the wake of widows of peasant society." Peter Franklin has written about the "liberation" of widowhood for rural women.[1] Assessments such as these seem to rest upon two presumptions: first, that sexual equality was more nearly approached among the peasant classes of the Middle Ages, and second, that widows were, of all women, the most powerful. I have argued elsewhere that social rank only minimally affected the social relations of the sexes in medieval England—that peasant women, townswomen, gentlewomen, and aristocratic women encountered roughly equivalent expectations and limitations.[2] In this essay, I want to suggest that our assessment of widows must also be more carefully nuanced, for widows, although able to take advantage of many new and unusual opportunities, were nevertheless restricted in important ways because of their sex. Widows had many opportunities, but not all took them up, and none were truly liberated.

To illustrate as fully as possible the experience of widowhood in the medieval English countryside, I shall focus upon the lives and activities of widows on the manor of Brigstock in the six decades that preceded the plague. As a case study, Brigstock will illustrate widows not only within a particular local context but also in actual action—allowing an assessment of practice as well as prescription. Brigstock, with its daughter settlement Stanion, lay in Rockingham Forest in the English Midlands. As in many forest communities, the inhabitants of Brigstock supported themselves in a variety of ways—arable farming, animal husbandry, fishing, poaching, even cloth working. They practiced an unusual inheritance custom that divided property between the younger son (who received his father's inherited lands) and his elder brother (who received any lands purchased by their father). The manor was heavily populated (with between 350 and 500 adult males) and under the demographic pressure typical of many preplague communities (population declined slightly and sporadically after the 1320s). Every three weeks, the people of Brigstock attended their manorial court—bringing complaints about bad debts and broken contracts, selling and leasing land, electing officers for local governance, reporting petty crimes and disturbances, and attending to a wide range of local matters. The surviving records of the 549 sessions of this court between 1287 and 1348 provide the raw material for reconstructing the experiences of widows in the community.[3]

Alice the wife of Peter Avice typified the public reticence of wives in Brigstock. She seldom brought business before the local court and often relied on her husband in such matters. Acting on her own, she paid six amercements for selling ale, she used the court to settle four disputes, and she once incurred censure for her disrespectful behavior toward the bailiff. Five other matters brought her to court accompanied by her husband; in 1292, they paid jointly for admittance to a quarter-virgate, and between 1295 and 1301, they together pursued four cases against other villagers. Over the course of her twenty-four years as a wife, Alice Avice accumulated a small court network of only twenty-two contacts with fourteen people. She interacted in court most frequently with her husband (eight contacts), who far outweighed in importance any of the other associations reflected in her court actions.[4] After Peter Avice died, however, Alice's public reticence was replaced by public assertion. Usually coming to court unaccompanied by others, she paid rent on her holding, she purchased and sold lands, she answered for various offenses associated with property ownership, she brought or responded to six complaints against other villagers, and she even acted on three occasions as a legal surety, guaranteeing that others would meet their legal obligations. During a widowhood that lasted eight years less than her marriage, Alice Avice developed a much larger court network than she had known as a wife: thirty-four contacts with twenty-five people. Her associations as a widow, moreover, were notable for their diversity rather than for their reliance on a single person. The records of the Brigstock court leave little doubt that the death of Peter Avice in 1316, no matter how personally distressing it might have been to his widow, left her in a new position of public authority. She accepted the responsibilities of a householder, she vigorously and effectively administered her holdings, and she actively participated in the social community of Brigstock.[5]

Many medieval countrywomen, like Alice Avice, faced years of widowhood at the end of their lives. The absence of marriage or death records makes it impossible to calculate precisely the usual duration of marriage on manors like Brigstock, but most marriages probably endured for little more than two decades. Of the fifty-three widows in Brigstock whose marital histories could be partially reconstructed from activities noted in the manor court, the gap between first citation as a wife and first mention of bereavement stretched from as little as two years to as much as forty-two years, but the median of fifteen years was quite close to the average of seventeen years. Because these calculations underestimate the actual duration of marriage, most marriages in Brigstock likely ended with the death of a spouse after the passage of about two decades.[6] Although very rough, these estimates match Zvi Razi's calculations for Halesowen, which suggest that, before the plague, marriages on that manor usually lasted about twenty-three to twenty-six years.[7] Moreover, an average marital duration of about twenty years likely characterized English rural communities throughout the preindustrial period; analyses of the information found in parish registers of early modern English communities suggest that most marriages in the sixteenth and seventeenth centuries also ended with the death of a spouse after about two decades.[8]

Were women more likely to be widowed than men? Although at least 12 percent of the women identified in the courts of Brigstock before the plague survived their husbands, no comparable figures for men are available because manorial records never mention male widowhood.[9] It is highly likely, however, that widowhood was a more temporary status for males than for females; studies of preindustrial European communities have shown that widowed men remarried more frequently and also more quickly than did widowed women.[10] Mortality rates dictated whether more men or more women were deprived of their spouses, but social custom invariably assured that more women than men remained alone. In Brigstock, widows often survived their husbands for considerable lengths of time. Of the fifty-three unremarried widows whose court activities could be reconstructed, the gap between first citation as a widow and last court appearance stretched from one to thirty-seven years, and the median of five years fell significantly below the average of nine years. Although experiences varied widely (doubtless reflecting the age at which a woman lost her husband), most widows in the community probably survived their husbands for at least several years, and possibly as much as a decade or more.

As suggested by the public activities of the widowed Alice Avice, widowhood brought medieval countrywomen new responsibilities and opportunities. Because rural households were built around the conjugal unity of husband and wife, bereaved wives necessarily assumed many of the functions of their dead husbands. Widows whose sons were too young to claim their inheritances usually took custody of minor heirs and controlled their conjugal estates until the heirs' maturity.[11] In addition, widows enjoyed dower rights that superseded the claims of heirs, whether minor or mature. Under the common law, a widow's dower extended over only one-third of her husband's property, but customary law often granted to widows as their "free bench" from one-half to all of their husbands' lands. As a rule, rural custom gave widows only the *use* of free bench lands, dictating that they were not to alienate such properties without the consent of their husbands' heirs; this right of use, however, often endured throughout the widow's life, regardless of either remarriage or the maturation of heirs.[12] As a result, widows controlled significant proportions of land in the medieval countryside; in many villages, 10 to 15 percent of all holdings were in the hands of women, most of whom were widows.[13]

Precisely because of the enhanced public stature that widowhood offered women, their experiences are especially difficult to trace in the records of manors like Brigstock. Wives and adolescent daughters, as dependents of householders, were regularly and reliably cited in manorial records by their dependency status, but widows, as independent householders, were often cited with no indication of marital status. Matilda Manning, for example, was invariably identified as "Matilda the wife of John Manning" during her married years (ten citations), but after her husband died, the manorial clerk usually identified her simply as "Matilda Manning" (9 citations) instead of indicating her widowed state by calling her "Matilda the widow of John Manning" (two citations).[14] Indeed, some widows, like Alice Goldhop, the widow of Hugh Helkok, resumed their former names after the deaths of their husbands. Unless the records have included some indication of widowed status (a clerical identification, a payment of relief or heriot, a transfer of free bench lands), the marital condition of such women cannot be precisely determined. If the record of Alice Goldhop's payment of heriot in 1322 had not survived, for example, historical reconstruction of her widowed status would have been impossible because she was never again specifically identified by the court clerk as a widow.[15]

As a result, many widows are doubtless hidden among the "women of unknown marital status" found in the reconstructed population of Brigstock. Some of these women were probably spinsters who grew beyond the authority of their fathers without ever coming under the authority of husbands. The experiences of those who remained perpetually unmarried are, with a few exceptional cases such as that of Cecilia Penifader, notoriously difficult to trace. But most "women of unknown status" were likely widows for whom bereavement brought new responsibilities and opportunities. Certainly, these women—whether spinsters or widows—were distinguished by their breadth and independence of public action from wives and adolescent daughters in the Brigstock samples.[16] To offset the obstacles posed not only by the obfuscation of widowhood in the extant records but also by the small numbers of cited widows found in the Brigstock samples, widowhood in Brigstock is best studied from a total reconstruction rather than a sampling. Some widows have doubtless remained untraced, but all of the criminal, litigious, and proprietal transactions of the 106 widows identified in Brigstock before the plague have been fully considered.

If all the women of Brigstock had reacted to widowhood with the vigor and independence of Alice Avice, our picture of the intersection of household status and female experience would be neatly completed: semiautonomous daughters, dependent wives, autonomous widows. Yet the realities of widows' lives were more complex and varied. Some women, like Alice Avice, assertively responded to the responsibilities of widowhood; others, however, seem to have taken little part in public affairs. Alice Avice's counterpart was Alice Penifader, who reacted to the death of her husband, Robert, in 1318 by withdrawal, not assertion; the Brigstock records note only her many excused absences from meetings of the court. Widowhood was an exceptionally varied status, with not only personality but also locale, socioeconomic standing, and age affecting each woman's response to the death of her husband.[17]

Locale profoundly shaped one of the most important decisions faced by rural widows—the choice either to remarry or to remain single. In villages where land was scarce, remarriage was frequent, but when land was readily available, widows remarried only rarely. With the economic diversity offered by its forest location and the ready access to property provided by the local market in land, Brigstock offered few economic incentives for remarrying. As a result, most widows remained single, only about one of every thirteen marrying a second time. The pastoral economy of Iver (Buckinghamshire) similarly discouraged remarriage.[18] But in other contemporary villages, remarriage was such a crucial means of redistributing resources that most widows married again. In early fourteenth-century Halesowen, for example, six of every ten widows remarried.[19] Although the connection between land availability and remarriage in the medieval countryside is clear, motivations are less certain. Perhaps widows were usually eager to remarry, but could only bargain successfully for new husbands when they controlled lands valued by prospective suitors.[20] Or perhaps few widows wished to remarry, but those in land-hungry villages were compelled to do so because of their extensive proprietal rights.[21] In either case, the very existence of the widowed state varied widely from village to village. In some communities, remarriage was so common that few women acted for long as widowed heads of household; when they remarried, they essentially resumed their prior status as wives. Other villages boasted many widows who, instead of remarrying, spent many years administering the households and properties left by their husbands.

Within a given village, the experience of widowhood varied dramatically according to the solvency of the household left by the husband. Widows of wealthier husbands who had planned carefully for their bereavement faced secure and settled prospects, but widows of poorer husbands often struggled for their basic livelihood with great difficulty. The effect of socioeconomic standing is clearly seen in the Brigstock records; just as male heads of lower rank households generally came less frequently before the court, so lower rank widows generated less court notice than widows of more privileged status. Two-thirds of officeholders' widows were noticeably active in the Brigstock court, compared to only one-third of the widows of men who never held local office.

Publicly active widows were, more often than not, widows of wealthy and influential men.[22]

The varied experiences wrought by socioeconomic status were compounded by age, since women widowed early in life faced more opportunities than those widowed in their later years. A widow's age strongly affected her likelihood of remarriage. Young widows, responsible for young children and all the economic resources left by their husbands, were more likely not only to be expected to remarry (placing their households again under the normative control of a male) but also to desire the emotional comfort offered by a second spouse. Older widows, whose grown children had already established separate homes, likely faced less pressure to remarry (because they controlled only small households) and also possibly were less interested in obtaining new partners. Remarriage in Brigstock was very rare, but most of the women who sought second husbands had apparently lost their first husbands prematurely.[23]

Age also probably affected the public presence of widows as reported in manorial courts. The ages of persons traced in the courts of Brigstock cannot be precisely calculated, but table 3.1 illustrates how men slowly withdrew from public life as they aged; each of the five men studied participated less in the basic political networks of Brigstock—acting as pledges, essoining friends from court attendance, serving as officers—during his later decades than he had done earlier. Henry Kroyl senior's life provides a particularly good example of this phenomenon because the marriage of his son Henry junior in 1319 clearly marked the beginning of his retirement. He had served his community as an officer (usually a juror or an affeeror) on twenty-three occasions in the ten years prior to his son's marriage; although he lived for a decade after the marriage, he never again took on official responsibilities. His three land conveyances in the 1309–19 decade similarly contrast with the single transfer of property accomplished in his last ten years, as do the three disputes that went to litigation in the former period as opposed to only one in the latter. Although Henry Kroyl senior remained an independent householder until his death in 1329, as he aged, he slowly withdrew from the public life of Brigstock. The same circumstances that encouraged his lessening interest in public matters also doubtless affected many widows, ensuring that elderly widows were less active than younger widows in community life.[24]

Because aging adversely affected economic productivity, elderly persons also numbered heavily among the poor of preindustrial communi-

TABLE 3.1. The Effect of Aging on Male Public Activity in Brigstock

Individual	First Decade of Court Activity	Second Decade of Court Activity	Third Decade of Court Activity	Fourth Decade of Court Activity	Fifth Decade of Court Activity
Richard Aylward, 1292–1335					
Pledger/essoiner	3	16	32	17	—
Officer	0	4	22	13	—
Total	3	20	54	30	—
Henry Cade, 1295–1336					
Pledger/essoiner	3	16	17	4	—
Officer	0	1	3	6	—
Total	3	17	20	10	—
William Durant, 1297–1337					
Pledger/essoiner	2	1	18	16	—
Officer	0	0	16	6	—
Total	2	1	34	22	—
Gilbert Son of Galfridus, 1287–1335					
Pledger/essoiner	11	28	28	31	3
Officer	0	9	23	21	7
Total	11	37	51	52	10
John Hirdman, 1303–40					
Pledger/essoiner	7	100	11	12	—
Officer	0	1	2	1	—
Total	7	101	13	13	—

ties. Both villagers and lords were concerned with care of those for whom age brought either poverty or disability. By restricting gleaning to the poor, local bylaws assured that such persons would receive basic sustenance. Seigneurial policies that replaced incompetent tenants certainly did not hurt manorial revenues, but they also provided secure maintenance for those unable to provide for themselves. The link between aging and poverty suggests that many of the apparent disabilities of widowhood (as seen in retirement contracts, work defaults, requests to be excused from court, and the like) were more often caused by age than by widowhood itself. One of the ironies of widowhood in the medieval countryside is the mingling of old age with access to new responsibilities and privileges.[25]

Because of the forces exerted by locale, socioeconomic status, and age, each new widow faced a unique situation. As long as she remained unremarried, however, she shared with all other widows the status of a female endowed with extensive public authority; as a result, widows fit awkwardly into the social hierarchy of the medieval world. In a society of male householders, they were female heads of households. In a legal system that so often distinguished clearly between the public rights of males and females, they took on some of the public attributes of men. In an economy that most valued landholding, their peculiar land claims threatened the proper devolution of assets from father to son. Because of the conjugal basis of the rural household, the death of a husband required that his wife replace him; their household was usually too discrete from kin to find his replacement among brothers, cousins, or even sons (for whom the attainment of householder status was associated with marriage, not inheritance). But when a widow assumed her husband's responsibilities, she became an anomaly—a householder who was not male. All widows in Brigstock did not fully utilize the public opportunities presented by their ambivalent status. Some asserted both domestic and public authority, others managed their households without much involvement in public matters, and still others might have retired from active management of their households. Few widows, however, totally eschewed the public opportunities of their new stature, and the overall patterns of their public activities were unlike those of either male householders or other women. Widows were never as publicly active and autonomous as male householders, but the breadth of their public actions as householders, as landholders, and as villagers clearly surpassed the more limited political, legal, economic, and social options of wives and adolescent daughters.

Widows as Householders

The political and legal activities of men in Brigstock expanded when they became married heads of households. Adolescent males were politically active as members of tithings, essoiners, attorneys, and pledges; married males could additionally participate in the official hierarchy of Brigstock by serving as bailiffs, affeerors, aletasters, and the like. Similarly, adolescent males accepted legal responsibility for their own affairs, paying fines, answering or bringing suits, or attending court if required to do so; married male householders shouldered further responsibilities not only for the corporate actions of their households but also occasionally for the independent offenses of their wives and children. When widows in Brigstock took over the households left by their husbands, they seldom retired meekly from all domestic duties. They did not, however, fully assume their husbands' privileges and obligations. Located awkwardly on the public spectrum between the extensive authority of male householders and the dependency of wives and children, widows took over many of the functions once undertaken by their husbands. Yet they acquired more responsibilities than privileges.

Because of the conjugal basis of the peasant household, widows' households were exceptionally diverse and unstable. The size and structure of all households varied with socioeconomic circumstances and the age of its head, but households headed by widows, ipso facto in the later stages of the household cycle, were especially variable. More often than not, widows either had married offspring established in separate households or else soon supervised the leaving of their children. Alice the widow of John Popelin of Iver might have been typical; one daughter had married a few years before John's death, and another daughter and a son married shortly thereafter.[26] Low replacement rates ensured that the households of many other widows were especially small; of every five widows, probably one had no living children and another had no living sons.[27]

Although widows lived in households that were often small and disintegrating, their public position was clear. On the one hand, they resumed all the legal options they had known when unmarried; widows, like adolescent daughters (but unlike some wives), owed suit to the court of

Brigstock, answered for their own crimes and offenses, resolved disputes through litigation usually unaccompanied by others, and freely concluded contracts or other agreements with their fellow villagers. On the other hand, widows also assumed control of their newly shattered conjugal households. Because households were formed at marriage and shaped around the conjugal unity of husband and wife, no other option was automatically available; sons, who established discrete households upon marriage, could not readily step into their fathers' places. When William Popelin married a few years after the death of his father John, for example, he did not assume domestic authority over his widowed mother, but instead lived separately from her.[28] Studies of the household structures of English villagers in the sixteenth through eighteenth centuries have shown that most widows remained in their marital households and did not retire into the households of married children.[29] The public activities of widows in early fourteenth-century Brigstock suggest that they, like their counterparts in early modern villages, normally took over the domestic responsibilities of their husbands.

Of the 101 unremarried widows in the community whose careers have been reconstructed, the public actions of only ten betrayed an unwillingness to meet their responsibilities as householders and, in most cases, the evidence of disability is quite minimal.[30] Three widows made arrangements for retirement, concluding maintenance agreements in which they granted property in return for guaranteed support. Matilda Cocus tried to arrange a pension with her son, but resumed control of her holding when the agreement soured; in 1311, an inquisition determined that she (widowed since 1302) could reclaim her land from her son because he had failed to provide her with the food and clothing he had promised. She was still managing the land herself several years later.[31] Emma Sephirde, after seventeen years of widowhood, divided some property *(placia)* between her sons in 1319, specifying that they were to give her a cartload of hay each year for the holding. Yet she continued to manage other lands on her own and, six years later, arranged for one son to enter the residue of her holdings after her death.[32] Emma With retired after her second husband died, not to her son's home but rather jointly with her son; in 1331, they both, acknowledging their poverty and inability to do services, granted their land away in return for an annual rent.[33] None of these widows successfully retired under the protection of a son, and all three seem to have been at a quite advanced age at the time they began to make provision for retirement. Aside from these three equivocal cases, no other hints of retirements appear in the reconstructed histories of Brigstock's widows.

Evidence of economic disability on the part of widows is also rare. Both Emma With (who claimed poverty in transferring her lands for an annual rent) and Matilda Cocus (who was cited after the maintenance dispute with her son for failing to find a servant for herding and plowing) might have been prompted to think of retirement because of problems managing their holdings. But the public activities of only one other widow betrayed any evidence of economic difficulties; Edith the widow of Gilbert Cocus claimed poverty in a plea she entered some nine years after the death of her husband. As with retirements, the evidence of economic disability is not only sparse but also ambivalent; claims of poverty accompanied the court actions of some demonstrably wealthy suitors, and male householders were also occasionally cited for work defaults.[34]

Another indicator of disability, the seeking of relief from the obligation of attending court, involved only six widows. Emma Werketon, whose son replaced her as court suitor, might have wished to withdraw permanently from public life. Five other widows paid fines to relax court suit temporarily (never more than one year), without specifying replacements. Fines to avoid court attendance, however, are uncertain indicators of public withdrawal because men frequently avoided attending court without jeopardizing their public status. Henry Cade, for example, was fined once to relax suit of court for a full year and frequently proffered excuses for not attending specific meetings; nevertheless, he served on several local juries during the course of his adult life.[35]

In contrast to the limited evidence suggesting that widows in Brigstock were unwilling or unable to assume the responsibilities of householders, the Brigstock records contain abundant examples of widows publicly acting as heads of households. For every widow who betrayed any difficulty managing her household, roughly three widows in the community capably assumed the duties of householders. As their husbands had done before them, many widows in Brigstock accepted responsibility for the actions of their dependents and their households. Only one widow paid an amercement for a misdemeanor committed by a member of her household, but many widows paid amercements for crimes associated with householding (see table 3.2).[36] The overall pattern of the reported criminality of widows generally follows the female norm; most citations against widows involved antisocial actions rather than personal attacks or thefts. Yet widows deviated from the expected pattern for females by the preponderance of amercements they paid for household offenses—for improper use of pastures, for misuse of their holdings or other property damage, and for allowing strangers to tarry overlong in their homes. Indeed, because widows seem to have been notably less criminal than other adults, over half of their criminal amercements covered such household offenses. All told, sixteen widows in Brigstock paid sums in the court for either the offenses of their dependents or crimes associated with householding. Another five widows similarly betrayed their householding responsibilities by paying rents noted in the one listing of rents extant for the manor.[37]

Moreover, other widows acted in court in a capacity that was unusual for women, but common for householders; they pledged for their dependents. Of the thousands of sureties recorded in the Brigstock court between 1287 and 1348, only 46 were offered by females and most of these were widows pledging for the petty crimes of their sons and daughters (see table 3.3). Of the twenty-four women accepted by the court as

TABLE 3.2. The Reported Criminality of Widows in Brigstock

Category	Widows		Female Norm (percentage)	Male Norm (percentage)
	Number	Percentage		
Crimes against the community				
Illegal pasturing	1	2.0	1.0	3.0
Misconduct in fields	5	11.0	38.0	9.0
Property damage	15	33.0	9.5	12.5
Insolence to officers	0	0.0	0.5	1.0
Rescue of seized property	3	6.5	2.0	5.0
Harboring strangers	10	22.0	3.0	8.0
Behavior that caused hue	2	4.0	15.0	18.0
Unjust raising of hue	3	6.5	8.5	2.5
Miscellaneous	0	0.0	5.5	3.0
Subtotal	39	85.0	83.0	62.0
Crimes against persons				
Attacks (and threats)	4	8.5	13	31
Hamsokens (housebreaking)	3	6.5	4	7
Subtotal	7	15.0	17	38
Total, all crimes	46	100.0	100	100

Note: For further information about female and male patterns of criminality, see the samples discussed in Bennett, *Women in the Medieval English Countryside*, 38–42. To provide the best comparison with these samples, only crimes reported against widows in the views of frankpledge have been considered. When possible, percentages have been rounded to produce integral numbers.

pledges, at least fourteen were widows, and the unknown marital status of nine other female pledges raises the strong possibility that they were also widowed heads of household. Only one woman who acted as a pledge was cited as being married, and the dating of that instance in 1348 (the year the plague arrived in England) lends doubt to this attribution that cannot be verified (because the 1348 court records are the last extant for Brigstock for several decades). The major criterion for acceptance of a female pledge was widowhood; women from various social strata (as shown by the official activities of either their husbands or other males of presumed relationship to them) acted in this capacity. Most of the recipients of female pledging were the dependents of their pledges; twenty-six of the forty-six cases (57 percent) explicitly involved a mother pledging for her child, and one case involved a probable, but unverified, mother-son tie. The rate of familial pledging by these widows was, in fact, probably much higher; in three other cases, the pledger and pledgee shared a surname, and other women might well have been pledging for servants. Finally, these widows usually only acted as sureties for the payment of the small amercements levied for petty crimes (thirty-eight cases) or baking activities (two cases). The few women who served as pledges in other sorts of legal transactions were personally involved in other aspects of the case. Emma Pote, Alice Avice, and Strangia Tulke were the original holders of the lands whose acquisition by another prompted their pledging activities, and Alice Somonor was a joint party with her son in the court plea that generated her pledge for his future appearance. Clearly, widows were accepted as pledges not because the court wished to extend to them a legal privilege usually reserved to males, but because the court expected them, as householders, to accept responsibility for their dependents.[38]

Counting widows, not incidents, table 3.4 summarizes the extant evidence on how the widows of Brigstock met their householding responsibilities. Even when indicators of retirement or disability are defined as broadly as possible, only 10 of the 101 widows in Brigstock betrayed an unwillingness to fulfill the duties of their deceased husbands. In contrast, almost one-third of the widows in the community demonstrably acted as heads of the households vacated by their husbands. This one-third, moreover, represents a minimum, since many widows quietly managed their households through many years without ever meriting notice by the Brigstock court. Consider, for example, Agnes the widow of Hugh Heyr who paid her husband's heriot in 1306 and next appeared before the court in 1311 when she was excused from attending a single session; although she had been attending court during the five years after 1306 and presumably resumed regular attendance after her single essoin in 1311, her reliable fulfillment of the obligation to attend court was not noted by the clerk of the manor court.[39] The predilection of manorial courts to record incapacity rather than competency suggests that most widows not cited for retirements or derelictions were, in fact, quietly meeting their householding responsibilities. Because the items considered in table 3.4 represent only brief incidents in the public careers of these widows, their full implications can best be seen in the reported activities of the three widows in Brigstock whose court citations have provided evidence of both disability and capability.

Paying her husband's heriot in 1302, Matilda Cocus first brought substantial business before the court in 1304. In that year, she pledged for a daughter guilty of trespass, she successfully defended (joined by her sons Walter and Henry and Henry's wife Beatrice) a land claim brought by Cristina ad Fontem, and she raised a just hue against her son Henry. Her difficult relationship with Henry came to a head six years later in the failed maintenance agreement of 1311. After resuming control of her lands, she probably used servants to maintain her lands (one was noted in 1313), and encountered no further difficulties until 1314, when she was cited for failing to provide a servant to do plowing and herding. In her last year of court activity (1315), she pursued cases against two villagers (one concluded successfully, the other's resolution unknown), and transferred a half rod of land to her son Henry. Although Matilda Cocus certainly encountered some difficulties during her more than dozen years of widowhood, her last court appearances show her to be still in control of her free bench lands and still independent of her sons (she never once, for example, sought pledging assistance from them).[40]

After her husband, Peter Swetman, died in 1302, Emma Sephirde resumed her own name, but retained clear authority over her offspring by virtue of her proprietal rights. In the first year of her widowhood, she transferred future rights in a *placia* with a curtilage and two rods from her free bench to her son Henry who promptly transferred the property to his brother Peter. Twelve years later, she gave a small house to her daughters Elicia and Agnes. Five years thereafter, she made the possible retirement provisions described above, dividing a croft between Henry and Peter with the stipulation that they provide her with a cartload of hay each year in return for tenure of the property. In 1319, she still,

TABLE 3.3. Female Pledges in Brigstock

Case No.	Pledge's Name	Marital Status	Rank[a]	Year of Entry	Relationship of Pledgee to Pledger	Transaction Requiring Pledge
1 a	Alice widow of Peter Avice	Widow	Upper	1316	Unknown (son?)	Land transaction
b				1317	Daughters	Land transaction
c				1328	Unknown	Petty crime
2 a	Elicia widow of Peter Aylward	Widow	Upper	1335	Son	Petty crime
b				1336	Son	Petty crime
c				1337	Son	Petty crime
d				1340	Son	Petty crime
e				1340	Son	Petty crime
3 a	Matilda Baker	Widow	Upper	1340	Son	Petty crime
b				1340	Son	Petty crime
c				1340	Son	Petty crime
d				1343	Unknown	Petty crime
e				1343	Unknown	Petty crime
f				1343	Daughter	Petty crime
g				1345	Unknown	Petty crime
4 a	Matilda Bate	Unknown	(Upper)	1337	Unknown	Petty crime
b				1344	Unknown	Petty crime
5 a	Margery Cocus	Unknown	(Upper)	1343	Unknown	Petty crime
b				1343	Unknown	Petty crime
c				1344	Unknown	Baking fine
d				1344	Unknown	Petty crime
6	Matilda widow of Peter Cocus	Widow	Upper	1304	Daughter	Petty crime
7	Margery Fory	Unknown	(Lower)	1345	Daughter	Petty crime

TABLE 3.3. Continued

Case No.	Pledge's Name	Marital Status	Rank[a]	Year of Entry	Relationship of Pledgee to Pledger	Transaction Requiring Pledge
8	Margery widow of William Golle	Widow	Upper	1343	Daughter	Baking fine
9	Alice (Goldhop) widow of Hugh Helkok	Widow	Upper	1322	Unknown	Petty crime
10	Alice widow of William Hem	Widow	Lower	1344	Unknown	Petty crime
11	Alice wife of Robert Kroyl	Wife (?)	Lower	1348	Child	Petty crime
12	Margery Laynde	Unknown	(Upper)	1335	Unknown	Petty crime
13	Alice Leche	Unknown	(Upper)	1343	Son	Petty crime
14	Emma Page	Unknown	(Lower)	1344	Unknown	Petty crime
15	Alice widow of Henry Pidenton	Widow	Upper	1337	Son	Petty crime
16 a	Emma widow of Thomas Pote	Widow	Lower	1320	Son	Petty crime
b				1320	Son	Land transaction
c				1321	Son	Land transaction
17	Unnamed mother of Emma Robin	Unknown	(Lower)	1331	Daughter	Petty crime
18 a	Alice Robin	Unknown	(Lower)	1339	Unknown	Petty crime
b				1340	Unknown	Petty crime
19	Alice widow of Robert Somonor	Widow	Lower	1317	Son	Plea
20 a	Matilda widow of Hugh Tubbe	Widow	Lower	1344	Daughter	Petty crime
b				1345	Unknown	Petty crime
c				1345	Daughter	Petty crime

TABLE 3.3. Continued

Case No.	Pledge's Name	Marital Status	Rank[a]	Year of Entry	Relationship of Pledgee to Pledger	Transaction Requiring Pledge
21	Strangia widow of Henry Tulke	Widow	Upper	1344	Son	Land transaction
22 a	Margery widow of John Werketon	Widow	Lower	1340	Daughter	Petty crime
b				1340	Unknown	Petty crime
23	Alice relicta . . .	Widow	Indiv.	1340	Unknown	Petty crime
24	Matilda Honie	Unknown	Indiv.	1344	Daughter	Petty crime

[a]All rankings have been derived from the official activity of the pledge's husband, except those placed in parentheses (for which no precise data were available).

however, held sufficient land to be included in the partial rental for that year, paying 12*d*. (the normal rent for a quarter virgate). In her last court appearance in 1325, she granted ownership of the residue of her properties to her son Henry, to be entered after her death. Throughout her long widowhood, she also intermittently sold ale (10 amercements) and bread (6 amercements). Emma Sephirde never paid amercements for her children, pledged for their crimes, or answered for the collective misdemeanors of her household, but there can be little doubt that she remained, throughout her long widowhood, not only independent of her children but also somewhat dominant over them.[41]

Alice Somonor's life as a widow was more difficult, and of the three, she was probably the least economically privileged (her husband never held local office). After her husband died in 1316, she had to be distrained for payment of heriot, and she and her son John (as coexecutors of the estate) faced three pleas of debt. During the course of one case, she pledged once for John's future appearance. Acting on her own, she also pursued (and lost) another plea. In December, 1318, she paid 3*d*. to be excused from court suit until the following Michaelmas, but she retained her landholdings (paying rent of 2*s*. in 1319) and presumably resumed attending court after her exemption expired in September 1319.

TABLE 3.4.   Widows as Householders in Brigstock

Categories	Number	Percentage of All Unremarried Widows
Evidence of disability		
Retirements	3	3
Economic problems	1	1
Avoidance of court suit	6	6
Total	10	10
Evidence of capability		
Paid fine for dependent	1	1
Paid fine for householder crime	15	15
Paid rent	5	5
Acted as a pledge	10	10
Total	31	31

Note: This table includes data only on the 101 unremarried widows reconstructed from the identified surnames of the manor (one widow who acted as a pledge was incompletely identified and is not counted here). This table excludes from subsequent subcategories a widow counted in a prior subcategory (i.e., a woman noted for both evidence of retirement and economic problems was counted in the retirement subcategory). Percentages have been rounded to produce integral numbers.

She also dispersed small properties through her children to third parties. In 1322, she transferred a *placia* and a *domus* from her free bench to her son Robert, who immediately conveyed the property to another person, and ten years later she gave a tenement from her free bench to her son Henry, who similarly transferred the property outside the family. Like Matilda Cocus, Alice Somonor encountered some problems during her public life as a widow, but she nevertheless retained her independence throughout her last appearances in the extant records.[42]

Most widows in Brigstock, then, probably remained independent heads of household until they died. Few remarried, few retired, and few failed to meet their legal obligations. But the widow as householder was both publicly and privately anomalous. On the public level, male control of the political structures of Brigstock was based on the assumption that all females were dependents of a male householder; women did not, for example, need to be inducted into tithings because they were presumed to be always under the authority of a father or husband. A widow, however, not only lived independently, but also, as a householder, met one of the prime prerequisites for attaining official responsibilities. Yet widows neither joined tithings nor served as officers. Even the pledging of widows was so restricted that it offered few opportunities for building networks of mutual assistance and cooperation within the manor. More influenced by gender than by household position, politics remained a male affair.

On the private level, the assumption that households would be headed by males meant that widows were never more than substitutes for their husbands. Created at marriage, households were permanently identified with the husband, whose authority extended, in some matters, even beyond death. As illustrated by the widow's use, not full control, of free bench lands, widows acted as their husbands' surrogates, but they could not fully emulate their husbands' authority. Moreover, their households were probably often smaller and poorer than they had been during the lifetimes of their husbands; heirs matured and claimed their portions of the familial property, and other children married and sought endowments. The tensions created by the widow's ambivalent authority during these years of household disintegration seem to have been quite considerable in Brigstock. Intrafamilial conflicts were rarely recorded in the Brigstock courts, accounting for less than 2 percent of all criminals studied and only 3 percent of litigants sampled. Widows, however, often came into formal conflict with family; 10 percent of all widows in Brigstock encountered at least one problem with children or kin that could not be resolved without court intervention (see table 3.5). Most of these disputes involved the disposition of land.

Widows as Landholders

In Brigstock, a widow's primary asset was her landed property. It has been suggested that widows and spinsters in some preindustrial villages were particularly active as moneylenders, but this was not the case in Brigstock; most of the widows involved in debt litigation before the manor court were defendants, not plaintiffs.[43] In medieval towns, widows often supported themselves by selling ale and other foodstuffs or by running the businesses of their deceased husbands, but commercial activity was less common among the widows of Brigstock. Both aging and widowhood seem to have discouraged commercial involvement. Most of Brigstock's alewives abandoned brewing for profit as they grew older, and few were still selling ale when their husbands died. Several of these quickly ceased brewing for profit when their husbands died, and only three women brewed for profit with any regularity as widows. Similarly, only five widows, accounting for 11 of 233 baking amercements, baked bread for profit. Perhaps the small, truncated households of widows not only required less income from food sales but also were less capable of sustaining commercial enterprises.[44] Widows were most active in the economy of Brigstock not as traders or sellers or moneylenders, but as landholders.

Insofar as husbands and wives shared a community of property, it was a community of assets, not authority. Both spouses contributed their property and labor to the venture, but only the husband effectively controlled the conjugal economy. A wife was, at best, her husband's subordinate partner in the control of their household's movable goods, landholdings, and labor resources. The inequality of this partnership was probably most apparent at the husband's death, when conjugal assets were divided and dispersed rather than delivered intact to the bereaved wife. A wife's death had no such effect on the continuation of the conjugal estate, but because a husband authoritatively controlled the household economy, its unity ceased when he died. Two basic principles guided the dispersal of a male householder's property in the medieval countryside: his widow had to be provided with a secure holding from the conjugal property sufficient to ensure her continued well-being (her free bench), and his heirs had to claim their inheritances as straightforwardly and as quickly as possible. The next generation was, in short, to move into ownership without threatening the maintenance of the *relicta,* the woman left behind.

These simple objectives were difficult to achieve. On the one hand, a widow provided with secure and ample tenure undermined the rights of her husband's heirs. If her ownership was complete, she could alienate lands or sell assets that her husband had intended for his heirs. If her settlement was too generous, she could delay for many years the devolution of substantial properties to the heirs of her husband. On the other hand, an heir who immediately entered the properties of the deceased also undermined the widow's security; no wise husband wished to leave his wife dependent solely on the goodwill of his heirs. Because no single system provided a foolproof solution to the dilemma posed by the legiti-

TABLE 3.5. Intrafamilial Conflicts of Widows in Brigstock

Widow	Nature of Conflict
Elicia the widow of Richard Aylward	Raised hue against her daughter (26/9/1338); suffered a housebreaking (hamsoken) committed by her son's wife (11/10/1342).
Mablia the widow of Adam Carpenter	Sued John and Richard Carpenter (relation unknown) to get her one-third of property (7/1/1328).
Edith the widow of Gilbert Cocus	Boundaries had to be placed between her land and that of her daughter (25/1/1301).
Matilda the widow of Peter Cocus	Raised a hue against her son Henry (17/9/1304); reclaimed land when Henry failed to fulfill a maintenance contract (15/7/1311).
Mablia the widow of Radulph Coleman	Simon Coleman (relation unknown) disputed her attempt to transfer land (28/1/1328).
Margery the widow of William Geffray	Daughter tried to claim her inheritance prematurely (6/7/1341 and 16/2/1343).
Agnes the widow of Hugh Gilbe	Paid for an inquisition to determine whether a certain property belonged to her or her son (3/6/1322).
Elicia the widow of William Helkok	Son prevented her attempt to sell free bench (17/8/1302).
Alice the widow of Gilbert le Heyr	Argued with nephew over land (2/11/1318).
Emma the widow of Thomas Pote	Boundaries had to be placed between her land and that of Richard, son of John Pote (relation unknown) (4/4/1321).
Matilda the widow of Hugh Tubbe	Raised a hue against her daughter (25/9/1343); attacked her son's wife (25/9/1343).
Alice the widow of Radulph Tulke	Cheated by son on two-step transfer of land (20/3/1315).

mate, but contrary, claims of widows and heirs, the tenurial rights of widows varied enormously from village to village. The widow's free bench could include one-third, one-half, or all of the conjugal holding. Most widows claimed their portions without paying entry fines (indicating their status as cotenants with their husbands), but widows on some manors were fined *pro introitu* (indicating that they were considered to be not cotenants, but heirs). Some widows held their free bench for life, but in other villages widows relinquished free bench holdings when they remarried or when heirs reached maturity. If a widow did keep her free bench after remarriage, her second husband sometimes could and sometimes could not claim the property if she predeceased him. The variability of custom, however, should not obscure the essential features of provision for widows. First, in all villages, widows of landholders were provided with properties separate from the claims of heirs; details varied over time and place, but the customs of all rural communities ensured that widows were not wholly dependent on the generosity of heirs. Second, most widows were custodians, not full owners of the lands designated for their maintenance; their rights of use could sometimes be passed to their second husbands or leased to others, but widows were not supposed to sell or otherwise to alienate their settlements.[45]

In Brigstock before the plague, the proprietal claims of widows provided them with more extensive landholdings than those available to other women. Wives, of course, could not independently control personal properties, and although adolescent daughters and spinsters managed their lands freely, these properties tended to be small parcels obtained through gift or purchase. Some heiresses obtained larger properties, but they usually married quickly. Widows, however, often enjoyed extensive control over extensive properties. First, widows resumed management of all personal properties that had been previously merged into the conjugal fund; a woman who independently acquired land (through purchase, gift, or inheritance) forfeited control of that land to her husband during her marriage, but regained full ownership when widowed. Second, widows also claimed free bench from their husbands' lands. The customs that governed the settlement of free bench in Brigstock, however, defy full reconstruction. Some widows paid heriots (a tax on the chattels left by the deceased), others paid reliefs (entry fines to the property), and still others were subject to no fines whatsoever. Some widows apparently claimed as free bench all of the heritable property of their youngest sons, but others claimed a third of the conjugal estate.[46] Nevertheless, all widows in Brigstock held their free bench for life, relinquishing such properties neither at remarriage nor at the maturation of their heirs. As a consequence of the claims of widows not only to resume full control of properties obtained in their own right but also to exercise temporary control over part or all of the conjugal estate, most female holders of large properties in Brigstock were widows. Of the sixty people listed in the partial rental that survives for Brigstock from 1319, eleven (18 percent) were women, of whom at least six were widows (and the unknown marital statuses of the remaining five women suggest that they, too, might have been widowed).[47]

Widows in Brigstock assertively managed the properties that fell under their control. Dying husbands probably hoped that their widows would quietly maintain the lands provided for them, eventually passing the property intact to their heirs. In Brigstock, such hopes were not always realized; half of the widows in the community brought some of their properties to the local land market (and half of their transfers explicitly identified the conveyed property as free bench land). Dying husbands also likely hoped that their wives would supervise the devolution of resources among their children, assuring that noninheriting offspring were provided with adequate portions or endowments. Although many widows in Brigstock went to court to grant properties to their children, others used the land market to their own advantage, buying, selling, and trading with their neighbors; well over half of the transfers initiated by widows conveyed land outside of the family.[48] To wield such control over their properties, widows in Brigstock devised four methods of circumventing the custodial restrictions of free bench tenure.

Although widows could not permanently alienate their free bench lands, they were free to lease them. Some leases specified terms, as when Margery the widow of John in Cimiterio, joined by her daughter Custancia, leased one acre to Robert Malin for a six-year term. Other leases were set to expire at the widow's death; in 1343, for example, Cristina the widow of Peter Tubbe leased one rod from her free bench to Walter ad Stagnum, specifying that he was to hold it until she died [*ad terminum vite sue sine alique contradictione aliter hominis heredis vel alterius*]. Although only a few such leases were recorded in the courts of Brigstock, many more agreements were probably never noted in the legal records of the manor because short-term leases required no enrollment. Leasing not only enabled widows to realize, at least temporarily, the capital value of their properties but also permitted them to profit from the upswing in land values in the late thirteenth and early fourteenth centuries. Widows, more likely than most to hold disposable lands that they could lease for a few seasons, might have been especially advantaged by rising land values in the half-century before the plague.[49]

Some widows in Brigstock also probably sold free bench lands, despite the customary restriction on such sales. Such efforts were eased in Brigstock by some confusion about the validity of sales of free bench; although a jury had accepted a widow's sale in 1297, another inquisition five years later determined that widows could not sell any part of their settlements.[50] Only one widow in Brigstock clearly alienated part of her free bench; in 1335, Alice the widow of Gilbert le Heyr transferred a *placia* from her free bench to John Hirdman. Other widows, however, clearly attempted to do so; Elicia Helkok's son had to pay for a court inquisition to prevent his mother from selling free bench lands, and both Mablia Coleman and Leticia Chapman endured similar challenges to their land conveyances. It is perhaps telling that about half of the transfers effected by widows in Brigstock made no mention of either free bench or the rights of heirs.[51] Some of these lands were properties that widows held in their own right and were free to alienate, but others might well have been free bench properties being transferred under the guise of normal conveyance.

In other cases, widows secured the right to alienate free bench lands from the eventual heirs of the properties. Because widows and heirs were sequential, not joint, owners of free bench properties, they seldom conveyed land jointly; heirs could, however, forfeit their future claims, leaving widows with unencumbered control of their free bench lands. Usually, the widow granted the free bench to the heir and received it back in full ownership. In 1317, for example, Isabella Leche gave two rods from her free bench to her son who immediately returned the property to her; she then sold part of the land to a neighbor.[52]

Finally, many widows who wished to convey free bench lands obtained the concurrence of the heir through two-step transfers that conveyed the property to a third party via the heir. In 1340, for example, Alice the widow of Henry son of Peter gave a tenement from her free bench to her son and heir John, who immediately transferred it to John Wolf. This method of circumventing free bench restrictions was especially popular in Brigstock; of the 106 grants made by widows, 37 (35 percent) thus conveyed free bench through the heir to a third party. These two-step transfers ensured that conveyances of free bench could not be later challenged by angry heirs, but they were not without danger. In 1315, Alice Tulke wanted to endow her daughter with a tenement from her free bench, but when she gave the property to her son Henry, he vilely [*viliter*] kept the tenement rather than passing it along to his sister. Alice Tulke's appeals to the court failed to bring her son to justice; because she had fully conveyed the property to him, he retained control of the holding.[53]

Widows, of course, freely managed any properties they held in their own right, but these four options—leases, surreptitious sales, receipts of full ownership from the heir, and two-step conveyances through the heir—also allowed them to use their free bench lands much like other landholders, independently disposing of small parcels at advantageous moments. Few acted precipitously.[54] Of the twenty-two widows for whom the timing of transfers could be established, only five conveyed any land within the first year of bereavement; the average interval between the beginning of widowhood and the first transfer of land was about seven years. Few sold or gave their entire property. At most, only thirteen widows might have conveyed their entire holdings, but eight of these arranged to retain use of the property for the duration of their lives. Few also came to the land market solely to arrange for the endowments of children. Only sixteen widows used land conveyances exclusively to grant holdings to their sons or daughters. Nevertheless, although widows seem to have been as eager as other landholders to control their properties fully, their land conveyances also betray the particular familial circumstances of their status.

As heads of disintegrating households, widows so often used the land market to provide for their children that their overall patterns of land conveyance are distinguished clearly from those of other traders (see table 3.6). Widows figured disproportionately as sellers or givers of land, but their prominence in this capacity does not suggest poverty or disability as much as the responsibilities of widows in the developmental cycle of the rural household. Managing households undergoing disintegration, widows were more interested in dispersing familial properties than in accumulation. Most often, widows granted such properties not to neighbors or friends, but to children. Some of these grants were the first steps of the two-step conveyances that transferred free bench through heirs to nonrelatives (twenty-nine grants), but most went either directly or indirectly to the widow's heir or other children (thirty-nine grants; the remaining five intrafamilial transfers represent receipts of land by widows).

And grants by widows, likely to come more often from large conjugal holdings, were more substantial than the usual small parcels transferred in Brigstock (although it should be emphasized that many of these larger grants provided for the widow's continued use of the property until her death). To a large extent, the widows of Brigstock adequately fulfilled the expectation that they would distribute resources among their children; of the fifty-four widows active in the land market, forty-one (76 percent) conveyed at least some land to their children.[55] As exemplified by Emma Sephirde's grants to two sons and two daughters, many provided for noninheriting children as well as allowing designated heirs to gain early access to some of their properties.

Yet the image of the altruistic widow dispersing properties among her children, though accurate, is incomplete. Because they supervised households undergoing disintegration, widows were especially active in intrafamilial conveyances, but such domestic concerns comprised only a part

TABLE 3.6.   Widows in the Brigstock Land Market

Category	Widows		Female Norm (percentage)	Male Norm (percentage)
	Number	Percentage		
Type of action				
Grantor	106	87	60	48
Receiver	16	13	40	52
All actors	122	100	100	100
Autonomy of actor				
Acted alone	65	53	60	88
Acted alone				
in two-step transfer	37	30	—	—
Acted jointly	20	16	40	12
All actors	122	99	100	100
Nature of grant				
Not intrafamilial	49	40	63	83
Intrafamilial	73	60	37	17
All grants	122	100	100	100
Size of grant (if known)				
Less than 2 rods	79	78	80	90
Over 2 rods	22	22	20	10
All grants of known size	101	100	100	100

Note: For further information about female and male patterns of landholding, see the samples discussed in Bennett, *Women in the Medieval English Countryside*, 32–36. Percentages have been rounded to produce integral numbers.

of their participation in the local land market. Thirteen widows transferred land directly to unrelated persons, and another twenty-one conveyed property outside the family using the two-step process involving
the heir.[56] Widows often provided for their children, but they also often
used land to their own advantage. The counterpoint to Emma Sephirde
might be Margery the widow of John in Cimiterio, who repeatedly alienated properties from her family. In 1332, she transferred first a rod and
then (joined by her daughter) one-half rod to John Broyer; in 1333, she
transferred to Cecilia Penifader two half-rods and, later in the same
court, a selion (strip); and accompanied by her daughter in 1335, she
sold one-and-a-half rods to Robert Malin and one rod to Cecilia Penifader and then leased an acre to Robert Malin for six years.[57]

As landholders, then, widows demonstrated the same ambiguities seen
in their householding activities. Although widows were not passive custodians of their lands, they also did not use their properties as freely and
as autonomously as did male landholders. Men in Brigstock used the
land market primarily to alter the size or configuration of their holdings.
By consolidating properties, selling small parcels, and offering short-
term leases, men constantly adjusted their needs and their resources.
Widows similarly traded land to their own advantage, but they were also
more bound than others by familial responsibilities. Just as widows were
partial householders, so they were partial landholders. Restricted by
both the tenurial limitations of free bench and the familial obligations
inherent to their status, widows nevertheless managed their estates as
vigorously and as independently as their circumstances allowed.

Widows as Villagers

Both daughters and wives were less active in the social circles of Brigstock than were men of comparable status. It is difficult to trace social
relations in court records, but the legal associations of women suggest
that they were considerably more oriented toward family than were
men; when a woman in Brigstock came to court to resolve a dispute, to
transfer land, to answer for a crime, or to conclude any type of legal
business, she was much more likely than a man either to deal with
relatives in these transactions or to rely on a relative for legal assistance.
Reported crimes also show that women were less active than men in the
community of Brigstock. The activities of widows in the Brigstock court,

however, suggest that their social experiences often more closely matched the male, rather than the female, pattern.

The court networks of wives, as illustrated by the associations formed by Agnes Penifader-Kroyl, were usually small and focused on their husbands. Indeed, wives' networks were even, in a sense, artificially inflated because they usually came to court accompanied by their husbands and dealt predominantly with the associates of their husbands. During her married years, for example, Edith the wife of Gilbert Cocus accumulated a small court network of only seven contacts with seven people, and in all but one of these associations she was accompanied by her husband. In widowhood, the court networks of women usually expanded in both breadth of acquaintance and frequency of contact. After her husband died, Edith Cocus independently associated with twelve people in court on thirteen occasions, raising a hue, pursuing two pleas, and seeking pledges for her court obligations. Her experiences were typical. Of the thirty women in Brigstock who were active in court as both wives and widows, most interacted as widows not only with more people but also on more occasions; nineteen women (63 percent) accumulated larger numbers of associates and contacts than during their married years. The larger court networks of widows were also usually acquired over considerably shorter periods of time—an average of only nine or ten years of widowhood as opposed to sixteen or seventeen years of married life.[58]

Moreover, the pledging associations of widows more closely paralleled those of male householders than those of wives or daughters. Widows, unlike other women, normally turned for pledging assistance not to male relatives, but rather to unrelated friends or neighbors (see table 3.7). Although daughters were often pledged by their fathers and wives often received such aid from their husbands, widows seldom turned to either brothers or sons for service as legal sureties. Since widows were householders, they had no household head whom they could use for legal assistance, so instead of turning (as was legally permissible) to other male kin, widows usually looked outside of their families for pledging assistance. Once the household basis of reliance on male kin was broken, the importance of such ties apparently weakened quickly. Probably the most striking aspect of the data shown in table 3.7, however, is not the divergence of the pledging associations of widows from those of wives and daughters, but their coincidence with the pledging patterns of male householders; 9 percent of widowed litigants used familial pledges, as opposed to 10 percent of male householders involved in the pleas sampled; 18 percent of both widows and male householders used familial pledges when amerced for petty crimes or offenses. The pledging associations of widows suggest, then, that their social experiences conformed more to the pattern associated with their household position than to the pattern of their gender.

Although the court networks and pledging associations of widows indicate that widowhood was a time of unusual social activity for women, many widows were markedly uninvolved in the public affairs of Brigstock. Fifty-four widows in the community rarely, if ever, used the resources of the court to adjudicate disputes, convey land, or register contracts, and they almost never merited legal notice for criminal actions or commercial sales. Such court activities indirectly reflect social relations, because each clerical notation of a land trade, broken contract, ale sale, and the like indicates an informal interaction between villagers. Men and women active in the society of Brigstock almost inevitably had some of their disagreements, crimes, contracts, and sales enrolled in the court record. As a result, the fifty-four widows who seldom merited court attention for such matters were, compared to other villagers, relatively inactive in the social life of Brigstock. Nothing suggests, it should be reiterated, that these widows were not privately active as householders and landholders, but they were probably not as publicly active in local society as other women and men. To be sure, these widows probably spoke with their neighbors and cultivated friendships outside of their families, but such associations, as indicated by the silence of the record, were comparatively limited in both breadth and depth. These women, it seems, took control of their free bench lands and retired to the private management of their households.

Court records, then, offer two contrary pictures of how widows fit into the social community of Brigstock. On the one hand, about half of the widows traced on the manor actively participated in the public life of Brigstock in ways that suggest that they were more independent of familial ties than most women. On the other hand, about half of Brigstock's widows were publicly inactive, rarely bringing any business before the local court. Two factors probably encouraged social inactivity. Some women became widows at an age of social withdrawal, not involvement. As illustrated by the male careers summarized in table 3.1, men withdrew from public activity as they aged, and it is likely that many widows did the same. Other widows supervised such poor house-

TABLE 3.7. Familial Pledging of Widows in Brigstock

| Category | Widows | | Percentage for Wives | Percentage for Daughters | Percentage for Male Householders |
	Number	Percentage			
Litigation					
Litigant used some familial pledges	3	9	32	33	10
Litigant used only nonfamilial pledges	30	91	68	67	90
Total litigants using pledges	33	100	100	100	100
Crime					
Familial pledges	7	18	75	56	18
Nonfamilial pledges	31	82	25	44	82
Total pledges	38	100	100	100	100

Note: For further information about patterns of familial pledging of wives, daughters and male householders, see Bennett, Women in the Medieval English Countryside, 84–85, 133–39.

holds that neither they nor their husbands were very active in public affairs; over two-thirds of the publicly inactive widows of Brigstock had husbands who never held local office.[59] When such factors, however, did not distract widows from the public realm, the Brigstock evidence suggests that widows often became so active in their communities that their social horizons had more in common with the experience of male householders than with those of daughters or wives.

As a householder, a landholder, and a villager, each widow in Brigstock personally experienced the inconsistencies of her status. She took on most of the responsibilities of householding, but accrued few of its adtvantages. She held extensive properties, but her control was limited by both tenurial restrictions and familial obligations. And she either participated more actively in public affairs than was common for other women or was exceptionally uninvolved in the social circles of her community. Widows, in short, certainly did not wholly step into the positions vacated by their husbands, but they also seldom meekly retired to the care of a married son. Faced with the expanded legal, economic, and social options of widowhood, most women in Brigstock actively exploited at least some of their new opportunities.

The particular customs and economy of Brigstock in the early fourteenth century probably promoted the autonomy and assertiveness of its widows. To begin with, the manor's diverse economy and active land market assured the very existence of widowhood, since remarriage was very common in areas where land was both precious and scarce; on land-hungry manors like Houghton-cum-Wyton (an open-field manor in Huntingdonshire), widows remarried so quickly that few women long experienced the status of widowhood.[60] Brigstock's active land market also probably assured that many widows were not solely dependent on inalienable free bench lands. Because some held properties acquired through inheritance or purchase that were not bound by the restrictions of free bench tenure and others devised methods of circumventing the custodial nature of free bench, the vigorous land market of Brigstock encouraged widows to be active, not passive, landholders. And Brigstock's custom of divided inheritance, which gave younger sons their fathers' inherited lands, might also have worked to the advantage of widows by more often placing them in control of minor heirs.

The activities of widows in Iver (a pastoral manor in Buckinghamshire) suggest, however, that the customs and economy of Brigstock caused differences of degree, not kind, in the experiences of widows in the medieval countryside. Iver, like Brigstock, was not a land-hungry agrarian community, but instead relied largely on animal husbandry and boasted a fairly active market in land. Widows in Iver only rarely remarried; of the thirty-four widows identified in the preplague records of the manor, only five (15 percent) sought second husbands. Iver, however, differed from Brigstock in its provisions for widows; a widow in Iver only claimed a third of her husband's properties, which third was, it seems, not formally separated from the tenement of the eldest son and sole heir. Because the widow's portion was intermingled with the heir's property, conveyances or leases of free bench were discouraged if not forbidden outright; no widow in Iver ever independently transferred lands explicitly identified as free bench. Yet Iver widows, like their counterparts in Brigstock, seldom retired from active management of their households and properties.[61]

As householders, Iver's widows never pledged for their children in the local court, but they were accorded the other responsibilities that usually fell to heads of households. Widows, as householders, were directly charged for the conduct of their dependents; in 1337 Katrina the widow of William Peys paid an amercement because she had not prevented her son from fishing illegally.[62] Similarly, Iver's widows paid amercements for offenses typically committed by households—the trespass of animals, the illegal felling of trees, and the failure to clean ditches.[63] Widows in Iver also often received full legal custody of their husbands' minor heirs. Women such as Alice the widow of John Sprot not only acquired physical custody of these children, but also obtained the right to administer their lands and properties. And Iver's widows took over another common responsibility of householders; they paid the merchets of their daughters.[64] Of the sixteen widows active in Iver between 1322 and 1348, nine were cited for such householder responsibilities, and only two evinced any interest in retirement. Neither case provides definitive evidence of any social expectation that widows should retire to the protection of their sons. Although Margery the widow of John Lawrence paid to relax her obligation to attend court in January, 1346, she was still sufficiently active to be fined several months later for failing to clean a ditch. And although Alice the widow of John Popelin contracted a maintenance agreement with a couple to whom she was not related in 1345, this retirement came after thirteen years of active widowhood.[65] As in Brigstock, the widows of Iver were not content to retire into households headed by their sons; instead, they usually took control of the truncated households left by their husbands.

As landholders, widows in Iver were less active than their counterparts in Brigstock, but they nevertheless managed their lands effectively. One-fourth of Iver's widows brought properties to the land market. Some transferred land directly to children, others transferred land through children to third parties, and still others directly conveyed property outside the family. None, it is worth noting, immediately transferred land after the death of her husband, and none conveyed away all of her property. Widows in Iver could not convey land as freely as widows in Brigstock, but they used their properties for essentially similar purposes—for maintenance, for profit through sales or leases, or for endowing their children.[66]

As villagers, the experiences of widows in Iver were as varied as those of the widows in Brigstock. As in Brigstock, half of Iver's traceable widows were inactive in the manor, appearing in court only once or twice to pay obligatory fines. Yet the other widows traced in Iver were quite active in the community, paying amercements for misdemeanors, pursuing disputes through litigation, and trading land with their neighbors. Like their counterparts in Brigstock, these active widows only infrequently relied on male relatives for legal assistance when they brought business before the court. The social experiences of widows in Iver varied enormously, but those who chose to be active in local affairs were often very active indeed.[67]

Widowhood in the medieval countryside has been so little studied by historians that the typicality of the activities of widows in Brigstock cannot be firmly assessed. The comparative experiences of widows in Brigstock and Iver suggest, however, that different customs of tenure and inheritance affected the options of widows, but did not alter their essential responsibilities and opportunities. One manor practiced divided inheritance; the other followed the custom of primogeniture. One offered widows easy access to land trading; the other more closely restricted the conveyances of widows. Yet in both communities, women stepped into new public roles—as householders, as landholders, as villagers—when their husbands died. On many medieval manors, few women lived for long as widows because they quickly found second husbands, but on those manors whose economies discouraged remarriage, widows were often active and powerful members of their communities.

Widowhood was not a time of absolute advantage for women in Brigstock. It probably often brought many personal and emotional problems; bereaved of their husbands, with whom they had shared many years and experiences, widows often also coped with the disabilities and frustrations of old age. This time of life also varied so enormously according to individual circumstances that not all widows were either willing or able to emulate Alice Avice's vigorous assumption of public responsibilities and opportunities. But despite much variety and much ambivalence, most widows took some advantage of the new public roles offered by their changed status, and in most instances, their public presence exceeded that of both daughters and wives. Widows were often heads of small, disintegrating households, but they were householders, neither semi-independent daughters nor dependent wives. Despite customs that restricted their control of free bench properties, widows' tenures were both substantial (exceeding those held by most daughters) and independent (as opposed to the submergence of wives' properties into the conjugal estate). Although some widows reacted to bereavement by withdrawing from village society, those widows who remained active in local life built social networks larger and more independent of kin than the associations formed by either daughters or wives. Although their public presence fell short of that typical of male householders, it surpassed the female norm. Widows, although certainly not liberated, were nevertheless the most publicly active of all women in the medieval countryside.

ABBREVIATIONS

BAS   Buckinghamshire Archaeological Society, 128/53: Iver court roll for 1332–1376.
NRO   Northamptonshire Record Society, Montagu Collection, Boxes X364A, X364B, X365: Brigstock court rolls for 1287–1348.
PRO   Public Record Office.

NOTES

With only a few changes, this article reprints, with permission from Oxford University Press, chap. 6 from Judith M. Bennett, *Women in the Medieval English Countryside: Gender and Household in Brigstock before the Plague* (New York, 1987).

1. Stenton, *The English Woman in History,* 76; Hilton, "Women in the Village," 97; Franklin, "Peasant Widows' 'Liberation' and Remarriage before the Black Death," 186–204.

2. Bennett, *Women in the Medieval English Countryside,* esp. 177–98.

3. For a fuller introduction to Brigstock and its records, see Bennett, *Women in the Medieval English Countryside,* esp. 10–16, 19–22.

4. Alice Avice first appeared in the Brigstock records in 1292, and she was widowed by 1316 (when the manorial clerk first identified her as a widow). Her marital court network included only one person, besides her husband, with whom she had multiple contacts (two contacts with Robert Moke). For examples of her activities in court as a married woman, see NRO, 5/4/1311 (ale amercement); 12/10/1302 (guilty of disrespect toward the bailiff and defendant in a plea of trespass brought by William Scharp); 6/3/1292 (acquisition of a quarter virgate with her husband); 10/11/1301 (separate pleas of trespass pursued with her husband against Alice ad Solarium and Mablia Tulke).

5. Widowed by 1316, Alice Avice last appeared in the courts of Brigstock in 1332. During widowhood, her court network included multiple contacts with five persons (her son Peter, a possible son Henry Grace, Galfridus ad Solarium, Adam Prepositus, and Adam Kyde). For examples of her activities in court as a widow, see NRO, verso of file 31 (payment of 2*s.* with Adam Kyde in 1319 rental); ?/3/1316 (transfer of three-and-one-half rods from her free bench to Henry Grace—possibly one of her sons—who then conveyed the property to her son Peter); 20/1/1317 (lease of a small *domus* for twenty years from Emma Scharp); 28/9/1331 (amercement for having an obnoxious dung heap); 21/9/1321 (plea of trespass against Emma Stoyle); 3/3/1317 (pledge for daughters Strangia and Alice in their receipt of land).

6. Both sides of this attempt to estimate the duration of marriages in Brigstock are subject to error. First, because few merchets were recorded in the Brigstock courts, a woman could have been married for many years before her first court appearance as a wife. Second, because all widows did not have to pay heriots or reliefs, many years could also elapse between the onset of widowhood and a court citation indicating the woman's changed status. But since more heriots or reliefs were paid than merchets, the termination of marriages can be more accurately dated than their beginnings. As a result, these calculations probably underestimate the normal length of marriage in Brigstock.

7. Razi never directly calculated the duration of marriage in *Life, Marriage, and Death,* but two sets of figures suggest the conclusions offered here. First, Razi calculated that most marriages occurred between the ages of eighteen and twenty-two, with young men being older than their prospective wives by several years (60–64). Second, Razi estimated that most twenty-year-old men in Halesowen had a life expectancy of twenty-five to twenty-eight more years (43–45). If we estimate from these figures that young men marrying at twenty-two could

expect to die at the age of forty-five to forty-eight, the duration of their marriages would be twenty-three to twenty-six years. Needless to say, this estimate is extremely rough, especially because it ignores female life expectancies (for which Razi gives no data). For a debate about the accuracy of Razi's calculations, see Poos and Smith, "Legal Windows?" and Razi, "Use of Manorial Court Rolls."

8. Stone (*Family, Sex and Marriage*, 55) estimated that "the median duration of marriage in Early Modern England was probably somewhere between seventeen to twenty years." See also Laslett, *Family Life and Illicit Love*, 184.

9. Of the 843 women identified in the reliable surnames of Brigstock, 106 are known to have been widowed at least once during their lives (12.5 percent). Male widowhood cannot be traced because a husband's public status did not change when his wife died—he paid no fines, he lost no lands, and he did not alter his position as head of household. If both sexes enjoyed roughly equal expectancies of life, about half of all wives and half of all husbands would have lost their spouses, but we simply have no data that allow us to calculate sexual differences in life expectancy in the medieval countryside (see Razi, *Life, Marriage, and Death*, 34–45). In his study of widowhood in rural France, Alain Bideau found that roughly half of all marriages were ended by the death of the husband; see "Widowhood and Remarriage," esp. 32–33.

10. Laslett, *Family Life and Illicit Love*, 200; Burguière, "Réticences théoriques," 41–48; Bideau, "Widowhood and Remarriage."

11. See Bennett, *Women in the Medieval English Countryside*, chap. 4, n. 12.

12. For some of the many discussions of the tenurial rights of widows, see Homans, *English Villagers*, esp. 181–82; Faith, "Peasant Families"; Shahar, *Fourth Estate*, 236–39. Variations in the customary laws that governed free bench will be more fully discussed subsequently.

13. Titow found that 9 to 15 percent of the tenants on the manors of the Winchester, Glastonbury, and Worcester estates were women (most of whom were widows); see *English Rural Society*, 87. At Waltham and High Easter in 1328, nearly one-fourth of the land was held by women (a figure that excludes landholding by wives, whose properties were explicitly identified under their husbands' lands); see Poos, "Population and Resources," 214–15. Hilton found that one in every seven tenants at Ombersley in 1419 was a widow; see "Women in the Village," 99. Barbara English found that women held one-sixth of the bovates and one-third of the cottar holdings in late thirteenth-century Holderness; see *The Lords of Holderness*, 191. Of the sixty persons listed in the Brigstock rental for 1319, eleven (18 percent) were women, of whom at least six were widows; see NRO, file 31. Similar rates have been found in early modern villages. In Aldenham between 1611 and 1701, from 10.4 to 18.2 percent of households were headed by widows (see W. Newman-Brown, "The Receipt of Poor Relief," 405–22). Laslett's survey of preindustrial households led him to conclude that about 13 percent were headed by widows (see "Mean Household Size," 147).

14. For examples, see NRO, 14/4/1317 (identified as wife); 20/7/1321 (identified as widow); 12/3/1322 (identified with no indication of marital status).

15. NRO, ?/2/1322.

16. For example, women of unknown status in the Brigstock samples were pledged by kin very infrequently (18 percent versus 46 percent of all female criminals; 14 percent versus 29 percent of all female receivers of land; 0 percent versus 24 percent of all female litigants). In the crime sample, women of unknown status were also much more likely than other women to be cited for crimes associated with householding.

17. Joel T. Rosenthal has described how the experiences of aristocratic widows were similarly varied and diverse in his article, "Aristocratic Widows." Probably widowed in the summer of 1318, Alice Penifader sought excused absences from several court meetings that autumn. In January, 1319, she (identified by the forename Dulcia) paid to be excused from attending court until Michaelmas, and in the following October (again identified as Dulcia), she was fined again to avoid court suit for a year. She never again merited notice by the clerk. See NRO, 31/8/1318, 4/1/1319, 4/10/1319.

18. The classic discussion of the effect of land availability on remarriage is Titow, "Some Differences Between Manors." See also Houston and Smith, "A New Approach to Family History?" 123–24; Faith, "Berkshire: Fourteenth and Fifteenth Centuries," 114; Ravensdale, "Population Changes," 197–225. For a general introduction to remarriage in early modern England (where remarriages constituted 25 to 30 percent of all marriages), see Schofield and Wrigley, "Remarriage Intervals." Eight of the 106 widowed women in Brigstock remarried (7.5 percent); 5 of the 34 widows traced in Iver remarried (15 percent).

19. Razi, *Life, Marriage, and Death*, 63.

20. Razi's finding that widows in Halesowen after the plague (when slackening demand for land had lowered the incidence of remarriage) gave birth to proportionally more illegitimate children lends support to the notion that most widows preferred to remain sexually active and, hence, likely preferred to remarry if they could find second partners. See *Life, Marriage, and Death*, 138–39.

21. The advantages of remaining unmarried were even evident to St. Jerome, who complained that widows failed to find second husbands because they preferred liberty over wifely submission [*et quia maritorum expertae dominatum viduitatis praeferunt libertatem*] (quoted in Shahar, *Fourth Estate*, 97).

22. Of the forty-five widows of officeholders, twenty-nine (64 percent) were active in local life, trading lands, pursuing disputes, committing offenses, and the like. Of the sixty-one widows of nonofficeholders, only twenty-three (38 percent) were active in such matters.

23. No data correlating age with remarriage are available for medieval English villages, but one study of rural remarriage has shown clearly that young widows

were especially likely to remarry and that age much less dramatically affected the likelihood of a widower remarrying (see Bideau, "Widowhood and Remarriage"; see also Schofield and Wrigley, "Remarriage Intervals," 213–19). Rosenthal found that age at widowhood influenced the likelihood of remarriage for aristocratic widows, see "Aristocratic Widows," 40. Data on four remarried widows in Brigstock are unavailable, but three of the other four survived their first husbands for exceptionally long lengths of time: six years, sixteen years, thirty-one years, and forty-two years.

24. It is, of course, possible that aging affected the status of women and men differently. Le Roy Ladurie claimed, for example, that elderly men in Montaillou were objects of ridicule whereas women gained, rather than lost, prestige as they aged (see *Montaillou,* 196, 216). This possibility cannot be checked for medieval English villages and received no attention in Laslett's lengthy discussion of aging in early modern England in *Family Life and Illicit Love,* 174–213. More than likely, customs in fourteenth-century Montaillou differed dramatically from practices in contemporary England because of social and demographic divergences between southern ("Mediterranean") and northern Europe. See Smith, "The People of Tuscany."

25. Richard Smith has described how the elderly constituted a significant portion of the rural poor because of the "poverty cycle" of conjugal households, see "Some Issues," 68–85; see also Clark, "Some Aspects of Social Security."

26. John Popelin paid a merchet for his daughter Isabella in 1327; his widow Alice paid a merchet for their daughter Johanna in 1334; when their son William married in 1338, Alice Popelin guaranteed his future inheritance of a semivirgate. See St. George's Chapel (Windsor Castle), IV.B.1 (merchets paid 17/10/1327 and 26/9/1334) and BAS, m. 20 (grant of land to William). The Penifaders of Brigstock provide another example of a widow's disintegrating household. When Robert Penifader died in 1318, his daughter Cristina was already married; his daughter Agnes married in the following year.

27. This statement draws on Wrigley's calculations that 20 percent of all couples in a stationary preindustrial population will have no children survive them, 20 percent will produce only daughters, and 60 percent will have at least one son survive them; see "Fertility Strategy."

28. William Popelin almost certainly did not live with his mother after he married in 1338; in 1345, she entered into a maintenance agreement with a married couple to whom she was not related. See BAS, m. 36: 5/12/1345.

29. Laslett has argued that both elderly women and men tended to live in their original households, although widows were sometimes incorporated into the households of their married children in order to make use of their assistance in child care (see *Family Life and Illicit Love,* 174–213). Richard Wall found not only that between 71 and 78 percent of all widows in the preindustrial English

villages that he examined continued to head their own households, but also that more widows than widowers remained independent householders (see "Women Alone in English Society").

30. The figure of 101 widows excludes 5 women who remarried so quickly and so permanently that their careers as widows were too brief for consideration. The careers of the other 3 remarried widows have been included in this analysis because they either lived alone for many years before remarriage or else survived their second husbands.

31. NRO, 15/7/1311, 3/1/1314.

32. NRO, 31/5/1319, 10/5/1325.

33. NRO, 6/9/1331.

34. NRO, 6/9/1331 (With); 3/1/1314 (Matilda Cocus); and 25/1/1308 (Edith Cocus). In the same court at which Matilda Cocus was amerced for not providing a servant for herding and plowing, William Golle paid a similar amercement. For an example of a man claiming poverty, see NRO, 17/5/1329 (grant of land by Henry Cocus). *Quia pauper* entries probably indicated not destitution, but rather temporary lack of resources (see Alfred E. May, "An Index of Thirteenth-Century Peasant Impoverishment?"

35. See NRO, ?/5/1309 (Emma Werketon); 14/12/1291 (Quena widow of Galfridus); 10/1/1298 (Alice ad Vinarium); ?/5/1309 (Agnes Geroud); 14/12/1318 (Alice Somonor); 4/1/1319 and 4/10/1319 (Alice or Dulcia Penifader). For examples from Henry Cade's long career, see his fine to relax court suit for a year in NRO, 15/12/1301, and his service as a juror in NRO, 13/5/1311.

36. PRO, SC-2: 194/65, 29/5/1299 (Letia Fox paid 3*d. pro Dulce serviente sua*).

37. See the verso of NRO, file 31. The six widows listed are: Alice Avice (who also paid an amercement for a householder crime), Isabella Leche, Alice Somonor, Emma Talboth, Emma Sephirde, and Alice Tucke.

38. Most instances of female pledging in Brigstock occurred in the decades immediately preceding the plague. At Wakefield, widows might have also been allowed to act as pledges. See Baildon, ed., *Court Rolls of the Manor of Wakefield*, vol. 2 (1297–1309), 36.

39. NRO, 29/4/1306, 3/6/1311.

40. For highlights of Matilda Cocus's career as a widow, see NRO, 6/7/1302, 26/5/1304, 24/7/1304, 15/7/1311, 3/1/1314, 27/2/1315, 14/8/1315.

41. For highlights of Emma Sephirde's career as a widow, see NRO, 7/9/1302, 9/5/1314, 31/5/1319, 10/5/1315.

42. For highlights of Alice Somonor's career as a widow, see NRO, 24/3/1317, 14/4/1317, 16/6/1317, 14/12/1318, 6/8/1322, 22/8/1332.

43. Hilton, "Women in the Village," 103–4 (Hilton does not discuss the marital status of the female moneylenders he describes, but they were almost certainly unmarried because wives could not contract debt agreements without

involving their husbands); Holderness, "Widows in Pre-industrial Society." Widows were defendants in eighteen of the nineteen debt cases involving widows reported to the court. In many of these cases, moreover, they were being sued for debts owed by their husbands.

44. See Bennett, *Women in the Medieval English Countryside,* chap. 5, n. 56, for the marital statuses of alewives. Of the 106 widows traced in Brigstock, 22 sold ale at least once (21 percent); of all the women identified in Brigstock, about one-third sold ale on at least one occasion. The three women who brewed intensely as widows were: Alice Goldhop the wife of Hugh Helkok, who acquired only one ale amercement when married and accumulated another thirty-seven during her widowhood; Margery the widow of William Durant, who brewed thirteen times as a wife and twenty-five times as a widow; and Matilda the widow of Hugh Tubbe, who accumulated ninety-three ale citations while married and brewed on thirty more occasions while widowed. Widows cited for commercial baking were: Alice widow of John Dogge (two baking amercements as a wife, one as a widow); Emma Sephirde widow of Peter Swetman (six baking amercements as a widow); Elicia widow of Richard Aylward (four baking amercements as a wife, two as a widow); Alice widow of Henry Pidenton (one baking amercement as a widow); and Strangia widow of Robert Pidenton (one baking amercement as a widow).

45. The variable customs that provided for widows have been much discussed in the historical literature. See, especially, Homans, *English Villagers,* 181–82 (where he claims that the variety of custom indicates its comparative unimportance); and Faith, "Peasant Families," esp. 91 (where she notes that, despite variety, provisions were "durable and firmly established"). Custom, of course, did not necessarily reflect practice. For example, Ravensdale's study of the remarriages of widows in Cottenham has shown that the lord of that manor usually waived (for a fee) the customary forfeiture of a widow's free bench if she remarried; see "Population Changes." It is worth noting that, since widows of all landholders could claim some portion of their husbands' properties, the only landless widows were widows of landless men. Faced with supporting themselves and their families without the wage-earning power of an adult male, such women probably numbered among the poorest members of rural society. But they appear rarely in manorial records because of their landless status.

46. Many of these differences likely arose from different tenures of land that were unspecified in the court records, but the results were certainly confusing to contemporaries; about one of every ten widows in Brigstock endured some sort of legal inquiry into her rights as a landholder (see table 3.5).

47. NRO, file 31.

48. Of the 106 widows studied, 55 conveyed land on at least one occasion (52 percent). Of the 106 conveyances made by these widows, 52 explicitly stated that the properties being conveyed were from the widow's free bench (49 per-

cent), and 67 (63 percent) conveyed land outside of the family (this figure includes transfers that conveyed land from a widow through the heir of her husband to a third party).

49. NRO, 17/2/1335 (Cimiterio), 1/8/1343 (Tubbe). Hilton found that many rural lessors were widows; see *Medieval Society,* 163.

50. NRO, 6/9/1297, 17/8/1302. Both inquisitions were held to determine whether a widow could sell half of her lands. Although neither explicitly mentioned free bench, both were implicitly considering free bench tenure.

51. NRO, 15/9/1335 (Heyr); 17/8/1302 (Helkok); 28/1/1318 (Coleman); 16/3/1302 (Chapman). Of the 106 conveyances made by widows, the clerk made no mention of free bench restrictions in 54 cases (51 percent). For examples of widows conveying land on other manors, see Jones, "Bedfordshire: The Fifteenth Century," 249–50; and Lomas, "South-East Durham," 300.

52. NRO, 20/1/1317.

53. NRO, 11/7/1340 (Alice, widow of Henry son of Peter); 20/3/1315 (Alice Tulke). An obvious but imponderable question about two-step transfers is: Who profited? Heirs, eager to realize the value of their inheritances, often might have pressured widows to release portions for immediate sale. Such impatience might have been the motive, for example, behind the transfer of future access to her free bench through the heir to a third party by Alice the widow of Adam Talbot; she retained effective control over the free bench land for her life, but the heir was able to realize immediately the value of the land (see NRO, 10/9/1333). But widows, desirous of more extensive control over their free bench lands, might have often coerced heirs into agreeing to alienations of their lands. Heirs almost certainly, for example, obtained no financial benefit from agreeing to two-step transfers that conveyed land to their noninheriting siblings (eight cases found in Brigstock). In the final analysis, of course, both a widow and the heir of her husband had to agree to the advantages offered by a proposed two-step transfer.

54. To be included in this analysis, a widow needed (*a*) to have paid a relief or heriot indicating the beginning of widowhood, and (*b*) to have transferred land on at least one occasion; twenty-two women met both these criteria.

55. However, sixteen of these forty-one widows conveyed land to children only as the first step of two-step transfers that conveyed land outside the family. To be sure, a widow's child might have profited as much from such a transfer as did the widow herself, but only twenty-five widows conveyed properties to children, which properties were subsequently retained by the children.

56. To look at the figures from a different perspective, of the fifty-four widows involved in land conveyances, sixteen conveyed land only to children, twenty-nine conveyed land only to nonrelatives (including those who used two-step transfers), and nine conveyed land to both relatives and nonrelatives.

57. NRO, ?/3/1332; 7/5/1333; 17/2/1335; 10/3/1335.

58. For Agnes Penifader-Kroyl, see Bennett, *Women in the Medieval English*

Countryside, esp. 129–39. These thirty widows include all widows who could be traced in the courts during both their married and their widowed years. Of these thirty, the breakdown was as follows: nineteen widows exceeded both the number of persons contacted and the number of contacts made during their married years; eight widows had smaller networks than they had built as wives; and three widows had networks equivalent to those of their married years. On the average, the traced careers of these women as wives lasted 16.9 years; their average career as widows lasted 9.5 years.

59. A widow was classified as publicly inactive if she never traded land and merited only one citation (essoin, plea, petty crime, or the like) after her payment of heriot or relief. Of the fifty-four inactive widows in Brigstock, thirty-eight (70 percent) had husbands who never held local office.

60. Only twelve widows were identified from the preplague records of Houghton-cum-Wyton, raising the possibility that many women were widows for so brief a time that their widowhoods escaped notice in the extant records. Of these twelve widows, three (25 percent) definitely remarried.

61. The composition of Iver's free bench is never explicitly described in the extant records, but one court entry implies that widows controlled an unseparated one-third of their husbands' holdings. In 1341, William le Coke's transfer of property to John Snape was followed by his widowed mother's conveyance of her right to one-third of the property (BAS, m. 24, 2/5/1341). Of the thirty-four widows in Iver, only sixteen can be fully studied because they lost their husbands during the well-documented years from 1332 to 1348. The subsequent discussion is based largely on the experiences of these sixteen widows.

62. BAS, m. 17, 7/5/1337.

63. BAS, m. 9, 5/5/1335 (animal trespass by Alice widow of Roger Scheperde); m. 40, 21/11/1346 (John Palmer cited for illegally felling trees on land of Dionysia widow of Salamon Blake); m. 20, 1/4/1338 (Juliana widow of Peter Godefrey cited for illegally felling trees on the tenement of her husband's heir); m. 41, 3/5/1346 (Margery widow of John Lawrence ordered to repair a ditch).

64. BAS, m. 21, 4/7/1338 (Sprot custody); m. 14, 7/10/1336 (merchet paid by the widowed Agnes Ram for her daughter).

65. BAS, m. 37, 14/1/1346 (Lawrence); m. 36, 5/12/1345 (Popelin).

66. The widows who transferred land in Iver were: (1) Alice Popelin, who (*a*) transferred a small parcel to her daughter Margery (BAS, m. 18, 14/7/1337, (*b*) transferred property to her daughter Johanna and her husband Peter Pekele (BAS, m. 19, 1/12/1337), and (*c*) granted future access to her messuage and semivirgate to her son William when he married (BAS, m. 20, 1/4/1338); (2) Alice Coke, who released her one-third right in a tenement to her son who then conveyed the entire tenement to John Snape (BAS, m. 24, 2/5/1341; (3) Cecilia Blanchard, who leased land to John Snape and sold another property to Peter

Peckele (BAS, m. 44, 4/12/1348); (4) Alice Shepherde (Bercarius), who (*a*) leased three rods to John Aleyn (BAS, m. 32, 9/11/1342), and (*b*) joined by her daughter, conveyed three rods outside of the family (BAS, m. 35, 27/9/1345). These four widows represent one-fourth of the sixteen widows whose careers could be reconstructed from the Iver records.

67. Katerina Peys, for example, was a widow by 1335 (BAS, m. 8, 7/7/1335) and remained active in the courts until her death by plague (BAS, m. 52, 6/5/ 1349). During her long widowhood, she brewed frequently (see BAS, m. 45, 15/6/1348 for one ale amercement), provided the lord with security that she would not remarry without permission (BAS, m. 12, 29/7/1336), pursued a debt dispute with Alice Gentyl (BAS, m. 17, 7/5/1337), raised a just hue against several men (BAS, m. 17, 8/5/1337), paid a fine for the illegal fishing of her son (BAS, m. 17, 7/5/1337), and paid for the trespass of a colt owned by her (BAS, m. 20, 1/4/1338).

BIBLIOGRAPHY OF SECONDARY WORKS
AND PRINTED SOURCES

Baildon, William Paley, ed. *Court Rolls of the Manor of Wakefield.* Vol. 2 (1297–1309). Leeds, 1906.

Bennett, Judith M. *Women in the Medieval English Countryside: Gender and Household in Brigstock before the Plague.* New York: Oxford University Press, 1987.

Bideau, Alain. "A Demographic and Social Analysis of Widowhood and Remarriage: The Example of the Castellany of Thoissey-en-Dombes, 1670–1840." *Journal of Family History* 5 (1980): 28–43.

Burguière. "Réticences théoriques et intégration pratique du remariage dans la France d'Ancien Régime—dix-septième-dix-huitième siècles." In *Marriage and Remarriage in Populations of the Past,* ed. J. Dupâquier, E. Hélin, P. Laslett, M. Livi-Bacci, and S. Sogner, 41–48. New York: Academic Press, 1981.

Clark, Elaine. "Some Aspects of Social Security in Medieval England." *Journal of Family History* 7 (1982): 307–20.

English, Barbara. *The Lords of Holderness, 1086–1260.* Oxford: Oxford University Press, 1979.

Faith, Rosamund. "Berkshire: Fourteenth and Fifteenth Centuries." In *The Peasant Land Market in Medieval England,* ed. P. D. A. Harvey, 107–77. Oxford: Oxford University Press, 1984.

———. "Peasant Families and Inheritance Customs in Medieval England." *Agricultural History Review* 14 (1966): 77–95.

Franklin, Peter. "Peasant Widows' 'Liberation' and Remarriage before the Black Death." *Economic History Review,* 2d ser., 39 (1986): 186–204.

Hilton, R. H. *A Medieval Society: The West Midlands at the End of the Thirteenth Century.* Cambridge: Cambridge University Press, 1966.

———. "Women in the Village." In *The English Peasantry in the Later Middle Ages,* 95–110. Oxford: Clarendon Press, 1975.

Holderness, B. A. "Widows in Pre-industrial Society: An Essay upon their Economic Functions." In *Land, Kinship and Life-Cycle,* ed. Richard M. Smith, 423–42. Cambridge: Cambridge University Press, 1984.

Homans, George C. *English Villagers of the Thirteenth Century.* New York: Harper Torchbooks, 1970.

Houston, Rab, and Richard Smith. "A New Approach to Family History?" *History Workshop* 14 (1982): 120–31.

Jones, Andrew. "Bedfordshire: Fifteenth Century." In *The Peasant Land Market in Medieval England,* ed. P. D. A. Harvey, 179– 251. Oxford: Oxford University Press, 1984.

Laslett, Peter. *Family Life and Illicit Love in Earlier Generations.* Cambridge: Cambridge University Press, 1977.

———. "Mean Household Size in England since the Sixteenth Century." In *Household and Family in Past Times,* ed. Peter Laslett with Richard Wall, 125–58. Cambridge: Cambridge University Press, 1972.

Le Roy Ladurie, Emmanuel. *Montaillou: The Promised Land of Error.* Trans. Barbara Bray. New York: Vintage Books, 1978.

Lomas, Tim. "South-East Durham: Late Fourteenth and Fifteenth Centuries." In *The Peasant Land Market in Medieval England,* ed. P. D. A. Harvey, 253–327. Oxford: Oxford University Press, 1984.

May, Alfred E. "An Index of Thirteenth-Century Peasant Impoverishment? Manor Court Fines." *Economic History Review,* 2d ser., 26 (1973): 389–402.

Newman-Brown, W. "The Receipt of Poor Relief and Family Situation, 1636–1690." In *Land, Kinship, and Life Cycle,* ed. Richard M. Smith, 402–22. Cambridge: Cambridge University Press, 1984.

Poos, L. R. "Population and Resources in Two Fourteenth-Century Essex Communities: Great Waltham and High Easter, 1327–1389," Ph.D. diss., University of Cambridge, 1983.

Poos, L. R., and R. M. Smith. "Legal Windows Into Historical Populations? Recent Research on Demography and the Manor Court in Medieval England." *Law and History Review* 2 (1984):128–52.

Ravensdale, Jack. "Population Changes and the Transfer of Customary Land on a Cambridgeshire Manor in the Fourteenth Century." In *Land, Kinship, and Life Cycle,* ed. Richard M. Smith, 197–225. Cambridge: Cambridge University Press, 1984.

Razi, Zvi. *Life, Marriage, and Death in a Medieval Parish: Economy, Society, and Demography in Halesowen, 1270–1400.* Cambridge: Cambridge University Press, 1980.

————. "The Use of Manorial Court Rolls in Demographic Analysis: A Reconsideration." *Law and History Review* 3 (1985): 191–200.

Rosenthal, Joel. "Aristocratic Widows in Fifteenth-Century England." In *Women and the Structure of Society,* ed. Barbara J. Harris and Jo Ann K. McNamara, 36–47. Durham, N.C.: Duke University Press, 1984.

Schofield, R., and E. A. Wrigley. "Remarriage Intervals and the Effect of Marriage Order on Fertility." In *Marriage and Remarriage in Populations of the Past,* ed. J. Dupâquier, E. Hélin, P. Laslett, M. Livi-Bacci, and S. Sogner, 211–27. New York: Academic Press, 1981.

Shahar, Shulamith. *The Fourth Estate: A History of Women in the Middle Ages.* Trans. Chaya Galai. London: Methuen, 1983.

Smith, Richard M. "The People of Tuscany and Their Families in the Fifteenth Century: Medieval or Mediterranean?" *Journal of Family History* 6 (1981): 107–28.

————. "Some Issues Concerning Families and Their Property in Rural England, 1250–1800," In *Land, Kinship, and Life Cycle,* ed. Richard M. Smith, 1–86. Cambridge: Cambridge University Press, 1984.

Stenton, Doris Mary. *The English Woman in History.* London: Allen and Unwin, 1957.

Stone, Lawrence. *The Family, Sex and Marriage in England, 1500–1800.* New York: Harper and Row, 1977.

Titow, J. Z. *English Rural Society, 1200–1350.* London: George Allen and Unwin, 1969.

————. "Some Differences Between Manors and Their Effects on the Condition of the Peasant in the Thirteenth Century." *Agricultural History Review* 10 (1962): 1–13.

Wall, Richard. "Women Alone in English Society." *Annales de Démographie historique* 1981: 303–17.

Wrigley, E. A. "Fertility Strategy for the Individual and the Group." In *Historical Studies of Changing Fertility,* ed. Charles Tilly, 135–54. Princeton: Princeton University Press, 1978.

Chapter 4

Opportunities for Medieval Northern European Jewish Widows in the Public and Domestic Spheres

Cheryl Tallan

With my children gathered around me, I sat upon the ground for the seven days of mourning, and a sad day it must have been to see me sitting thus with my twelve fatherless children at my side.

—Glückel [1932] 1977, 152

Glückel of Hameln, early modern Europe's best known Jewish widow, begins her description of widowhood on a note of deep sorrow. Bereft of her husband, she grieves for herself and for her children. Yet, while obviously affected by the death of a husband whom she loved, Glückel could not permit herself an extended period of grieving. After the thirty days of mourning prescribed for a widow according to Jewish law, Glückel had to carry on her late husband's business and assume responsibility for her eight unmarried children.

Some Jewish widows in northern Europe of the eleventh, twelfth, and thirteenth centuries appear to have taken on duties similar to Glückel's upon their husbands' death. Working through family connections, they assumed positions of importance and influence in both the public and the domestic spheres—although like most medieval Jews, both men and women, their access to power and authority in the public domain was limited.[1]

A good source of information on northern European medieval Jewish widows is the responsa literature.[2] These collections of questions sent to medieval rabbis and their answers concern all matters of importance to the medieval Jewish community—affairs of ritual, marriage and divorce, community organization, business, taxation, and relations between Jews and non-Jews (Weinryb 1967, 400). Though every responsum focuses on a legal problem, the questions brought to the rabbi, as well as the surrounding material that the petitioners used to prove their cases, contain valuable information of cultural, political, economic, historic, and sociological interest.

Medieval rabbis addressed many questions concerning widows. Frequently, widows and other claimants disputed over the widows' rights to the portions of their late husbands' estates decreed to them according to Jewish law. In these cases, the rabbis had to choose between the rights of the widows and those of the heirs or the creditors. Circumstances of the widows' remarriages were also common causes of conflict between them and their late husbands' heirs. Controversies dealing with matters specific to Jewish law, such as the levirate widow—the widow of a man who sired no children who must marry or be released by his brother—and the 'agunah—the woman whose husband has disappeared and who cannot remarry until he is declared legally dead—often came to the rabbis for decisions. Since problems of the 'agunah and the levirate widow are specific to widows, and inheritance problems are widespread among them, the amount of information about widows in the responsa is large, perhaps greater than the amount about other medieval Jewish women, both married and unmarried.

Documents of non-Jewish origin such as notarial records, court documents, and reports of royal investigations complement the material on Jewish widows found in the responsa literature. This material is primarily economic, dealing with business affairs and the provision of credit.

Using all of these sources, both Jewish and non-Jewish, a picture emerges of the northern European Jewish widow as a woman who, in the domestic sphere,[3] played an active role in advancing her own, as well as her children's, interests; enjoying a position of power and authority far greater than that of her married sisters. In the public sphere, however, Jewish widows, like all Jewish women in medieval northern Europe, were restricted by Jewish law and custom. Women could not be community leaders, religious officials, or even witnesses in a court of law. Access to public authority in these communities was generally restricted to men, although widows sometimes did use family connections to achieve goals and influence non–family members in the public sphere.

While wives were under their husbands' authority within the domestic realm, widows, who were autonomous, could be very powerful and commanding. They could, in medieval northern Europe, act as heads of the family and guardians of their minor children. They could thus plan marriages, make educational arrangements, and have complete control over their children until the children reached majority or married. Some widows were very active and successful in business and used their wealth both for family and for personal purposes.

The opportunities for power available to medieval Jewish widows were many and diverse. Certain widows could, as widows still do today, partially fill their late husbands' leadership positions by giving advice to their followers. After the death of Rabbenu Tam (d. 1171, Troyes, France), a prominent Jewish sage and leader, "the scholars asked his wife about his practices" (Urbach 1980, 61).[4] A similar case occurred among the Karaites (a heterodox Jewish sect) of Spain in the late eleventh or early twelfth century. The Rabbanite Ibn Daud described the position of the widow of Abu'l-Taras thus:

> When Abu'l-Taras passed on to hell, he was survived by his accursed wife, whom [his adherents] used to address as *al-Mu'allima* and on whom they relied on for authoritative tradition.[5] They would ask each other what *Mu'allima*'s usage was, and they would follow suit. (Ibn Daud 1967, 95)

These two widows exercised authority in the public sphere, giving advice that was accepted by their late husbands' followers on matters similar to those on which their husbands had ruled. But while they ultimately did achieve important and influential positions of their own, these women came to their status as widows—that is, through family connections.

Other widows acted as the representatives of their families in community matters. Andrée Courtemanche found in Manosque, France, at the turn of the fourteenth century, two Jewish widows, Rosa and Baceva, who represented their families before *sindici yconomici* (1987, 555–56). Though these widows had adult children (Rosa, three sons; Baceva, a married daughter), it was the widows themselves, and not their children, who acted as heads of their respective families.

Most widows, however, did not act in public. They acted in private, as did wives, and put pressure on other members of their family to act in such a way that the widows achieved their goals. For example, in eleventh-century France, a business agreement existed among a certain widow, her son-in-law, and their partner. A dispute arose between the widow and the partner, and her son-in-law supported her claim. He protested to the partner and the partner replied: "Must I allow her [the mother-in-law] to take, through you, her share of the assets in my hands...?" (Solomon ben Isaac [1943] 1967, no. 72]).

In addition to personal influence, the most important source of some widows' power was the significant amount of money or assets they could control. The Jewish widow could not inherit from her late husband. But, on his death, she received the equivalent of the amount stated in her *ketubbah,* her marriage document.[6] The money and assets the Jewish widow received as payment of her *ketubbah* belonged to her absolutely and did not revert to her late husband's heirs on her death or remarriage. While she remained a widow, she could sell, lease, or mortgage them; give them away; or leave them to anyone she wished.

Around the turn of the twelfth century in Germany and about a century later in northern France (see Freimann 1950, 374–76), the *ketubbah* value was set at fifty pounds silver for the *nedunya',* the dowry, and fifty pounds silver for the *tosefet ketubbah,* the additional amount specified by the groom.

> I considered the question of the custom among us to write in the *ketubbot* of women, "this *nedunya'* that she brings with her [consists of] silver, gold, clothing, and bedding to a total value of fifty pounds." [We write the phrase] even if she can't bring with her [even] four pounds worth. On what authority do the recent generation of rabbis write in this way?... [The answer is] since the whole matter depends only on custom, the rabbis of the recent generation were concerned with the betterment of the daughters of Israel so that they should not be so easy to divorce. Accordingly, they [the rabbis] decreed that the *ketubbot* should be written in the same manner for poor as for rich and that the *nedunya'* should be equal for all and also that the *tosefet* that he [the groom] added from his own [possessions] they decreed should be equal for all. (Freimann 1950, 374, quoting Rabbi Eliezer ben Natan [d. 1170])

But since one hundred pounds silver was such an enormous amount of money, the payment of the total amount must have been uncommon. Except among the very rich, the husband's estate would be worth less than one hundred pounds so that, in general, all the husband's assets would come to the widow as payment of her *ketubbah* (see Freimann 1950, 382).

This bright picture of the widow's situation may have existed more in theory than in practice. Although in northern Europe the Jewish widow, except among the very rich, was entitled to all of her husand's assets as payment of her *ketubbah,* heirs and creditors of her late husband sometimes tried to claim part or all of it. Occasionally, her husband attempted to give away portions of his estate during his lifetime or on his death bed (see Tallan 1989, 64–67). Depending on the circumstances of the case and the customs of the specific community, sometimes the rabbis ruled in the widow's favor and sometimes in favor of the heirs or creditors.

Yet, despite such attempts to remove some possessions from their control, it seems likely that medieval Jewish widows might have been in charge of much of their late husbands' assets. This put significant economic and social power in the hands of these widows. One late tenth- or early eleventh-century German responsum depicted a widow who clearly had command of all the assets left by her husband. This responsum stated that the husband "took his will and gave it to his wife so that she would take charge of it and of her sons all her days" (Müller 1966–67, no. 85). A different widow living in eleventh-century Germany exercised her right to give away some of her assets by choosing to give a gift of land to one son and nothing to the other (Aptowitzer 1938, 179 no. 12).

As guardians of their minor children, widows often used their assets to control their children's lives.[7] For example, one widow in thirteenth-century Germany arranged her son's education. In this case, the son took his mother to court over an inheritance he felt was due him. In her testimony, she stated: "Your father did not bequeath you anything and even if he did bequeath you [something] I spent a lot [of money] on you for I raised you and had you taught until you were thirty years old" (Meir ben Barukh, 1969–70, no. 245).

In their role as head of the family, medieval Jewish widows could also contract marriages for their children. An English betrothal contract of 1271 reads:

> On Friday, the third day of Shevat in the year 31 of the six thousand [5031] we, the undersigned, having received a blessing from a *minyan*[8] of ten persons constituted ourselves as a *Beth Din* (Court of Justice) to arrange matters between R. Benjamin the son of Joseph Jechiel and Belassez the daughter of Rabbi Berechya (Benedict). The

said Belassez has betrothed her daughter Judith the daughter of Hayim to Aaron the son of Benjamin upon the following conditions.

The said Belassez promised to the said Aaron as a dowry twenty marks sterling and the twenty-four books (of the Bible) properly provided with punctuation and the *Masora*[9] and written on calfskin: on every page there are six columns, and the *Targum*[10] of the Pentateuch and of the *Haftaroth*[11] are all therein written separately. From today Belassez had handed to Benjamin the said book to keep for the use of the young couple. She has further handed to him the said twenty marks that they may be lent out on interest to non-Jews until the young Aaron his son is grown up....

> Judah son of Rabbi Meir
> Abraham Hayim son of Rabbi Joseph, Rabbi
> Joseph son of Rabbi Joshua. (Adler 1939, 43–45)

A responsum from thirteenth-century Germany describes another marriage agreement.

> Rabbi Eliezer and Marat Miriam vowed to join together Itzak the Levite, her son, and Gotlin, his daughter. Together, they would give to the couple three pounds, on condition that, God forbid, if one of them [of the young couple] should die [before the marriage], the surviving one will take one half of the three pounds for himself [or herself] and the interest and half the three pounds will be returned. (Meir ben Barukh 1969–70, no. 981).

In times of grief also, Jewish widows could accept the responsibility for their family. This continued even after a child's marriage or death. One Jewish widow had to pay her married son's burial costs: "Here is a case before us in which a mother lent [money] to bury her son" (Meir ben Barukh 1969–70, no. 926).

These widows, in arranging family matters, were acting in the domestic realm; they were making decisions about the fates of members of their immediate families and advancing their family's interests. These decisions were authoritative; they were, for example, binding on their minor children. Whether such widows as those I have mentioned had the authority to act as they did because they were legal heads of their families, or whether they wielded power because they possessed the families' financial assets, is, however, difficult to judge.

Many medieval Jewish widows used their assets for purposes other than family ones. One late twelfth-century French woman, probably a widow, gave money to charity.

> A question concerning a woman who set aside twelve pounds for the charity fund: She gave the money to Reuben to lend out under the conditions that he could keep half the profit. He would give the money from the charity fund's portion of the profit to scholars that he chose. After a time Reuben said: "Aside from what I have distributed to the scholars, I have earned an additional four pounds for the charity fund." These four pounds were added to the loan in his name such that the principle of the loan was sixteen pounds. (Meir ben Barukh 1969–70, no. 147).

This woman used some of her assets to generate money for scholars. For medieval Jews, giving money to scholars was extremely laudable; this act may well have raised the woman's status in the community.

Other responsa depict widows using the assets received from their *ketubbah* to increase their own wealth. A twelfth-century French widow started by trading and went on to money lending. She stated: "[T]here only remained from my husband nine *qav* of grain.[12] I sold it and worked to make my nest-egg grow and also borrowed from others and [lent that money out] and made a profit with that also and now I have approximately thirty pounds" (Meir ben Barukh 1969–70, no. 502). Another case involving a widow who traded came before an eleventh-century French rabbi.

> A question concerning Reuben's widow who claims from Simon's widow: "[The assets of] of our partnership were in your hands. Before we came to divide it, you took for yourself a pound of silver from the partnership and the rest we shared. I now claim the half-pound that is owing to me." Simon's widow replies: "It is true that there was a partnership between me and your husband. I had many claims against him and he against me and so we went to court. We bound ourselves with oaths. Through the court we made a compromise [and agreed] that he should give me a pound of silver and thus he would be acquit-

ted in a binding manner from these claims. This is what he said to me: 'Since [the assets] of the partnership are in your possession, either take two pounds of silver from the partnership or I will give you a pound of silver from the money I have at home.'" Now one of the witnesses of that compromise agreement testifies as [to the truth] of her claim. [Simon's widow states further]: "After this compromise Reuben, your husband, obtained his supplies from me and gave me from his assets silk equal to a value of a half-pound silver. He went out on the road and sin overtook him and he did not return." (Meir ben Barukh 1969–70, no. 876)

The original partnership had probably been between Reuben and Simon. Simon's widow most likely received her husband's portion of the partnership after his death as all or part of the settlement of her *ketubbah*. It seems, however, that, after Simon died, Reuben was agreeable to continuing the partnership with Simon's widow, who was an active rather than a silent partner in this trading venture. After Reuben's death, the partnership dissolved and the assets were divided, perhaps since there was no man left to do the traveling.

Another means of increasing assets available to medieval Jewish widows was moneylending. The English widows were especially active. Among the wealthiest of these widows was Licoricia of Winchester, a well-known businesswoman whose clients included the clergy of the local cathedral. The comparatively modest sum Licoricia had to pay in taxes gives evidence of royal participation in the success of this widow's business, and the fact that her five sons—all prominent moneylenders— invariably describe themselves as sons of Licoricia rather than of their father attests to her role as head of the family (Adler 1939, 39–42).

Many sources show that continental European Jewish widows also lent money for profit. Jordan's research on moneylending in Picardy, France, in the mid-thirteenth century, establishes that, of the seventy-five Jewish lenders identified in his source by sex, thirty-five were women (see Jordan 1978, 56). Though these women were not classified according to marital status, it is quite likely that some of them were widows. Emery found that in Perpignan, Spain, during the thirteenth century, twenty-five women, mostly widows, participated in sixty-one loans (see Emery 1959, 26). In her research on women and credit in Manosque, France, at the turn of the fourteenth century, Courtemanche discovered that four women, among whom two certainly and another probably were widows, monopolized 70 percent of the Jewish female moneylending activities (see Courtemanche 1987, 555).

Not all moneylending widows operated alone; some acted together with their sons, other family members, or even acquaintances. In the mid-thirteenth century, the principal resident of the small Jewry of Bedford was a widow who, aided by her sons Jacob and Benedict, managed a loan office on an extensive scale (Adler 1939, 36). A responsum from thirteenth-century Austria showed Jewish women (not identified as to marital status, though some at least were probably widows) in an informal moneylending network. A young man whose father had died gave his money to his aunt to keep for him, since he was afraid that the duke might otherwise claim it.

> She [his aunt] told him that she gave twelve pounds of his money to one Jewess for half the profit and such and such an amount to another Jewess. Afterwards she died and she had not instructed her daughter [as to the whereabouts of the money]. (Isaac ben Moses 1862, no. 762)

These English and continental European widows who earned income by trading and moneylending might, and probably did, use part or all of that money for family expenses such as dowries, education, and burial costs for their children and grandchildren. But it is likely that they used at least some of it for themselves. If they wanted to remarry, for instance, they had to provide their own dowry. Some also used their money for clothes, jewelry, and other luxury goods. One woman in eleventh-century France entered a second marriage with "jewels and clothing and the remainder of [the] assets of silver and gold and all that she had" (Meir ben Barukh 1969–70, no. 880). She could have received these goods at or during her first marriage, or used some of the assets available to her during her widowhood to acquire them.

But not all widows were rich. Although they do not appear frequently in the responsa, it is likely that there were many poor widows.[13] We find one in a query that came before a thirteenth-century German rabbi: "A question concerning three brothers: one has nothing but what he earns teaching, the second has approximately fourteen *zeququim*,[14] and the third is rich and he is not here. They have an old mother who claims support from them for she is poor" (Meir ben Barukh 1969–70, no. 541). In some medieval Jewish communities, poor widows who either had no children or family or whose children or family could not or would not support them, could be supported from the charity fund (see Levitas 1972, 811). These widows must have led desperate lives.

Any generalizations about medieval Jewish widows have to be gross oversimplifications. Location, era, level of organization of the community, type of family structure, socioeconomic status of family, involvement of levirate or not, age and personality of the widow, length of widowhood, and the possibility of remarriage all determine the experience of Jewish widows. These considerations also shape the range and amount of public and domestic power available to widows. But the historical material available today shows that medieval Jewish widows could, indeed, wield authority and power, both in the public sphere and in the domestic realm. In economic relationships, widows might act on their own; the large amounts of money they controlled made them important and influential members of family and community. They could also, as representatives of their late husbands, make decisions that were binding on non–family members.

While the authority and power of the medieval northern European Jewish widow was limited to certain, specific areas within the public sphere, within the domestic realm it was not. Widows could be their children's guardians and so could arrange family affairs. They could use the money received from their *ketubbah* for family expenses, personal use, or charity.

The position of medieval Jewish widows can be described as intermediate between that of married Jewish women and adult Jewish men. Since medieval Jewish widows could exercise formal power in the domestic realm, they were in a stronger position than their married sisters who were restricted to informal power and influence. But widows could not truly (with rare exceptions) exercise any formal power or authority in the public sphere, for they were barred from all official positions in the political and religious institutions that governed Jewish medieval life. Under Jewish law and custom, these functions were exclusively the business of men.

NOTES

Professor Martin Lockshin, Professor Johanna Stuckey, and Dr. Elizabeth Cohen, all of York University, provided helpful comments on previous drafts of this essay, for which I am truly grateful.

1. Power is here defined as "the ability to act effectively, to influence people and decisions, and to achieve goals" (see Erler and Kowaleski 1988, 2). Authority is here defined as the right to make decisions binding on others (see Erler and Kowaleski 1988, 1).

2. It should be noted that there are several limitations in the use of the responsa literature as a historical source of information on medieval Jewish widows. First, the date of composition and the location of origin of a responsum is often unknown. With the early responsa, all that is certain is that the question was sent to a certain rabbi who lived at a certain time in a certain place. Second, in order to guarantee the anonymity of the petitioners, they were given common Biblical names: Reuben, Simon, Rachel, and Leah were most often used. Thus, it is impossible to identify them with any known historical personalities. Third, the responsa deal more often with problems of the rich than the poor, for, in general, the more property, the more litigation. Therefore, rich widows appear more frequently than poor ones.

3. In analyzing the data found in the sources, the theoretical frame of public or domestic is fruitful. As Rosaldo explains: "An opposition between 'domestic' and 'public' provides the basis of a structural framework necessary to identify and explore the place of male and female in psychological, cultural, social, and economic aspects of human life" (1974, 23).

4. All translations from Hebrew or Aramaic were done with the help of Prof. Martin Lockshin, York University. I am also very grateful to Prof. Lockshin for explaining to me many of the intricacies of Jewish law as they pertain to women and in other areas.

5. *Al-Mu'allima*: Arabic feminine for 'the teacher' (Ibn Daud 1967, 95 n. 54).

6. The total amount of a *ketubbah* would include an amount equivalent to the bride's *nedunya'*, her dowry, plus the *'ikkar ketubbah*, the two hundred *zuzim* from her husband prescribed in the Babylonian Talmud, the late fifth-century compilation of Jewish law. By the medieval period, this two hundred *zuzim* was worth very little (Agus 1939–40, 250, 252). In most cases the amount specified in the *kettubah* also included the *tosefet ketubbah*, the additional amount the groom promised to provide on the dissolution of the marriage by divorce or by his death.

7. Often the guardians of minor children were relatives of their late father rather than the widow.

8. A *minyan* is a quorum of ten adult males. This quorum is necessary, according to Jewish law, for public synagogue services and certain other religious activities.

9. The *Masora* is a set of comments to the Biblical text of a technical, linguistic nature.

10. The *Targum* is the traditional Aramaic translation of the Biblical text.

11. The *Haftaroth* are selections from the Prophets read in the synagogue on all Saturdays and holidays.

12. A *qav* is a Hebrew measure of volume. Nine *qav* equal approximately twenty liters.

13. For a description of poor widows and their children in the medieval Jewish Egyptian community, see Goitein 1967–83, 3:302, 304–5.

14. According to Prof. Joseph Shatzmiller, University of Toronto (personal communication), a *zaquq* was equivalent in value to a mark.

BIBLIOGRAPHY

Adler, Michael. *Jews of Medieval England*. London: Edward Goldston, 1939.

Agus, Irving. "The Development of the Money Clause in the Ashkenazic Ketubah." *Jewish Quarterly Review* 30 (1939–40): 221–56.

Aptowitzer, Victor. *Mavo le-Sefer Raviah* (Introduction to the Book of Raviah [Rabbi Eliezer ben Joel ha-Levi]). Jerusalem: Meqize Nirdamim, 1938.

Courtemanche, Andrée. "Les femmes juives et le credit a Manosque au tournant du XIVe siècle" (Jewish Women and Credit in Manosque at the turn of the fourteenth century). *Provence Historique* 37 (1987): 545–58.

Emery, Richard. *The Jews of Perpignan in the Thirteenth Century*. New York: Columbia University Press, 1959.

Erler, Mary, and Maryanne Kowaleski, eds. *Women and Power in the Middle Ages*. Athens, Ga.: University of Georgia Press, 1988.

Freimann, A. "She'ure ha-Ketubbah be-Ashkenaz ve-Tsorfat bi-Yeme ha-Benayim" (Amounts of the Ketubbah in Germany and in France in the Middle Ages). In *Alexander Marx Jubilee Volume*, ed. Saul Lieberman, 2:371–85. New York: Jewish Publication Society, 1950.

Glückel of Hameln. *The Memoirs of Glückel of Hameln*. Trans. M. Lowenthal. New York: Shocken, [1932] 1977.

Goitein, Solomon. *A Mediterranean Society*. 5 vols. Berkeley: University of California Press, 1967–88.

Ibn Daud, Abraham. *The Book of Tradition*. Trans. and ed. Gershon Cohen. Philadelphia: Jewish Publication Society, 1967.

Isaac ben Moses [known as 'Or Zarua']. *She'elot u-Teshuvot* (Responsa). Zhitomir, 1862.

Jordan, William Chester. "Jews on Top: Women and the Availability of Consumption Loans in Northern France in the Mid-Thirteenth Century." *Journal of Jewish Studies* 29 (1978): 39–56.

Levitas, Isaac. "Community: Middle Ages." *Encyclopaedia Judaica*. New York: Macmillan, 1972.

Meir ben Barukh [known as Maharam]. *She'elot u-Teshuvot ha-Maharam, defus*

Prague (The Responsa of Maharam, Prague edition). Ed. M. Bloch. Jerusalem: n.p., 1969–70.

Müller, Joel, ed. *Teshuvot Hakhme Tsorfat ve-Lotir* (Responsa of the Sages of France and Lotharingia). Jerusalem: n.p., 1966–67.

Rosaldo, Michelle. "Women, Culture, and Society: A Theoretical Overview." In *Women, Culture, and Society,* ed. Michelle Rosaldo and Louise Lamphere, 17–42. Stanford: Stanford University Press, 1974.

Solomon ben Isaac [known as Rashi]. *Teshuvot Rashi* (The Responsa of Rashi). 2 vols. Ed. I. Elfenbein. Jerusalem: n.p., 1967.

Tallan, Cheryl. "Medieval Jewish Widows: Powerful, Productive, and Passionate." M.A. thesis, York University, 1989.

Urbach, Efraim E. *Ba'ale ha-Tosafot* (The Tosafists). 4th ed., rev. 2 vols. Jerusalem: Mosad Bialik, 1980.

Weinryb, Bernard. "Responsa as a Source for History (Methodological Problems)." In *Essays presented to Chief Rabbi Israel Brodie on his 70th Birthday,* ed. H. J. Zimmels, J. Rabbinowitz, and J. Finestein, 399–417. London: Soncino, 1967.

Part 2
Noble Widows

Chapter 5

Other Victims: Peeresses as War Widows, 1450–1500

Joel T. Rosenthal

Historians treat war as though it were an exclusive men's club. A moment of reflection should remind us that women and children, as well as men, knew of war in the Middle Ages, as in other times. Society often wore a martial guise, and neither age nor gender offered a guarantee of immunity. The people of fifteenth-century England lived in a world filled with those who had been called, or who had volunteered, to heed the summons of king and country, or of nobleman and retinue, or of captain and free company, or of urban watch and ward for city walls and gates. As our world is still filled with the veterans of the Second World War, of Korea, and of Vietnam, so theirs was populated by those who had served with Henry V on St. Crispin's day, or with Talbot at Clermont, or with Warwick at St. Albans or with Edward IV at Tewkesbury. And in this brief litany of battle and military glory, note that I have only listed some of the winners. What of those who stood with the duke of Clarence when he was ambushed and fatally wounded at Baugé in 1421, or with the great earl of Shrewsbury when he fell at Castillon in 1453, or with the 'Kingmaker' when he died at Barnet in 1471? Such veterans of the battlefield surely knew the bitter dregs of defeat: some paid with their heads, many with their patrimony, some perhaps were luckier and got away with just a temporary blow to social status, ego, and the purse. And among both groups—the winners and the losers—there was pain and suffering, physical as well as social and economic. Battlefields were surely no less grisly then than they have become in more advanced ages; some escaped, some died, and some survived to come home wounded, maimed, and disfigured. What must life have been like in those days for those who lived but who were never whole again?[1]

Thus far I have been referring to men who—with varying degrees of voluntarism and enthusiasm—actually showed up on the field of battle. Many others—men and women, young and old, rich and poor—were also touched by war. What of those who had to stand by and watch as armies marched up and down, fighting across their fields or in their streets? What of those whose hard-won stores and goods were embraced by the iron grip of the passing quartermaster? And what of the many who never saw troops engage in actual combat, but who still lived through the dangers and alarms of war; how many times between the death of Edward IV in April, 1483, and Henry VII's triumphant entry into London after Bosworth did the citizens of the city spring to guard their walls, patrol their gates, and arm their militia, lest a siege or armed assault really came to pass? It never did; but the constant preparations alone were costly and disruptive. Finally, among these introductory reflections, what of those who suffered at one remove because loved ones, protectors, and breadwinners had become involved in a dangerous game in which they ultimately proved to be losers? This essay focuses upon the widows of those English peers who died, between 1450 and 1500, either in battle, or directly afterwards as part of the summary punishments of victory and defeat, or in political executions, or in politically inspired mob violence and lynchings. When men went to war, or when war came to them, they placed their political choice and their own safety on the line. But many of them also left hostages to fortune, wives and children, mere pawns in a larger game. These vicarious and dependent victims of war ran their own risks and might have been called upon to face, over a much longer span than their fallen fathers and brothers, the full consequences of battle and defeat.

The Wars of the Roses, for men at the very top of their society, were very sanguinary. Taking into account the different categories of violent death I have just enumerated, some sixty-two peers and peers' direct heirs fell within a period we can think of as the long generation of the half-century.[2] Some men died with all the drama we expect from such tales as the *Song of Roland* or *The Cid*. Sometimes death was incorporated in a scenario worthy of a Victorian melodrama, as when John, ninth lord Clifford, slew the young earl of Rutland at Wakefield. Clifford refused to show mercy, despite the earl's tender years, saying that Rutland's father had previously slain Clifford's father (or so the popular histories told the tale).[3] Sometimes the victim turned out to be nobody's friend, especially after death. Where was the venerable British tradition of fair play toward a scrappy loser when the body of Richard III, now with neither royal crown nor any signs of birth defects, was "slung naked, across the saddle of a horse, the arms and legs hanging on either side . . . abused and insulted . . . [with] a halter . . . round the dead king's neck"?[4] But regardless of which narrative style or dramatic backdrop sets the tone for any particular peer's death, stone dead—as was remarked some two centuries later—hath no fellow. The Wars of the Roses were obviously bloody—despite occasional revisionist efforts to minimize such realities—and their confrontations were scattered across the realm, from Tewkesbury in the west and Barnet in the south to Hedgeley Moor and Hexham in the north, and they occurred, off and on, for over thirty years, from the first battle of St. Albans in May, 1455, to the battle of Stoke in May, 1487. They were nasty, brutish, and protracted.[5]

The wars claimed, directly and indirectly, some sixty-two peers and peers' heirs (in addition to a number of younger sons).[6] Since the peerage in the second half of the fifteenth century usually numbered about three or four dozen men, summoned to any given session of the House of Lords, the casualty list represents a significant bloodletting, drawn out though it was. For convenience we can divide the half-century into four intervals: (1) from 1450 to the accession of Edward IV in March, 1461, (2) from Edward's accession to his reacquisition of the throne in April, 1471, (3) from that date until the battle of Bosworth in August, 1485, and (4) after Bosworth to the end of the century. Within each of these shorter intervals, the toll among the peers and their heirs (who left widows) was, respectively, twenty, twenty, five, and four. Of this grand, albeit lugubrious, total of forty-nine, thirty-four died in battle or immediately afterwards, and fifteen by miscellaneous or scattered executions. While many aristocratic families totally escaped the carnage, others gave more than their full share, and the aristocratic necrology includes two Cliffords, two Percies of Northumberland, Richard duke of York and three of his sons, three Beauforts, and three Welles.

But our interest here is not in the violent deaths of the peer, per se. It is, rather, in those whom the victims of the field and the block left behind, that is, their widows. Most of the dead men had been married at the end, and most of them had been well into their years of maturity, years when wives, children, and the continuity of the patrilineage and the transmission of the patrimony should have been a major part of their orders of the day. Only six of the sixty-two aristocrats died unmarried (and they died at an average age of twenty-six).[7] Of the rest—a sizeable and statistically significant universe of married men—the average life span was forty-three. Violent death often came to the young, as we would expect; but it also fell upon such aged stalwarts as lord Bonville at sixty-eight or sixty-nine, the earl of Northumberland at sixty-three, lord Rivers at sixty-one, and the duke of Norfolk at seventy.[8] Since peers and men of property mostly married by their late teens or early twenties, it is no surprise to discover that twelve of the dead were already in a second marriage and one, at his death, was in his third.

From dead peers we can move to surviving peeresses. It is only in this sideways fashion that we manage to cross the great divide in the quality and the quantity of historical data, going from the sunlit slopes whereon lie the materials about mens' lives to that shadowy ground whereon rests much of what we know about their wives. The lives of aristocratic wives, or aristocratic widows as they are represented here, are relatively obscure, better illuminated than the lives of their less prominent sisters, but invariably poorly illuminated when compared to those of their husbands. We usually know something of the peeresses' social status, some details of their father's identity, and of their family of origin. We less frequently know the date of their marriages, which means that we are generally ignorant regarding duration. We do know, usually with fair precision—sometimes to the hour—when it ended, though their subsequent lives frequently are again shadowy affairs.[9]

Thus we work, as we have come to expect, with data and sources that present women largely as defined by their husbands' identities, careers, and fates. Though there are a few fifteenth-century women with a flair for self-expression, for example, Margaret Paston or Margery Kempe, they are unusual (though probably not all that anomalous, had we more information). Most women of the time have almost no (recorded or preserved) independent voice at all. My universe, in this essay, consists of a specific kind of aristocratic wife or peeress; she who survived a man who died in or as a direct result of war. This defines her in terms of a negative and usually an involuntary action on *his* part. It also, implicitly, advances the idea that her marriage to our unfortunate peer—the activity that makes her part of our universe—stands out as the prime or model experience of *her* life. For many of the forty-four aristocratic widows whom we can identify, it may well have been the prime experience, in both its length and the centrality of such marriage-related experiences as the bearing of children and in the formation or fixing of her ego identity. But for many other women, the particular marriage that is of interest here may not have been nearly as critical or as central. We run risks when we categorize women as *their husbands' other,* risks that we would not have to take were we dealing with men. If we have little alternative, we at least should be explicit about our difficulties.

Of these forty-four military and/or political widows, thirteen came to our critical or definitional marriage after a prior marriage. Moreover, some of the thirteen prior marriages had been of longer duration than those with our peers, and some had produced the children who, in turn, would help fix her identity and her loyalty through the entire span of her life. And, of greater significance perhaps in judging how war-widowhood affected the entire course of her (remaining) life, twenty-one of the forty-four widows remarried (including five of the thirteen who had also been married before).[10] Of the twenty-one who remarried, four went on to remarry more than once, and one woman, Katherine Neville, had the peculiar fortune of losing one husband in battle (William Bonville, lord Harrington, killed at Wakefield in December, 1460), and then of marrying a second peer (William, lord Hastings) who was eventually to suffer death by execution.[11] With the twenty-one women who went from widowhood to remarriage, it is not so easy to determine which chapters of life, in retrospect, were the main chapters. In a few cases, we know that a later marriage produced more children and, therefore, may have played a role, in her entire life story, of more importance than the union we are looking at. Also, of course, some of our critical or definitional marriages (i.e., marriages to the peer who died in war) were short, while a subsequent one may have been of considerably greater duration. In general, womens' lives can be perceived as a life line or vector composed of discrete or discontinuous segments, in contrast to the linked serial episodes that represented a man's life line.[12] Any particular marriage could be forever, or, on the other hand, each marriage could be but one short chapter of the entire volume, and this was even more the case with our war widows than for any other group or any random assortment of women. Given the untimely and abrupt end of the particular marriage we are concerned with, the episodic nature of life must have been much in mind. Had discontinuity not figured so markedly in their biographies, these women would not figure here.

The material presented in table 5.1 gives a brief idea of the scope of the problem for the upper classes. It particularly highlights (col. 2) the close proximity of the deaths of so many men—and the sudden plunge

TABLE 5.1. Peers and Their Heirs Who Died by Violence

			Her Marital Career		
Peer or Heir	Died	His Last Wife	Married Before	Married After	Her Death
Deaths to the accession of Edward IV					
William de la Pole, duke of Suffolk	5/50	Alice Chaucer	B, A[a]	—	5/75
James Fiennes, lord Say & Sele	7/50	Emiline Cromer	—	—	1/52
Thomas, lord Clifford	3/55	Joan Dacre	—	—	survived him
Henry Percy, earl of Northumberland	5/55	Eleanor Neville	B	—	survived him
Edmund Beauford, duke of Somerset	5/55	Eleanor Beauchamp	A	B	3/67
James Tuchet, lord Audley	9/58	Eleanor Holland	—	—	survived him
John, viscount Beaumont	7/60	Katherine Neville	A, B	A	after 1483
Humphrey Stafford, duke of Buckingham	7/60	Anne Neville	—	A	9/80
Thomas, lord Scales	7/60	Esmayne Whalesburgh	—	—	survived him
John Talbot, earl of Shrewsbury	7/60	Elizabeth Butler	—	—	2/64 or later
William Bonville, lord Harrington	12/60	Katherine Neville	—	A	11/1503
Richard Neville, earl of Salisbury	12/60	Alice Montague	—	—	1462
Richard, duke of York	12/60	Cecilly Neville	—	—	5/95
William, lord Bonville	2/61	Elizabeth Courtenay	A	—	10/71
John Grey, lord Ferrers of Groby	2/61	Elizabeth Wydvill	—	A	6/92
John, lord Clifford	3/61	Margaret Bromflete	—	B	4/93
Randolf, lord Dacre	3/61	Eleanor FitzHugh	—	A	after 5/68
John Neville	3/61	Anne Holland	A	A	12/86
Henry Percy, earl of Northumberland	3/61	Eleanor Poynings	A	—	2/84
Lionel, lord Welles	3/61	Margaret Beauchamp	B, A	—	after 6/82
From the accession of Edward IV to the Battle of Tewkesbury (5/1471)					
James Botiller, earl of Ormond	5/61	Eleanor Beauford	—	B	8/1501
William Herbert, earl of Pembroke	7/61	Anne Devereaux	—	—	6/86 or after
John de Vere, earl of Oxford	2/62	Elizabeth Howard	—	—	1475 or later
Aubrey de Vere	2/62	Anne Stafford	—	A	4/72
Robert, lord Hungerford	5/64	Eleanor Moleyns	—	B	1476

Thomas, lord Roos	5/64	Philippa Tiptoft	—	B, B	1/87 or later
Hugh Neville, lord Latimer	7/69	Joan Bourgchier	—	—	10/70
Humphrey Stafford, earl of Devon	8/69	Isabel Barre	—	B	3/89
Richard Wydville, earl Rivers	8/69	Jaquetta of Luxemburg	A	—	5/72
Thomas Talbot, lord Lisle	3/70	Margaret Herbert	—	B	before 1503
Richard, lord Welles	3/70	Margaret Strangeways	B	—	5/75 or later
Robert, lord Welles	3/70	Elizabeth Bourgchier	—	—	10/70
John Tiptoft, earl of Worcester	10/70	Elizabeth Hopton	B	A	6/98
William Bourgchier	4/71	Anne Wydville	—	B, A	survived him
Humphrey Bourgchier, lord Cromwell	4/71	Joan Stanhope	—	B	5/90
John Neville, marquis Montague	4/71	Isabel Ingoldsthorpe	—	B	5/76
William Fiennes, lord Say & Sele	4/71	Margaret Wykeham	—	B	5/77 or later
Richard Neville, earl of Warwick	4/71	Anne Beauchamp	—	—	9/92
Edward, prince of Wales	4/71	Anne Neville	—	A	3/85
John, lord Wenlock	4/71	Agnes Danvers	B, B, B	—	6/78

From Tewkesbury through the Battle of Bosworth

William, lord Hastings	6/83	Katherine Neville	A	—	11/1503
Anthony Wydville, earl Rivers	6/83	Margaret Fitzlewis	—	B	survived him
Henry Stafford, duke of Buckingham	11/83	Katherine Wydville	—	A, B	after 1500
Walter Devereux, lord Ferrers	8/85	Jane —	—	B, B, B	after 1512
John Howard, duke of Norfolk	8/85	Margaret Chedworth	B, B	—	1494

After Bosworth to the end of the fifteenth century

John de la Pole, earl of Lincoln	5/87	Margaret Wydville	—	—	after 1493
Francis, viscount Lovel	1487?	Anne Fitzhugh	—	—	after 1495
John Radcliffe, lord Fitzwalter	11/96	Margaret —	—	—	survived him
James Tuchet, lord Audley	6/97	Joan Bourgchier	—	—	3/1532

aA means a previous or subsequent husband was a peer or a peer's son, B means a commoner.

into widowhood of so many women. It also gives an indication of how the critical aristocratic marriage fit into the entire life pattern, running both before the marriage with the peer, in some instances, and afterward, in others, and before and after, for a few. Only eighteen of the widows who constitute the universe under examination were married solely to the peer whose death brings them into focus here.

Of the range of questions that we might put to the data about the women's lives, only a few offer much promise of amplification. Though our major concern might be whether politicomilitary widowhood shattered their lives and whether the lives could be knitted up again, we mostly have to swim around in the shallow sides of the issues. What was the interval between the instance of widowhood and remarriage? But even here, poor data and variations of behavior hamstring efforts to offer any sort of general statement. Some widows waited but a year or two: the duke of Buckingham was executed in November, 1483, and Katherine Wydeville remarried Jasper Tudor, the new duke of Bedford, by November, 1485. This was obviously among the speedier cases. However, most widows (and presumably widowers) who did remarry did so within a few years, and we should be careful not to read the tale of one marriage—either positive or negative—from the speed with which the next was entered.

We have reasonable information regarding a widow's absolute survival after the aristocratic marriage, whether her remaining years were spent in celibate isolation or in a subsequent marriage; we know less about the intervals between marriages. For the forty women about whom we can speak, the duration of survival—of outlasting the critical husband in the competitive game of life—was fairly impressive. Of our forty widows, fifteen survived for a decade or less, ten lived between ten and twenty years after the peer had been killed, and fifteen outlasted him for more than two decades. The dead peers themselves had had an average life span of about forty-three years (which was about a decade below the average life span of all the fifteenth-century peers, these men included). Since 62.5 percent of their widows (twenty-five of forty) outlived them by at least a decade, many of our widows must have lived to at least half a century, if not more.[13] And what seems a reasonable assertion for a group of forty women must have been all the more so for those women who outlasted him for twenty years or more. The champions in this category survived the instance or moment of widowhood for about a third of a century. James Audley was executed for treason in June, 1497, and his second wife, Joan Bourgchier, survived without further marriage until her death in March, 1532. However, three of the five women who lasted thirty years or more did remarry, and two of them bore children in a subsequent marriage.

The life of the widow, as I have argued elsewhere, was some odd combination of good news and bad news. We must not overemphasize her relative autonomy nor—even at the upper levels of society—her affluence. For some women at the top there were powerful as well as ameliorating factors. Many of the widows were already heiresses in their own right, coming as they did either from aristocratic or substantial gentry backgrounds. Others were already widows, and in six such instances the previous husband had likewise been a peer (including Henry V's brother John, duke of Bedford).[14] Comely dower portions were apt to be part of the trousseau such women had brought to what is, for us, the operative marriage. Other aristocratic widows, if not heiresses, were nevertheless daughters of aristocratic or upper-class houses and they may have come to the marriage with handsome settlements in lands, cash, or convertible assets and prospects. The sum total of these factors gives us a group of women whose widowhoods—long or short—and whose years of isolation and beareavment—few or many—were at least relatively free of the worst forms of economic distress.

This may be true, but it is still an assertion in need of some qualification and some relative evaluation. At best it is a reflection of the socioeconomic position of peeresses, not of marital status. Furthermore, the rich had their own versions of need, and social demotion, rather than genuine hunger, was also a legitimate worry in a world of hierarchy, inherited status, and deference. Because we are not dealing with just a random group of peers, we are also dealing with a group of widows who sometimes entered their new state under the peculiar burden of a sentence of attainder and forfeiture that had been levied upon the husband either before, at the time of, or even appreciably after his death. In these instances, the road ahead—for her and for their children who might hope to reclaim the patrimony—could be a rocky one, with no guarantee of a successful passage. Men who died before the reaccession of Edward IV were mostly called upon to pay for their mistakes with their lives, though the king did not always rush to summon their sons and heirs to his side. But after 1470 or 1471, attainder—that fell and dreaded sentence upon family blood and estates—was used more and more, and, even if a widow were exempted from its sharpest teeth, her lot was hardly apt to be an easy or a happy one. The loss of honors and estates was not intended as merely symbolic deprivation.

The widow claimed her one-third share of her husband's estates, according to law, and from this she supposedly was able to support herself and to raise her minor children. Sometimes the recovery of her dower share proved to be quick and simple, while in other instances she faced both delay and oppressive supervision. Conversely, the ease of recovery was not always related to the degree of political favor in which he had stood at his end. The earl of Oxford was a dedicated Lancastrian, and he and his son had paid with their heads for the family commitment in February, 1462. But by March 1, 1462, we discover that Anne, "late the wife of Aubrey de Veer [the earl's son], who died without issue by her," was receiving shares of the lands they had held together in five counties.[15] This was an easier passage than that of Eleanor, widow of James Butler, earl of Wiltshire, "attainted of high treason by authority of Parliament." In her case, lord Wenlock was appointed governor of the lady and of her jointure, "with the sole power of appointing and removing servants and officers."[16] But one family's misfortune was often the fuel by which another's rise was powered. The duke of Somerset was killed in 1455. Though his widow received valuable grants in 1456, she came in for really generous treatment in 1460, when she was given substantial blocks of lands, now in the king's hands, because of the "high treason, insurrection, and rebellions" of the duke of York and the earl of Warwick.[17]

In the early 1460s, Elizabeth Wydeville had supposedly been suing for some share of the forfeited possessions of her late husband, the Lancastrian John Grey, lord Ferrers of Groby, when Edward IV's eye fell upon the young widow and mother and she more than regained lost ground. But other women also pleaded a poverty that was probably very real, and their problems were rarely solved in such fairy-tale fashion. Even hard-hearted and tight-fisted Henry VII made a special and uncharacteristic dispensation that Anne Fitzhugh, widow of Francis, lord Lovel, should not suffer because of the sentence of forfeiture and attainder levied upon him for his sustained support of the Yorkist cause.[18] Wives were easily tarred with the brush that had obliterated the husband, and many of them had to survive uneasy if not dangerous times. Even the widows of such great men as the duke of York and the earl of Salisbury had, immediately after their husbands' deaths, to lay low and just hope for powerful friends and better days.[19]

An affluent widow presumably weighed a number of variables when she assessed an opportunity to remarry. Of our universe, twenty-one women did remarry, while twenty either chose not to or died before they got around to it.[20] Some second marriages were of goodly duration and seem to have been successful, as far as we can judge such matters across the flickering lights of five intervening centuries. Some women went, unknowingly, from one set of troubles to another, though many years might have separated their sets of woes. I have already referred to Katherine Neville, who lost two husbands in the wars.[21] Her marriage to William Bonville, lord Harrington, lasted only two years before his death in 1460. By February, 1464, she was married to lord Hastings, and they had nineteen conjugal years and at least four children before he was executed in June, 1483. She lived for another twenty-one years. Her troubles were heavy but not without some parallels. Another Katherine Neville had married John, viscount Beaumont, and, after his death at Northampton in 1460, she married (as her fourth husband) John Wydeville, a younger son of earl Rivers.[22] He was beheaded in August, 1469, along with his father, and the aged Katherine (rather belatedly) bowed out of the marriage game. Margaret Herbert, daughter of the earl of Pembroke, married Thomas Talbot, lord Lisle, and he was killed in his family's running feud with the Berkeleys in 1470 (after about four years of marriage). Her second husband, Henry Bodrugen, died in 1503 while in exile because of treason, but, as she had predeceased Bodrugen, she was at least spared some of his final woes.[23] Elizabeth Hopton also had two husbands who were killed. The first was the earl of Worcester, which suffices to make her part of our group, and, twenty-five years later, it was Sir William Stanley, younger brother of the earl of Derby, executed by Henry VII for treason.[24] So, whatever good news there was during the long interval, some tales of remarriage did not end happily ever after.

Several aristocratic widows talked about taking the veil, though it is hard to know whether this meant real enclaustration or a simple widow's vow of chastity.[25] Elizabeth Wydeville had entered an adventurous new life, as Edward IV's queen, but eventually she too wound up, once more, a grieving widow and a poor old woman, unloved, untrusted, impoverished, and under virtual house arrest within Bermondsey Abbey.[26] Others lived out their widowhood in a more prosaic fashion. Eleanor, daughter and heiress of Sir William Moleyns, married Robert, lord Hungerford (and lord Moleyns, executed in 1464), and then Sir Oliver Maningham, and when she died in 1476 she requested burial at Stoke Poges, with her grandfather and grandmother, her father (d. 1425), and her father's first wife Margaret (her mother?). Hungerford went to lie in his family's great chantry chapel in Salisbury Cathedral, so the union was not visibly continued after death, though their family peerages had been merged (in their eldest son's titles) and the union had produced at least three sons.[27] Lord Wenlock's wife was not so impressed with his de novo peerage, and when she died, seven years after Wenlock's death at Tewkesbury in 1471, she requested burial with a previous and non-noble husband, Sir John Fray, chief baron of the Exchequer and then dead for some twenty years.[28] And in a last exercise of wifely power, the countess of Salisbury (Richard Neville's widow) sought burial with her ancestors in their ancestral burial house at Bisham; her older Montacute pretensions outweighed his newer Neville ones. He, in fact, was reinterred with her in 1462, in her family house, after a funeral procession that was a high water mark of early Yorkist pomp and pageantry.[29] These biographical snippets shed some light on the extent to which a widow's life was bound up and subsumed into her husband's life. And, though the general answer has to be in favor of his superordinate status, the details indicate that variety was permissible and even that her identity (or at least that of her paternal family) could sometimes remain distinct or even emerge as dominant.

Beyond this, and other such bits and scraps of information about the lives of men and women and then of women alone, it is hard to go. We constantly want to ask: What was her life *really* like, after he went off to war and came home nevermore? What did she think of his cause, and of the fatal attraction of that cause? Of this, we know virtually naught, and maybe the loving gibes of Hotspur's wife about war and marital entanglements in *Henry IV,* part 1, are as close to the ambivalent truth as anything we can decipher from the historical sources regarding women's views of war. But we also know that such a woman as Queen Margaret of Anjou could play a significant role in stoking the fires of partisan politics. On the other hand, Elizabeth Wydeville turned, in no significant interval, from the role of Lancastrian widow to that of Yorkist queen. Party lines could be fuzzy, determined as they were by such large measures of personal ties or personal aversions, and women do not seem to have been any more orthodox or steadfast than their fathers, brothers, and sons during the vicissitudes of these years. Anne Holand married and buried John Neville and then married his uncle, John, lord Neville (killed at Towton); this sounds incestuous, albeit politically consistent. How-

ever, her husbands represent the two different (and divergent) branches
of the Jesse tree of the Nevilles that sprang from the first earl of
Westmorland (Ralph Neville, d. 1425), and Anne had no more trouble
hopping fences than she did in obtaining the requisite ecclesiastical dis-
pensations. Great widows who survived to become matriarchs, such as
Cecilly Neville (d. 1495), widow of Richard, duke of York (executed
1460), were clearly bastions of political and partisan devotion. But some
qualification is also in order. In a world where one or perhaps two of
Cecilly's sons had killed a third, and where the youngest labeled his
oldest brother a bastard and his mother a whore, and then caused two
of his nephews to disappear (if not worse), we find that we are able to
check our impulse to sing a paean for family loyalty.[30]

In a final effort to assess the quality of these widows' lives we can turn
to some last wills of both the peers and their peeresses. Unfortunately,
whether due to the random survival of records or to a correlation between a violence-prone personality and a reluctance to make a last will,
we have a smaller proportion of wills for either these particular peers or
for their widows than we have for the entire universe of fifteenth-century
peers and peeresses. Furthermore, in assessing the material in the wills
that have been preserved, such variables as the interval between his death
and hers, her subsequent marital career, and the identity (as well as the
age and sex) of her heir(s) and nearest survivors all become important
factors. Though few of our peers expected to die when and as they did,
most must have realized that they were about to venture into what we
might label as a high-risk situation. Nevertheless, only a handful have
left us very much, and even their records shed little light, beyond the
obvious formulaic conventions, about marriage and the marital partner.
William Herbert, earl of Pembroke, was beheaded in 1471 by Robin of
Redesdale's rabble (or "primitive rebels," if we prefer); his will was
dated two years before. He spoke in a tender if manipulative fashion
regarding his wife, Anne Devereux: "and wyfe, that ye remember your
promise to me, to take the ordre of wydowhood, as ye may be the better
mayster of your owne, to performe my wylle and to helpe my children,
as I love and trust you."[31] Whatever substance lay behind this fairly
common sentimentality (and its efforts toward posthumous social control), she was alive and (still) unmarried in 1486. The couple had produced a son and six daughters, and the earl was concerned that his
daughters be married as he wished. Since he and Anne had been married
for fourteen years when he wrote the will and sixteen when he died, at

least some of the girls were still below marriageable age. Anne was not named as an executrix. But this was hardly out of the ordinary. Nor was there much in the will of Anthony, second earl Rivers, concerning his widow. She simply received some personal and household items, including all the plate given her at their marriage, which was his second and had only run for some three years.[32] At least lord Say and Sele gave her land, for life, plus the residue of his estate, and made her one of his executors. She, at her death some eighteen months later, repaid his faith by choosing a common burial ground, the popular aristocratic site of the Grey Friars, Newgate.[33]

Do the widows' own wills open a wider window into the experience of marriage, widowhood, and alienation or psychic and social reintegration than do those of their late husbands? We can be fairly certain, by now, that the answers are hardly likely to be strongly positive or dramatic. As I have said, our widows as a group left very few wills. Moreover, a will is a valuable document for decoding and assessing the testator's views of his or her *final* life situation; it is much less useful when read as a photographic plate on which to seek the total record of a relationship and feelings that stretch back to youth or girlhood. Thus, when we look at the will of Anne Neville, duchess of Buckingham, we must not only take into account that she had outlived the duke by twenty years after his death at Northampton in 1460, but that, in the interval, she had married and again outlasted William Blount, lord Mountjoy. She left a very nice will, opening with gifts to her grandson, the young duke (who would be executed by Richard III three years later) *if* he honor her wishes. But "if my sonne of Bukkyngham interrupt or sett my last will . . . thanne the bequest . . . be voide and of noon effect."[34] Then there were bequests to her daughter, lady Beaumont, to a younger son, to a daughter-in-law, to a step-daughter by her Blount marriage, and to a grandson. No direct reference at all was made to the late lord Mountjoy, while Buckingham, as her "moost dere and best biloved husband," was the long-gone beneficiary of the endowed chantry services. Her bequest embraced cash, land, the usual medley of personal items (including a pair of silver basins "wherein I used to wash"), and a collection of service books, volumes of saints' lives, a New Testament, and "a book of French called Lucum." But this is a comely will from a rich old lady, and pretty much what we might expect.

In fact, other widows' wills are not all that different from that of the duchess. Lady Hastings remembered many relatives and distributed a vast panoply of personal possessions. Because we know that she had lost two husbands in battle or by execution, we look with particular interest at her prefatory comments: "nothing is more certain than deth and nothing more uncertain than the houre of deth."[35] But, alas, despite her grim personal experiences with such trite realities, this was but a pious convention, uttered in almost identical fashion by many of her contemporaries of both sexes with no comparable draughts from her bitter autobiographical cup. Again, there is little reference to husbands dead for two or three or even four decades. This seems a common theme: few signs of the grief, or of the need to accept new responsibilities, or of the painful efforts that had once been made to pick up the threads. The last wills of the war widows carry few distinct touches when set against those of aristocratic widows in general. Perhaps if we had some material preserved from their salad days of bereavement we might detect a different flavor. When Cecilly Neville, dowager duchess of York, died in 1495, she had survived many close relatives who had died in the wars: a husband, three sons, a brother, nephews, and any number of brothers-in-law, cousins, and so forth. But she looked to the future, as much as a will can, as well as to the past; there were bequests to Henry VII, to the prince who would become Henry VIII, to Queen Elizabeth (her granddaughter), to Prince Arthur, and to others who mainly belong on the more recent stage of the Tudor dynastic drama.[36] There was little of either York or Lancaster; old woes were perhaps best left unrehearsed, old sorrows unspoken.

In conclusion, we have to accept that this glimpse at the lives and fortunes of these war widows is tantalizing rather than satisfying. We have enough data to raise and to examine many questions, to resolve almost none. I began by asserting that war touched women in numerous ways, and not the least of these was in her wife-widow capacity. As in most other areas, she is most readily approached in terms of her existence as her husband's other, and in this regard her role or status as a war widow represents no major departure.

Given our sources, it is almost impossible to catch the full force of her bereavement. Men and women in late medieval society were socialized not to give vent to excessive expressions of personal feeling.[37] The liturgy and the ecclesiastical calendar both exerted an anaesthetizing effect. Chantry licenses and chantry prayers—at least as the written sources filter them for our perusal—are controlled and relatively unemotional.

We can only guess at the waves of stoicism or rage or grief that were unleashed by the news of a husband's death. In addition, we know that news could travel quickly, just as we know that rumor or false versions of events could outstrip more authentic information.[38] Did families know when their men were about to engage in battle, or were messengers' dispatches to the corners of the realm concerning the tallies of the wounded, the missing, the captured, and the dead likely to come as bolts from the blue? Obviously, neither her petition for her dower share nor her last will is apt to be of much guidance when we concern ourselves with such questions.

Widowhood, by itself, poses some peculiar problems. I began by talking about war, and the instances of widowhood we have been looking at all stemmed, directly or indirectly, from the breakdown of civil order in late Lancastrian, Yorkist, and early Tudor England. However, widowhood was a fate that befell about half of any group of married women who lived to their mid-twenties or beyond. This means that war widows probably had much in common with other widows and with other groups—define or choose them as we will—of women. War was the operative factor in some respects, a mere formal cause in others. Had we picked up this same group of women at the time of their first marriages, and had war not entered the realm with such fratricidal clamor, we would not have found them all to be widows, and those who would have suffered such a fate for "natural" reasons would presumably have suffered it at more advanced ages. But many would, nevertheless, have become widows, though admittedly later rather than sooner. War widowhood meant widowhood at a younger age; the husbands died about ten years below the average for the peerage, and we can extrapolate accordingly for her, both regarding the duration of the terminated marriage and her age at the point of its termination. And younger widowhood meant more minor children and younger children, more years of vulnerability, of being supervised and dependent. If the men who died in the wars had an average life span of forty-three years, their widows probably had been averaging in their mid to late thirties when disaster had befallen them. They lived, on the average, another fifteen years, for a total span of about fifty. Of course, the obverse is that war widows had a longer span after the incidence of the widowhood of interest to us in which to get on with a new (or a left-over) life.

This is thin material on which to construct serious demography, though it is worth a few lines of speculation. War cut off their marriages when the women were, on the average, somewhere between half and two-thirds of the way from cradle to grave, and when they probably had about as many years of marriage (and motherhood) behind them as they had of survival ahead. So if widowhood was a common lot, war did serve to bring them to it sooner and to leave those who never remarried in it longer.

Modern historians sometimes have the luxury of studying a many-sided relationship between women and war: feminist peace movements, wartime opportunities and women's expanded role in the labor force, wartime strains upon the nuclear family and traditional sexual mores, and so forth. For fifteenth-century England, there are no such topics. I have alluded to Hotspur's wife and her distinctly anti-heroic views of war. On stage, the scene is usually presented as a bittersweet love scene, with eroticism being used to blunt the edge of her scorn and hostility. Perhaps we are too sentimental; if young lady Percy were depicted as a serious pacifist and/or a feminist, how much would the entire complexion of her assault change? On the other hand, contemporaries had no doubts about identifying Margaret of Anjou as a devoted supporter if not an outright instigator of violence, bloodshed, and martial and partisan vengeance. She more than deserved her widow's weeds, they said, for her ridicule of the duke of York's decapitated head after his death at Wakefield. As there are no simple answers or easy generalizations about the statistical material we have looked at, nor to the qualitative issues about women's life-styles and adjustments, neither is there one to the entire issue of how war and war widowhood affected lives. Some of the answers and ramifications are too obvious to need elaboration. Others remain beyond us. All fifteenth-century women—rich or poor, maid, wife, or widow—were going to find difficult stretches in the course of their journeys. Our aristocratic war widows came in for even more than the ordinary share of misfortune. Some surmounted it while others never rallied or perhaps were quite willing, after such a blow, to accept their fate and to withdraw from the race. Without romanticizing those who stayed behind (or who were left behind), we should at least note their continuing presence and the way in which they were called upon—like it or not—to bear the consequences of their men's foolishness. War was better for the winners than the losers, no doubt, as it was probably better for men than for women. For the latter it was often just one additional burden—and perhaps an irremediably heavy one—that many women—without advice or consent—were forced to shoulder.[39]

Thanks to some recent scholarly work, there is one final issue we can address. Because of the nature of late medieval sources, we now have some studies of the widows of village or manorial or peasant society.[40] Such works suggest that for a widow of any substance remarriage was the most likely fate, and that elderly widows were usually provided for by dying husbands and surviving children. While it is hardly my intention to denigrate the circumstance of the widow, nor to deny the peculiar opportunities for independence offered by her new status, I wonder if an approach by way of economic and social history, from the ground up, offers a picture of too much integration and of too little alienation. This is speculation, rather than an assertion of fact or of a fully formulated hypothesis. But it reminds me of two important points on which I might close.

One is the extent, once again, to which the nature of the sources— almost never of explicit concern here—governs our ability to offer questions, let alone to extract answers. The other has to do with the tangled threads between gender and class.[41] Were aristocratic widows (and their lives and experiences) more like aristocratic men than they were similar to their less prosperous (but perhaps less constrained) sisters? To some extent, further research may resolve these issues. But to some extent, I suspect, there will always be room for variations in approach and in interpretation. In that respect, at least, the history of medieval women and widows is a typical and proper segment or case study in the larger enterprise of historical research and interpretation.

NOTES

A shorter version of this essay was read at the University of Toronto's conference on War in Medieval Society, February, 1986. This essay is reprinted, with permission, from *History* 72 (1987): 312–30.

1. See C. T. Allmand, ed., *Society at War: The Experience of England and France during the Hundred Years' War* (Edinburgh, 1973), especially chap. 1 ("Late Medieval Attitudes to War") and chap. 5 ("War and the Civilian Population"); John Gillingham, *The Wars of the Roses: Peace and Conflict in Fifteenth-Century England* (Baton Rouge, 1981), 1–14; Anthony Goodman, *The Wars of the Roses: Military Activity and English Society, 1452–1497* (London, 1981), 196–226.

2. On peers and mortality, see K. B. McFarlane, "The Wars of the Roses," in *England in the Fifteenth Century* (London, 1981), 231–61; Colin Richmond,

"The Nobility and the Wars of the Roses, 1459–1461," *Nottingham Medieval Studies* 21 (1977): 71–86.

3. The accounts of Leland, Hall, and Hollinshed—all long after the fact and without contemporary documentation—are cited in Vicary Gibbs *et al., The Complete Peerage* (London, 1910–59), 3:293.

4. See R. A. Griffiths and Roger S. Thomas, *The Making of the Tudor Dynasty* (Gloucester, 1985), 164–65; Charles Ross, *Richard III* (London, 1981), 225 (with a reference to the "prolonged posthumous humiliation" heaped upon both body and reputation).

5. The deaths run, in chronological order, from the lynch mob execution of the duke of Suffolk, on Dover sands on May 2, 1450, to the beheading of James Tuchet, seventh lord Audley, for treason, at Blackfriars, London, June 28, 1497.

6. Among the younger sons, we can number Humphrey (executed 1471), son of James, fifth lord Audley (ex. 1459), and Ralph Percy (ex. 1461–62), son of Henry, fifth earl of Northumberland (ex. 1459). See table 5.1 for the forty-nine peers and peer's heirs who died with surviving wives. There were thirteen other men who either survived their (last) marriage or who had never married. In addition, there are a few cases where the information is simply beyond recovery.

7. The peers who never married were John Courtenay, earl of Devon (ex. 1471); Thomas Percy, lord Egremont (ex. 1460); Edmund, earl of Rutland (ex. 1460); Henry Beaufort, third duke of Somerset (ex. 1464); Beaufort's brother and heir, Edmund, fourth duke of Somerset (ex. 1471); Edward, earl of Warwick (ex. 1499), son of George, duke of Clarence.

8. For the old men, see J. T. Rosenthal, "Old Men's Lives—Elderly English Peers, 1350–1500," *Mediaevalia* 8 (1982): 211–37.

9. The basic biographical material for the peers and their wives/widows is from Gibbs, *Complete Peerage*. Some of the peers are known to have married women whose ultimate fate cannot be determined. Among these "lost" women are the second wife of James Audley (ex. 1459); Joan Dacre, wife of Thomas, eighth lord Clifford (ex. 1455); Margaret, second wife of John Radcliffe, lord FitzWilliam (ex. 1496); and Esmayne Whalesburgh, wife of Thomas, seventh lord Scales (ex. 1460).

10. See the material as set out in table 5.1.

11. Besides Katherine Neville, who lost two husbands, other women suffered more than a fair share of personal grief from the wars: Eleanor Neville, wife of Henry Percy, fifth earl of Northumberland (ex. 1455) and mother of Ralph Neville (ex. 1461–62); Eleanor Moleyns, wife of Richard, third lord Hungerford (ex. 1464), and mother of Thomas (ex. 1469); Margaret Herbert, daughter of William, earl of Pembroke (ex. 1471) and wife of Thomas Talbot, viscount Lisle (ex. 1470); Isabel Barre, wife of Humphrey Stafford, earl of Devon (ex. 1469) and daughter-in-law of William Stafford (ex. 1450 by rebels in Kent); Elizabeth Howard, wife of John de Vere, twelfth earl of Oxford (ex. February 26, 1462)

and mother of Aubrey, John's first son and heir apparent (ex. February 20, 1462); Anne Stafford, wife of Aubrey de Vere and daughter of Humphrey, first duke of Buckingham (ex. 1460) and sister of Humphrey Stafford, killed with his father; and Eleanor Holand, wife of James Tuchet, fifth lord Audley (ex. 1459) and mother of Sir Humphrey (ex. 1471).

12. This is discussed in a more general fashion in Joel T. Rosenthal, "Aristocratic Widows in Fifteenth-Century England," in *Women and the Structure of Society,* ed. B. J. Harris and J. K. McNamara (Durham, N. C., 1984).

13. Of the fifteen widows who survived by a decade or less, six lived for one to five years, nine for six to ten; of the ten who outlived their husbands by eleven to twenty years, five lasted for eleven to fifteen years, and five for sixteen to twenty years.

14. She was Jaquetta, daughter of Pierre de Luxembourg, count of St. Pol. Bedford died in September, 1435, and by March, 1437, she was married to Richard Wydeville. He, as earl Rivers, was executed after the battle of Egecote, August 12, 1469, and she lived until at least May, 1472.

15. *Calendar of the Patent Rolls, 1461–67* (London: Her Majesty's Stationery Office, 1897), 76.

16. Ibid., 178; also 6, 24, 108, 181, 196, 298; *Patent Rolls, 1476–85,* 436, 496.

17. *Calendar of the Fine Rolls* (Her Majesty's Stationery Office), 19 (1452–61): 63, 261, 268, 272.

18. *Patent Rolls, 1485–94,* 304; *Rolls of Parliament* (London, 1783), 6:503. Royal generosity was not likely to be very expensive or risky; Lovel had no children and his heirs were two married sisters. His widow, daughter of lord Fitzhugh and Alice Neville, was still alive in 1495.

19. The life of the countess of Warwick, after the "Kingmaker's" death, was adventurous and unenviable, see P. M. Kendall, *Warwick the Kingmaker* (London, 1957), 327–29; see also William Campbell, ed., *Materials for a History of Henry VII* (London: Rolls Series, 1873–77), 2:66, 84, 211–12.

20. See B. A. Holderness, "Widows in Preindustrial Society: An Essay upon Their Economic Functions," in *Land, Kinship, and Life Cycle,* ed. R. M. Smith (Cambridge, 1984), 428: "the first weapon in the armoury of the widow was remarriage."

21. Katherine Neville was the daughter of Richard, earl of Salisbury, and Alice Montacute. She married William Bonville by 1458, and he died, s.p.m., in December, 1460. She was married to Hastings by February, 1462, and he was beheaded for treason in June, 1483.

22. This Katherine Neville was the daughter of Ralph, earl of Westmorland, and his second wife, Joan Beaufort, daughter of John of Gaunt. She married John Mowbray, duke of Norfolk, Sir Thomas Strangeways, viscount Beaumont (ex. 1460), and then John Wydeville, Edward IV's young brother-in-law. On the political marriage between the twenty-year-old bridegroom and the bride, now

about sixty-five, see Charles Ross, *Edward IV* (London, 1975), 93. Unfriendly eyes saw that as a *maritagium diabolicum*.

23. W. Campbell, *Materials,* 1:315, 328, 2: 118, 186, 244.

24. For her first husband, see Rosamund J. Mitchell, *John Tiptoft 1427–1470* (London, 1938); for her second (and his fatal flirtation with rebellion and treason), see W. A. J. Archbold, "Sir William Stanley and Perkin Warbeck," *English Historical Review* 14 (1899): 529–34.

25. The widows of the earl of Shrewsbury and of lord Welles both sought to take the veil; see James Raine, Jr., ed., *Testamenta Eboracensia* (Surtees Society, no. 45, 1865), 3: 335, 343.

26. For Elizabeth Wydeville's unhappy end, see Agnes Strickland, *Lives of the Queens of England* (London, 1905), 3:376–80.

27. Michael Hicks, "Chantries, Obits, and Almshouses: The Hungerford Foundations, 1325–1478," in *The Church in Pre-Reformation Society: Essays in Honour of F. R. H. Du Boulay,* ed. C. M. Barron and C. Harper-Bill (Woodbridge, 1985).

28. J. S. Roskell, "John lord Wenlock of Someries," in *Parliament and Politics in Late Medieval England* (London, 1981), 2:229–65. For Lady Wenlock's will, see Public Record Office (London), Wills of the Prerogative Court of Canterbury, 34 Wattys. She asked for burial beside Sir John Frey, "my last husband," and a priest was to pray for Frey, Wenlock, and Sir John Say, "my husbands." Her daughters were by Frey and her first husband, Thomas Baldington.

29. The description of the reburial of the earl of Salisbury and his son is reprinted, see Edith Rickert, *Chaucer's World* (New York, 1948), 407–10. The earl's son Thomas, also a casualty of Wakefield, was reburied with him at the same time.

30. Family loyalty is treated (though mainly from the male perspective) by J. A. F. Thomson, "The Courtenay Family in the Yorkist Period," *Bulletin of the Institute of Historical Research* 45 (1972): 230–46. Such women as Elizabeth Wydeville, the duchess of Buckingham, and Katherine Neville, widow of the duke of Norfolk, "changed sides" with successive husbands. What we cannot determine is the extent to which such behavior was a real issue in contemporary eyes. After all, how many times did peers do the same, with fewer external pressures?

31. Prerogative Court, 28 Godyn.

32. Prerogative Court, 44 Milles.

33. London, Lambeth Palace Archives, Archiepiscopal Registers: Arundel, I, 190b–191a.

34. Prerogative Court, 2 Logge. For the dowager duchess' continuing identification as a Stafford, rather than as a Blount, see Carole Rawcliffe, *The Staffords, Earls of Stafford and Dukes of Buckingham, 1394–1521* (Cambridge, 1978), 87–88.

35. Prerogative Court, 7 Holgrave.

36. Prerogative Court, 25 Vox.

37. S. L. Thrupp, *The Merchant Class of Medieval London, 1300–1500* (Ann Arbor, 1948), 200–201.

38. C. A. J. Armstrong, "Some Examples of the Distribution and Speed of News in England at the Time of the Wars of the Roses," in *Studies in Medieval History Presented to F. M. Powicke,* ed. R. W. Hunt, W. A. Pantin, and R. W. Southern (London, 1948); Michael Bennett, *The Battle of Bosworth* (Gloucester, 1985), 1–15.

39. See F. R. H. Du Boulay, *An Age of Ambition* (London, 1970), 107–9, for the widow of Thomas Denys, murdered in 1461: she "made such piteous moan and said that she knew not how to do for money" (quoted from Paston Letter, no. 400). In 1427, a Breton robbed and murdered a London widow, without Aldgate. When he was apprehended, the women of the parish stoned him to death, "and thus this fals thefe endede his life in this worlds, for his falseness." And so sisterhood and xenophobia joined hands; see F. W. D. Brie, ed., *The Brut* (Early English Text Society, o.s. 136: 1908), 11: 442–43.

40. See Holderness, "Widows"; Peter Franklen, "Peasant Widows' 'Liberation' and Remarriage after the Black Death," *Economic History Review* 39 (1986): 186–204; Cicely Howell, *Lands, Family, and Inheritance in Transition: Kibworth Harcourt, 1280–1700* (Cambridge, 1983), 255–61; Margaret Spufford, *Contrasting Communities: English Villages in the Sixteenth and Seventeenth Centuries* (Cambridge, 1974), 88–90, 112–16, 161–64.

41. See the recent discussion by Mary Beth Rose, "Making Gender the Question," *Journal of British Studies* 28 (1986): 335–44.

Chapter 6

Widows in the Chronicles of Late Medieval Castile

Clara Estow

Widowhood in the Middle Ages, given its complexity and uniqueness, is a rich area of study for modern scholars. In the otherwise limiting and rigid society of medieval Europe, a woman's identity was altered in significant ways by widowhood. A widow assumed social, legal, and economic responsibilities that set her apart from the rest of adult female society. In certain regions, she was expected to carry on her husband's official and military obligations. The status of widow also denoted a separate category in moral and ecclesiastical treatises. The widow, never the widower, was placed among the defenseless, or *miserabiles personae,* and was deemed in need of moral guidance, and many a moralist showed concern for the virtue and welfare of the woman who found herself alone.

The recurrent mention of the widow in legal, moral, and historical literature testifies to medieval society's recognition of the uniqueness of her role. It also reflects society's desire to regulate widowhood. This essay will present several examples from Castilian historical literature of the late Middle Ages that illustrate the complexity of the widow's role. The main sources used here are the chronicles of Pedro I, Enrique III, and Juan II. These chronicles were composed between the last third of the fourteenth century and the first half of the fifteenth by Pero López de Ayala and Fernán Pérez de Guzmán.[1]

A word about these sources. Medieval chronicles offer a rich reservoir of historical material. They inform the reader rather accurately about major political and military events of the periods under discussion and identify and rank the most important individuals associated with a given policy or issue. The most accomplished ones, such as those used in this

153

essay, also offer a complex picture of the forces and individuals that helped to shape a particular reign.

Since chronicles are essentially concerned with recording change through time, they cannot help but tackle certain matters, such as widowhood, in a dynamic fashion. Consequently, chronicles are the best sources of information on how widowhood affected the public lives of certain prominent individuals. This, however, does not mean that historical chronicles are the ideal sources for social history. By design, the scope of most chronicles is limited to recounting the deeds of the mighty. Their protagonists are all individuals who have distinguished themselves, and it is their individuality or uniqueness that appeals to the authors.

The narrative structure of medieval historical accounts tends to be largely chronological, horizontal, and linear, betraying a marked disinterest in and unconcern for patterns, groups, types, and other broad categories that might illuminate patterns of social behavior. The widows in this essay are, thus, as much the product of the genre in which they appear as of the social class to which they belong.

Historical literature, its limits notwithstanding, challenges the researcher in the opposite way from another great body of primary source material from the Middle Ages, the collections of legal codes, *fueros, cortes* documents, court rulings, and other records detailing legal principles and expectations. This is the documentary evidence that L. Sponsler, H. Dillard, and M. Ratcliffe have studied so profitably. The most obvious difference between the two types of sources is that, while historical literature highlights the experiences and uniqueness of individuals, legal treatises and the legal tradition—by recording the normative and ideal—often erase important differences and project a uniformity and universality seldom enforceable and rarely achieved. Used with caution, legal documentation can aid us in reconstructing the concerns and preoccupations of medieval society. The legal tradition, however, should never be used as a living portrait of a particular society.

A rich, third source of documentary material for social history is the record of letters, financial agreements, commercial and real estate transactions, wills, marriage contracts, and other legacies of daily life now being unearthed and studied seriously by a growing number of Spanish medievalists. Last, there is the artistic legacy of the Middle Ages, the books, poems, treatises, and the visual and plastic arts, that further enhance our understanding of the role of the widow in the Middle Ages (see, for example, Graiño 1984). Given the variety of available sources, selecting only one makes a great deal of difference in our fair and accurate understanding of the medieval widow. Again, given the source material used in this essay, all the widows discussed here will be rich, powerful individuals; their behavior is noted precisely because of their wealth and power. And while each woman is unique, they all have their widowhood in common.

Both López de Ayala and Pérez de Guzmán show some discomfort with the widows they describe, in part because of a tacit acknowledgement that widowhood was a legal anomaly and an unnatural state brought about by the disruptions of the natural bond expected to prevail in the adult relationship between the sexes—that is, matrimony. These chroniclers also perceived widowhood as unnatural because of a much more threatening and compelling reason: while her widowhood lasted, the widow was a newly empowered authority figure, not only within her own household but also in the eyes of the outside world. The death of a husband gave the woman a new legal persona and assigned her a number of duties, rights, and responsibilities not associated with her prior to or during her marriage. As her husband's surrogate, she was expected to act on his behalf. His death promoted her to principal family decision maker, a status she retained pending either remarriage or the majority of her male children. Consequently, a woman during widowhood was able to enjoy a degree of autonomy and independence associated only with men.

This is not to say that, in an essentially patrilineal society like medieval Castile, widowhood, even among the aristocracy, did not carry its share of undesirable traits and stigmas. It was viewed by many as a dangerous and undesirable state. We need only think of Endrina's plight in the *Libro de Buen Amor;* although she was young, noble, intelligent, beautiful, and rich, she was anxious about her reputation, the management of her estate, and her diminished patrimony. In fact, given these burdens, it is not surprising that medieval accounts laud so few widows; Queen María de Molina (d. 1321) stands out as a notable exception.[2]

The opening chapters of Pero López de Ayala's chronicle of the reign of Pedro I of Castile offer several instructive episodes revolving around the figure of the widow. The author begins the narrative with the death of Pedro's father, King Alfonso XI, who succumbed to the plague during his army's siege of Gibraltar in 1350. Pedro, the sole legitimate heir, was soon crowned in a routine and fairly orderly ceremony in Seville (*Crónica,* 401–4). No one challenged Pedro overtly because there was no question of his legitimate right to the throne. Alfonso, however, had left behind a messy domestic situation that would have dire ramifications for the future of Castile.

There were two women prominent in Alfonso's life: his wife María, daughter of the king of Portugal, and his mistress, Leonor de Guzmán. Alfonso and María, who were first cousins, wed in 1328.[3] María bore the king at least two children, but only the second, Pedro, survived. The author of the account of Alfonso's reign, displaying strong admiration and respect for Alfonso, reports that the king grew frustrated over his wife's inability to bear him an heir, citing this as the reason the king sought children elsewhere. The sympathetic chronicler thus manages to turn a weakness in Alfonso's character into a virtue by skillfully shifting the blame for Alfonso's infidelities to Queen María. The chronicler is also full of praise for Leonor de Guzmán, the woman Alfonso was fortunate to find; she met royal expectations in every way.

Leonor de Guzmán was a wealthy Andalusian from Seville who became Alfonso's mistress not long after Alfonso's marriage to María. She was a widow, a fact that did not escape the attention of the narrator. A widow, rather than a virgin or a married woman, was the more suitable partner for an extramarital affair. The chronicle reports that "she sought to be of good service to the king, whenever he needed her. . . ."[4] In fact, for some twenty years, Leonor de Guzmán was Alfonso's constant companion. She lived and traveled with him, and had at least ten of his children, two of whom preceded Pedro into the world. Leonor's influence over Alfonso was widely recognized and just as impressive to her contemporaries as to the modern reader, as much for its depth as for its duration. They went everywhere together, even on military campaigns. In the course of their relationship, Leonor received large grants and privileges from her consort; so did her children, relatives, and a wide circle of retainers. The prestige and royal largesse she and her extended family enjoyed helped to promote them to the first ranks of Castilian aristocracy, a status their descendants would enjoy well into the modern age. Leonor was, it should be noted, the matriarch of the bastard Trastamaran royal line, rulers of Castile from 1369 until the death of Ferdinand the Catholic in 1516.

Needless to say, what was at times extravagant royal favoritism toward the Guzmáns fueled the animosity of Leonor's rival, Queen María. This circumstance made for an explosive family dynamic. Relations between the two sides deteriorated after Alfonso's death and eventually plunged Castile into a bloody civil war.

During Alfonso's life, María's situation was inherently an unhappy one, less for the loss of her spouse's affection—there is no reason to suppose that their marriage was more than a union of mutual convenience—than for the loss of her status and influence. María, while officially wife and queen, was relegated to a secondary role because of her husband's disinterest. After the birth of Pedro in 1334, she seldom, if ever, saw the king. She might have decided, for her own reasons, to stay away from court; but it is more likely that she was kept away. By having to live apart from the king—and his peripatetic court—she was deprived of whatever access or influence cohabitation might have afforded her. She was also cut off from the means to enhance her own power and prestige, which were secured, generally, through royal largesse and patronage. López de Ayala recognizes María's plight, although the chronicler does not show great personal sympathy for her. The overall impression he conveys is that, unlike Leonor, she was not an admirable figure.

Ayala, however, was deeply interested in the situation created by Alfonso's unconventional preferences and attributes to the queen and her household an attitude of hatred and resentment toward the mistress and her family.[5] We know that Alfonso himself recognized the political and domestic difficulties he had created; shortly before his death, he had urged Leonor to attempt to repair the rift between herself and Queen María by swiftly paying homage to the new king.[6] This advice would have been both unthinkable and irrelevant had Alfonso lived. Leonor, as his favorite, did not need the good will of the queen. María's role in Castilian affairs had been largely diplomatic, reproductive, and ceremonial, and she had already fulfilled her duties by bringing Castile and Portugal closer for a time and by bearing a royal heir. Without the active backing of her husband, she wielded little power in her own right. The king's death, however, shifted the balance in her favor, as Alfonso's anxious entreaty to his mistress had predicted. María, widow of the king, would prove to be a much more formidable character than María, out-of-favor queen consort.

A second interesting aspect of Alfonso's premature death was that each woman could justly call herself his widow and, in fact, each set out to compete for power and authority: Leonor struggled to retain hers;

María to assume her rightful share. For a few years following Alfonso's death, these women, more than sixteen-year-old King Pedro himself and his advisers, attempted to control the future of Castile.

Leonor, in spite of her intelligence, and perhaps because of her great influence, prestige, and considerable number of armed retainers, chose not to heed Alfonso's advice and refused to pay homage to the new king. She sought refuge instead in one of her holdings, the heavily fortified castle at Medina Sidonia. There, she prepared to resist the inevitable opposition that had begun to form against her and to attract to her side as many members of the quarrelsome Castilian nobility as she could. Only when one of her principal supporters defected, and she received assurances that neither she nor her children would be harmed, did she agree to travel to Seville. Her children stayed behind at Medina Sidonia, from where they proceeded to their various strongholds to prepare for war. Not surprisingly, the opposition, which claimed to represent the interests of the newly crowned Pedro, was directed by Queen María, and administered by one of her more loyal followers, her cousin and adviser Juan Alfonso de Alburquerque. By all accounts, the actual running of royal affairs during the first two years of Pedro's reign was carried out by the queen and her principal adviser. The pair decided to confront and disband the Guzmán family forces by sieging their strongholds. One by one they surrendered, giving the royal party an early and easy victory.

Meanwhile, for María, victory brought with it the surrender of Leonor, who was kept under house arrest in Seville to prevent her from meddling in court affairs. She nonetheless was allowed frequent visitors, among them her newly rehabilitated children. What was a comfortable confinement came to an end when Leonor was blamed for engineering the marriage of her eldest son, Enrique, to Juana Manuel, the daughter of one of Castile's most influential powerbrokers. This wedding, the terms of which had been negotiated during Alfonso's lifetime (*Crónica,* 408–9), was Leonor's undoing. Upon release of news of the consummation of the marriage, Leonor's autonomy, her perceived ability to act in Alfonso's stead—bypassing royal approval of the marriage by the new king—must have sharpened her enemies' suspicions. Implementing the marriage contract showed that she was acting as surrogate of the dead king, suggesting to her rivals—including King Pedro—that she, more so than her children, was a threat to royal authority. Her fortunes deteriorated even further when two of her major allies among the Castilian *ricoshombres* died unexpectedly. In captivity and without the protection of the powerful, Leonor's situation became bleak. Although neither the date of her death nor many other details related to it have been established with absolute certainty, it is generally accepted that she was killed by an executioner in the employ of Queen María (*Crónica,* 412–13).[7]

While López de Ayala makes clear that Leonor's death sentence came from María, he also tries to implicate Pedro in the decision. Whether mother and child acted in concert on this matter is less important than the deed itself. It is interesting to note that, in the seventeen or so months that Leonor was captive, her children behaved seditiously on more than one occasion. Ayala's account, written a generation after the events themselves, views the killing of Leonor as an outrageous act and "predicts" that it will have grave consequences for the future of the realm. Equipped with exquisite hindsight, he uses Leonor's death, somewhat inaccurately, as the beginning of Pedro's difficulties. The historian treats the rebelliousness of Leonor's children as the direct result of the unjust death of their mother. What is important for our purposes, though not for Ayala's, is that Leonor's children had already exhibited seditious and unreliable qualities before their mother's death. It is difficult to imagine that Pedro's circle of advisers would decide that Leonor, and not her children, had to go. Her elimination makes sense only if we think of her as continuing to represent the figure of the king, able to act as a state within the state, to the detriment of royal authority. In that respect, Leonor de Guzmán, widow of Alfonso XI, would have remained a threat perhaps more serious than her children. In every other sense, her belligerent children were as much the cause of political instability as their mother. They, however, were spared.

It is not inconceivable that Queen María's order to execute Leonor was motivated exclusively by jealousy; it is, however, unlikely. María, no doubt, had every reason to resent her former rival, but as she was no longer the powerless and marginal figure she had been during her husband's reign, she had to consider matters of greater political importance than avenging her pride. In fact, even Ayala acknowledges her central role in the running of Castilian affairs for at least the first two years of her son's rule. During that period, Pedro was reportedly pursuing a carefree and trivial existence, showing little inclination for statecraft. Queen María was, by all accounts, in charge. Her enhanced prestige resulted in, among other things, marriage proposals from individuals who, because of their lineage, could have aspired to the Castilian crown should anything unexpected happen to Pedro.[8] María's decision to kill

Leonor, then, must have come as a result of a genuine political threat rather than from a simple desire for revenge. Moreover, had she wanted only revenge, she could have had Leonor killed immediately after Alfonso's death or shortly after the death of her important allies. Instead, María waited many months to do it, and the death sentence, one may suppose, was triggered by a completely new set of circumstances.

María, formidable for the first time when widowed, succeeded in becoming a significant figure in Castilian politics. Her first two years as queen mother were, by far, her most distinguished. There are indications, however, that her influence had begun to wane sometime before Leonor's death. In this respect, her final victory over her rival might very well have been a hollow one. María's own importance diminished as Pedro displayed a new, willful assertiveness and a serious interest in the business of government. The first rift between mother and son resulted from Pedro's rejection of the French princess Blanche de Borbón, who had become Pedro's wife in 1353. Queen María was one of the principal architects of this union, behind which was a diplomatic alliance between Castile and France—and was seriously displeased when Pedro abandoned his bride shortly after elaborate wedding celebrations at Valladolid. María, no doubt, was Blanche's protector. María's disapproval of her son's behavior and his subsequent policies was so intense that, at times, she formed political and military alliances with Pedro's bitterest enemies, Leonor's children.

While the failure of the marriage between Pedro and Blanche was the catalyst for the rift between mother and son, their deteriorating relations actually resulted from another development that was much more detrimental to the political interests of Queen María. What made Pedro such a reluctant husband was that a year before the wedding, in the spring of 1352, he had met and fallen in love with María de Padilla, a young woman whose early experience at court is reminiscent of Leonor de Guzmán's. María de Padilla had a large family, and just as Leonor's had done in the court of Alfonso XI, María de Padilla's relatives managed to position themselves firmly at court during the first year of her liaison with Pedro. The success of the Padillas, perhaps a declaration of independence from maternal control for Pedro, marked the end of Queen María's role of royal surrogate. Pedro was ready to assume control of the government and, as the adult male child of a widow, he was no longer bound by the will of his mother. María and Alburquerque, failing to persuade Pedro to return permanently to his wife, joined in the mounting opposition to the king in a broad coalition that included most adult children of Alfonso and Leonor.

Pedro was able to defeat his enemies by the late fall of 1355. In a gesture of generosity, he allowed his mother to remove herself to Portugal. Queen María died in her native land in 1357. It is interesting, and ironic, to note that Portuguese historian Fernão Lopes, a contemporary of Ayala, relates that Pedro, after his mother's death, dispatched ambassadors to Portugal to bring back her remains. In the presence of great lords and prelates, he had Queen María interred next to Alfonso XI's tomb in Seville (Lopes 1966, 154). A number of stories circulated about María's presumed loose character and, after Pedro's death, about the illegitimacy of his birth. Although there might be some truth to the former, the latter charge has been completely rejected as propagandistic and false.[9]

Another instructive example of widowhood in historical literature of the late Middle Ages is the case of Catalina of Lancaster, Queen of Castile from 1390 to 1418. Catalina (granddaughter of Pedro I) was the wife of Enrique III of Castile, king from 1390 to 1406. The diplomatic marriage that united Catalina and Enrique was the principal clause of the treaty of Bayonne, negotiated in 1387, which settled English claims to the crown of Castile. The English, who had married into the royal family of Castile during the reign of Pedro, felt entitled to the crown following the usurpation of the throne by the bastard Enrique of Trastamara, Leonor de Guzmán's and Alfonso XI's illegitimate son, in 1369.[10]

At the time of the nuptials, Catalina was fourteen and Enrique several years her junior. Enrique, known in history as the Ailing (*el Doliente*) was a sickly youth, the victim of a stroke that affected his speech. His physical condition was the source of much court interest and intrigue, although there was never any question about his vigor; in 1405, the queen gave birth to their third child and first son Juan, who was subsequently sworn in as heir to the throne. A year and a half after the birth of Juan, Enrique died, making complicated provisions for the future of the kingdom. His will stipulated a somewhat unique distribution of power. Queen Catalina and the king's brother, Fernando, would share the leadership of the kingdom in the capacity of equal coregents. They would determine policy and control expenditures (*Crónica de Enrique III*, 263, 264–70). As stipulated in the *Siete Partidas*, the education of the heir was entrusted to two distinguished individuals who would oversee the boy's upbringing. Amidst open suggestions by a faction of the

Castilian aristocracy that Fernando wrest control of the realm from his coregent, the first clash between Fernando and Catalina developed over the matter of custody of the infant king. Catalina refused to give up the child, a stand that Fernando decided to respect. Aside from whatever attachment Catalina might have had for the infant, her control over him was of crucial importance. While she, in her own right—as Pedro I's granddaughter—might have considered herself the legitimate ruler of Castile, her subjects thought otherwise. She was queen consort and, just as in the case of María of Portugal, her influence depended on her husband's good will. While her husband was alive, Catalina displayed a strong will and a decisive personality. I have written elsewhere about the active role she took in the upbringing of her son, at times countermanding her husband's explicit wishes (Estow 1982). After her husband's death, she became even more active.

It was incumbent upon Enrique's widow to redefine her role, given the new political circumstances. The choice of issue on which to take an independent stand, custody of her son, was a rather fortunate one; even Catalina's detractors and competitors found it difficult to criticize her. In some respects, she was taking advantage of the ambiguity in Castilian legal tradition regarding the role of royal tutors. These individuals were expected to guard and educate their young ward, but also to rule on his behalf until he reached his majority.[11] In this particular case, however, such ambiguity was removed when Enrique stipulated that Catalina and Fernando would be coregents responsible for administering the state and, by inference, having authority over the king's tutors. Catalina's reluctance to give up physical custody of the child to his appointed guardians confirms her desire not to separate the function of ruling from the function of educating the child; she intended to retain both. Fernando, however, was not pleased, and Catalina's resolve on this matter, which she was able to maintain until Fernando's death in 1416, was the first in a series of disagreements between the regents.[12]

In the historical account of the reign of Enrique III, the disagreements between Fernando and Catalina are reported in a manner unflattering to the queen. It relates how she had been instrumental in persuading her Castilian subjects to subsidize Fernando's campaign against the Muslims and wished to travel south to Andalucía to be near the coregent, for the better management of the realm. And while Fernando is reported to have agreed to her plan, the Royal Council did not. She was seriously criticized for putting the well-being of the young king in jeopardy, as it was assumed that she would take him along. Ultimately, she was kept from carrying out her plan (*Crónica de Juan II*, 283). She resigned herself to staying in Segovia while Fernando distinguished himself in battle. In 1407, to settle an uneasy relationship, the two regents decided to cooperate by dividing the kingdom into two discreet geographic areas. Catalina retained the northern region, while Fernando administered from Toledo southward.

Catalina did not enjoy a good reputation among her subjects, nor did she receive kind treatment from the otherwise able Pérez de Guzmán, historian of her son's reign. She is portrayed as highly superstitious and suggestible, open to the influence and manipulation of self-seeking and ruthless courtiers (*Crónica de Juan II*, 283). The two courtiers on whom the chronicler bestowed most of the opprobrium were women, without whose counsel, the account informs us, Catalina never acted. One of these counselors had to be removed from court, following the resolution by the royal council of her pernicious influence on the queen. This episode, which ocurred around 1408, coincided with the decline of Catalina as an important political force within Castile and signaled the political triumph of Fernando. The reversal did not lead to Catalina's total eclipse; she continued to be recognized in her role as coregent and was used, in her official capacity, on a number of important occasions, in particular when Fernando needed money. In 1411, for example, she was the cosignator of a petition initiated by Fernando to raise additional revenues to fight against the Muslims.

Eventually, Fernando, through a combination of military success, raw ambition, and heightened prestige after his being chosen king of Aragon in 1412, gained the upper hand. Catalina was never able to persuade the royal council, or her subjects, that she was fit to rule. It was almost immaterial whether she actually was. Official support for Fernando never diminished. She died two years after he did, in 1418, leaving behind both a bad reputation and an heir whose reign would be the longest—and one of the most ineffective—of the Trastamaran dynasty. Juan II would rule Castile in his own right from 1419 to 1454. As for Catalina, she is best remembered from the unflattering portrait drawn by Pérez de Guzmán (*Generaciones y semblanzas*, 700). To him, she was fat, manly, somewhat irrational, and a heavy drinker. Her courageous defense of her prerogatives and the political vision she tried to implement receive no positive consideration. Pérez de Guzmán makes clear that Catalina should have spent her time in more appropriately frivolous pursuits, leaving the serious business of government to those better equipped to handle it.

The women whose lives are recounted in historical literature are hardly ordinary women. Each was able to assume a persona independent from her spouse, and each was able to command, at least for a time, the attention of the realm. The fact that neither María nor Catalina is remembered with affection might well be the result of these women's assertiveness rather than their inadequacy. Their morality was also questioned—another way, one may suppose, for the chroniclers to dismiss or ignore their other efforts and achievements. By concentrating on their virtue or lack thereof, these writers could then ignore the real significance of these women in their respective ages. For a time, these women were able to enjoy the full extent of royal power. This privilege came to them only because of their widowhood. Even Leonor, whose tale was written by a political ally, is shown more affection than respected, treated as a forlorn widow rather than as the formidable power broker and matriarch that we now recognize.

In their portrayal of royal widows, the medieval Castilian chronicles cited in this essay no doubt reflect the prevailing values and mores of their time. Their rather predictable degree of discomfort in relating the behavior of their aristocratic subjects serves to highlight the conflicting attributes and expectations of the role. Aside from the obvious incongruity of a female figure embodying the fullness of royal authority in what was essentially a patrilineal society, the chronicles convey an obligatory sense of sympathy, in recognition of the sorrow and suffering brought on by the loss of a spouse. What is more striking, however, is the unstated assurance derived from the knowledge that the exercise of royal power by a widow—like the sudden empowerment brought on by widowhood in general in the absence of adult male children—was a temporary anomaly, an interim situation to be endured in anticipation of the restoration of the natural state of affairs, more often than not achieved with the coming of age of a male heir. In this regard, the demise of Leonor de Guzmán, Queen María, and Queen Catalina must ultimately have been received with a general sense of relief, for their removal from power (or their death) precipitated a return to normalcy. That their heirs caused great turmoil and hardship, as was the case with Pedro I and Enrique II, is an irrelevant fact that does not diminish the degree of discomfort associated with the full exercise of royal authority by a widow.

NOTES

1. All references to Ayala's work are to the edition of Cayetano Rossell, cited hereafter in the text as *Crónica*. There is a new edition of Ayala's account, *Coronica del rey don Pedro,* ed. Constance Wilkins and Heanon M. Wilkins (Madison: The Hispanic Seminary of Medieval Studies, 1986). A new approach to the chronicle appears in Louise Mirrer-Singer, *The Language of Evaluation: A Sociolinguistic Approach to the Story of Pedro el Cruel in Ballad and Chronicle* (Amsterdam: John Benjamin, 1986). The account of Enrique III's reign was written mostly by Ayala, and that of the reign of Juan II by Ayala's nephew, Fernán Pérez de Guzmán.

2. The reassessment of the role of María de Molina in Castilian affairs is long overdue. The only study of her eventful life and reign is M. Gaibrois de Ballesteros 1936.

3. The details of Alfonso's marriage to María are recounted in *Crónica de Alfonso,* 209, 212, 218.

4. " . . . et porque el Rey era muy acabado hombre en todos sus fechos, teniase por muy menguado porque no avia fijos de la Reina; et por esto cató manera como oviese fijos de otra parte" [and because the King liked to do everything well, and felt diminished for having had no children with the Queen, he sought ways of begetting them elsewhere] (*Crónica de Alfonso,* 227).

5. There is only one study of their relationship, see Ballesteros-Beretta 1932. See also Moxó 1975.

6. *Crónica de Alfonso,* 390–91. Five years before his death, the king had already begun to make provisions for Leonor's safety. Negotiating a possible marriage alliance for Pedro with both the English and the French, Alfonso had the latter agree to offer sanctuary to Leonor and her children should they require it. See Daumet 1898, 12; *Crónica,* 408–9.

7. Fernão Lopes, the fourteenth-century Portuguese historian, does not believe that María ordered Leonor's death. See Lopes 1966, 154.

8. Juan Nuñez de Lara and Ferran of Aragon were the two suitors (*Crónica,* 407). This account states that Pedro had taken ill and was not expected to recover.

9. Queen María became the target of gossip largely in an effort by Pedro's enemies to discredit him through her. The king's illegitimacy was a favorite theme. One version suggested that he was the child of a Jewish couple, substituted for Queen María's only child, who was female. A second emphasized Pedro's bastard origins by claiming that his father was Juan Alfonso de Alburquerque, Queen María's cousin (see Russell 1955, 17, n. 12). Aside from her presumed relationship with Alburquerque, María was also linked with a Martín Alfonso Tello, killed at the battle of Toro (see *Crónica,* 471).

10. Pedro's daughter Constanza had married John of Gaunt, Duke of Lancas-

ter. When the treaty was signed in 1387, Gaunt agreed to abandon his claims to the crown (see Russell 1955, 149–71).

11. On this ambiguity, see García de Valdeavellano 1973, 437.

12. Fernando often complained publicly about Catalina; however, he also took credit for having negotiated the custody battle in her favor. He writes: "E para conplazer . . . a la dicha señora reyna, yo con buena entencion e por quitar los dichos ynconvenientes e peligros que la dicha disension e discordia podria recrecer, trabaje e tove maneras entre la dicha señora reyna e los dichos [tutores] como ella toviese e criase al dicho senor rey don Juan . . ." [And to please . . . the said Queen, I with good intention and in order to remove the said inconveniences and dangers that the said dissension and discord might reawaken, worked and negotiated between the said Queen and the said [tutors] so that she was able to keep and bring up the said King, don Juan]. The rest of the letter is an attack on the good judgment of the queen; see Torres Fontes 1964, 427.

BIBLIOGRAPHY

Ayala, Pero López de. *Crónica del rey don Pedro*. Ed. Cayetano Rossell. Crónicas de los reyes de Castilla. Biblioteca de autores españoles 66. Madrid: Rivadeneyra, 1956.

Ballesteros-Beretta, Antonio. "Doña Leonor de Guzmán a la muerte de Alfonso XI." *Boletín de la Real Academia de Historia* 100 (1932): 624–32.

Crónica de Alfonso XI. Biblioteca de autores españoles 66. Madrid: Rivadeneyra, 1953.

Crónica de Enrique III. Biblioteca de autores españoles 68. Madrid: Rivadeneyra, 1953.

Crónica de Juan II. Biblioteca de autores españoles 68. Madrid: Rivadeneyra, 1953.

Daumet, Georges. *Étude sur l'alliance de la France et de la Castille au XIVe et au XVe siècles*. Paris: É. Bouillon, 1898.

Dillard, Heath. *Daughters of the Reconquest: Women in Castilian Town Society, 1100–1300*. Cambridge: Cambridge University Press, 1984.

Erler, Mary, and Maryanne Kowaleski, eds. *Women and Power in the Middle Ages*. Athens, Ga.: University of Georgia Press, 1988.

Estow, C. "Leonor López de Córdoba: Portrait of a Medieval Courtier." *Fifteenth Century Studies* 5 (1982): 23–46.

Gaibrois de Ballesteros, Mercedes. *María de Molina*. Madrid: Espasa-Calpe, 1936.

García de Valdeavellano, Luis. *Curso de historia de las instituciones españolas*. 3rd ed. Madrid: Ediciones de la Revista de Occidente, 1973.

Graiño, Cristina Segura, ed. *Las mujeres en las ciudades medievales. Actas de las terceras jornadas de investigación interdisciplinaria.* Madrid: Universidad Autónoma, Seminarios de Estudios de la Mujer, 1984.

Labarge, Margaret Wade. *A Small Sound of the Trumpet: Women in Medieval Life.* Boston: Beacon Press, 1986.

Lopes, Fernão. *Crónica de D. Pedro.* Ed. Guiliano Macchi. Rome: Edizioni dell'Ateneo, 1966.

Moxó, Salvador. "La sociedad política castellana en la época de Alfonso XI." *Cuadernos de Historia* 6 (1975): 187–325.

Pérez de Guzmán, Fernán. *Generaciones y semblanzas.* Biblioteca de autores españoles 68. Madrid: Rivadeneyra, 1953.

Russell, P. E. *The English Intervention in Spain and Portugal in the Time of Edward III and Richard II.* Oxford: Oxford University Press, 1955.

Shahar, Shulamit. *The Fourth Estate: A History of Women in the Middle Ages.* Trans. Chaya Galia. London: Methuen, 1983.

Sponsler, Lucy A. "The Status of Married Women under the Legal System of Spain." *Journal of Legal History* 9 (1982): 125–52.

Stafford, Pauline. *Queens, Concubines, and Dowagers: The King's Wife in the Early Middle Ages.* Athens, Ga.: University of Georgia Press, 1983.

Torres Fontes, Juan. "La regencia de don Fernando de Antequera." *Anuario de Estudios Medievales* 1 (1964): 375–429.

Chapter 7

Noble Widowhood in the Thirteenth Century: Three Generations of Mortimer Widows, 1246–1334

Linda E. Mitchell

Studies of the legal questions concerning widowhood and female inheritance in medieval England, both before and after Magna Carta, have revealed one dimension of widows' lives.[1] Medieval widowhood's social context has, however, remained obscure. In a period of scholarship on the Middle Ages that emphasizes a contextualization of historical experience, an examination of the histories of three generations of widows in their legal and historical milieus is enlightening. These widows' experiences indicate how noble widows interacted in their families, with their tenants and dependents, and with the larger world of the central courts and the Crown.

Historians usually divide medieval law into two discrete categories: feudal and customary, or public and private. The first category describes law relating to the system of military and political obligation between the king and his nobles and between a lord and his knights. The second contains laws regarding inheritance, secular considerations in marriage, and land tenure. English common law, developed after the Norman Conquest, achieved a blending of feudal and customary law for the free Anglo-Norman people who lived in the English kingdom and its environs—Wales, Scotland, and Ireland. All landholders in England held land more or less directly from the king, even when intermediaries existed, so common law dealt with the relation between the Crown and the people. The hegemony of the king over all lands held in his kingdom also placed virtually all interactions regarding land tenure into his hands and, ultimately, into his courts.[2]

The common-law formulas of dower and inheritance, as defined by medieval legal theorists Glanville and Bracton and interpreted by Pollock and Maitland in the nineteenth century, have long been included in standard legal histories of England.[3] Historians have discussed the paradox that, in a society based upon military tenure, the common-law protection of widows' and heiresses' rights to family property overrode the feudal requirements of the tenant's military service to his lord (see Plucknett, *Legislation*). Widows have been discussed in the context of political or politicofamily histories, but writers often ignore their day-to-day activities, focusing instead upon either widows' divisive influence in their families (for example, when they "denied" the rightful—i.e., male—heir of his inheritance by continuing to live and keep their dowers)[4] or upon their contribution to the spiritual life of the family through religious devotion or extensive donations to ecclesiastical institutions.[5]

How did widows actually cope with the perils and opportunities of their unique status? Unlike daughters, who were under the legal protection of their fathers or guardians, and wives, who were an extension of their husband's legal "personality," widows could act legally and socially in their own right. They could pursue cases in court, gain control over their own remarriages, purchase the guardianship of minor children, and act as heads of their households. Other activities were, however, denied them: acting as jury members or judges, attending royal councils and parliaments, leading troops, and working as royal administrators in the exchequer or chancery. The laws that both protected and sanctioned widows, however, still never fully defined them with the same concreteness as it did men (who were completely independent) and single or married women (who were completely dependent). Widows' legal boundaries were both fluid and ambivalent and their activities reflect this ambivalence. In this essay I will address two questions: how successful were noble widows in acting in the more public sphere of the law courts, as landlords, and as the heads of their households and, conversely, to what degree did traditional views of women as legally and socially inferior hamper them?

Historians ascribe to widows contradictory positions. Some scholars concentrate on medieval conceptions of women as inferior and minimize the importance of widows' activities and effectiveness in the public milieu. They thus deny widows any possibility of being seen as legitimate contributors to medieval society.[6] Others emphasize instead the protection afforded widows under common law, downplaying the belief in female inferiority and thus viewing these independent women's abilities more positively.[7] Still other studies simply perpetuate inaccuracies about female legal competence in the Middle Ages or assume that later policies that restricted women's rights to inherit land must have been active at an earlier period.[8] Less general and more rigorous scholarship has now replaced many of these earlier views, but conclusions are still often made based upon past assumptions rather than new evidence.[9]

The feudal ideal required the survival of male heirs and sufficient adult men in the family in order to remove women from its sphere. Women could not bear arms or lead troops, so the military nature of feudal holdings prevented women from performing the duties of the fee. Social attitudes, combined with Paulistic antifeminism in the Church, considered women to be both incapable of performing any public service and dangerous in the public sphere. Medieval English common law thus contradicted both feudal and social attitudes about the inappropriateness of women as landholders, but the contradiction was accepted by the ruling class and even strengthened through Magna Carta, a document created by the same barons who relied upon feudal custom to survive. In reality, the medieval noblewoman governed when her husband was away, defended the family property, and commanded the respect of kings and barons alike. She was, moreover, expected by her husband and her peers to perform all these duties efficiently and with skill.

A discussion of noblewomen's position in society based only on legal status provides an incomplete picture of medieval widowhood. In this study, I have used a variety of documents to reconstruct the activities of three, thirteenth-century widows belonging to the powerful Mortimer family. In the voluminous records of the central courts, the itinerant courts of assize and eyre, secular and ecclesiastic cartularies, and the extensive printed collections of chancery records (Close, Patent, Charter, and Fine Rolls, and *Inquisitions Post Mortem*), I have found evidence, concerning these and other widows, to combat the social view of women as inferior to men.[10]

The principal wealth of the Mortimer family lay along the border between England and Wales, but its members held lands and maintained influence throughout the kingdom. Thus the Mortimer widows are typical of other baronial widows in thirteenth-century England. The sources I reviewed revealed widows' specific activities: when, why, and how they acquired their dower properties, what obstructions they encountered, how successful they were against other litigants, how they protected their holdings, and how they interacted both with their families and with the king and other landholders. The picture that emerges from this material shows noble widows not as women constrained by the social view of female inferiority or of female legal incompetence, but as women who created their own niche in the social scheme, however undefined their role might have been.

The three women I discuss played a vital role in the development of the Mortimer family's power and influence. In the brief biographical sketches[11] and the more detailed discussion of their activities in widowhood that follow, I will show that not only did they bring royal alliances to the lords of Wigmore, enrich the family's landed wealth, and give birth to the individuals who further enhanced the prestige of the family, but they also, as widows of three successive generations of Mortimer lords of Wigmore, interacted in much broader fields of public life. Their court appearances in dower suits, their relations with the Crown, and their methods of dealing with tenants, estate officials, and fellow landholders all show them to be experienced and competent members of the baronage. Their story has gone untold not because it is insignificant but because they were the women, not the men, of the household and, moreover, women who were incorporated into the family from outside (see fig. 7.1). Gladys Du ap Llewelyn ab Iowerth, Maud de Breouse, and Margaret de Fiennes are not unique in thirteenth-century England; they are simply three women out of a large population of dowagers who went about the daily business of maintaining their property, associating with their families, and dealing with their tenants and fellow landholders. As such, they might be seen as typical examples of the behavior and activities of many noble widows in the thirteenth century.

Gladys Du (Dark-eyed Gladys) was the daughter of Llewelyn ab Iowerth, Prince of Wales, and his second wife Joan, illegitimate daughter of King John. In 1215, Gladys became the second wife of Reginald de Breouse, the lord of Abergavenny, Gower, and Bramber in Wales, an important baron of the Welsh March. Although Reginald had children from his previous marriage, this union was barren. Reginald died in 1227; three years later, Gladys married Ralph Mortimer, Lord of Wigmore, another marcher baron. Thus Llewelyn succeeded in joining the Welsh royal house with two of his most powerful neighbors. The marriage between Gladys and Ralph lasted sixteen years and produced at least three children, sons Roger (born ca. 1232)[12] and Hugh and daughter Joan. Gladys did not remarry after Ralph's death in 1246; she remained active until her own death in 1251. All three children contrib-

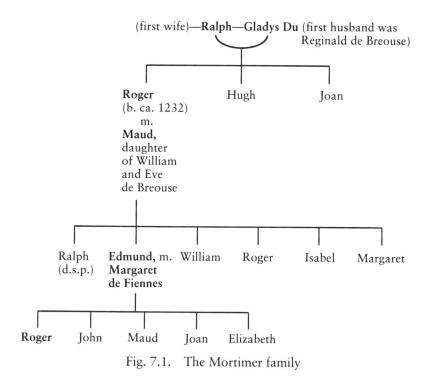

Fig. 7.1.   The Mortimer family

uted to the family's alliances along the Welsh marches. Hugh, who
founded the lordship of Chelmarsh in Shropshire, married Agatha de
Ferrers, one of the seven coheirs of Sibyl la Marshal, daughter of Earl
William le Marshal, while Joan married Peter Corbet, lord of Caus in
Shropshire. Roger, the heir of Wigmore, made a brilliant marriage to
Maud de Breouse, the granddaughter of Reginald de Breouse (therefore,
step-granddaughter of Roger's mother), and coheiress not only of the
Breouse lordship of Abergavenny but also of William le Marshal, Earl
of Pembroke, through her mother, Eve la Marshal. By means of this
marriage, Roger more than doubled the wealth and prestige of the Mor-
timer family, making him "one of the great architects of the late medieval
March."[13]

Roger married Maud de Breouse in 1247, a year after his father died.
Mother and daughter-in-law seem to have gotten along fairly well, something that cannot be said about Gladys's relations with the rest of her

step-grandchildren. Maud must have been a number of years older than Roger; she was the eldest of the four sisters and her father died in 1230, two years before Roger was born. They had an eventful married life lasting thirty-five years and producing six children who survived infancy: sons Ralph (who died before inheriting), Edmund (originally destined for the Church but ultimately his parents' heir), William (who died without issue in 1297), and Roger (first lord of Chirk in Shropshire); and daughters Isabel (who married John Fitz Alan, lord of Oswestry and Clun in Shropshire and de facto Earl of Arundel) and Margaret (who married Robert de Vere, heir apparent of the Earl of Oxford). Although frequently subject to attack from the Prince of Wales and often from their marcher-baron neighbors, Roger and Maud managed to keep their vast estates—Wigmore, one-fourth of Abergavenny, and one-fifteenth of the Earldom of Pembroke and Striguil and the lordship of Leinster in Ireland—more or less intact. Roger died in 1282, before the Edwardian conquest of Wales, and Maud achieved control of her inheritance as well as dower from Roger's holdings. She never remarried, although she lived another nineteen years, and was very active in managing and administering her considerable inheritance. At the time of her death, in 1300 or 1301, Maud must have been close to eighty years old.

In 1285, Margaret de Fiennes and Edmund Mortimer were married by the arrangement of Edward I's wife, Eleanor of Castile, who was Margaret's cousin. Unlike Gladys and Maud, Margaret was not native born, although her family had established a cadet branch in England well before her arrival. She was one of a number of Queen Eleanor's relations—among them Margaret's sister Joan, Isabel de Beaumont, and Clemencia de Avaugour—whom Eleanor had brought to England, with the intention of marrying them to English barons.[14] As longtime supporters of Edward before he achieved the throne, the Mortimer family must have been ideal for Eleanor's plan. During their nineteen-year marriage, Edmund and Margaret produced five surviving children: sons Roger and John, and daughters Maud, who married Theobald de Verdon, and Joan and Elizabeth, who became nuns at Lingbrook. Edmund died in 1304, still a relatively young man; his widow survived him by thirty years. Margaret never remarried and seems to have spent her widowhood very much involved in her elder son's life and activities. When Edward II confiscated Roger's lands in 1322, Margaret's were forfeited as well. Edward pardoned her the following year but did not return her property. When Roger and Queen Isabella returned from France, deposed Edward, and gained control of the government with Isabella as regent for the young Edward III, Margaret's confiscated lands were returned. Her fortunes continued to be tied to those of her son; after Roger was executed in 1330, Margaret was imprisoned. She must have been quite elderly by then, but was considered sufficiently threatening to be shuttled from castle to castle and finally locked up in Elstone nunnery, where she died in 1333 or 1334.

Each of these three women represents, in her own way, a type of alliance that the English baronage often made. Gladys, as the progeny of the Welsh royal house, linked an important Anglo-Norman Marcher lordship with its volatile neighbor. Llewelyn had married all of his daughters to marcher barons, but none of these alliances was effective in defusing the enmity between the Welsh and the Anglo-Normans. Mortimer's success in acquiring Maud, the heiress of a great barony, for his young son was a boon to the family's fortunes and influence. The Mortimers became established as a principal family in the March of Wales because of this alliance, which not only provided them with landed wealth but signaled the decline of earlier great families, such as the Breouses and the Marshals, who disappeared because of failures in the male line. Once established, the Mortimers consolidated their influence and prestige through an alliance with the royal family, in the person of Margaret. This alliance demonstrated their social standing, even if it did not add significantly to their wealth.

Although all three women led rather different lives during their marriages and participated in different activities during their widowhoods, they exemplify the range of involvement of medieval noble widows in the private lives of their families and the public arenas of land management, interactions with individuals outside the family, and relations with the king and his courts. The three Mortimer widows followed a fairly consistent pattern of behavior during the years immediately after their husbands' deaths. What happened thereafter usually depended on how long the widow lived and her resources. The first action of all three women was to consolidate their dower holdings and any holdings that originated with them—*maritagium,* previous dower, inheritance, and the like.[15] Since the Mortimers were tenants-in-chief, the king granted dower to the widow, a process made more complicated if the heir was a minor in wardship. Both Henry III and Edward I granted dower promptly, or at least granted temporary seisin of land for the widow's maintenance if an inquisition had been ordered. Since none of the Mortimer widows had nominated dower, they used the standard "reasonable" dower formula of one-third of the total estate.[16] Once the king had assigned dower from the demesne property held in chief, the widows began the typical procedure of purchasing writs to acquire dower from tenants, the heir, and lords other than the king, and to recover lands escheated by accident, or lost through involuntary demise or trespass. These actions provide interesting insights into widows' relations with their families.

Gladys, as mother of the next generation of Mortimers, had few problems in acquiring her dower property. The king, soon after Ralph's death, granted her the manor of Stretfeld and part of the honor of Bisleg, Gloucestershire (*Close Rolls*, 452–53, 484). Roger, her son, was a minor, so she did not have to litigate against him but Gladys did sue tenants in Sussex and Hereford for dower from their small holdings (Just 1/4 ms. 21 [Bedford Eyre of 1247]; *Berkshire Eyre*, 206–7, 247–48). Gladys's real difficulties lay with the step-grandchildren from her first marriage. As soon as Ralph Mortimer died, the Breouse heirs—except her daughter-in-law Maud—entered Gladys's Breouse dower property. From 1247 until her death, Gladys struggled to recover her rightful dower from her first marriage with middling success. The heirs (represented by their husbands) obstructed the suits through default, argument, and outright trespass. They denied her issues (profits and rents) from the property and argued against the validity of her claims. Clearly, Humphrey and Eleanor de Bohun and William and Eve de Cantelou resented having to give up their inherited property to their step-grandmother when Gladys had substantial dower from her second husband.

Maud and Roger Mortimer were conspicuously absent in these dealings. Although one cannot know for certain, it is possible that their impulses were somewhat more generous than Maud's sisters and brothers-in-law. This generosity becomes more plausible when Maud and Roger's actions regarding their own children are revealed. In an age in which younger sons were systematically disinherited and daughters received only small marriage portions in land or cash settlements, Roger and Maud gave each of their sons substantial holdings and their daughters significant *maritagia* from their combined landed wealth.

Rather sadly, Maud's sons and daughters did not reciprocate in this parental concern; she experienced real difficulty in acquiring her dower, especially when she had to negotiate with her heir Edmund for her due in lands demised during Roger's lifetime.

By following one such case, from its first appearance in the rolls of the court of common pleas to its disappearance from those records, it is possible to see the various ways in which Edmund, as the heir, hindered Maud from enjoying her rightful seisin. The case began in the Trinity term of 1283, when Maud sued her younger son Roger for dower in various manors, demised to him by his father, in Shropshire, Worcestershire, and Herefordshire (CP40/50, m. 26). Roger pleaded for a view of the land in question, a typical maneuver that adjourned the case to the next session. In the following two terms, Michaelmas 1283 and Hillary 1284, Roger vouched his brother Edmund to warranty (CP40/51, m. 46d; CP40/52, m. 40). This action was entirely appropriate, since Roger was merely a tenant in fee of Edmund, who was the actual heir of the land. The case again adjourned in order for the sheriff to summon Edmund to court. At each of the next three sessions, Edmund defaulted (did not respond to the summons; CP40/53, m. 26, 26d; CP40/54, m. 50; CP40/55, m. 34d, 35, 107d). During the Trinity term, the sheriff of Shropshire claimed the writ came too late for the summons, then admitted that he did nothing about the summons in the Michaelmas term (CP40/54, m. 50; CP40/55, m. 34d). The sheriff of Worcestershire said that Edmund had no lands in his county with which to make a distraint, but the court determined that a distraint could be made in Hereford instead (CP40/55, m. 107d). Maud even "won" her dower in Hereford during the Michaelmas term, due to Edmund's default. He must have subsequently regained seisin of the property she had won by pleading for a replevin of the land in the king's court, because in the very next session, Hillary 1285, Edmund appears against Roger arguing against both Roger's vouch of warranty and Maud's dower suit (CP40/57, m. 24d). The court found in favor of Roger because he had a charter for the litigated property, but adjourned the dower case until a later session. Maud's suits continued to appear in all the sessions for 1285 and until Easter 1286. They were respited by the court until later dates; Edmund defaulted again; finally, he denied any further warranty to Roger and put himself on the country (CP40/58, m. 35d; CP40/59, m. 12, 40d; CP40/61, m. 7d; CP40/62, m. 25d, 37d, 64d). At this point Maud's plea against Roger for dower disappears from the records. Presumably some agreement was made between both parties; it is unlikely that Edmund won any of his arguments against warranting his brother because Roger had charters and could produce witnesses. Edmund's actions simply delayed the proceedings and probably substantially increased the cost of Maud's attempt to claim her dower.

This case, which continued for three years in the court rolls, was only one of the cases Maud fought with her children for her dower. In all of the litigation her son Edmund was the main antagonist; he refused to warrant his siblings and deliberately obstructed the continuance—and the conclusions—of the cases. In his efforts to avoid giving Maud any additional dower, Edmund might have been assisted by the very sheriffs whose duty it was to ensure the smooth passage of writs and the continuance of cases. Edmund defaulted so many times, in the case discussed here and in the other dower cases in which he was vouched to warranty, that the collusion of the sheriffs in not properly executing the writs is a real possibility.[17] Thus, Maud was battling not only with her stubborn son, but with an inefficient system as well.

Edmund was probably motivated in his attempt to prevent his mother from receiving any more dower by the enormous size of her personal estate. Between her own inheritance and her dower, Maud controlled more than half of the lands over which Edmund was titular lord. He received no income from her seisin and he had no control over any changes Maud might make in her own property, although she could not alienate or lay waste to any of her dower. Maud's longevity must also have been a source of frustration for Edmund: it denied him the bulk of his inheritance for most of his adult life. He enjoyed his seisin a mere three years before his own death.

Edmund's wife, ironically, benefited most from Edmund outliving his mother. Through joint seisin with her husband and dower from the rest of the estate, Margaret controlled about half of the Mortimer inheritance.[18] Margaret's activities in the years after Edmund's death follow the usual pattern: the king informed the escheators to return Margaret's property, which she held in chief—through her joint seisin with Edmund—and to grant her dower in England, Ireland, and Wales (*Close Rolls* 1302–7, 171, 175–76, 274–76; CAPW, 89–90). In a rather atypical move, Margaret also demanded the custody of one of the three Mortimer castles in Wales (SC8/156, no. 7775);[19] King Edward gave her Radnor Castle. The usual dower pleas appear in the rolls, initially between Margaret and the army of guardians and custodians of her son's estate, since he was a minor in 1304, but in 1306 Margaret and Roger reached a compromise about her dower holdings (Harley 1240, fol. 67v). Since she controlled so much of Roger's inheritance, Margaret could choose to be generous to her son without endangering her independence. In the years that followed, Margaret protected her property but the antagonism that marked Maud's relations with her heir were absent in Margaret's interactions with Roger. Her difficulty, rather, lay with the king himself.

In 1322, Margaret's son, Roger, was imprisoned in the Tower for his role in the rebellion against Edward II and the Despencers.[20] As a result, his properties were forfeited to the Crown and Margaret's dower was included in the forfeit. He escaped in 1323 and fled to France, where other surviving rebels and Edward's queen, Isabella of France, joined him. Roger and Queen Isabella became lovers. Together they plotted the overthrow of Edward II and, in 1326, led the invasion force from France. The rebels were successful; they deposed Edward (probably murdering him) and Isabella became regent for the young king, Edward III.[21]

Between 1322 and 1326, Margaret petitioned Edward II for the return of her dower (SC8/61, no. 3028; SC8/62, no. 3076; SC8/63, no. 3110; SC8/127, no. 6346) but, despite Edward's mandate to that effect to the custodian of her Radnor properties, she apparently never received seisin. As Mortimer's mother, the supporters of the Crown must have considered Margaret suspect. Indeed, Edward II had good cause for concern. In 1326, the warden of Radnor arrested Margaret, charging her with holding meetings with "suspected persons," and shipped her off to Elstowe Abbey by Bedford (*Patent Rolls* 1324–27, 206). Margaret remained imprisoned and did not recover her dower until Roger and the Queen returned and assumed the governance of England as regents for Edward III.

The process of acquiring and reinforcing dower rights for each of these three women followed a fairly standard formula. Once the king had granted them dower from lands held in chief, they began to claim dower in property held by tenants of the heir and by family members granted land before the head of the household's death. This process, beginning immediately after their husbands' deaths, could continue for years; the assumption that dower cases were cut-and-dried formalities in which the heir summarily granted dower to the widow is not an accurate portrayal of the situation.[22] Many issues that affected the family contributed to lengthening the process whereby a widow acquired her dower. If the heir had to contend with a dowager who was a stepmother rather than his biological mother, as in Gladys's case, his antagonism toward her might cause him to obstruct her seisin all through her life, first by refusing to grant her dower, then by contesting her seisin through litigation and outright trespass. Since a widow who was also an heiress gained control of her inheritance, like Maud, she might have to contend with a disgruntled son who saw his own inheritance dwindling away into the hands of his mother and his siblings. The generous parent who demised extensive property to her younger children might find that generosity working against her when she sued them for dower. Even mothers who faced little opposition from their heirs often compromised, as Margaret did, on the amount and extent of their dower holdings, an arrangement that invariably favored the heir rather than the dowager. Moreover, once she had acquired her rightful dower, a widow had no guarantees that her seisin would remain uncontested by heirs frustrated by her longevity or anxious to develop the property.

The acquisition of dower and the reinforcement of other claims to land were not the only activities of the noble widow who remained single. She had to appoint bailiffs to oversee the property; manage a household; raise younger children; sometimes arrange marriages or control wardships; transact business with tenants, fellow landholders, and the Crown; pay debts; and perform service for property held in fee or contribute to the service owed by the heir. In short, she lived the life of a baron, with all of its responsibilities and usually with few of the rewards important men enjoyed. Gladys, Maud, and Margaret all accepted such responsibility when they refused to remarry.

Widows occasionally received gifts and respites from debts or other favors from the king, although the king was never as generous as he was with his male barons. In some instances, the king acquitted widows of specific services, most often of the common summons to hear pleas in the king's court from which, as women, they were traditionally barred. Maud received her quittances in 1287 and twice in 1292 (*Close Rolls* 1279–88, 471; 1288–96, 262, 271).[23]

A common gift from the king was wood from the royal forests. In 1248, Gladys received twenty quarters of timber from Penbury forest; Maud received ten timber oaks from the royal park of Pederton in 1300 (*Close Rolls* 1247–51, 66; *Patent Rolls* 1292–1301, 501). Henry III respited Gladys from hambling her dogs (maiming their feet so that—presumably—they could not chase the king's deer) and Edward I granted Maud's request of murage (a toll paid for the repairing of town walls) for her men of Radnor for seven years (*Close Rolls* 1247–51, 379; *Patent Rolls* 1281–92, 69). Other common marks of royal favor included respite from debts for a specified number of years (Maud owed the king £73 2s. 4d. in 1287 [E159/61, m.18]), and grants of fairs and markets in towns the widow controlled (Margaret was granted both a fair and a market at Kingeslane, Herefordshire, and a fair at Radnor [Harley 1240, fol. 73r]).

Maud, as a great landholder in her own right, was particularly burdened with all the duties of a tenant-in-chief. Once she had sworn not to remarry without the king's license and performed homage for her inheritance, she was expected to provide the king with counsel, pay her scutage, send her men-at-arms to war, guarantee the king's writ, and keep the king's peace. Maud's duties as tenant-in-chief began almost immediately after Roger's death. In March, 1283, Edward I ordered her to send soldiers to Montgomery, where he was amassing an army (Welsh Rolls, 280–81). In 1287, at the height of the Welsh war, Maud was required to victual the army from her market-sellers of Radnor; to send three hundred foot soldiers to the king's aid; to dispatch men, horses, arms, and aid to Gilbert de Clare in the campaign against Rys ap Meredoc; and to spend the winter in Wales, along with the other barons of the March, in order to repulse Rhys' attacks (Welsh Rolls, 308, 311–16). The king again ordered Maud and the other Marcher lords to remain in Wales in 1294, and he respited her from all pleas except dower, novel disseisin, and darrein presentment for the duration of her time there (Welsh Rolls, 350–51; CP40/106, mm. 71, 89).[24] In 1297, when Edward was going overseas, he requested that Maud send some of her men to advise and consult with Prince Edward (*Close Rolls 1296–1302*, 132).

Maud also received some of the benefits of being the King's loyal tenant. Even before Roger died, Henry III granted her land valued at £100 from the property of outlawed supporters of Simon de Montfort (Harley 1240, fol. 35r). As soon as she was widowed, Edward gave her a wardship worth £60 a year for at least six years (*Patent Rolls 1281–92*, 8, 115) and later granted her escheated manors in fee farm (SC8/312, no. E-26).[25] In another circumstance the king also treated Maud like his other barons, summoning her to his court *quo warranto* to defend her Marcher liberties. She was in court twice, arguing that her family had always held their land as Marcher lords, free from the king's writ, but the decision of the court on the legitimacy of her claim is lost (Just 1/302, m. 38d; Just 1/740, m. 46).

Maud was not the only dowager/heiress to serve her lord. Any woman who held property in chief or any tenure other than dower had to perform service of some kind. Even widows who held only dower property had to contribute to the heir's required service. Margaret, for example, was ordered to send one hundred footmen to the king at Newcastle-upon-Tyne in 1317 to aid in the Scottish war (*Close Rolls 1313–18*, 562–63) and in February, 1322, she was ordered to send two hundred men from Radnor—her dower lands—to the king, probably against her own son, who was an ally of the Earl of Lancaster against the Despencers (*Patent Rolls 1321–24*, 74). By requiring Margaret to provide military service from her dower lands, the king could threaten her position. If she refused to provide men-at-arms, her lands could justifiably be forfeited. Margaret's activity in the rebellion against Edward II and her subsequent imprisonment because of her support for her son illustrate that a rebel-lious dowager could be considered dangerous to the security of the king just as a female supporter of the royal cause could be considered an ally.

The extensive rolls from the royal central and itinerant courts of medieval England give the impression that litigation was a national pre-occupation. Women were far from exempt in this supposition. Although men outnumber women in the court rolls, a significant proportion of litigants in these records are female. Since the system did not permit wives and unmarried women to appear without a husband, father, or guardian, the women who litigated by themselves were invariably wid-ows, nuns, or abbesses. Litigation over dower might be the most frequent case involving a widow, but it was not the only case. Dowagers often returned to court to protect their property from encroachment. Con-versely, heirs sued dowagers for waste and destruction of their property, and other tenants sued widows for entry into their dower holdings. When a dowager was also an heiress, these cases increased in both quan-tity and scope. Other than dower, widows became involved in the same types of cases as their male peers. Their degree of activity depended upon the amount of land they controlled and the quality of their seisin, not their gender. It is possible, however, that the medieval social view of women as weak, inferior, and ineffective might have hindered widows' ability to receive justice in cases other than dower. If a woman was perceived as being less powerful than a man in the same situation, then her antagonists, as well as the officers of the court, might have exploited that perception and prevented her from keeping what was hers by right.

Gladys, Maud, and Margaret may have had difficulties with family, but their relations with their tenants seem to have been remarkably free from strife.[26] Gladys, although she had many problems with her step-grandchildren, pursued only one case outside her family involving the default of feudal and military service by two of her knights (KB26/135, m. 24; KB26/141, m. 23d). This apparent lack of difficulty with tenants had nothing to do with length of widowhood. Although Maud survived her husband by nineteen years (fourteen more than Gladys survived Ralph), she engaged in little litigation with tenants who were not members of her family.[27] Other than demanding that former bailiffs in Juteberg, Worcestershire, render accounts for their periods of service (Maud vs. Geoffrey de Parco, CP40/92, m. 140d [1292]; Maud vs. John de Juteberg, CP40/122, m. 163 [1298]), and one case of a widow suing her for dower from lands Maud held as guardian of the heir (CP40/101, m. 31d), Maud's actions against tenants originated in properties she held in conjunction with other coheirs of her inheritance. For example, Maude shared two cases of trespass and distraint of cattle and one of novel disseisin with fellow Marshal heir, Joan de Valence, and her husband, William (Tenants of Aure, Gloucs. vs. Maud and William and Joan de Valence, CP40/93, m. 81, 96d and CP40/98, m. 77; Maud and William and Joan vs. John ap Adam and his wife Elizabeth, CP40/106, m. 86d and CP40/107, m. 99d; Maud and William and Joan vs. John de Aure and Richard de Cany, Just 1/283, m. 8d). Maud pursued enough cases in court to justify retaining full-time attornies in her household, but they seem to have been employed more for the battles between her sons Edmund and Roger and other Mortimer family members than for suits with her own tenants. Margaret's early years of widowhood follow a similar pattern, revealing only two cases, both involving the la Poer family, one in which she sued the dowager for waste of her lands and another in which she was sued for novel disseisin (Margaret vs. Margery la Poer, CP40/163, m. 246d; Alina la Poer vs. Margaret and others, Just 1/1331, m. 54).[28] Relations with the la Poers must have been amicable nonetheless, because Margaret demised one of her dower manors to them a few years later (*Patent Rolls* 1313–17, 106). Since, during fully half of her widowhood, Margaret did not have access to her property, it is difficult to know if she would have experienced the comparatively trouble-free seisin enjoyed by her predecessors.

The public records of medieval England—plea rolls, charters, and chancery records—reveal a picture of medieval noble widowhood that contrasts sharply with that presented by the feudal ideal. Although it recognized the need to protect widows and to provide them with subsistence, feudal or chivalric conceptions presented no clear-cut role, delineated no niche, into which these women fit. The idea of an independent woman, particularly one who controlled a great deal of land, was antithetical to the feudal ideal. This exclusionary principle was not entirely displaced by the common law's protection of women. Medieval English common law did recognize a widow's rights to dower and control of her inheritance, but still retained the concept of female inferiority in the larger social scheme and, thus, left the dowager's place in the social and political milieus unclear. Women's prohibition from acting as jurors and magistrates, leading armies, and participating in royal councils is well known. This historical preoccupation with magisterial roles, however, ignores the daily activities of public life, such as suing in court and holding property, or siding with a son in a baronial rebellion, which had an important impact on the lives of the populace. At this level of the public sphere, widows appear in virtually every type of action, from suing for dower to suing for trespass or nonpayment of service, and from receiving gifts of the king to receiving summonses to send men to arms. The records show that noble dowagers such as Gladys, Maud, and Margaret could be devoted to their families but still encounter difficulties with them. They managed their own property and punished those who impinged upon their rights or neglected their dues and services. They performed the duties expected of landholders of their class and met the social and political obligations that being a landholder entailed. Ordinary women of the noble class routinely engaged in public activity, whether it involved sending troops or protecting the king's writ. Although custom hampered their activity by emphasizing their social inferiority, these women were not reticent about protecting their own rights and privileges in court, and they did so competently and effectively. Even though noble widows could not participate in many of the activities in which their husbands and sons took part, such as sitting on royal councils or being appointed as royal officials, they still played their own social, economic, and political roles. Their baronial duties and their activities as landlords were comparable to those of their male peers.

Medieval dowagers, despite constraints imposed on them by common law, made significant contributions to their community. As landholders, patrons, household managers, and parents they influenced the lives of their children, tenants, and dependents. As tenants-in-chief and royal subjects, they fulfilled baronial responsibilities and interacted in the world of the court and politics. Noble widows such as Gladys, Maud, and Margaret Mortimer maintained high social visibility. Their roles might have been ill defined, but the very ambivalence of their position gave noble widows the opportunity to create their own social role.

ABBREVIATIONS

Berkeshire Eyre	*Roll and Writ File of the Berkeshire Eyre of 1248.*
CAPW	*Calendar of Ancient Petitions Relating to Wales.*
Close Rolls	*Calendar of Close Rolls Preserved in the Public Record Office.*
CP40	Great Britain, Public Record Office, manuscripts of the Court of Common Pleas.
E159	Great Britain, Public Record Office, manuscripts of the King's Remembrancer.
Harley 1240	Great Britain, British Library, manuscript in the Harlein Collection, no. 1240.
Just 1	Great Britain, Public Record Office, manuscripts of the itinerant justices.
KB26	Great Britain, Public Record Office, manuscripts of the Court of the King's Bench, Henry III.
Patent Rolls	*Calendar of Patent Rolls Preserved in the Public Record Office.*
SC8	Great Britain, Public Record Office, manuscripts of Ancient Petitions made to the King.
Welsh Rolls	*Calendar of Various Chancery Rolls A.D. 1277–1326.*

NOTES

1. See, for example, Biancalana, "For Want of Justice"; Buckstaff, "Married Women's Property"; Kenny, *History of the Law;* Loengard, " 'Of the Gift of her Husband' "; Walker, "Feudal Constraint."

2. An exception, of sorts, was land held in socage tenure, which retained some local legal relationships. Most nobles did not hold land in socage; it was more typical of the free peasantry. Disputes regarding socage land did, however, appear in the central courts. It was not totally free from common-law control.

3. Common-law dower required the heir to give the widow use of one-third of her late husband's property, except the main residence of the holding (the "capital messuage"). Inheritance law required primogeniture for land held in fee, but partible inheritance among female heirs if no direct male existed.

4. See G. H. Orpen, whose *Ireland under the Normans* is still the standard text, despite his obvious sympathy with English colonial interests in pre-republican Ireland. In his chapter on the Marshal family in Ireland and the division of the late Earl's estate (3:49–78), Orpen blames female inheritance and the granting of dower to widows for the dissolution of English power in Ireland, completely ignoring the documentary evidence that shows these same widows and heiresses as responsible and concerned landholders.

5. For example, Michael Altschul's excellent study of the Clare family is nonetheless androcentric; Countess Maud, a widow for twenty-five years, is depicted—aside from her dower-related battles with her son Gilbert—primarily as a patroness of monasteries and a supporter of her pluralist son Bogo. Although Maud did, indeed, give richly to the Church and provided handsomely for her son, she also spent a great deal of time managing her properties and engaging in public activities.

6. See Cecily Clark's and Robert Palmer's convictions that female independent activity was always undermined by social attitudes toward women, no matter what the law said, in, respectively, Fell, with Clark and Williams, *Women in Anglo-Saxon England*, 164; Palmer, *Whilton Dispute*, 147.

7. For example, Labarge, *Small Sound of the Trumpet*, 34.

8. In "Sanctity and Power," McNamara and Wemple imply that entail of property in order to bar female inheritance was a legal possibility in twelfth-century England. The concept of fee tail did not appear until the *De Donis* statute of Edward I in 1290, and the strict entail was a much later phenomenon. Heiresses abound in the thirteenth and fourteenth centuries.

9. A common assumption that widows, especially if they were young, almost automatically remarried, was made as recently as this past year in Mertes, *English Noble Household*, 54. After Magna Carta, which forbade the king to force widows to remarry and ensured that they would not have to pay an outrageous sum to retain their autonomy, remarriage by widows, unless they were truly children at the time of their husbands' deaths, seems to me to have become more a matter of personal preference among the nobility. I have found many instances in which a widow retained her single status for thirty or even forty or more years.

10. For a larger study, see Linda E. Mitchell, "Widowhood in Medieval England: Baronial Dowagers of the Thirteenth-Century Welsh Marches" (Ph.D. diss., Indiana University, 1990).

11. The geneological material upon which these biographies are based is from G.E.C., *Complete Peerage*, 9:274–83.

12. Roger was about fifty years old at his death in 1282 according to G.E.C., *Complete Peerage*.

13. Davies does not mention that Mortimer's success stemmed primarily from his wife's inheritance and is completely silent about Maud's nineteen-year wid-

owhood, during which her son was unable to solidify his position in her lands (*Lordship and Society,* 25).

14. See discussion of this in Parsons, *Court and Household,* 45, 46, 47–48, 52, 53–54.

15. *Maritagium* was the Latin legal term for what we now call dowry, the property that a wife brings to her marriage.

16. Nominated dower was specific property named by the husband as his wife's dower at the time of their marriage. This differed from reasonable dower, which was an unspecified one-third of the husband's total property at the time of the marriage (before Magna Carta, 1225) or during the marriage (after 1225).

17. For a discussion of the corruption of thirteenth-century sheriffs, see Morris, *Medieval English Sheriff,* 210–11.

18. At least according to Holmes, *Estates,* 10–11.

19. See also CAPW, 260.

20. Hugh Despencer the Elder, Earl of Winchester, and his son, Hugh the Younger, became great favorites of Edward II after the death of his first favorite, Piers Gaveston. Their rapacious greed—and Edward's indulgence—contributed to the rebellion of Thomas, Earl of Lancaster, and his followers in 1321, known as the "Despencer Wars." Lancaster was killed and the rebellion crumbled. Many of the "Contrariants" were imprisoned or executed.

21. Mortimer and the Queen retained power for only another three years before Roger met the same fate as his enemies, the Despencers. Edward III, supported by his friends, Richard de Bury, William de Montague, and Robert Ufford, and with papal approval, effected a coup in October, 1330, that toppled Mortimer and the Queen. Roger was executed and Queen Isabella retired from public life to Castle Rising.

22. In her article, " 'Of the Gift of her Husband,' " Janet Senderowitz Loengard discusses the difficulties widows had in acquiring their dowers during the reign of King John. Although Magna Carta, as well as the personality of Henry III, alleviated some of the most glaring of the king's abuses against dowagers, heirs still had free reign to obstruct and interfere in widows' dower cases to the best of their ability, with few sanctions against such actions.

23. These are the only quittances of Maud's listed in the printed Close Rolls; she might have received yearly acquittals but they were not included in the calendar. I consider this conviction that female barons never participated in royal councils to be a problematic issue, since the only available evidence is negative evidence—quittances from summonses—rather than absolute strictures against female participation.

24. Novel disseisin was one of the "petty" assizes created by Henry II. If a tenant was forcibly evicted from his property without having lost a court case to a plaintiff, then he purchased a writ of novel disseisin. Novel disseisin is

probably the most common civil case in the courts of medieval England. Darrein presentment was another "petty" assize that sought to determine who had last presented a cleric to a particular ecclesiastical living. There is a question in the Welsh Rolls whether the list of landholders sent to Wales was for 1292 or 1294. As the entries in the Common Pleas roll for Michaelmas 1294 are the only indications that Maud was ever respited for pleas, I believe that the summons to Wales probably occurred in 1294 rather than 1292.

25. In 1297 she paid £50 for farm of the manor of Aure.

26. This was different than other noble widows, who often litigated against tenants and were sued themselves.

27. This might seem like a predictable pattern for female litigation but it is actually rather unusual. Other subjects in my dissertation evidence far more acerbic relations with their tenants, especially when they are heiresses as well as dowagers.

28. In the latter case, the plaintiff did not prosecute and the case was dismissed.

BIBLIOGRAPHY

Altschul, Michael. *A Baronial Family in Medieval Europe: The Clares 1217–1314*. Baltimore: Johns Hopkins University Press, 1965.

Biancalana, Joseph. "For Want of Justice: Legal Reformes of Henry II." *Columbia Law Review* 88, no. 3 (April, 1988): 433–536.

Buckstaff, Florence Griswold. "Married Women's Property in Anglo-Saxon and Anglo-Norman Law and the Origins of Common-Law Dower." *Annals of the American Academy* 4 (1893): 233–64.

Calendar of Ancient Petitions Relating to Wales. Ed. William Rees. Cardiff: University of Wales Press, 1975.

Calendar of Close Rolls Preserved in the Public Record Office, Henry III–Edward II, 1242–1247. 23 vols. London, 1892–1938.

Calendar of Patent Rolls Preserved in the Public Record Office, Henry III to Edward II, 1227–1327. London, 1894–1966. *Henry III, 1216–1272*, 6 vols.; *Edward I, 1272–1307*, 4 vols.; *Edward II, 1307–1327*.

Calendar of Various Chancery Rolls A.D. 1277–1326. Hereford, 1912.

Davies, R. R. *Lordship and Society in the March of Wales, 1282–1400*. Oxford: Clarendon Press, 1978.

Fell, Christine, with Cecily Clark and Elizabeth Williams. *Women in Anglo-Saxon England and the Impact of 1066*. Bloomington: Indiana University Press, 1984.

G.E.C. *The Complete Peerage of England, Scotland, Ireland, Great Britain, and the United Kingdom*. 2d. ed. 13 vols. London: St. Martin's Press, 1910–40.

Great Britain. British Library. Harlein Manuscript 1240.

Great Britain. Public Record Office. Manuscripts of Ancient Petitions made to the King, Edward I–Edward II. SC8.

Great Britain. Public Record Office. Manuscripts of the Court of Common Pleas, Edward I. CP40.

Great Britain. Public Record Office. Manuscripts of the Court of the King's Bench, Henry III. KB26.

Great Britain. Public Record Office. Manuscripts of the itinerant justices, Henry III–Edward I. Just 1.

Great Britian. Public Record Office. Manuscripts of the King's Remembrancer. E159.

Holmes, G. A. *The Estates of the Higher Nobility in Fourteenth-Century England.* Cambridge: Cambridge University Press, 1957.

Kenny, Courtney Stanhope. *The History of the Law of England as to the Effects of Marriage on Property and on the Wife's Legal Capacity.* London: Reeves and Turner, 1879.

Labarge, Margaret Wade. *A Small Sound of the Trumpet.* Boston: Beacon Press, 1986.

Loengard, Janet Senderowitz. " 'Of the Gift of Her Husband': English Dower and its Consequences in the Year 1200." In *Women of the Medieval World: Essays in Honor of John H. Mundy,* ed. Julius Kirshner and Suzanne F. Wemple, 215–55. Oxford: Basil Blackwell, 1985.

McNamara, JoAnne, and Suzanne Wemple. "Sanctity and Power: The Dual Pursuit of Medieval Women." In *Becoming Visible,* ed. Renate Bridenthal and Claudia Koontz, 90–118. Boston: Houghton Mifflin, 1978.

Mertes, Kate. *The English Noble Household, 1250–1600.* Oxford: Basil Blackwell, 1988.

Morris, W. A. *The Medieval English Sheriff to 1300.* Manchester, 1927. Reprint. New York: Barnes and Noble, 1968.

Orpen, G. H. *Ireland Under the Normans.* 4 vols. Oxford: Clarendon Press, 1920.

Palmer, Robert C. *The Whilton Dispute, 1264–1380.* Princeton: Princeton University Press, 1984.

Parsons, John Carmi. *The Court and Household of Eleanor of Castile in 1290.* Toronto: Pontifical Institute of Medieval Studies, 1977.

Plucknett, T. F. T. *The Legislation of Edward I.* Oxford: Oxford University Press, 1962.

Pollock, Sir Frederick, and Frederick William Maitland. *The History of English Law Before the Time of Edward I.* 2d ed., reissued with a new introduction by S. F. C. Milsom. Cambridge: Cambridge University Press, 1968.

Roll and Writ File of the Berkshire Eyre of 1248. Ed. M. T. Clanchy. Selden Society vol. 90. London: Selden Society, 1973.

Walker, Sue Sheridan. "Feudal Constraint and Free Consent in the Making of Marriages in Medieval England: Widows in the King's Gift." *Historical Papers* (Saskatoon), 1979: 97–110.

Part 3
Widows and the Law

Chapter 8

Widows as Disadvantaged Persons in Medieval Canon Law

James A. Brundage

Help for disadvantaged widows has long held an honored place in Judeo-Christian morality. The Hebrew Scriptures, long before the time of Jesus, had commended those who assisted widows and assured the devout that God was especially attentive to the prayers of widows, orphans, and other victims of misfortune.[1] Jesus and his early followers likewise ascribed great moral value to the prayers and pious gestures of poor widows and commended those who assisted them.[2] From the beginning, Christian communities assumed responsibility for helping and protecting the widows of their members, and programs to assist widows furnish the earliest examples of organized Christian charity.[3] All of this rested squarely on the Jewish tradition of solicitude for the *anawim*, the holy poor.[4]

It is no great surprise, therefore, that as the Christian Church developed a legal system, the moral obligation to assist widows who suffered social and economic misfortune became a topic of ecclesiastical legislation and that canon law showed particular solicitude for protecting the legal rights of widows in distress. Thus in 451, for example, when the fourth general council of the Church, meeting at Chalcedon, forbade bishops, monks, and clerics to involve themselves in property management and worldly business, the council fathers pointedly made an exception for those who gave legal advice and assistance in litigation to "orphans and widows and those persons without means who rely especially on ecclesiastical assistance."[5]

The belief that the Church had special rights and obligations to watch over and safeguard the interests of widows and other disadvantaged persons remained an established element of ecclesiastical doctrine during the early Middle Ages, but until the mid-twelfth century it had neither any intellectually coherent definition of its objectives nor any regular and effective procedures for achieving its goals. While early medieval prelates often took their obligations as guardians of widows and orphans seriously enough, they lacked settled institutional devices to put them into practice. The effectiveness of the Church's intervention depended upon the interest and energy of individual bishops and other authorities in dealing with particular situations that happened to attract their attention. No regular system for referring such matters to Church authorities existed, and ecclesiastical policy was, in any case, only vaguely defined. It was far from clear when, under what circumstances, and to what extent bishops and others ought to intervene, nor were the limits of their obligations defined with precision. The protection of widows and orphans did not, and in fact could not, find clear and detailed legal expression until the Church's own system of law had developed and matured into a coherent form. Only then could effective institutional means for implementing this noble but ill-defined goal begin to develop.

The mature phase of the development of canon law commenced with the appearance, about 1140, of the *Concordia discordantium canonum* by Gratian, a jurist about whom, unfortunately, we know very little.[6] Gratian's book, which is conventionally referred to as the *Decretum,* not only brought together a vast body of ecclesiastical laws, regulations, and statements of aspirations, but also attempted to analyze their content and to organize them into a coherent, intelligible whole. Gratian's *Decretum* was an impressive intellectual achievement, whose very shortcomings and lacunae furnished the starting point for further analysis and showed where the law required additional development.

Bishops, according to Gratian, had a general obligation to defend and protect the poor;[7] Rufinus, a law professor and early expositor of Gratian's text, added that a bishop who failed, despite repeated warnings, to fulfill this obligation could, on that account, be deposed from office.[8] The general obligation to defend the poor, moreover, entailed a specific obligation toward widows and orphans who needed safeguards against oppression by the rich and powerful.[9] Stephen of Tournai, another academic lawyer who analyzed the implications of Gratian's treatment of this topic, subsumed widows and orphans within the larger category of *miserabiles personae,* a label that corresponds closely to the modern term *disadvantaged persons.*[10] He added that the bishop's obligation to help the disadvantaged took priority over nearly all other demands upon his resources. It was more important for a bishop to assist the disadvantaged than, for example, to beautify churches and, if a choice had to be made, then the available resources should be allocated to poor relief, rather than to enriching God's temples with marble and other ornaments.[11]

Although the care of *miserabiles personae* was an important obligation of the bishop, the authoritative commentary on the *Decretum* written by Johannes Teutonicus noted that he need not carry out this duty personally: the bishop could, and indeed ought to, delegate responsibility for poor relief to his subordinates, especially the archdeacons and archpriests, who acted as the bishop's agents at the local level.[12] But the obligation to assist widows and orphans was not limited to the bishop and his immediate agents: all clerics shared in the bishop's duties toward the disadvantaged, and every village priest, every monk, every clergyman whatever his rank or authority had a responsibility to devote a share of his time and resources to this purpose, whether specifically commissioned to do so by the bishop or not.[13]

The legal texts, moreover, specified in some detail—if not always quite consistently—how relief of widows, orphans, and others was to be financed. The most important source of funds for this purpose was the tithe, a 10 percent tax on many kinds of agricultural produce and other personal income. Essentially, the rules prescribed that one-fourth of the tithe revenue of each parish was to be devoted to poor relief.[14] Those were the principles. The practice was far more complicated.

The rules that Gratian cited and that his expositors commented upon had originated in the early Church. By the mid-twelfth century, when Gratian wrote, circumstances had changed radically and these rules represented ideals that, in practical terms, could no longer be implemented precisely. Still, the old rules continued to provide rough guidelines for the allocation of diocesan and parochial revenue and the enforcement through legal process of clerical obligations to furnish poor relief.[15]

My particular concern here, however, is not with poor relief in general, but quite specifically with the role of the medieval clergy and church courts in furnishing widows, as well as orphans and indigents, with legal counsel and representation and, thus, assist them in protecting their personal and property interests. The special involvement of the clergy in this particular type of poor relief began, as I have mentioned, with the Council of Chalcedon and was reiterated by other early medieval councils and Church authorities, several of whom Gratian cites.[16] This clerical obligation became increasingly prominent in the late twelfth century and the thirteenth century, when legal processes, both in church courts and civil tribunals, became increasingly complex and it accordingly became progressively more difficult for litigants to defend their interests without expert advice and assistance. And as legal counsel and representation came to require more precise and extensive knowledge in order to be effective, clerics with advanced legal training were also tempted to devote their skills full-time to the practice of law, to the detriment of their priestly and spiritual rules. Popes and councils in this period, therefore, reiterated the rules of the early Church with increased concern. The Third Lateran Council in 1179, for example, decreed that

> Clerics in the subdiaconate and above, and also those in minor orders, who are supported by ecclesiastical stipends shall not presume to appear as advocates before secular judges in worldly matters, save on their own behalf or in the interests of their church, or perhaps on behalf of disadvantaged persons who are unable to manage their own litigation.[17]

Those who failed to observe this prohibition, the canon continued, should be punished and should forfeit their clerical status. Half a century later, Pope Gregory IX repeated the council's prohibition and added that beneficed clerics who, contrary to law, not only persisted in this behavior but also represented adversaries of the church in which they held preferment, were to lose their benefices.[18]

Canonists and theologians alike elaborated on these and related passages in the canonical texts concerning jurisdiction over widows. Johannes Teutonicus deduced from Gratian's texts that civil and ecclesiastical courts shared in the obligation to protect widows and other persons liable to oppression.[19] The difference between the two jurisdictions in this respect was a matter of degree, according to Cardinal Hostiensis and other writers: ecclesiastical courts had a special responsibility toward *miserabiles personae,* so that they constituted the forum of last resort. Thus, if secular judges in the ordinary course of proceedings failed to do justice to a widow, she could appeal their decision to the church courts, which had the right to intervene and to overrule the civil courts when necessary to protect the rights of the disadvantaged.[20]

These jurisdictional claims seem to have been predicated on the canonists' belief that their system of law was better equipped than that of secular judges to protect the weak from oppression by the strong, but it also raised serious questions about how far the power of canonical judges extended and what were its limits.[21] Pope Innocent IV, in his *Apparatus* on the *Liber Extra,* analyzed these issues in some detail. Innocent asserted that the pope had jurisdiction over all matters involving widows, but that as a favor to civil judges he permitted them to deal with these matters in the ordinary course of events. If, because of the negligence of the civil courts, a widow was unable to get justice in their forum, however, she retained the right to appeal to the ecclesiastical judges to secure the justice that she was entitled to.[22] Innocent further claimed that church courts had the right to intervene in any proceeding where secular judges failed to do justice, but distinguished between cases involving *miserabiles personae* and those involving ordinary litigants. In general, he maintained that canonical judges ought to intervene in a case only when the appellant had exhausted all available avenues of appeal in the civil courts, but that widows or other *miserabiles personae* had the right of immediate appeal to the church courts from first instance decisions and did not have to wait, as other litigants did, until the civil appeals process had run its course.[23]

But could every widow claim the protection of the canonical courts in all situations? Was the wealthy widow of a great magnate entitled to the same canonical protection as the indigent widow of a poor peasant? Was the claimant who was attempting to secure possession of a rich inheritance or a mighty castle to be accorded the same consideration as the widow who needed help to secure a hut to live in and food to keep her and her children from starvation? Circumstances must surely alter cases. So thought Pope Innocent IV: widows came under the jurisdiction of church courts, he declared, only when it was obvious that they could not secure justice elsewhere. The protection of the Church should be reserved, he thought, for the deserving poor alone, not for every woman who had suffered tragedy in her life or for those who were poor because they were too shiftless to work. Disputes involving persons who were technically *miserabiles personae* were not automatically cognizable in the ecclesiastical courts: their hardship had to be real before the Church would intervene.

The criteria to be considered in determining whether the Church was justified in intervening to protect a particular widow, according to Innocent and other canonists, included not only the widow's social standing and economic resources, but also the kind of hardship she had suffered. Where she was the victim of negligence on the part of a secular judge, for example, she was entitled to seek redress from the church courts, regardless of her social rank.[24] Likewise, if she had been dispossessed of property by violence, the Church had a clear obligation to protect her. Thus, Honorius III ruled that Queen Berengaria, the widow of the English King Richard I, was entitled to bring a possessory action before the ecclesiastical courts in order to recover a castle that had been taken from her by force.[25]

There was thus nothing automatic about a widow's entitlement to seek adjudication of her complaints before ecclesiastical judges. She not only had to have a cognizable grievance, but she also had to take the initiative in petitioning for redress. Canonical judges would take action only after the widow had lodged a petition with them and after they had made a preliminary determination that her situation warranted their intervention.[26]

These legal technicalities meant that, in practical reality, most widows needed advice and assistance from someone knowledgeable in the law if they were to avail themselves of the protection that church courts offered them. Where and how were widows, especially poor widows who lacked influential connections, to find the aid of counsel learned in the law? And, having found it, how were they to pay for it? Medieval canonists adopted, at least in principle, answers to both questions that they found in Roman law.

The answer to the first question, how and where widows were to find expert legal advice, lay in the courts themselves. Roman magistrates, at least by the time of Ulpian (ca. 160–228), had on equitable grounds adopted the practice of designating court-appointed advocates for litigants who were unable to find counsel by themselves.[27] By the late fourth century, an imperial rescript broadened this practice further by requiring judges to assure at least a rough parity of legal advice and representation through the process known as "distribution of counsel." This meant that the judge in each case was responsible for seeing not only that both parties were represented, but also that each had the service of advocates of approximately equal experience and skill, so that neither party monopolized the services of the most talented, skilled, and resourceful members of the local bar.[28] By the end of the twelfth century, law professors were teaching budding canonists that church courts ought to follow these same practices.[29] Early in the thirteenth century, Pope Honorius III (1216–27) had adopted this teaching as official papal policy.[30] The poor litigant was, of course, the main beneficiary—as the civilian law teacher, Azo (ca. 1150–1230) remarked, the rich can always find lawyers, for their money will attract them;[31] indeed, given the small size of the practicing bar in many medieval courts, a wealthy and unscrupulous litigant could easily retain the services of all the locally available legal talent, a practice that the law sought to discourage.[32]

Disadvantaged litigants, in contrast, often needed help in securing legal advice, and that help was not always voluntary. The law authorized judges to place pressure on advocates to agree to furnish their services to widows and disadvantaged litigants; an advocate who failed to comply with a judicial order to do so might be disbarred.[33] Canon law permitted clerics to appear in either church courts or civil courts in order to assist widows and other poor persons;[34] indeed, it attempted, although without great success, to discourage the clergy from practicing law for any other purpose.[35]

The difficulties that poor widows experienced in finding legal aid to press their claims in court had to do with the second question I posed, namely, how this assistance was to be paid for. The prevailing opinion among academic lawyers was that advocates and others should charge no fees for the services they rendered to the poor, but ought to furnish their help gratuitously as an act of charity. Moreover, advocates were told, God had given them the pearl of knowledge; contribution of their services to the poor was their way of repaying that debt.[36]

This advice may have been morally sound, and certainly the principle seems praiseworthy enough in the abstract, but legal practitioners and even a few theologians were aware that it could be implemented only sparingly in the real world. Medieval society produced enough poor people, widows, orphans, and other worthy candidates for legal services to consume the time of the advocates who practiced in the courts. "No one," declared Thomas Aquinas, "can help every indigent," and therefore, he continued, "an advocate is not always obliged to furnish assistance to the poor."[37] Precisely how far the advocate's duty to represent disadvantaged clients should extend, however, remains a difficult question, about which, as the United States Supreme Court has recently demonstrated, opinions remain sharply divided.[38]

To this day, opinion remains similarly divided over the question of whether the moral obligation to assist widows and other disadvantaged persons in securing their rights makes it necessary for authorities to facilitate legal assistance to claimants who contemplate bringing action against the authorities themselves. Medieval canonists sometimes dealt with this question in the context of a bishop's obligation to help *miserabiles personae*. Hostiensis maintained that the bishop's duty to assist the disadvantaged required him to make the services of an advocate available to disadvantaged persons, even when the indigent was pressing a claim against the bishop himself.[39] Canonical treatment of the general issue more often centered, however, on a slightly different problem: could the advocate ethically assist an indigent to bring an action against the church from which he himself held a benefice? Bernard of Parma thought that he could not and, indeed, that he must not do so, on pain of forfeiting his benefice, since he would be showing ingratitude, in the technical sense, to the institution that supported him.[40] Hostiensis analyzed this problem in quite considerable detail and suggested that if the advocate, after examining the matter closely, concluded that the litigant had a persuasive claim, then he was morally obliged to assist the action. This obligation was binding on the advocate, however, only if the prospective litigant could find no one else to represent him. In that situation, the advocate's duty to help the poor took precedence over his obligations to the church in which he held office.[41]

It seems clear from all of this, then, that canonical provisions for furnishing legal assistance to widows responded not only to an evident need in medieval society but also to perennial ethical issues in legal practice about which opinions remain divided to this day. The canonistic texts and commentaries examined here tell us how medieval law dealt with these issues and what differences of opinion emerged among the classical writers on these problems. What they do not tell us is how effectively the principles discussed by the jurists were implemented in practical reality.

Evidence bearing on that problem certainly exists in the records of medieval courts, but scholarly exploration of those records has barely begun. It does seem clear, however, from some preliminary soundings that lawyers in medieval canonical courts did, at least occasionally, act for widows and other poor clients without fee and the evidence does not suggest that they handled these cases any less diligently than others for which they were paid.[42] It may well be, in addition, that young lawyers who were just beginning to practice dealt in disproportionate numbers with cases involving poor widows and that novice lawyers treated such cases as a means for building experience and acquiring a reputation.

Substantial work, however, remains to be done on the surviving records of litigation in medieval canonical courts before these and other impressions about the implementation of the theories of the academic canonists can be adequately verified and further details of the canonical protection of widows can be more fully explored.

NOTES

1. Thus, e.g., Exod. 22:22–24; Deut. 10:18, 26:12; Jer. 7:6–7; Ps. 24:16, 33:7, 145:9; Prov. 12:9, 28:6; Eccles. 4:13, 9:15. The entire book of Job is, in effect, a commentary on the theme that virtue emerges from poverty and misfortune.

2. Thus, e.g., Mark 12:38–40, 42–44; 1 Tim. 5:3; James 1:27.

3. 1 Tim. 5:3–16.

4. Mollat, *Les pauvres,* 18.

5. Council of Chalcedon (451) c. 3, in *Conciliorum oecumenicorum decreta* (cited hereafter as *COD*), 64–65. Roman jurists had taught long before Chalcedon, and, indeed, long before Christianity became the established religion of the Roman world, that equity required magistrates to see to it that the poor and disadvantaged had legal assistance and representation when they appeared in court; see, Ulpian, *De officio proconsulis,* bk. 1, in Digest 1.16.9.5; *Ad edictum,* bk. 6, in Digest 3.1.1.4. Roman law texts are cited here from the critical edition of the *Corpus iuris civilis* by Mommsen, Krueger, Schoell, and Kroll.

6. Noonan, "Gratian Slept Here."

7. Gratian, *Decretum,* D. 84 pr., c. 1, citing the authority of Pope Gregory the Great.

8. Rufinus, *Summa decretorum,* D. 84 pr., 174.

9. D. 87 pr., c. 1–2, relying upon the authority of Pope Gelasius I.

10. Stephen of Tournai, *Summa,* D. 87 pr., v. *viduis,* 109.

11. Stephen of Tournai, *Summa,* D. 86 c. 18, v. *ornare templum dei,* 108.

12. Johannes Teutonicus, *Glossa ordinaria,* D. 84 c. 1, v. *pauperes.* The *Glos. ord.* to the *Decretum* and other texts of the *Corpus iuris canonici* will be cited throughout from the four volume edition published at Venice in 1605.

13. Rufinus, *Summa,* D. 87 pr., 178–79; Johannes Teutonicus, *Glos. ord.,* D. 86 c. 26, v. *tutelas.* Johannes added that poor clerics themselves had a right to be represented in litigation; *Glos. ord.,* C. 5 q. 3 c. 3, v. *quia episcopus.*

14. Gratian, C. 12 q. 2 c. 26–27, 29–30; c. 28 allocates one-third of the tithe

revenue to be used jointly for maintenance of the church fabric and the needs of poor.

15. For further details, see Tierney, *Medieval Poor Law*, 68–79.

16. D. 86 c. 26 (Council of Chalcedon); D. 87 c. 8 (Fourth Council of Toledo); D. 88 c. 1 (Pseudo-Melchiades).

17. 3 Lateran Council (1179) c. 12, in *COD*, 194; X 1.37.1. Note also X 3.50.1, drawn from a Carolingian Council at Mainz.

18. X 1.37.3; *Regesta pontificum*, no. 9569.

19. Johannes Teutonicus, *Glos. ord.*, D. 87 c. 1, v. *plus tamen;* C. 23 q. 5 c. 23, v. *oppressos.*

20. Hostiensis, *Summa aurea,* fol. 75rb. Likewise Johannes Teutonicus, *Glos. ord.*, C. 24 q. 3 c. 21, v. *pauperem;* Bernard of Parma, *Glos. ord.*, X 3.39.4, v. *non permittas,* and X 5.40.26, v. *personarum vel rerum* and v. *viduis.*

21. Tierney, *Medieval Poor Law*, 14–15.

22. Innocent IV, *Apparatus,* X 2.2.11, v. *terminetis,* fol. 198rb: " . . . papa iurisdictionem habet super viduas, sed de gratia defert iudicibus secularibus, ut non procedat iudex ecclesiasticus, nisi propter negligentiam laici iudicis." Similar, but less explicit, claims may be found in Johannes Teutonicus, *Glos. ord.*, D. 87 c. 3, v. *nos* and D. 87 c. 6, v. *mancipiis;* as well as Bernard of Parma, *Glos. ord.*, X 2.2.11, v. *terminetis.*

23. Innocent IV, *Apparatus,* X 1.29.38 §§1, 3, fol. 142ra–va. In effect, Innocent assimilated *miserabiles personae* to the clergy and argued that widows and others in this category ought to have the same access to ecclesiastical jurisdiction that clerics did; see Génestal, *Le privilegium,* 1:57–58.

24. X 2.2.11.

25. X 2.2.15.; Tierney, *Medieval Poor Law*, 17–19; Innocent IV, *Apparatus,* X 1.29.38 §4, fol. 142va; Bernard of Parma, *Glos. ord.*, X 2.2.11, v. *in iustitia.*

26. Innocent IV, *Apparatus,* X 2.2.11, v. *terminetis,* fol. 198rb; cf. Beaumanoir, *Coutumes,* 1:157.

27. Ulpian, *Ad edictum,* bk. 6, in Dig. 3.1.1.4.

28. *Corpus iuris civilis,* Codex 2.6.7.1 (Valentinian and Valens, 370).

29. Bernard of Pavia, *Summa,* 23.

30. X 1.32.1; Bernard of Parma, *Glos. ord.*, X 1.32.1, v. *implorando;* Geoffrey of Trani, *Summa,* X 1.37 §5, 127; Innocent IV, *Apparatus,* X 1.37.1 §3, v. *pro miserabilibus,* fol. 165rb. The policy continues in modern canon law, but with an unexpected twist: whereas the 1917 *Codex iuris canonici Pii X,* can. 1914–1916, stipulated that poor persons were entitled to free legal assistance as a right, the 1983 revision (*Codex iuris canonici auctoritate,* can. 1649) permits courts to furnish poor litigants with legal assistance as a favor.

31. Azo, *Summa super Codicem,* 28.

32. Vivianus Tuschus, *Casus,* Cod. 2.6.7, comments on this practice, noting

that judges had the power to punish those who attempted it; see Bataillard, *Les origines*, 100–101.

33. Geoffrey of Trani, *Summa*, X 1.37 §1, 126; Hostiensis, *Summa*, lib. 1, tit. *De postulando*, §§2, 3c, fol. 62ra–rb.

34. Bernard of Parma, *Glos. ord.*, X 1.37.3, v. *nulla nocere* and *pro seipso;* Geoffrey of Trani, *Summa*, X 3.50 §1, 126.

35. I have dealt with this aspect of the matter elsewhere; see Brundage, "The Monk as Lawyer."

36. Raymond of Penyafort, *Summa*, 2.5.39, col. 518; Hostiensis, *Summa*, lib. 1, tit. *De postulando* §2, fol. 62ra; Jason de Mayno, *Commentaria*, § *tripli vero* [Inst. 4.6.24], no. 54, fol. 199vb.

37. Thomas Aquinas, *Summa theologiae*, 2–2.71.1 concl.

38. The court divided 5 to 4 on the question of whether an unwilling attorney can be required to represent an indigent client; Brennan, J., writing for the majority, held that 28 U.S.C. §1915(d) did not compel a lawyer to represent an indigent client in a civil action. The district court, according to the majority, has a statutory right to "request" such assistance, but may not penalize an attorney for refusal to comply with the request. Stevens, J., joined by Marshall, Blackmun, and O'Connor, maintained in a dissenting opinion that the appellant's admission to practice implied an undertaking to represent indigent litigants when asked to do so; see Mallard v. U.S. District Court, No. 87–1490 slip op.

39. Hostiensis, *Summa*, lib. 1, tit. *De postulando* §8, fol. 63rb.

40. Bernard of Parma, *Glos. ord.*, X 1.37.3, v. *contra ecclesiam.* This gloss makes an interesting use of the Roman law concept of the "gratitude" that a freedman owed throughout his lifetime to the person who had freed him.

41. Hostiensis, *Summa*, lib. 1, tit.*De postulando*, §8, fol. 63ra.

42. Helmholz, "Ethical Standards," 289.

BIBLIOGRAPHY

Assises des bourgeois. See *Recueil des historiens des croisades.*

Azo. *Summa super Codicem, Instituta, Extraordinaria.* Turin: Apud haeredes Nicolae Beuilaque, 1578. Reprint. Turin: Bottega d'Erasmo, 1966.

Bataillard, Charles. *Les origines de l'histoire des procureurs et des avoués depuis le Ve siècle jusqu'au XVe.* Paris: Cotillon, 1868.

Beaumanoir, Philippe de. *Coutumes de Beauvaisis.* 2 vols. Ed. A. Salmon. Paris: A. et J. Picard, 1899–1900.

Bernard of Parma. *Glossa ordinaria to Decretales Gregorii IX.* In *Corpus iuris canonici.* 4 vols. Venice: Apud Iuntas, 1605.

Bernard of Pavia. *Summa decretalium.* Ed. E. A. T. Laspeyres. Regensburg: Josef Manz, 1860. Reprint. Graz: Akademische Druck- und Verlagsanstalt, 1956.

Bosl, Karl. "Das Problem der Armut in der hochmittelalterlichen Gesellschaft." *Sitzungsberichte der österreichischen Akademie der Wissenschaften,* phil.-hist. Kl. 294, pt. 5. Vienna: Verlag der Oesterreichischen Akademie, 1974.

Brundage, James A. "Legal Aid for the Poor and the Professionalization of Law in the Middle Ages." *Journal of Legal History* 9 (1988): 169–79.

———. "Marriage Law in the Latin Kingdom of Jerusalem." In *Outremer: Studies In the History of the Crusading Kingdom of Jerusalem Presented to Joshua Prawer,* ed. B. Z. Kedar, H. E. Mayer, and R. C. Smail, 258–271. Jerusalem: Yad Izhak Ben-Zvi Institute, 1982.

———. "The Monk as Lawyer." *The Jurist* 39 (1979): 423–36.

Codex iuris canonici Pii X pontificis maximi iussu digestus, Benedicti papae XV auctoritate promolgatus. New York: P. J. Kenedy & Sons, 1918.

Codex iuris canonici auctoritate Ioannis Pauli PP. II promulgatus. Vatican City: Libreria editrice Vaticana, 1983.

Conciliorum oecumenicorum decreta. 2d ed. Ed. Giuseppe Alberigo et al. Freiburg in Breisgau: Herder, 1962.

Corpus iuris canonici. 2 vols. Ed. Emil Friedberg. Leipzig: B. Tauchnitz, 1879. Reprint. Graz: Akademische Druck- und Verlagsanstalt, 1959.

Corpus iuris civilis. 3 vols. Ed. Theodor Mommsen, Paul Krueger, Rudolf Schoell, and Wilhelm Kroll. Berlin: Weidmann, 1872–95.

Decretales Gregorii IX. See *Corpus iuris canonici.*

Génestal, R. *Le privilegium fori en France du Décret de Gratien à la fin du XIVe siècle.* 2 vols. Bibliothèque de l'école des hautes études, sciences religieuses, vols. 35 and 39. Paris: Ernest Leroux, 1921–24.

Geoffrey of Trani. *Summa super titulls decretalium.* Lyon: Roman Morin, 1519. Reprint. Aalen: Scientia, 1968.

Gratian. *Decretum.* See *Corpus iuris canonici.*

Hanawalt, Barbara A. *The Ties that Bound: Peasant Families in Medieval England.* Oxford: Oxford University Press, 1986.

Helmholz, Richard H. "Ethical Standards for Advocates and Proctors in Theory and Practice." In *Proceedings of the Fourth International Congress of Medieval Canon Law.* Monumenta iuris canonici, Subsidia, 5: 283–99. Vatican City: Biblioteca Apostolica Vaticana, 1976.

Herlihy, David. "Marriage at Pistoia in the Fifteenth Century." *Bullettino storico pistoiese* 74 (1972): 3–21.

———. *Medieval Households.* Cambridge, Mass: Harvard University Press, 1985.

———. "The Medieval Marriage Market." *Medieval and Renaissance Studies* 6 (1976): 3–27.

Hostiensis. *Summa aurea.* Lyon: Joannes de Lambray, 1537. Reprint. Aalen: Scientia, 1962.

Innocent IV. *Apparatus toto orbe celebrandus super V libris decretalium.* Frankfurt am Main: Sigismund Feyerabendt, 1570. Reprint. Frankfurt am Main: Minerva, 1968.

Izbicki, Thomas. " 'Ista questio est antiqua': Two Consilia on Widows' Rights." *Bulletin of Medieval Canon Law* 8 (1978): 47–50.

Jason de Mayno. *Commentaria super titulo de actionibus.* Lyon: A. Vincent, 1539.

Johannes Teutonicus. *Glossa ordinaria to the Decretum Gratiani.* In *Corpus iuris canonici,* 4 vols. Venice: Apud Iuntas, 1605.

Liber extra. See *Corpus iuris canonici.*

Little, Lester K. *Religious Poverty and the Profit Economy in Medieval Europe.* Ithaca, N. Y.: Cornell University Press, 1978.

Le livre au roi. See *Recueil des historiens de croisades.*

Mollat, Michel. *Les pauvres au moyen âge: Étude sociale.* Paris: Hachette, 1978.

Mallard v. U.S. District Court. U.S. Supreme Court. Slip Opinion 87-1490.

Noonan, John T., Jr. "Gratian Slept Here: The Changing Identity of the Father of the Systematic Study of Canon Law." *Traditio* 35 (1979): 145–72.

Raymond of Penyafort. *Summa de penitentia.* Ed. Xavier Ochoa and Aloisio Diez. Universa biblioteca iuris, vol. 1, tomus B. Rome: Commentarium pro religiosis, 1976.

Recueil des historiens des croisades. Lois, 2 vols. Paris: Imprimérie royale, 1841–43.

Regesta pontificum romanorum inde ab anno post Christum natum MCXCVIII ad annum MCCCIV. 2 vols. Ed. August Potthast. Berlin: Rudolf de Decker, 1874–79.

Rufinus. *Summa decretorum.* Ed. Heinrich Singer. Paderborn: F. Schöningh, 1902. Reprint. Aalen: Scientia, 1963.

Sheehan, Michael M. "The Influence of Canon Law on the Property Rights of Married Women in England." *Mediaeval Studies* 25 (1963): 109–24.

Las siete partidas del rey don Alfonso el Sabio, cotejadas con varios codices antiquos por la Real Academia de la Historia. 3 vols. Madrid: Imprenta real, 1807.

Stephen of Tournai. *Die Summa des Stephanus Tornacensis über das Decretum Gratiani.* Ed. Johann Friedrich von Schulte. Giessen: Emil Roth, 1891. Reprint. Aalen: Scientia, 1965.

Thomas Aquinas. *Summa theologiae.* In *Opera omnia, iussu edita Leonis XIII.* 48 vols. Rome: Riccardo Garoni, 1882–.

Tierney, Brian. *Medieval Poor Law: A Sketch of Canonical Theory and Its Application in England.* Berkeley: University of California Press, 1959.

Vivianus Tuschus. *Casus Codici.* In *Corpus iuris civilis,* 5 vols. Lyon: Apud Iuntas, 1584.

Walker, Sue Sheridan. "Free Consent and Marriage of Feudal Wards in Medieval England." *Journal of Medieval History* 8 (1982): 123–34.

———. "Widow and Ward: The Feudal Law of Child Custody in Medieval England." In *Women In Medieval Society,* ed. Susan Mosher Stuard, 159–72. Philadelphia: University of Pennsylvania Press, 1976.

Chapter 9

Widows Not So Merry: Women and the Courts in Late Medieval France

Harry A. Miskimin

French women during the later Middle Ages had standing before the law courts and they used it. One cannot read the registers of the Parlement of Paris without being struck by the very substantial number of cases that involve women either as plaintiffs or as defendants, but the reasons for this apparent litigiousness are not entirely clear. Did an insensitive society attempt to exploit women, especially widows, and thus drive them into the courts, or were women themselves the aggressors, seeking advantage through the judicial system? Not surprisingly, the cases and decisions preserved in the registers of the Parlement of Paris suggest a balance between these two poles, and both extremes are in evidence. Widows sometimes seem to have been the victims of rank exploitation, yet, at other times, they emerge as dishonest manipulators of the judicial process. Widows occasionally challenged other widows within the same family and sometimes they mounted legal assaults against their own sons. Beyond doubt, however, is the fact that widows frequently brought or argued cases before the highest French court and did so in the expectation of a favorable result.

Disputes often revolve around a widow's dower rights and her endeavor to protect them from greedy family members or collateral heirs. Yet, in some, the widow is revealed less as the passive recipient of property from father or husband than as an actor in her own right. On January 20, 1302, for example, the widow of Raoul Goatre, arguing for herself and her children, prevailed in Parlement over the Abbot and Convent of St. Geremer de Fly and overturned an earlier inquest regarding the control and mineral rights of an iron mine (AN X^{la}4, 50v [20 January 1302]). Pending the results of a further inquest to be undertaken at the expense of the convent, the widow reestablished her right to work the mine and draw iron from it.

I do not wish to imply that the widow actually worked with pick and shovel in the mine, but her role as entrepreneur and economic actor seems clear. Indeed, many of the cases that involve widows establish or reiterate significant points of law, and some contribute to the long process whereby the Crown deepened its control of the judicial system. Tension between ecclesiastical and secular courts was virtually perpetual during the High Middle Ages as crucial disputes traversed jurisdictional lines. Many such cases involved women. Rights of inheritance of feudal property might well turn on matters of marriage, legitimacy, or heresy. Should they be heard in the ecclesiastical courts as issues of faith or the sacraments, or in the royal Chambre des Comptes as direct concerns of the Crown and the military security of the country? What rights of appeal might exist from one set of courts to the other? Should appeals from the ecclesiastical courts be directed to the Court of Rome or to the king and who should decide? The path toward definition was long and troubled, yet early in the fourteenth century, a property case pitted John de Bailly, clerk at St. Germain-des-Pres, against one Johanna la Bouchière in a dispute regarding two houses and a rent of one hundred nine livres parisis (AN X^{Ia}4, 66r [20 December 1304]). The court, albeit the secular arm, of St. Germain had divided the properties between the two parties and Johanna had appealed the case, first to the Châtelet of Paris, and thereafter to the Parlement. The Parlement, after due consideration of the evidence and presentations, quashed the ruling of the court of St. Germain and absolved Johanna from its terms. The records of Parlement do not clarify the basis underlying this decision, though the fact that the initial ruling was rendered by the secular court of St. Germain suggests that the dispute did not entail religious doctrine or the sacraments. On the other hand, the fact that one of the parties was a cleric opens the possibility that the case might have proceeded through the ecclesiastical judiciary. Conflict concerning appeals from the ecclesiastical courts persisted during the subsequent century-and-a-half, and it was but temporarily resolved when the Pragmatic Sanction of 1438 eliminated the possibility of appeal to the Court of Rome, and, thus, placed the French Crown at the apex of the ecclesiastical judiciary by default (*Ordonnances*, XIII, 267–91 [7 July 1438]).

Widows, by definition, were frequently parties in suits concerning inheritance and their court battles did much to establish the appropriate rules of succession. These disputes determined the common law of inheritance and that law became the standard for the transfer of feudal and other property at death. Let us consider one of many such cases. On November 28, 1304, Parlement decided a case resulting from the simultaneous deaths of Jean, Lord of Boychavoine, and his son, Egidius, in the Flemish wars. Peter, Jean's second son, had won a lower court ruling according him the succession to the lands of Boychavoine, but Lady Ronaucourt, Egidius's widow, by reason of her dower and in the name of her children, appealed in the Parlement of Paris (AN X^{la}4, 66r [28 November 1304]). The initial problem for the court was to determine who was the most proximate heir to feudal property, and it reversed the judgment of the lower court and ruled in favor of Lady Ronaucourt and the children, her wards. The court records do not specifically mention whether there was a male child nor the ages of the children; the use of the masculine plural, *liberos,* however, implies the existence of at least one male child.

Note that the property at issue was that of Jean and not that of his son Egidius and that both father and son appear to have died at the same time. This implies that Egidius, although the firstborn son, had not inherited his father's property at the time of their mutual deaths. As a result, the widow was asserting a dower right over the property of her father-in-law to the detriment of his second son, Peter. The property at hand was feudal; the most common succession path made the fief descend to the eldest son.[1] Since Egidius died before inheriting, one could certainly argue that Peter stood in his stead as the eldest son. Under Norman custom, however, the children could take the place of their father when nonfeudal property was transferred; in that case, Egidius's male children would hold his place and compete with his brothers for their grandfather's property, but not so under the custom of Paris and not so for fiefs.[2] The Parlementary registers do not detail the reasons behind the judgment in favor of Lady Ronaucourt and her children, so we are left to speculate.

Complex as this case is, however, the ruling by Parlement was at variance with the practice followed in the royal succession at the deaths of Philip IV and his son, Louis X. Louis left a daughter by his first wife and his second wife was pregnant at his death; the child was a male but died almost immediately.[3] The succession then passed to Louis's brother Philip, who in turn died leaving five daughters; his brother Charles took the throne and ruled until 1328 when the line ceased.[4] It was this series of deaths that gave credence to Edward III's claim to the throne of France as the closest male relative of Philip IV by way of Isabella, Philip's daughter and Edward's mother. Under the custom of Paris, women could transmit rights that they could not possess; if followed, this custom would have given the crown to Edward.[5] Instead, of course, the crown went to the collateral line in the person of Philip VI Valois. Edward would later use this apparent irregularity to woo the Flemish to his side in the Hundred Years War by declaring himself the legitimate heir to France.

The parallels between the royal succession and the case of Boychavoine, while not exact, are interesting. Lady Ronaucourt's victory in Parlement meant that a woman and minor children could inherit feudal property in preference to the oldest surviving son. If grandchildren could inherit feudal property, the case in favor of Edward III's claim to the throne of France was strengthened. If, on the other hand, as the lower court had ruled, the property passed to the next adult male heir, in this case Peter, the behavior of Philip V and Charles IV in disinheriting their royal nieces was vindicated and the transfer of the royal succession to Philip VI Valois was justified.

At the very least, Lady Ronaucourt's victory in 1304 established a somewhat troublesome precedent for the Valois when they later disputed Edward's claim to the French throne.

Succession and inheritance disputes affected many important and unresolved areas of the law. In January, 1401, Parlement gave its ruling in a case that pitted the custom of one region of France against that of another [AN X^{la}48, 271r–273v [22 January 1401 N.S.]). Such cases could only be resolved through appeal to a national court acting beyond the local custom and thus enhanced the importance of Crown and Parlement in providing and defining the ultimate law of the land. In this case, Maria de Bethune, widow of Eustace de Vouldenaro, sought to protect her property and dower rights. She said that, when she married, her dower had been arranged according to the custom of Champagne and Brie, and, therefore, that the Chateau de Marolio in Brie was hers as dower. She further claimed half of the remainder of Eustace's hereditary lands and said that Margaret de Vouldenaro, her deceased husband's sister, and Margaret's husband Jean de Nigelle were entitled to the other half. Despite her right, she said that Jean de Nigelle and Philbert, husband of Eustace's other sister, Johanna, had kept her from her inheritance and that Nigelle had driven her people from the Chateau de Marolio by armed force. As a result of the later behavior, Maria had filed a charge of *excessum* against him.

Nigelle's wife, Margaret, counterclaimed that the death of Eustace made her the most proximate heir under the custom of Burgundy, where most of the property was located, and further claimed that, since Maria had failed to make timely notice of the death of Eustace as required by Burgundian custom, Maria had forfeited her right to the succession. To further complicate matters, Maria and Nigelle, the principle opposing parties, each had letters from the Parlement sustaining their respective position in the conflict. The court considered the evidence, the testimony, and the contradictory letters and ruled that Maria had possession and seizin of the Chateau de Marolio in Brie and half the moveable goods according to the custom of Champagne and Brie. Additionally, the court ruled that, since Eustace's marriage had been arranged in Brie, Nigelle and his wife were barred from the succession to his goods. Maria was thus put in possession and seizin of half of the fruits, profits, and emoluments of the disputed property for the term of her life and the court undertook to maintain Maria in those rights against Nigelle and his wife. The court also upheld Maria's letters from Parlement ordering Nigelle and his wife to honor their agreement with Maria in regard to her dower, ordered restoration of the arrears of fruits and emoluments, and charged Nigelle with court expenses. The case is interesting for a variety of reasons. It seems apparent that Maria's weakness as a widow was exploited by Nigelle when he forcibly expelled her from Marolio, which had, in fact, been the home in which she had lived. The court guaranteed her right to the chateau and imposed royal power to prevent Nigelle from again barring her access. Also at issue in the conflicting claims was the legal significance of a written contract specifying the terms of the dower; when the court ruled in Maria's favor, it sustained the value of a written document over personal testimony and, thus, took a step toward modern practice and away from the medieval norm of according greater credence to personal testimony. The most significant element of the case, however, lay in the decision as to which custom should prevail. The location of the property would normally have determined the applicable custom, but Maria was successful in her argument that the custom of Champagne and Brie that had governed her marriage should also govern her dower rights as a widow. As noted, when Maria brought her claim to the Parlement, she appealed beyond the local courts and, as a consequence, strengthened the role of royal justice.

Since marriages often traversed the lines between legal jurisdictions, dower cases, as a class, frequently touched such matters. Widows thus tended to instigate legal actions that had the effect of augmenting the role of centralized royal justice. If this be so, it was equally true that claims based on conflicting customs forced the central judges to know and comprehend a multitude of diverse regional laws so as to choose among them. The obvious difficulties of knowing the subtleties of each of the many regional customs ultimately frustrated the royal judges and led to the demand for a general codification of custom across France. The *ordonnance* of Montils-les-Tours in 1454 commanded that codification and, in so doing, initiated the events that would convert custom to written law and thus to a law subject to correction and revision by the Crown (*Ordonnances*, XIV, 284–314 [April, 1454], item 125).

Women and widows, though rarely actors in the wars of the later Middle Ages, were certainly affected by them. Court records reveal some of the war-related problems confronted by women and the judgments often make women participants in interesting innovations of law or adjustments to long-standing custom. A case decided by Parlement on July 9, 1401, set Agnes de Yuriaco, widow of Jean de Melles, seneschal of Ponthieu, against her son, Alard de Melles (AN X^{1a}48, 331r–332r [9 July 1401]). She had letters of July 2, 1381, assigning to her thirty livres tournois rent as dower; the letters had been confirmed and authenticated by Jean's last will and testament. In addition, she claimed that Jean had agreed that, if the local custom was repugnant to such a dower, she should have, through his pledge, all of his moveable goods as an alternative payment. At Jean's death, Alard had taken possession of the property and had obtained a court order from the Bailli of Amiens according her the rent and the arrears.

Alard disputed the claim, noting that the lands at issue were in Flanders, Cassel, Guienne, Boulogne, and Calais and, thus, in the hands of the English. Custom, he said, accorded his mother half of all fiefs and a third of the hereditary lands. In addition, he said that there were five sons and several daughters from the marriage; that custom gave the eldest son all lands save the fifth part; that Jean and Agnes had specified the exact division; that the fifth part had been given irrevocably to his siblings in accord with his parents' wishes; and that all his remaining lands were in conquered territory.

The moveable goods, by his accounting, came to 3,000 livres tournois, none or very little of which came from the lands that he had inherited. Alard said his mother had no cause of action and that the court should absolve him; failing that, the court should take into account the military exigencies, custom, and the prior distributions and charge Agnes expenses. The court ruled that Alard must pay fruits, revenues, and emoluments from the lands in Guienne and Boulogne for three years and the remaining share of the moveables to his mother. He was thereafter absolved from any further imprecations.

In this case, the court was compelled to make a ruling in equity since no law or custom was precisely tailored to the situation. Jean and Agnes were themselves apparently uncertain whether custom would uphold the initial rent and hence specified the alternative claim on the moveable goods. Alard, perhaps cynically, cited custom, which would have accorded Agnes half of the fiefs and a third of the hereditary lands, in his effort to avoid additional payment since the lands in question were held by the English. No one disputed Agnes's right to a dower share. Confronted by military exigency and seeking fairness, the court made a compromise ruling, offering Agnes three years equivalent of the rent and a final cash payment while freeing Alard from further claims. The solution was probably fair, but it was not based on existing law. The ruling thus weakened the fixity of custom, opened opportunities for new activities by the Crown unbounded by law, and heightened the role of the royal courts as the source, rather than the interpreter, of law.

As the loss of revenue-producing lands through war posed problems for the court, so too did the subsequent recovery of territory from the enemy. On August 14, 1451, Parlement decided a case regarding such recaptured lands [AN X^{1a}80, 74r–76r [14 August 1451]). Katherine of Alençon, Duchess of Bavaria, sought to regain her lands in Normandy from the Duke of Alençon. The court had given her possession of lands near Caen on September 13, 1415, but the English had captured Normandy and "kept it for a long time." After its return to obedience, Katherine again got court orders dated July 28 and September 2, 1450, giving her the lands. The Duke opposed these letters, and that brought the matter before the Parlement.

In his defense, the Duke of Alençon said that Katherine's letters were invalid because they had been obtained before the English were expelled and that he had gotten to the lands by military force when she was unable to do so. He also claimed that he had constructed certain castles for the defense of the disputed lands and that he had been there long enough to gain possession and seizin of the lands under the custom of Normandy. His presentation was apparently not very effective; the court ruled in Katherine's favor and condemned the Duke to expenses.

As in the previous case, the court faced something of a dilemma. There was no doubt that Katherine's claim to the lands was strong and certain in 1415, but more than thirty years had passed under English occupation. The duke based his claim on his participation in the reconquest, on adverse possession through his construction of castles, and on the perfectly legitimate assertion under custom that he had been possessed and seized of the lands for the requisite year and a day and that that fact validated his claim. Once again, the court was compelled to make a ruling more in equity than in strict construction of existing law. The surviving records do not reveal the family relation between Katherine and the duke in much detail, nor do they explain the reasoning underlying the decision. Even so, however, one must grant a degree of justice to the duke's argument. The court's ruling seems more an effort to restore the parties to their condition before Henry V's invasion than to respond to established custom. Such problematic cases contributed to the elevation of the royal courts by extending their authority to areas where the application of law merged with the creation of law.

Some matters brought before the court clearly served to strengthen both the king and the conception of centralized law; others produced more ambiguous effects. Consider the coinage for example. From at least the beginning of the fourteenth century, the French Crown had sought to impose and enforce control over the coinage and had asserted the right to determine the circulation value of precious metal. From the time of Philip the Fair, French kings had claimed the right to issue fiat money, albeit one stamped on precious metal or alloy as opposed to the modern use of paper bank notes.

Such fiscal freedom would have been of great utility to royal governments enmeshed in war and desperately seeking funds for its conduct. One can with reason, of course, argue that the ability to finance war is an uncertain benefit and that an impoverished state is often more peaceful and less dangerous than a rich one. So be it, but the economic difficulties at the end of the Middle Ages did not result only from war. Plague followed upon plague after the initial visitation in the late 1340s, and with plague came deep economic, social, and psychological disruptions. Depopulation meant that food cost less and that wages were high in the immediate wake of the plagues. People, fearful of death, could thus afford to seek relief in luxury or piety, and each depended on services provided by the Italian south. Money flowed from the northwest of Europe toward the south- and northeast in search of luxuries or as papal remittances.[6] The persistent drain of precious metal reduced the available money supply and thereby lowered the vitality of the French and other economies and led to economic contraction. Note that this result need not necessarily follow from an outflow of bullion. In modern times, the money supply is quite distinct from the bullion supply, since modern government has both the right and the power to issue fiat currency—to say that a scrap of greenish paper will circulate at a value of one, ten, or even one hundred dollars. Medieval governments still struggled to gain that fiscal freedom and medieval women played an important role in limiting the use of fiscal expedients by initiating actions in the royal courts.

Legal obstacles to the creation of fiat money derived from certain provisions of canon law; the closing of a contract and the extinction of a debt due in the future required that the payment be made in money equivalent to that in use at the inception of the contract. This rule emerged from the Digest and the Glossators, found further articulation in the pronouncements of Popes Innocent III and Gregory IX, and even occurred in certain early fourteenth-century *ordonnances* of Philip IV.[7] Economic necessity, military exigency, and the conscious efforts of a series of French kings had combined to challenge the old laws. The crown sought to impose, through statute law, a legal tender monetary standard with a value set by the king. The result was a period of confusion in the law as interested parties endeavored to assert one or the other of the two legal treatments of contract and payment. Women were often among those affected.

One of the principal areas of conflict concerning payment lay within the family. Dowery and dower disputes proved to be fertile breeding grounds for court conflict, as wives, widows, and heirs demanded vindication before the courts. There were many such cases, of course, but let us consider just a few in detail. On February 13, 1451 N.S., the two sons of Claudia de Rossillone prevailed in Parlement as her heirs in a long-standing dispute (AN X[la]80, 3v–11r [13 February 1451 N.S.]). Claudia had married in 1412 and her husband, Armand, had burdened his estate with a rent of three hundred livres tournois in a dower contract. Since his chateau was insufficient, other lands and all moveable goods were pledged. Claudia's sons claimed a payment of four thousand old scuti of 64 to the marc of gold, a sum affirmed in Armand's will of 1421. Claudia had gotten court orders from Parlement in and after 1431, and had gotten the Bailli to attach certain lands; this latter was accomplished in 1435, after her death in the preceding year. The case had apparently remained in the courts ever since. Claudia's sons demanded payment of the rent, arrears, and so forth with precise specification of the money by weight (AN X^{la}80, 7v). Despite the counterclaims by Armand's relatives that there were other heirs, that the dower exceeded custom, and that such an enormous sum would inequitably disenfranchise the others, the court ruled for Claudia's sons. Further, the payments were carefully structured to reflect the intrinsic value at the time of origin. The arrears were estimated in three different royal moneys. The final sum was to be paid in royal money equivalent to that, be it gold or silver, having course at the time that the said arrearages occurred. They were to be calculated with respect to the price of the silver marc and in accordance with the royal *ordonnances* on the money.

This case exhibits the manner in which a widow's dower rights could conflict with currency legislation and interfere with the effort to develop a true, legal tender currency. Similar problems could arise with regard to doweries as opposed to dower. Some six months after Parlement decided in favor of Claudia de Rossillone and her sons, it settled an extremely complex litigation between two of the most powerful families in France (AN X^{la}80, 51v–69r [21 July 1451]). The family Daulphine had, in effect, died out, leaving only the Bishop of Albi, Robert Daulphine, and Jacqueta Daulphine, Abbess of St. Menulph. The Montispensiers claimed the property by marriage to Johanna Daulphine, noting that the last surviving Daulphines were in orders and thus barred from inheriting feudal property.

Robert Daulphine acceded rather easily to most of these claims, but he demanded payment of his niece's dowery as her next of kin; he also sought recovery of some land unjustly taken from him by Guillaume de Vienne, Lord of St. George. As the case unfolded, it turned out that there were a long series of unpaid doweries that dated back to June 22, 1361, when Bevaldus Daulphine married Johanna de Forez, siring a daughter who subsequently married Louis Bourbon, a Montispensier cousin. The court-imposed settlement was extremely convoluted; the underlying property was divided among the many heirs generated by both families. The various current beneficiaries were required to pay shares of the dowery of Johanna de Forez in proportion to their part of the inheritance of Johanna Daulphine. They were further required to do so in money having course as of June 22, 1362, the marriage date, or the equivalent value determined after the price of the marc of gold and the royal *ordonnances* of the time (AN X^{la}80, 68v). An unpaid dowery contracted at the marriage of Margarita Daulphine in 1404 was to be paid by the current heirs on a proportional basis in money having course at the time of that marriage or in equivalent value determined by the price of the silver marc and the royal *ordonnances*. Robert Daulphine was allowed to retain certain lands for his lifetime, but the court ruled that the Lord of St. George was Johanna Daulphine's heir and, thereby, apparently denied Robert's claim to his niece's dowery. Note the implications of these two last cases that settled property claims in money current at the inception of marriage contracts. The scarcity of precious metal and coin was at its most severe in the mid-fifteenth century and the need for transactions cash accordingly intense. For over a century, the Crown had sought to establish a fiat currency that could easily have alleviated such a shortage, yet the same crown, in its judicial manifestation as the Parlement, was in effect annulling its own currency *ordonnances* by making contract settlements dependent on the intrinsic metal content of the coins in circulation. Fiat and intrinsic systems could not coexist, and it was not until the sixteenth century that fiat currencies became general.

French women were rarely highly visible participants in the power politics of the later Middle Ages, yet their role in the formulation and application of the law was far greater than their political profile would suggest. In the few cases considered here, women were formidably present in defining the currency and frustrating the crown's attempt to create fiat money. Others, among them Johanna la Bouchière, participated in decisions that defined the relationship between secular and ecclesiastical courts. Lady Ronaucourt's success in claiming her husband's father's property helped to establish precedents for subsequent cases of succession, although rule by precedent was not a direct method of establishing law in France; parallels with the royal succession could have been drawn from this case. Marriage across the borders of regional customs led women to make claims that entailed conflict of customs and, thus, contributed to the pressures for a general codification of customs in France. The latter was commanded in 1454 and, in fact, brought to fruition in 1510 for Paris and, shortly after, for much of the rest of France. Both as property holders in their own right and as dower recipients, women were involved in litigation arising from military disruption. Since the underlying circumstances were too irregular to be covered by existing custom, such litigation was often settled in equity rather than strict law. This, in turn, expanded the role of royal justice and simultaneously cast the king as the author of a new and more flexible law, increasingly detached from the constraints of divine, natural, or customary sanctions. At the extreme, the bearers of the oriflamme were tempted to cast off the fetters that the gods impose on those impious enough to steal the fires of heaven and to claim divine power for earthly rule beyond the law.

ABBREVIATIONS

AN   Archives Nationales.
Ordonnances   *Ordonnances des rois de France de la troisième race.*

NOTES

1. See Ourliac and Gazzaniga 1985, 320–28.
2. See Ourliac and Gazzaniga 1985, 321–22.
3. See Perroy 1965, 72–74.
4. Perroy 1965, 72–74.
5. See Ourliac and Gazzaniga 1985, 326.
6. See, for example, Miskimin, 1975 and 1984; Day 1978; Munro 1983.
7. See Cazelles 1966, 83–105, 251–78; Timbal 1973, 336–37.

BIBLIOGRAPHY

Archives Nationales. Ser. X^la, vols. 4, 48, 80.
Day, John. "The Great Bullion Famine of the Fifteenth Century." *Past and Present* 78 (1978): 1–53.
Cazelles, R. "Quelques réflexions à propos des mutations de la monnaie royale française (1295–1360)." *Le Moyen Age* 72 (1966): 83–105, 251–78.
Miskimin, H. A. *The Economy of Early Renaissance Europe, 1300– 1460.* Cambridge: Cambridge University Press, 1975.
———. *Money and Power in Fifteenth Century France.* New Haven: Yale University Press, 1984.

Munro, John. "Bullion Flows and Monetary Contraction in Late Medieval England and the Low Countries." In *Precious Metals in the Later Medieval and Early Modern Worlds,* ed. John Richards. Durham: Carolina Academic Press, 1983.

Ordonnances des rois de France de la troisième race.

Ourliac, P., and J.-L. Gazzaniga. *Histoire du droit privé français.* Paris: Albin Michel, 1985.

Perroy, E. *The Hundred Years War.* New York: Capricorn Books, 1965.

Timbal, P.-C. *Les Obligations contractuelles d'après la jurisprudence du Parlement, XIIIe–XIVe siècles.* Vol. 1. Paris: C.N.R.S., 1973.

Part 4
Widows in Literature

Chapter 10

Mystical Inspiration and Political Knowledge: Advice to Widows from Francesco da Barberino and Christine de Pizan

Liliane Dulac

Translated by Thelma Fenster

Written about a century apart, the *Del Reggimento e Costumi di Donna* by Francesco da Barberino (hereafter *Reggimento*)[1] and the *Livre des Trois Vertus* by Christine de Pizan (hereafter *Trois Vertus*)[2] offer resemblances striking enough to call for comparison. Whether a direct filiation exists between the two texts is a question that no doubt remains impossible to decide conclusively. Still, in the absence of internal proof—quotation or literal borrowing—and of any extratextual information, a study of parallels may be undertaken, one that nonetheless brings out—and rather sharply, I believe—the particular characteristics of each of these two pieces devoted to the education of women. The present investigation will concentrate on the examination of one shared theme, that of widowhood.[3]

The following categories cover a collection of fairly general traits that suggest or permit comparison of the two texts:

1. Allegory,
2. The organization of the addresses to widows,
3. Didactic address, and
4. Communication.

The relationship between the two works for widows is less at the level of their doctrinal content than at that deeper level where, for both

Francesco da Barberino and Christine de Pizan, the signs of another truth, the quest for another perfection and another knowledge, are revealed.

Allegory

Francesco da Barberino

Allegorical characters are numerous and their role is fundamental in Barberino's work. Madonna, protectress of the writer, along with the personified virtues that she delegates to his side, are, with the author himself, the actors in scenes that introduce or interrupt the narrative, as if the text were being written before the reader's eyes. It is by studying the allegory that each author's particular inclination becomes clear.

In Barberino's case, the work at hand and the book to be written inscribe themselves in a project of a divine nature. In a dialogue, Francesco and the entities Piatate and Cortesia (Piety and Courtesy) repeat Madonna's initial prayer (*Proemio,* ll. 3–9). The discussion concerns a twin quest proposed by Madonna: literary (that of the book to be done), and mystical (that identified with the feminine inspiration of the book). The didactic ambition is but the pretext for a transcendental quest. The ardor of creation is at the service of Madonna's hoped-for human revelation.

> Ella ci manda attè, chè si ricorda,
> Ed anco Amor la ne fe' memorare,
> Della inpromessa ched ella ti fecie,
> Di mostrar sè attè tutta ben chiara,
> E d'ascoltari, e di far tuo piaciere
>
> (*Del Reggimento,* 215, ll. 34–38)

[She sends us to you, because she recalls, as love too made her remember, the promise that she made you to present herself to you in all her clarity, and to listen, and to grant your wishes.]

Upon the intercession of this High Authority, who presides over every destiny and every creation, Francesco undertakes to write an uplifting work destined for a female public. But Madonna herself must remain in the realm of a fictional "character," of an allegorical figure who is at

once present and absent, influencing her humble servant without revealing herself.

Parla, risponde; che eser[e] ciò non può,
Però ch'io non volglio eser conosciuta

(Proemio, 6, ll. 6–7)

[Speak and respond; for that cannot be so since I do not wish to be
known.]

That is the source of the contradictoriness of Francesco's situation:
addressing human creatures in the treatise he is composing, he translates
into clear language Madonna's necessarily veiled language. The essential
problem is that of making a literary transcription of an inspired and
inspiring word, thus freezing it in writing.

I' non so ch'io mi parli,
Che fanciullo sono;
Nientemeno, pensando che voi dite,
Ghe nommi fia mestier(e) pensare o dire,
Ma sol[o] volgier la penna

(Proemio, 11, ll. 33–37)

[I do not know what I am saying; for I am nothing less than a child,
believing what you say: that it is not my place to think or speak but
only to wield the pen.]

In the course of the interludes (*Del Reggimento,* Parte Sesta, 213–19,
ll. 1–115) interrupting the widow's laments, Piatate and Cortesia progressively liberate Francesco from his earthly chains through a mystical
ascesis that raises him up to Madonna. The poet undergoes an entire
series of tests (the test by fire, the test of the mountain, bad weather, the
sword test, and the river passage—216, ll. 63, 62–63, 81) within a
Dantesque schema, crossing the "dark forest" and the "bitter forest" to
reach Madonna's sweet and ineffable presence.[4]

Face to face with the allegorical figure, Francesco celebrates the divine
beauties of the lady and devotes to her a paean of praise (*laude*—221–
23, ll. 150–218), in which he repeats his oaths of adoration and submission. Madonna answers (223–24, ll. 219–49), exalting her own omnipo-

tence and kindness, which have allowed the meeting between a human being and a celestial Virtue. She inspires in her initiate the energy necessary to the pursuit and accomplishment of his work.

> La mia potenza è di gran maravilglia.
> Tu ài veghiato per avermi assai,
> E di mie *laude* assai ti se' disteso.
> In guidardone ti giuro e prometto,
> Che, settù fai te capacie di tanto
> Quant'io sarò a donar larga e libera,
> Tu porterai tuo intendimento assai.
> Vattene omai, e pensa di ben fare...
>
> (224, ll. 236–43)

[My power is of great wonder. You have kept vigil to have me, and you have long toiled over my praises. In reward I swear and promise you, that, if your abilities can sustain the breadth and generosity I can provide, your wisdom will grow profoundly. Take your leave now, and concentrate on good works...]

To Francesco's declarations of allegiance, made earlier,

> Io vi rispondo, ch'io son lo suo servo
>
> (215, l. 32)

[I reply to you, that I am her servant,]

the lady replies with her unconditional support and assistance:

> Che chi mi serve, mai nollo ingannai.
>
> (224, l. 249)

[He who serves me, I have not deceived.]

After that purifying conversation with Madonna, Francesco returns to his work.

> Sanza più dire i' men vado a seguire
> Quell'ovra che da voi si mosse e move.
>
> (225, ll. 251–52)

[Saying no more, I leave to continue / That work which by you was inspired and continues.]

Most of the instructions given to widows are generally placed in the mouth of the author, who speaks in his own name. Yet Costanza[5] (Constancy), inseparable companion to the widow, still a prey to grief, remains her tutelary angel throughout the sixth part. This chapter ends with an apologia for Costanza:

Però prego e consilglio ciaschuna,
Che mentre vive sec' agian Costanza;
Ch' ell è virtù che tutte molto avanza.

(242, ll. 109–11)

[Thus I beseech and advise each one, that, while in life they keep Constancy with them; For she is a virtue that mightily betters all women.]

The role given to the allegorical figure of Costanza is that of providing exemplary exhortation and sermon. She is adviser and confidante to a woman entering a painful phase of her life. Her speeches, marked by resolution, lead the royal widow, who has not yet found the equilibrium necessary to the execution of her new duties, toward perseverance and wisdom (209–10; 226–27).

Christine de Pizan

Allegory is just as essential to the *Trois Vertus,* as the title of the work suggests. In Christine's text, however, the allegorical episodes are not very developed, as the discourse is always expressly that of Reason, Rectitude, and Justice, those daughters of God, who continue the work of education begun in the *Cité des Dames* (*City of Ladies*). The author is composing at the dictation of the *Virtues,* who entrust their powers to Charity and Prudence. Thus, it is *Worldly Prudence* who gives to the young lady and to the lady of princely birth seven teachings on the *art of governing oneself and of governing others:*

Si nous convient d'ores en avant parler de la leçon et des enseignemens que Prudence Mondaine lui amoneste, lesquelx enseignemens et amonicions ne se different ne departent de ceulx de Dieu, ains en viennent et dependent. Si dirons et parlerons du sage gouvernement et maniere de vivre qui lui aduisent selon Prudence. (Bk. 1, chap. 9, [41])[6]

[Now we must speak of the example and the teaching that Worldly Prudence imparts to her. These teachings and warnings do not differ from God's; rather, they come from them. We will speak of the wise governance of life that Prudence's teachings advise.]

The allegory, without any sort of staging to adorn the account, serves as support for the author's didactic intentions. It is put to the service of a moral and political pedagogy whose principles will guide women of every rank, especially princesses.

... il est de neccessité que ceulx et celles, tant femmes comme hommes que Dieux a establiz es haulz sieges de poissance et dominacion soient mieulz moriginéz que aultre gent afin que la reputacion d'eulx en soit plus venerable et que ilz puissent estre a leurs subgiéz et a ceulx qui les frequentent et hantent si comme mirouer et exemple de toutes bonnes meurs, s'adrecera nostre leçon premierement a ycelles, c'est assavoir aux roynes, princepces et haultes dames; et puis ensuivant de degré en degré chanterons semblablement nostre doctrine en tous les estaz des femmes afin que la discipline de nostre escole puisse estre a tous valable. Si dirons doncques en ceste maniere. (Bk. 1, chap. 1, [9])

[Necessarily, both men and women whom God has placed in the high seats of power and rule should be more knowledgeable than others so that their reputations are more respected and so that they may be as mirror and example of every good habit to their subjects and to those who visit them. Our teaching will be addressed first therefore to those women, that is, to queens, princesses, and high-placed ladies. Then, proceeding step-by-step, we will tell of our doctrine among women of all estates, to make the teaching of our school applicable to all. That is how we will proceed.]

The address to the widowed princess opens upon a declaration that takes up once more, in part, the introductory statement of intention, for it is in the repetition of identical formulas that the symbolic power of the personifications must be sought.

> ... mais afin que notre doctrine soit en tous les estas des dames valable, dirons encores a ce propos parlant aux dictes princepces et grans maistresses vesves, tant aux joennes comme aux anciennes en difference de leurs aages. (Bk. 1, chap. 22, [82])

> [But so that our doctrine may be useful to women of all estates, we will once again take up these issues, speaking to princesses and great ladies who are widowed, young and old, according to the differences in their ages.]

The didacticism can be less austere when the allegorical figures address widows of the middle class. The rigor and severity of the ideal proposed to women do not forbid tenderness and emotion, recalling Christine de Pizan's autobiographical pages.[7]

> Chieres amies, nous, meues par pitié de vous cheues en l'estat de veuveté par Mort, qui despoillees vous a de voz mariz, qui qu'ilz fussent, ouquel estat sont livréz communement maintes angoisses et moult d'anuyeulx affaires. (Bk. 3, chap. 4, [188])

> [Dear friends, we, moved by pity for each of you fallen into the state of widowhood because Death has deprived you of your husbands, whoever they may have been—fallen into that pitiable state where much anguish and many trying problems afflict you. . . .]

The Organization of the Addresses to Widows

In Barberino's work and in Christine de Pizan's, widowhood is presented first as an event followed by:

1. a lament,
2. a consolation, and
3. finally, by instruction proper.

But the proportions among these parts are very different in the two treatises under study. The evocation of grief and affliction, as well as the consoling speech, are the occasion for a very developed dramatic presentation in Barberino, whereas, in the *Trois Vertus*, the depiction of grief is but a rapid introduction to the teaching. But, in spite of divergences in content and proportions, certain striking analogies in the composition of the two addresses justify an attempt to define elements that vary within the common framework. We dare not put forward the hypothesis that the *Reggimento* was one of the sources of the *Trois Vertus* without asking: Could the analogies between them be those of a tradition, of the laws of a genre?

Francesco da Barberino

Lament

Before removing herself from the sight of others by retiring to her chamber, where her widowhood relegates her, the lady makes plain her own physical and moral decay. Her cries and sighs are part of a conventional ritual. Long, despairing laments recount the joys of the past as compared with the solitude of the present. Tender plaints escape from her lips, suggesting that she still has the leisure to give free rein to her pain before she turns more calmly to the duties of her estate. Her sadness takes the form of a desire to join her dead husband and of praise for his perfections. Evoked in the main are his wisdom and his distinguished qualities as a leader.

> Ov'è la gran larghezza ed honore,
> C'a tutti usavi e facievi a potere?
> Ov'è 'l gran senno ella gran provedenza,
> Che sempre uscia di tutte l'ovre tue?
> Ov'è la giente chetti seguitava?
> Ond' averanno gli amici e parenti
> Lo grande aiuto, soccorso e consilglio
> Che ricevièn dattè, dolcie singniore?
>
> (207, ll. 35–42)

[Where is the great largesse and honor, which you extended and offered to all? Where is the great wisdom and profound foresight, which issued from all your works? Where are the people who followed you? From where will friends and family have the solid hand, succor, and counsel they received from you, gentle lord?]

That praise foreshadows elaborations to come in Costanza's consolation and in Francesco's teaching.

Consolation
The widow's lamentations are interrupted by the allegorical figure of Costanza, whose speech is fashioned around the theme of the husband. The widow must, in some way, become identified with the image left by her deceased husband, and she must be ready to guide the peoples that her husband led so well. Moreover, it is as if the sovereign had passed from the world just when his kingdom was most prosperous.

> Elle suo' terre non lassa con briga,
> Nè lor gravati, ma ricchi e potenti,
> C'ancor porranno attè molto ben dare.
>
> (210, ll. 21–23)

[He leaves not his lands in want, nor his people burdened, but rich and strong, so that they will be able to give you much.]

The memory of a husband haloed in glory serves Barberino's didactic design. The lady succeeds a prince whose conduct she must imitate and whose friendships she must perpetuate.

> Elegga de' milgliori e più fedeli,
> E di color c'amaron lo marito,
> Alquanti assuo continovo consilglio;
>
> (232, ll. 25–27)

[Choose the best and most faithful and those who loved your husband, as well as his continued council.]

In the *Reggimento*, the narrative proceeds harmoniously, as the dramatic staging and instructions progressively prepare the lady for her responsibilities. Her sadness disappears. It is smothered and will finally be extinguished by Costanza's advice. The princess will cede to the demands of social life.

In the writing of both authors, the didactic portion proper is organized, at least in principle, according to the same categories defined by social status and age. That is undoubtedly the plan Barberino has in mind in the prologue of the sixth part, which addresses widows:

E qui si tratta di tutto suo stato,
E como s'ella è vecchia,
E como s'ella è mezana,
E como s'ella è giovane, . . .

(203, ll. 4–7)

[And here is addressed every status, be she aged, be she middle-aged,
be she young, . . .]

In fact, Barberino will hardly talk about any but the widowed princess, or about the woman of high nobility, and middle-aged, upon whom the responsibilities of power may rest. The Italian writer, intermediary between humanity and Madonna with divine knowledge, is much more interested in his book's ultimate conclusiveness than in the character of the widow.

Christine de Pizan

In Christine's work, the speech of the Virtues is centered entirely upon the social situation of the widow—whether she is a princess [*baronnesse*], of the merchant class, or of the people—and on her age. Christine applies that schema in a much more concrete and realistic fashion than Barberino does.

Widowed princesses

The personal grief of the widow and the scrupulous completion of customary mourning rituals are legitimate manifestations of sensibility and propriety. But any tragic representation of emotion or staging of despair is eschewed by Christine, who prefers sober reserve and restrained comportment to a crescendo of plaints. The drama of widowhood is enacted only against the perspective of a completely uncertain and far-away future.

The *lament* essentially contains recommendations about the conduct to adopt in the event of widowhood and the list of obligations that the princess cannot avoid.

> . . . se il avient que la sage princepce demeure veuve, n'est pas doubte qu'elle plaindra et pleurera sa partie si que | bonne foy le donne; se tendra closement meismement un temps après le service et obseques,

a petite clarté de jour, a piteux et adoulé habit et attour selon l'onneste usage. Si n'obliera pas l'ame de son seigneur, ains en priera et fera prier tres devotement par grant soing en messes, services, aumosnes, offerendes et oblacions, et moult la fera recommander a toutc gent de devocion. (Bk. 1, chap. 22, [83])

[If it happens that the wise princess becomes a widow, there is no doubt that she will weep and lament her loss, as good faith allows. She will remain sequestered for a time after the burial service, in dim light and in mourning costume, as proper decorum demands. She will not forget her lord's soul; she will pray and have prayers said very devoutly and caringly at masses, and through services, alms, offerings, and oblations, commending his soul to all devout people.]

In the *consolation*, Prudence, helped by the princess's father-in-law and friends, combats the debilitating effects of a suffering that has lasted too long and is finally to be condemned, in order to prompt the lady to react without delay.

Si convient que elle prengne autre maniere de vie, ou grever pourroit son ame et sa santé, si n'en seroit pas de mieulx a ses nobles enfans, qui encores ont tout mestier d'elle. (Bk. 1, chap. 22, [83])

[She must adopt another manner of life, lest she damage her soul and her health. (Her continued grieving) would not be much better for her noble children, who still have great need of her.]

The responsibilities that fall to the widow appear at first to be only a remedy for a fruitless affliction. In the end, the lady, concerned about her duties, is constrained to dominate her feelings and is led progressively to defend the interests of her estates.

ceste dame, ainsi amonnestee de raison et de bon conseil, pour au-cunement mieulx passer ceste grant tribulacion, se prendra a donner de garde de ses besoignes. (Bk. 1, chap. 22, [83])

[The lady, thus advised by reason and good counsel to help her better pass through this period of great tribulation, will devote herself to guarding her own interests.]

Lament and consolation rapidly give way to the presentation of the responsibilities that weigh upon a sovereign, that is, to the *teaching* proper.

The chapter devoted to widows *des communs estas* [of the common estate] is not organized according to that schema, however. Lament, consolation, and instruction mix indistinctly. The loss of the husband, already so painful, delivers the widow over to multiple torments. Financial worries will track her, along with the evil done by others and the humiliations she will suffer. The Three Virtues, sympathetic, teach her the way to be strong and they lead her to fight back. Christine proposes remedies for all the evils, attacks, and cruelty. Against ignorance and fear she opposes knowledge and lucidity.

> Et pour ce que vous avez besoing d'estre armees de bon sens contre ces pestillences et toutes autres qui avenir vous peuent, nous plaist vous amonnester de ce qui vous puet estre valable,... (Bk. 3, chap. 4, [189])

> [And because you need to be armed with good sense against these plagues and all others that may come to you, it pleases us to instruct you in what may be valuable for you,...]

Didactic Address: A Narration

The didactic address begins like a narration in following the order of situations and events that widowhood brings. But more generally, it may be partly composed of small stories. Faced with a given event or situation, the widow will act in accordance with advice given her in order to obtain a specific, often implicit, result. Thus Christine, in speaking about widows of the bourgeoisie or those of the people, distinguishes three sorts of evil:

> —*durté* [hard-heartedness],
> —*divers plaiz et demandes de pluseurs gens ou fait de debtes ou de chalanges de terres ou de rentes* [various suits and demands by many people concerning debts or challenges over land or income from rent], and
> —*mauvais language* [bad language] (Bk. 3, chap. 6, [189–93])

for which she proposes appropriate remedies: confidence in God, gentleness, and a defensive politics.

The narrative element may be very marked. The author, by way of giving information, recalls the savoir-faire and perfect life of *royne Jehanne* (Queen Jeanne) *royne Blanche* (Queen Blanche), and the *duchesse d'Orleans* (duchess of Orleans).[8] Elsewhere Christine details the visits to the princess by the women of the village for the purpose of offering small gifts (chap. 1, 23). Barberino, writing in another register, ends the sixth part of his narrative with a story (*Del Reggimento,* Parte Sesta, 238–42), that of the heroic widow who, with weapons in hand, resists the amorous advances of the king's son, who has been courting her since her youth. She refuses the love and marriage offered by a man whom she surpasses in common sense and intelligence but whose social standing is higher than hers.

> Ella, tuttochè fosse gientil donna,
> Et an' di gran lingnaggio,
> Non però era possente inver lui;
> Però pensava con senno passare.
>
> (239, ll. 27–30)

[She, although a woman of noble spirit, and of notable lineage, was, nevertheless, not his equal; thus she decided to overwhelm him with wisdom.]

We may thus compare Barberino's and Christine's texts by bringing together their most characteristic elements, that is, their *characters* and *events*.

Characters

The number and diversity of characters with whom widows must deal characterize their social relations, presented as desirable or inevitable for women.

In Christine, the contrast is clear between the very diversified society that constitutes the princess's sphere of activity (from the ordinary people to the principals and wise men of the council) and the reduced relations envisaged for the widow of middle-class status. For the latter, with the exception of relatives and servants, preferably of the female sex, only *coustumiers* (those who call regularly) and *clers* (priests) are specifically evoked (chap. 3, 4). If we place Barberino's and Christine's addresses side by side, in particular where they deal with a lady of high rank, common categories are of course discernible, essentially those of members of the family: husband, children, and relatives of the husband and of the widow herself. In return, certain differences are telling: Barberino will frequently have characters appear, such as the housekeeper, nursemaid, childrens' governess, and chambermaid, who constitute the widow's household; Christine scarcely speaks of any but the collective *gens de son hostel* [the people of her household; chap. 1, 23], but in return she details other groups of people who are defined by their position outside the household. For example, there are vassals of all ranks with whom the sovereign, retired to her land, has friendly commerce:

—*les officiers et leurs femmes* [officials and their wives],
—*les dames et les damoiselles du païs et les bourgoises* [the matrons and young women of the countryside, and merchant women],
—*les petites femmes de village* [the village women], and
—*les acouchees, et povres et riches* [women who have taken to their beds, both the poor and the rich].

But the princess, who holds the reins of government, must also enter into relations with various people whose role or central importance is political.[9] The order in which these men appear conforms to a hierarchy:

1. those who participate in the government, the barons and advisers of the council;
2. those who fight, that is, *les chevaliers, escuiers et gentilz hommes* [the knights, squires, and gentlemen]; and
3. *le peuple enfin* [finally, the people] (chap. 1, 22).

These three categories—advisers, soldiers, and the people—are invited to demonstrate toward the reigning princess and her children the equal virtues of fidelity and loyalty. The woman who wants to oversee her domains will have to be surrounded by administrators and by officers who are especially honest: *principaulx de ses hommes* [her chief men], *baillifs de ses chatellenies* [administrators of her properties], and marshals (chap. 1, 23).

If Barberino's text completely ignores any of the lower class, such as the villagers, he does introduce (but in a way that is much vaguer than

Christine's) a series of political men, who must assume the tasks that power imposes and who replace the deceased sovereign in his different activities during the minority of the royal children:

1. a great lord who exercises the functions of an interim prince,
2. members of the council,
3. very many *officiers* [officials] and agents, [and]
4. zealous administrators who watch carefully over the finances. Most important, all these dignitaries will be men who can be trusted. (Parte sesta, 231–35, ll. 1–96).

These differences in the list of characters summoned by Barberino and Christine form a coherent ensemble. In fact, the one situates the widow, though a princess, in the interior life of her house, while the other, on the contrary, puts her directly in contact with the society for which she has responsibility. The exemplary princess of *Trois Vertus* lives a life of public appearance. Her residence is a meeting place. She herself moves about at will. The frequent use of verbs such as *come, visit,* and *receive* is entirely meaningful in that regard.

Voudra estre par eulx et par leurs femmes visitee souvent, et bonne chiere leur fera; les dames et les damoiselles du païs et les bourgoises s'assembleront aucunes fois vers elle, si les *recevra* joyeusement et honnourera chascune selon son droit, et les mandera pour en estre acompagnee quant seigneurs ou estrangiers devront *venir* vers elle. A ceste noble bonne | dame meismement les petites femmes de village, qui l'aimeront de tout leur cuer, lui aporteront aucunes fois de leurs petiz presens comme fruis et autres choses, et elle les fera *venir* vers elle et les vouldra veoir, *recevra* joyeusement leurs chosetes et de pou de chose fera grant conte et grant feste . . . (Bk. 1, chap. 23, [87–88])

[She will wish to be *visited* often by her men, and she will greet all graciously. Ladies of rank, young women from the country, and townswomen sometimes will assemble before her. She will *receive* them joyfully, and will honor each one according to what is due her, and will send for them to join her company when noblemen or foreigners are *to come* before her. Even the common women of the village, who will hold her in great affection, sometimes will bring her small presents—fruit or other little things—and she will have these women come before her, will wish to see them, will *receive* their gifts enthusiastically, and will make much out of trifles.]

Events, Activities

Examining the *Reggimento* and the *Trois Vertus,* we can state a first, clear divergence. Barberino envisages only situations or events that are not very precise (for example, an official who acts badly and must be replaced, or imprudent acts that put the reputation of a widow in danger). Without ignoring those possibilities, Christine puts forward some well-defined troubles. The material obstacles that the widowed sovereign comes up against thread through the narrative: enterprises that menace her widow's dower and her goods, dissension between barons, attacks from enemies, internal revolts, extortion and the theft of taxes by farmers (chap. 1, 23). Elsewhere in the work, Christine paints a picture of the perils that threaten widows of a lower station: assaults by *felons* [traitors] against their goods, lawsuits, . . . (Bk. 3, chap. 4).

Francesco da Barberino
Barberino's concern is to offer widows a life ideal turned inward toward family and hearth (*Del Reggimento,* 232–33, ll. 24–57). Their duties and occupations are very clearly defined. They must see to the education of their children—or better, have them brought up by experienced tutors; the mother's role sometimes seems limited. Does she have the right to inculcate in her sons notions of justice and wisdom? Probably, but her right of reprimand is contested.

> Ma sovra tutte cose faccia loro
> Amici di ragione e di giustitia,
> E che canminin per la via d'Iddio,
> Facciendoli correggiere al maestro;
> Chè rado madre ben corregie loro.
>
> (234, ll. 69–73)

[But above all make them friends of reason and justice, and make them walk the road of God, leaving discipline to their master; since rarely does a mother discipline them well.]

Strict and austere conventions regulate the existence of widows of all ranks. They must bend to prudent reserve where men are concerned and abstain from all superfluous familiarity; they may barely receive a priest at home.

> Parli con preti e con riligiosi,
> Ne' suoi consilgli, anzi le chiese loro;
> chè troppo farli a suo' magion venire
> Per loro honore ed ancor di lei,
> Usi lo men che puote.
>
> (237, ll. 25–29)

[Speak with priests and men of religion for advice in their churches; so be in the habit, for their honor and yours, of having them come to your house as seldom as you can.]

Stripped of a smart appearance, these widows don the sad and heavy mask of mature age. The windows and doors of their dwellings put a barrier between them and the outside world. They are counseled to appear as seldom as possible at the window.

> ... Alle finestre
> O per le vie rade volte si truovi;
>
> (237–38, ll. 29–30)

[Seldom should you find yourself at your windows or out of doors.]

The doors seem to be the guardians of an always-menaced honor. They open just a crack, to allow the poor to pass through.

> Faccia serrar le suo' porti per tempo,
> Ettardi avrire; e cautamente guardi
> Che non s'inchiuda lo serpente in casa.
> Limosiniera lei convien chessia,
> Ma guardi chi le vien però in casa.
>
> (238, ll. 44–48)

[Keep your doors locked all the time, and open them hesitantly; and cautiously watch that the serpent isn't closed up in the house. Giving alms is a good idea, but be careful who enters the house.]

The perils against which the widow is warned to be on her guard are of a moral order especially. She does not personally have to confront events that thrust her onto the stage of a social or political life in which her role might compare with that of a man. Such an eventuality is not envisaged by Barberino, not even for the widow of high rank, whose sphere of activity will remain very limited. Scarcely anything is asked of her but to put herself wisely in the hands of officials who will act for her. It is useful to note that the verbs *choose, place, create,* and *find,* are used constantly to designate the princess's responsibilities [*elegga, ponga, faccia uficiali, truovi, chosi*].

Successfully choosing the members of her council, the agents of her lands, and especially the man who will take the place of her son (233, ll. 35–46)—those summarize the almost unique activities constituting the political duty of the widowed sovereign. Her competence and her prudence will be judged by the number of qualified dignitaries that she has designated to govern in her stead.

> E tanti e tali attutti ufici ponga,
> Che non bisongni lei di que' pensare.
>
> (232–33, ll. 33–34)

[And put in charge only those whom you do not need to watch over.]

The following comparison of two short passages from Barberino with one of Christine's is interesing because of their remarkably similar advice to widows on the choice and maintenance of personnel.

Del Reggimento

> Ma sovra tutti truovi un *principale,*
> Acchui melglio convengnia tal uficio,
> Il qual tenga de' suoi filgluoli il loco;
> E, *mentre dura buono, honori lui;*
> Quando *faciesse il contrario,* il rimuova.
> . . . *Ponga fedele e cauta giente e buona,*
> Loro e tutti altri *riciercando* spesso;
>
> (233, ll. 35–39, 49–50)

[But over all these offices find an overseer who is best suited for this position, and who would take the place of her sons. And so long as he does well, honor him. When and if he does the opposite, remove him. . . . Engage faithful, careful, and honest people, often questioning them and all the others.]

Le Livre des Trois Vertus

Si mandera tantost les principaulx de ses hommes et aussi tous les prevosts et baillis de ses chastellenies, si vouldra savoir par *bonne enqueste* comment ilz se sont portéz le temps passé; et s'ilz sont preu-dommes s'informera des coustumes du païs. Et se *yceulx officiers sont bons ilz ne se bougeront*, et | se *mauvais sont les ostera* et mettra nouveaulx de qui elle aura bonne relacion. (Bk. 1, chap. 23, [86])

[Immediately she will summon her chief men, as well as all the marshals and bailiffs of her properties. She will inquire thoroughly how they have conducted themselves in the past, and if they are trustworthy she will ask them about the local customs. And if the officials are good, they will not be dismissed; if they are bad, she will remove them and replace them with men of whom she will have good report.]

Christine de Pizan

Christine, too, stresses withdrawal, that caution necessary to widows in many situations: these are defensive stances, justified by woman's multiple inferiorities in the social world. She refers specifically, moreover, to the difficulties that the customs of the time entail for women.[10]

The widow who is a princess and *young* remains, for all practical purposes, under the constant tutelage of those around her. But the constraints to which she submits are not nearly as rigorous as those that inhibit Barberino's widow. The most one must do in Christine's view is to avoid numerous visits by men. The precautions that the young woman takes have no other function than to assure her tranquility and good reputation. She is not forbidden peaceful pleasures, games, or conversations; the enthusiasms of youth, to which she might give herself in private, are not eliminated as long as she adopts a respectable demeanor and a reserved attitude (Bk. 1, chap. 23).

The *widow of modest rank* has no better arm against the cruelty of those who want to crush her than the silence of her house. That strategic isolation is proof of wisdom. Opposed to *fouler* [to trample underfoot, hence, to ruin] is *eschiver* [to avoid, flee from]. These verbs, repeated in a chiasmus, open and close a short passage on the benefits of retreat.

> ... que vous avisiez par bonne prudence et sage gouvernement comment vous vous deffendrez de ceulz qui trop vous vouldront *fouler:* c'est assavoir que vous *eschivez* leur compagnie, ne avoir que faire avec eulx se vous pouez; vous tenir closement en voz hostelz, ne prendre debat a voisin ne a un ne aultre, ne meismes a varlet ne a chamberiere; tousjours parler bel et garder vostre droit,—et par ainsi faire, et par pou vous mesler avec diverses gens se besoing ne vous en est, | *eschiverez* que vous ne soiez *folees* ne suppeditees par aultrui. (Bk. 3, chap. 4, [190])

> [... that you learn through prudence and wise governance how to defend yourself against those only too willing *to trample you under-foot:* that is, you must *avoid* their company, have nothing to do with them if you can, stay privately in your own house, not involving yourself in an argument with a neighbor, not even with a servant or chambermaid. Always speak graciously and look after your rights— by so doing and by not mixing with various people unless you must, you will *avoid* being taken advantage of or *ruined* by others.]

In any case, consideration of concrete social conditions in the *Trois Vertus* serves *action* more than it does *passivity*. Barberino does not do that; he situates his counsel much more in the absolute, even though he is sketching a picture of contemporary Italian customs.[11] In Christine's work, the steps recommended to widows are often very precise; even women of the middle class are advised to fight for their rights. That fight supposes courage, knowledge, and the sort of initiative that are very often identical to those of men (Bk. 3, chap. 4).

Knowledge
Thus, the multiplicity of activities required demands a knowledge that widows either possess or must possess. Competence of that kind is not absent from the model proposed to the *middle-class widow* who will have to defend herself before the law, in spite of all the difficulties that such an enterprise can have for a woman (ignorance and the necessity

to entrust oneself to others, others' bad faith in regard to the widow).
But the lady is invited to fight like a man: she will consult men of law,
watch closely over the progress of her case, and she will defend herself
and respond aggressively, should the situation demand it.

> Si lui convendra bien pour ces choses faire, et pour resister a tous les
> autres enuis se a chief en veult venir, que *elle prengne cuer d'omme,*
> *c'est assavoir constant, fort et sage,* pour avisier et pour poursuivre
> ce qui lui est bon a faire, ... (Bk. 3, chap. 4, [191–92])

[In order to do these things, and to avoid all further trouble so as to
succeed, she will have to take on the heart of a man, that is, a constant, strong, and wise heart, for taking counsel and for pursuing
what is good for her.]

Christine will deal rapidly with the case of women of the *petty and*
middle nobility who administer their own property.

> ... et que elle *sache* tout le fait de son gouvernement, si que dit est
> devant, des le vivant de son mary, c'est afin que se veuve demouroit,
> que elle ne fust pas trouvee ignorant de *savoir* son estre, si que chascun
> la voulsist foler et enporter sa piece. (Bk. 2, chap. 9, [152])

[And let her *be informed* about governing, as described above, while
her husband is alive so that, if she becomes a widow, she won't be
lacking in *knowledge* about her situation, so that others will cheat her
and take away her portion.]

But the necessity for *competence* is especially evident in the case of the
princess, who will be a woman of *grant savoir* [great knowledge]. The
address concerning high-ranking widows is very revealing. The princess
will not only ask for advice; she *will know.* The use of words like *wise,*
knowledge, prudent, and of the verb *to know* is particularly pertinent.

> Et pour ce, la dame qui sera toute *sage,* sera si bonne moyenne entre
> eulx par son *prudent* maintien et savoir—pensant le mal qui pourroit
> venir de leurs debas, veu son enfant encores joenne—que bien les
> *saura apaisier.* (Bk. 1, chap. 22, [84–85])

[The *wise* lady will be such a good mediator by her *prudent* conduct and her *knowledge* that she will *know how* to reconcile them, as she keeps in mind the trouble that could come from their quarrels, considering the youth of her child.]

In case of war,

... bien aura besoing la *prudent* dame qui desirera garder le bien de ses enfans, | qu'elle mette a oeuvre son grant *savoir*. (Bk. 1, chap. 22, [85])

[The *prudent* lady wishing to protect her children's rights must employ her very great *wisdom*.]

Prudence

Everything occurs as if the widowed sovereign were the custodian of a perfect wisdom, acquired in the course of lessons from Prudence, whose commandments she has progressively assimilated since childhood. The chapters devoted to the reigning princess serve as a conclusion to Prudence's admonitions.[12] The noble lady has both experience and a body of knowledge, which allow her to govern. The order of the widow's activities follows broadly the order of Prudence's teachings.

I. Lessons of Wordly Prudence (Bk. 1: 7 teachings)
   A. The family
      1. Chap. 13: Attitude toward the husband, first teaching.
      2. Chap. 14: Attitude toward the husband's relatives, second teaching.
      3. Chap. 15: Education of children, third teaching.
   B. The outside world: a "wise conduct"
      1. Chap. 16: Attitude toward ill-intentioned subjects, fourth teaching.
      2. Chap. 17: How to earn the affection of one's subjects, fifth teaching.
   C. A wise government
      1. Chap. 19: Finances, sixth teaching.
      2. Chap. 20: Generosity of the princess, seventh teaching.
II. Duties of the Widowed Princess (Bk. 1, chaps. 22–23, [82–90])
   A. The family
      1. Duties toward the deceased husband

2. Duties toward the children
3. Duties toward the husband's relatives
B. The outside world: a wise government
    1. The defense of rights: a politics of gentleness
    2. How to *tenir en amour* one's subjects[13] [keep one's subjects loyal] in order to maintain peace
       a. How to reduce one's enemies to silence
    3. Administrative and financial problems
       a. The fight against dishonest tax collectors
       b. The generosity of the princess

Action and Language

The widow of high status must find good servants who will support her but who will not exercise the prerogatives of power in her place. She will herself act, hence the use of verbs indicating effort: *si mettra toute peine* [she will take pains to], *prendra grant cure* [will take great care to], *s'en travaillera* [she will work at], *avisera* [will consider], *engardant et deffendant son droit* [protecting and defending her right] (Bk. 1, chap. 12). She will act upon men and things. The program imposed upon the widowed sovereign is coherent to the extent that her prudence rests upon the powers of speech. The princess will know how to speak to family members and to quarreling barons, in order to keep peace among them. She will speak to everyone—knights, noblemen, the people—and she will obtain their assistance when circumstances turn against her.

The words she utters, eminently effective, have as their essential attributes *reason* and *love*. If the *logos* is the expression of a commanding political wisdom, it is even more the *doulce parole* [kind word] that speaks of and inspires love.[14]

> ... parlera a eulx maintes foiz par bel, en disant par doulces paroles qu' il ne leur vueille anuier se adonc sont aucunement grevéz pour les grans charges de la guerre ou d'autres affaires,...(Bk. 1, chap. 22, [85])

> [... she will speak to them kindly, saying, with kind words, that she hopes no harm will come to them if they are sometimes afflicted by the great burdens of war or of other matters, ...]

As such, her speech is presented not as the political instrument of a sovereign who, because she is a woman, is weak, but perhaps, on the contrary, as a way of assuring a peaceful government when seignorial unkindness, more readily imagined to be masculine, evilly pushes the people toward discontent and revolt.

> Et telz manieres de *paroles* leur *dira* la sage princepce qui pourront estre valables | en tel cas, car ce les esmouvra a plus voulentiers y mettre du leur et a les garder de rebellion, lesquelles rebellions avien-nent le plus souvent en peuple par estre trop oppresséz de seigneur et menéz par *rudesce*. Et n'est pas doubte que estre extimé ne pourroit le bien que telle princepce peut faire en royaume ou contree. (Bk. 1, chap. 22, [86])

> [The wise princess *will speak* to them using *words* that are useful in such cases, for that will move them to give of themselves more will-ingly, and it will keep them from rebelling. Rebellions occur most often when the people are oppressed by their lord and ruled in an *unkind way*. There is no doubt that the good done by such a princess for the kingdom or for the country would be inestimable.]

The importance given to the word very narrowly recalls what Christine de Pizan will say elsewhere about the exemplary sovereign or about great heads of state, such as Charles V, noteworthy for an elo-quence that is counted among the essential political instruments. From the all-powerful *logos* emanates the right order in families, in society, and in the kingdom, so much so that the ideal of the widowed sovereign in the end differs very little from what will be the ideal of a *great king*, who reigns through the strength of his speech.[15]

Communication

The *Reggimento* and the *Trois Vertus* are presented as addresses made by characters in the text, the author himself in the first case, allegorical figures in the second. It is nevertheless fruitful to examine closely who is speaking, and to whom, in each of the two *Instructions to Widows*.

Francesco da Barberino

From beginning to end, the *Reggimento* is relentless in casting the poet as a player in the text. He is the one who says "I" in order to address the reader and at the same time the one who is designated by his own name. He is the subject, both in the speeches to the reader and in the prayers to Madonna.

Francesco and his audience

Francesco summons a fictitious reader to view the staging of a painful sadness, the object of a detailed description. The drama of widowhood upsets a woman's personality, and her appearance and bearing change fiercely. Direct appeals to the listening audience give more pathos to the story. Francesco talks to his reader in order to evoke pity for the widow, represented in the company of *Costanza*, in the miniature of his manuscript.

> Priegovi che guardiate suo'fighura,
> E quella di Costanza,
> E udiate il gran pianto
> Che questa donna fa del suo marito.
>
> (204, ll. 16–19)

[I request that you look upon the depiction of this woman, and upon that of Constancy, and that you listen to the profound tears of this woman for her husband.]

Verbs of the senses, used in the imperative form, and repeated like a litany—*vedi, vedi, ascolta ed odi*—punctuate the description of tears and cries (204–5).

The work of writing never ceases to be brought into question by the interventions of the writer, who comments upon his role as author/actor within the space of the story. Like the leader of the chorus in classical drama, Francesco speaks monologues in a stage whisper and, at the same time, witnesses the drama that he is in the midst of creating. Sometimes he leaves the stage, suspending his narration just at the most emotional moment, in order to fly away toward Madonna. The widow's sadness and her retirement give the poet a pretext for his departure.

Udite *io* tutte queste e molt' altre
Paro[l]e, pensando che nanzi che questa
Donna si possa ben raconsolare,
Passerà molti giorni; . . .
. . . e disiderando *io*
Dopo tanto dolor recreare alquanto:
Muo[v] omi da questa contrada, ed intendo
Di ciercar tanto, ch'i truo[v]i la mia donna;

(211–12, ll. 1–4, 7–10)

[Having heard all these and many other words, I realize that many days will pass before this woman can console herself . . . and I, desiring after so much pain to recreate the same: I am leaving this countryside and intend to search until I find my lady.]

Digressions in the first person thus play the role of a hinge between the story proper and the mystical quest.

The author interrupts the instructions to widows with thoughts about the organization and interest of his work. These preoccupations of an aesthetic order lead Barberino to prohibit from his narrative certain teachings already present in the *Documenti d'Amore,* and to abridge tiresome developments.[16]

Chè poner qui d'ongni cosa trattato
Temo non men di dispiacier di troppo,
Che blasmo aver di manco o difetto:
Tant'è la giente acconcia a poco bene.

(234–35, ll. 89–92)

[For me to write down here everything I have discussed I fear no less than the intemperate displeasure of others and the blame for errors or defects: So much are people prepared for little good.]

Francesco and the Virtues

In the dialogues with the allegorical Piatate and Cortezia, the character of Francesco is presented by name and according to his function

Francesco sono

(213, l. 14)

[I am Francis];

"Donzelle, i' son ben un che faccio un libro"

(214, l. 19)

[Young ladies, I am actually one who is putting together a book.]

before evoking the difficulties of his work in a personal mode. The preface of the *Reggimento* is constructed around the theme of the command to carry out the work by human means, thus necessarily limited ones for a celestial power. But that theme continues throughout the book, so much that the object of the narration becomes a meditation on the work in progress and on woman. Situated at a point of juncture for the two characteristics of *language*—divine by its inspiration, human or popular by its destination [*E parlerai sol nel volgar toscano; Del Reggimento*, 15, l. 39]—the author takes on the figure of a hero: he possesses the power of the explanatory *word*, a privilege conceded to him by Madonna.

Madonna, or qui non so io ch'io mi *parli;*
Vinto m'avete nella prima giunta,
Vinto m'avete più poi nel parlare.

(220, ll. 141–43)

[My lady, at this moment I do not know what I am saying; you have defeated me on the first encounter. You have defeated me even more in speech.][17]

The poet takes up his quest by celebrating the link, made by faith and love, that he enjoys with the celestial personifications who associate him with the world of supreme truths. It is in Francesco that the quality of wisdom will burst forth.

Tu mi *parl'* ora sicome *savio*

(221, l. 148)

[You speak to me now like a sage.]

Christine de Pizan

The address of the *Three Virtues,* on the contrary, leaves little place to the character of the author. Of course, the allegorical figures who say "we" speak as *subjects,* as an ordinary intervention about the organization of the treatise shows.

> Pour rendre nostre oeuvre plus accomplie au prouffit de tous les estas des femmes, parlerons aux veuves des communs estas, . . . (Bk. 3, chap. 4, [188])

> [In order to make our work more complete and beneficial to all ranks of women, we will speak to widows of the common estate.]

It is the three *Virtues,* or their deputies Charity and Prudence, who take charge of instructing widows. That subject of the narrative opens the chapters, assures transitions, and apportions the teachings.

> Parlé avons. (Bk. 1, chap. 22, [82])

> [We have spoken.]

> Si dirons ainsi. (Bk. 1, chap. 22, [82–83])

> [We will say thus.]

> Si dirons un petit, puis qu'entrees sommes, au propos de la joenne princepce veuve; et puis dirons de joennes máriees. (Bk. 1, chap. 23, [89])

> [We will speak a while, since we have begun the matter, about the young widowed princess, and then we will speak of young married women.]

In another instance an *I,* which seems to be a *lapsus,* reveals the personal author under the allegorical trio. Christine forgets the fictitious "we" of the allegories making the address, while citing princesses already evoked in other parts of the treatise, or in other works.

Ces voies bonnes et convenables sceurent bien tenir les tres nobles
roynes de France et princepces en leur veuvage, que j'ay cy devant
nommees, ... (Bk. 1, chap. 23, [88])

[The very noble queens and princesses of France, whom I named
before, knew how to keep to these good and appropriate paths in their
widowhood, ...]

That lapsus may underline the small importance of this character—be it
Virtue or *Author*—to whom the responsibility for instruction falls. The
character never takes itself to be the object of its own discourse and stays
discreetly in the background, as if to leave in the light the lesson being
enunciated.

The quite opposite traits of the two texts must not mask the fact that
the *subjectivity* of the *Reggimento* is of a very special nature. On the one
hand, the author, who inserts himself into his work, and under his own
name, speaks about the attributes of his "charge," without there being
anything truly personal in it. If Barberino talks about a "here" and a
"now," the place and time of writing, nevertheless that localization has
nothing at all individual about it. The subjectivity that is so openly staged
remains abstract. And on the other hand, the didactic discourse itself has
no explicit relation to a real experience, at least in the chapters that are
of interest here. The narrative is atemporal, like the celestial truths of
which it is the translation.

The *Trois Vertus* proceeds quite differently. In it very clear allusions
appear to a time, a country, a society. The models cited are historical
figures (the queens Jeanne and Blanche), and the customs criticized are
those of contemporary France.

Si ne voldra nullement que ses prevostéz soyent baillees pour argent
aux plus offrans et derreniers encherissans, si comme on fait commun-
ement maintenant en France, et pour ce a eu telz sieges en assés de
lieux de tres mauvaise ribaudaille, mengeurs de gens et pires que
larrons, car il n'est mauvaistié qu'ilz ne facent pour tirer argent. Et se
nous disons voir, l'experience commune le certifie. (Bk. 1, chap. 23,
[86–87])

[She will not want her offices sold to the highest bidder, as is commonly done now in France—the reason why such high seats are occu-

pied widely by riffraff who swallow people up and who are worse than thieves, for there is nothing they won't do for money. The truth we speak is verified by everyday experience.]

The experience described is, indeed, one that Christine shares with her French public. The very precise nature of the instructions given by the Three Virtues multiplies opportunities for such comments, in particular about the sphere of the judiciary.

> ... l'autre que il convient que elle se mette en dongier d'autrui pour faire solliciter ses besoignes, et gens sont communement mal diligens des besoingnes aux femmes et voulentiers les trompent et mettent en despens .viii. sols pour .vi.; et l'autre qu'elle n'y puet a toutes heures aler comme feroit un home, et pour ce est le meilleur conseil que elle laisse avant aler aucune partie de son droit, mais que ce ne soit a trop grant oultraige que elle s'i fiche. (Bk. 3, chap. 4, [190])

[Further, she must risk putting herself in the hands of others who will solicit on behalf of her needs, and people are commonly negligent about womens' needs, tricking them willfully, and charging them 8 for 6. Further, she may not come and go at all hours like a man and so the best advice is that she relinquish part of what is due her, as long as doing so doesn't cause her very great harm.][18]

Certain elements individualize the address even more because they are about *feelings* rather than *knowledge*. That is especially so for certain images, with emotional value, that go far beyond the common attitudes of pity and lament. Thus, all the *tres mauvaise ribaudaille,* the riffraff who purchase offices, are never described except in terms that translate indignation and anger. In another vein, when the middle-class widow is being advised to defend herself, that is done through strong comparisons that show the humiliation suffered by the resigned woman.

> ... non mie comme simple femme s'acroupir en pleurs et larmes sans autre deffense, comme un povre chien qui s'aculle en un coignet et tous les autres lui cuerent sus. (Bk. 3, chap. 4, [192])

[... not as a simple woman cringing in tears and weeping, without defense, like a poor dog who cowers in a corner while all the others attack him.]

Against that discreet but clear personal note from the author there is, at another pole of the communication, a certain representation of the intended public: it is much more consistent in the *Three Virtues* than in the *Reggimento*. To be sure, in his preface, Francesco is aiming at a female public for whom his teaching, because it is written in the vernacular, will be accessible. But in the course of the teaching itself, the person addressed remains indistinct. The author deals with the problem of widowed women but he does not speak to them directly, evoking them in general only in the third person. That style is equally frequent in the *Three Virtues*. However, in the advice given to middle-class widows, the second person dominates. When questioned, these women clearly become the principal recipients of the instruction, instead of simply being its object. In the most touching moments, apostrophe is frequent.

Car par ainsi faire *entre vous, femmes,* trouveriez assez de gens sans pitié qui le pain vous osteroient de la main et vous reputeroit on ignorans et simples, ne ja pour ce plus de pitié ne trouverez en ame. (Bk. 3, chap. 4, [192])

[For in so doing, *dear women,* you would find many pitiless people who would snatch the bread from your hands. They would think you ignorant and simple, nor would a single one of them pity you the more for that.]

That form of challenge underlines the most important part of the advice given: women are invited to take matters into their own hands for their own protection. The apostrophe, in the *second person* and in the *plural,* is doubly the opposite of the third-person subjunctive categorical injunctions that are almost constant in Barberino. Widows are, thus, collectively granted the dignity of a veritable social category—which no doubt signifies that woman is no longer thought of exclusively or especially in the isolation of her private life, and no longer is she thought the better for being more retiring. Wisdom demands that she fight on the stage of the world against the dangers that menace all women who are alone, whatever their individual qualities may be.

The didactic, particularly moral, discourse can attest only to an absolute confidence in its own utility and truth. Without that double certitude what would be left of the genre? That is perhaps the origin of the traditional recourse to allegory, whose function seems most of all to be that of guaranteeing, through the symbol, the authenticity of what is said, of what the personality of the individual author would be insufficient to establish.

Compared with the *Reggimento,* Christine de Pizan's treatise seems slim from that point of view. Its mystical inspiration is singularly reduced, to the point where the *Three Virtues* differs little from a discourse whose human origin is clear. Yet its tone is assured and commanding. For, corresponding to the weakening of divine caution, is a validation of another sort, one that is based upon the will to adapt a doctrine closely, making it a lesson for a public composed of women in a society at a specific historical moment. Whether that realistic and utilitarian project achieves more or less exactitude in describing the social categories it aims at is not at issue here. Its ambition rests upon a notably solid belief in an efficient word that is less the translation of immutable celestial truths than a human instrument formed by reflection and experience. In that way, the didactic discourse of the writer, Christine de Pizan, is related to the political eloquence of the prince himself.

NOTES

Translated from "Inspiration mystique et savoir politique: les conseils aux veuves chez Francesco da Barberino et chez Christine de Pisan," first published in *Mélanges à la mémoire de Franco Simone: France et Italie dans la culture européenne, I Moyen Age et Renaissance,* Bibliothèque Franco Simone, vol. 4 (Geneva: Slatkine, 1980), 113–41. Translations from Italian were kindly provided by Wayne Storey.

1. All references are to the 1875 edition of *Del Reggimento e Costumi* (Baudi di Vesme); I was not able to consult regularly the 1957 edition by Sansone. Da Barberino's work may have been written toward 1324–25. [Christine de Pizan wrote the *Trois Vertus* in 1405.—*Trans.*] Consult the bibliography at the end of this essay for studies devoted to Francesco da Barberino. The reader may profitably consult the pages devoted to Francesco da Barberino in *Grundriss der Romanischen Literaturen des Mittelalters,* Heidelberg, 1 (1968): 94–96; 2 (1970): 138–41.

I am deeply grateful to my colleagues Marthe Molinari and Jean Lacroix, professors at the Université Paul Valéry de Montpellier, for having given me access to works written in Italian. Jean Lacroix read my translation of several chapters from the *Del Reggimento* with constant and generous care, and he initiated me into the thought of the Italian poet.

2. All references are to Christine de Pizan, *Le Livre des Trois Vertus,* ed. Charity Cannon Willard, text established with Eric Hicks. For information concerning *The Book of the Three Virtues* and the role of women, consult the bibliography.

3. See *Del Reggimento,* ed. Baudi di Vesme, Parte Sesta, Parte Settima, 203–49. I will be concerned more particularly with the sixth part, 203–42. Also see F. da Barberino, *Del Reggimento,* ed. Sansone, Parte Sesta, 116–40, Parte Settima, 141–45; Christine de Pizan, *Le Livre des Trois Vertus,* pt. 1, chaps. 22–23, pt. 2, chap. 9, pt. 3, chap. 4.

4. "Vienten con noi per questa selva schura," 215, l. 40 [Come away with us through this dark wood]; "Quanto ancor dura questa selva amara?" 218, l. 86 [How much more is there to this bitter wood?]

5. Francesco da Barberino, *Documenti d'Amore,* pars secunda, reg. 9, pars tertia, Constantia, 303–46.

6. Cited text is taken from ms. 1528 of the Boston Public Library, the manuscript used by Willard and Hicks for their edition. I thank them for having made available to me a copy of their manuscript transcription. Page numbers from their edition appear in brackets following the book and chapter numbers from the *Trois Vertus.* [*Translator's Note:* translations into English from the *Trois Vertus* are my own but they have benefited from Professor Willard's translation, *A Medieval Woman's Mirror of Honor.* I thank Professor Willard for having given me access to the translation while it was still in the proof stage.]

7. The widowhood theme is central in Christine de Pizan's writing. See the following in particular:

Le Livre de la Mutacion de Fortune: vol. 1, 1959, ll. 1159–1460; vol. 3, 1964, ll. 6989–7052 (the widow and lawsuits)

Le Livre de la Cité des Dames: The Book of the City of Ladies, trans. E. J. Richards (New York: Persea, 1982): Empress Nicole, 32–33; Queen Fredegonde, 33–34; Queen Blanche, mother of St. Louis, 34; Queen Jeanne d'Evreux, wife of Charles IV le Bel, 34; her daughter, Blanche of France, wife of Phillip, Duke of Orleans, 34; Blanche of Navarre, wife of Phillip VI of Valois (Christine writes in error that Blanche is the wife of King John), 34; Marie of Blois, wife of Louis I of Anjou, 34–35; Beatrice, Countess of La Marche, wife of Jacques II of Bourbon, 35

Le Livre des fais et bonnes meurs du sage roy Charles V (cf. notes and alphabetic table II, 219–77): Semiramis, Bk. 1, chap. 15, fol. 12v–13; Fredegonde, Bk. 1, chap. 23, fol. 19a–v; Scismonde, daughter of the Prince of Salerno, Bk. 2, chap. 55, fol. 60–62; general advice to women of all ranks, Bk. 3, chap. 18, fol. 78v–79.

L'Avision-Christine: First part: Complaint of an Allegorical Figure, *Libéra,* the Crowned Lady, 95, who says, "I am like the widow, abandoned by her father, whom everyone attacks and no one pities." (I thank Christine Reno for having brought the theme of the allegorical Widow to my attention.) Third part: 154 (widowhood, lawsuits): "And then vexations leapt at me from everywhere, and, just as this is the food of widows, litigation and lawsuits surround me on all sides"; 159, ballade, ll. 1–2: "Alas, where then will poor widows find comfort, stripped of their holdings?" On Christine's lawsuits, see *Le Livre des Fais et Bonnes Meurs du Sage Roy Charles V, 1, XVI–XVII* (introduction by the editor, S. Solente).

8. Cf. *La Cité des Dames,* Bk. 1, chap. 13: *La royne Jehanne:* Jeanne d'Evreux; *La royne Blanche:* Blanche of Navarre[?]; *La duchesse d'Orleans:* Blanche of France, wife of Phillip, Duke of Orleans.

9. Mombello, "Quelques aspects"; Gauvard, "Christine de Pisan."

10. A number of works contain information about women and widowhood in the Middle Ages: see Bouteillier, *Somme Rural; Le Songe du Vergier;* De Montaiglon, ed., *Le Livre du Chevalier* (on widowhood: 220–24). Some recent critical works include: Bell, *Women;* Metz, "Le Statut de la femme"; Rosambert, *La Veuve en droit canonique;* Stuard, ed., *Women in Medieval Society.*

11. On women and widowhood in Italy, see Cecchetti, "La donna"; Chojnacki, "Patrician Women"; Ercole, "L'Istituto," esp. 190–257; Rossi, "Statut juridique"; Tamassia, *La Famiglia Italiana,* esp. 325–59.

12. Bk. 1, chap. 23, [89]: "Et cy est la fin des enseignemens que Prudence donne a la sage princesse, qui est en eage de congnoistre le bien et le mal" [And this is the end of the teaching that Prudence gives to the wise princess who is old enough to know good and evil.] See Brucker, "Prudentia/Prudence."

13. Cf. *Le Livre des fais et bonnes meurs du sage roy Charles V,* Book 2, pt. 3, 8: The passage at 28–30, which begins as follows, is to be compared with the chapters devoted to the widowed princess: "cy dit comment le roy Charles tenoit ses subgiez en amour et preuves que ainsi doie estre fait" [here it is told how King Charles kept his subjects loyal and it is shown that it must be done thus].

14. Concerning gentleness in speech, see *Le Livre du chemin de long estude,* ll. 5655–5704.

15. On language, see *Le Livre du corps de policie,* Bk. 1, chap. 25, 80–83; *Le Livre de la paix,* 165–69.

16. See for example 204, l. 28, and 234, ll. 75–85.

17. Translation suggested by my colleague, M. Jean Lacroix: "Madonna, à présent en ces lieux, je ne sais qui parle par ma bouche" [l. 141]. "Vous m'avez ensuite bien davantage vaincu par votre parler" [l. 143].

18. Cf. *La Mutacion de Fortune,* Bk. 3, ll. 6989–7052.

BIBLIOGRAPHY

Bell, S. G. *Women from the Greeks to the French Revolution: A Historical Anthology.* Los Angeles, 1973.

———. "Christine de Pizan (1364–1430): Humanism and the Problem of a Studious Woman." *Feminist Studies* 3 (1976): 173–84.

Bibliothèque de l'Arsenal (Paris). Ms. 3356.

Bibliothèque Nationale [BN]. Ms. BN ff. 452.

———. Mss. BN ff. 1091, 1177, 1180, 22937, 25294.

Bouteillier, J. *Somme Rural.* Ms. BN ff. 21010.

Brucker, Ch. "Prudentia/Prudence aux XIIe et XIIIe siècle." *Romanische Forschungen* 83 (1971): 464–79.

Carstens-Grokenberger, D. *Buch von den drei Tugenden in portugiesischen Uebersetzung.* Münster, 1961.

Cecchetti, B. "La donna nel Medioevo a Venezia." *Archivio Veneto* 31 (1886): 33–69, 307–49.

Chojnacki, S. "Patrician Women in Early Renaissance Venice." *Studies in the Renaissance* 21 (1974): 176–203.

da Barberino, Francesco. *Del Reggimento e Costumi di Donna.* Per cura del Conte C. Baudi di Vesme. Collezione di Opere Inedite o Rare. Bologna, 1875.

———. *Documenti d'Amore.* Rome, 1905–27.

———. *Reggimento e Costumi di Donna.* ed. G.E. Sansone. Collezione di "Filologia Romanza," no. 2. Turin, 1957.

De Montaiglon, A., ed. *Le Livre du Chevalier de la Tour Landry.* Paris, 1854.

de Pisan [Pizan], Christine. *L'Avision-Christine.* Ed. Sister M. L. Towner. Washington, D.C.: Catholic University of America, 1932.

———. *Le Livre du Chemin de long estude.* Ed. R. Püschel. Berlin, 1881.

———. *Le Livre de la Cité des Dames.* Ms. BN ff. 607.

———. *Le Livre du corps de policie.* Ed. R. H. Lucas. Geneva, 1967.

———. *Le Livre des fais et bonnes meurs du sage roy Charles V.* 2 vols. Ed. Suzanne Solente. Paris, 1936–40.

———. *Le Livre de la Mutacion de Fortune.* Ed. Suzanne Solente. Paris, 1959.

———. *Le Livre de la paix.* Ed. Charity C. Willard. The Hague, 1958.

———. *Livre des Trois Vertus.* Ed. Charity C. Willard with Eric Hicks. Paris, 1989.

———. *The Medieval Woman's Mirror of Honor: The Treasury of the City of Ladies.* Ed. Madeleine Cosman and trans. Charity C. Willard. New York, 1989.

Ercole, F. "L'Istituto dotale nella pratica e nella legislazione statutaria dell'Italia superiore." *Rivista italiana per la scienze giuridiche* 45 (1908): 191–302; 46 (1910): 167–257.

Finkel, H. "The Portrait of the Woman in the Works of Christine de Pisan." Ph.D. diss., Rice University, 1972.

Gauvard, Claude. "Christine de Pisan a-t-elle eu une pensée politique? A propos d'ouvrages récents." *Revue Historique* 250 (1973): 417–30.

Grundriss der Romanischen Literaturen des Mittelalters, Heidelberg, 1 (1968): 94–96; 2 (1970): 138–41.

Hentsch, A. *De la Littérature didactique du Moyen-Age s'adressant particulièrement aux femmes.* Halle, 1903.

Laigle, M. *Le Livre des Trois Vertus de Christine de Pisan et son milieu historique et littéraire.* Bibliothèque du XVe siècle, vol. 16. Paris, 1912.

Le Songe du Vergier. Ms. BN ff. 24290.

Lorcin, Marie-Thérése. "Les échos de la mode dans le *Livre des Trois Vertus* de Christine de Pizan: Le corps paré, ornements et atours." *Razo* (Nice) 7 (1987): 89–94.

———. "Pouvoirs et contre-pouvoirs dans le *Livre de Trois Vertus.*" *Revue des Langues Romanes* 92 (1988): 359–68.

Metz, R. "Le Statut de la femme en droit canonique médiéval." *Recueils de la Société Jean Bodin* 12 (1962): 59–113.

Mombello, G. "Quelques aspects de la pensée politique de Christine de Pizan d'après ses oeuvres publiées." In *Culture et politique en France à l'époque de l'Humanisme et de la Renaissance,* 43–153. Accademia delle Scienze di Torino, 1971.

Monfrin, J. Review of Francesco da Barberino, *Reggimento e Costumi di Donna* (Edizione critica a cura di G. E. Sansone). *Le Moyen Age* (Brussels) 13 (1958): 606–11.

Reno, Christine MacArdle. "Self and Society in L'Avision-Christine of Christine de Pizan." Ph.D. diss., Yale University, 1972.

Rosambert, A. *La Veuve en droit canonique jusqu'au XVIe siècle.* Paris, 1923.

Rossi, G. "Statut juridique de la femme dans l'histoire du droit italien," *Recueils de la Société Jean Bodin* 12 (1962): 115–34.

Solente, Suzanne. *Extrait de l'Histoire Littéraire de la France,* vol. 40. Paris, 1969.

Stuard, Susan Mosher, ed. *Women in Medieval Society.* Philadelphia, 1976.

Tamassia, N. *La Famiglia Italiana nei secoli XV e XVI.* Milan-Palermo-Naples, 1911. Thomas, A. *Francesco da Barberino et la Littérature provençale en Italie au Moyen-Age.* Paris, 1883.

Willard, Charity Cannon. "A Fifteenth Century View of Women's Role in Medieval Society: Christine de Pizan's *Livre des Trois Vertus.*" In *The Role of Women in the Middle Ages,* ed. R. T. Morewedge, 90–120. Albany, 1975.

———. "The Manuscript Tradition of the *Livre des Trois Vertus* and Christine de Pizan's Audience." *Journal of the History of Ideas* 27 (1966): 433–44.

Chapter 11

Why is Doña Endrina a Widow?
Traditional Culture and Textuality in
the *Libro de Buen Amor*

Louise O. Vasvari

The *Don Melón–Doña Endrina* (M-E) episode, the longest passage of the *Libro de Buen Amor* (*LBA*), is a much amplified adaptation of the twelfth-century Latin *Pamphilus* (*PA*). There are two immediately striking innovations in the M-E, whose text is almost double that of the *PA*. The pastoral names of the protagonists, Pamphilus and Galatea, have been discarded in favor of the Spanish vegetal-animal names *Melón* 'melon/badger' and *Endrina* 'sloe plum.' In addition, while the Latin Galatea was a virgin, the Castilian Endrina becomes a widow, with a considerable portion of the amplification focusing on both private and public aspects of her extremely youthful widowhood. Both Endrina's onomastic singularity and her condition as a widow have tended to be interpreted as mutually confirming signs of author "Juan Ruiz's" supposed "realism" or moral and didactic superiority to his Latin model, the so-called elegiacal comedy, which belonged to a literary tradition characterized by cynical plots and much sexual punning.

In this essay, I will explore the connotations of Endrina's widowhood within the *LBA* as well as its extratextual referentiality within a larger poetic tradition. I propose to show that the emphasis on Endrina's marital status is one of the cueing devices (or specific instructions) embedded in the text that signals how the episode was likely to have been interpreted by its contemporary audience, who would have shared the "depth of resonance" of her widowhood, which could not have been arbitrarily suspended by the author.

In the *PA*, the hero, with the aid of an astute old bawd, seduces the rich young virgin Galatea in 780 verses. In the *LBA*, it takes Don Melón, the secular alter ego of the first-person clerical protagonist of the rest of the work, the Archpriest of Hita, twice as many verses to achieve the same end. Much of the expansion is due to the enlarged role of the go-between, here called *Trotaconventos* 'convent-trotter,' who, in the guise of a peddler, visits Endrina on several occasions. Via a dialectic exchange of Aesopic fables with the young widow, the old woman awakens her sexual interest in Don Melón. She convinces Endrina to visit her garden to taste of its fruits and to "play ball." Don Melón soon appears, ready to burst the door down as if he were an animal in heat. He takes the lady by force and she laments her fate to the unsympathetic Trotaconventos, who advises her to keep quiet about it. The tale ends either with the marriage or with the continued relationship of the lovers, depending on how we interpret (891a) *en uno casados son* (v. Corominas).

Although the *M-E*'s basic plot and pseudodramatic structure follow that of the *PA,* it also owes much both to popular and literary tradition, in general, and to the Latin *De Vetula* in particular—in which the lady who is the object of the first-person narrator's passion appears first as a virgin and later as a widow. A comparison of the *De Vetula* and the *LBA* will not only help shed further light on the connotations of Endrina's status but also on the theme of the whole work. I will try to show that these connotations are further reinforced by an analysis of the depiction of other young (and not so young) widows in medieval literature in general, and in the *LBA*'s own mention of widows in several passages. I will also study the traces of oral tradition in the episode. In part because the *M-E*'s basic source is clearly a Latin text, previous critics, beyond noting the bawd Trotaconventos's use of proverbial language, have disregarded the potential influence of traditional sources in the episode. I will try to show that these sources, such as proverbs, traditional lyrics, and other residually oral genres, although not readily discernible to modern readers, were as obvious to the *LBA*'s original, informed audience as the plot outline offered by the Latin text.

Previous scholarship has tended to propose moralizing connections between Endrina's peculiar name and her condition as widow. Spitzer (1934) interpreted the *endrina,* arbitrarily choosing the supposed symbolism of the plant's white flower rather than the ripe fruit's blue-black hue, as an allusion to the lady's innocence, hardly credible of a sexually experienced widow. Lecoy (1974, 318) approved of the transformation in the *LBA* of the heroine from virgin to widow, commenting that it diminished, somewhat, *l'odieux* of the sexually explicit adventure of seduction and rape of the *PA*. More helpful was his observation that it allowed for the bawd Trotaconventos to make some realistic comments about Endrina needing a man's protection.

Lida de Malkiel (1940) was the first to suggest the important potential antecedent for Endrina's widowhood in the tradition of the *Matron of Ephesus*. However, she failed to note the extreme misogyny as well as frequent obscenity of the tales in that tradition, which potentially undermines her claim that the widow Endrina's name was a morally significant symbol for the delicate nature of feminine honor, through which the author sought to orient his public from the beginning to the didactic significance of his characters.[1] Cirot (1943) admired the character of Endrina as an illustration of the superior morals of Spanish womanhood in the early fourteenth century. Similarly, Lázaro Carreter (1951) applauded Endrina's rejection of her suitor's first kiss as an example of "moral muy española." Hart (1959, 95–97) said that Endrina's widowhood represents exactly the opposite of what Lecoy claimed because the Church, although it did not actually prohibit widows from remarrying, did exhort them to lead a life of chastity, contemplation, and devotion dedicated to the memory of their husband. This attitude was symbolized by the turtledove, which was considered the model of fidelity and monogamy. Therefore, Trotaconventos's reference to Endrina as *tortollila* (757ab) is ironic, as Endrina's aversion to remarriage, if real, is based only on the fear of losing her rights of inheritance. Zahareas (1965, 152–58) was the first scholar to point out that, while Galatea is never described, Endrina's portrait is developed both physically and emotionally. Trotaconventos senses that she can exploit the young widow's sexual restlessness when, on her second visit, she calls Endrina *gordilla,* a word with sensual implications. Ferraresi (1976, 235 n. 81), basing her arguments on those of Hart, claimed that the seduction of a widow would have been considered morally even more odious than that of a virgin like Galatea. Gilman (1976) suggested that the widowed heroine is named Endrina because, like the plum, she is covered in black, but did not venture reasons for her widowhood. In a later article (1983), he described the episode as "at once a tender and humorous garden allegory" (247). He did, however, make the important point that "Juan Ruiz's" deviation from tradition consists in exploiting the ambiguous category of widowhood, a category less personal and domestic than social, in that the barriers to a widow's sexual satisfaction are neither a husband, as in the tradition of courtly love, nor virginity, but only public opinion.

While not studying Endrina's widowhood per se, I have tried to show in a recent study (Vasvari 1988) that her name, as well as that of all the other characters in the episode, had not only horticultural but erotic connotations, with roots in traditional culture. If this interpretation is correct, it would discredit the claim that Endrina's characterization as a widow is meant to signal the moral intention of the work, but would still leave open the question of why she was transformed into a widow. In the single most illuminating contribution to date to this puzzle, Rico (1967) demonstrated the probable contamination of the *PA* by the *De Vetula* in a number of the *LBA*'s innovations, including, in the matter of the heroine's widowhood, a connection I will investigate further.

Medieval society was based on distinct estates or orders. These designated a great variety of social functions not limited to class but extended to every group and profession, from estates of the realm, the different orders of chivalry, orders within the Church, the various trades, the state of virginity, matrimony, and widowhood, and even the state of sin. What in medieval society established a unity among these meanings of estate is the belief that they all were part of an immutable institution ultimately divine in origin. While men would be classified according to their class or employment within society (priest or warrior, merchant or student, etc.) women, who did not generally have roles in public life, were classified according to the stages of their private lives: virgins, wives, widows, or nuns. Widowhood constituted a category of relatively enviable legal, economic, and sexual independence in comparison to that of all other women, and hence one of potential threat to the patriarchal social order. In literature, this reality was reduced to two contradictory stereotypes that allowed little latitude for personal invention by authors. They were, on one hand, the depiction of the chaste and disconsolate widow, faithful to the memory of her husband, and, on the other, of the lustful and debauched widow. The former is celebrated in moral tracts and occasionally in the lyric, as in the tradition of the chaste turtledove (see Gericke in this volume).[2] Far more prevalent, however, is the denunciation of widows, a part of the larger medieval misogynist tradition of antifemale and antimatrimonial satire that dominated ecclesiastic, moral, and scientific writing, but also prevalent in the genres of the so-called bourgeois realism, such as the comic tale, the fabliau, and the farce. The widow was, thus, a stock character with an internal coherence that varied only with the genre and type of discourse in which she appeared, and that left little latitude for personal invention of authors.[3]

Widows in Popular and Literary Tradition

The so-called Debate about Women, a conflict between two diametrically opposed attitudes toward women, raged from the time of St. Jerome (ca. 340–420) to the end of the Renaissance. Invectives as well as panegyrics of women were, for the Middle Ages as for Antiquity, *topoi,* which avoided any nuanced aspects of the subject, limiting discussion to one of two opposed opinions, with invective, however, far outnumbering panegyric.[4] The debate takes on new force in the twelfth century, with the idealistic attitude represented in courtly literature, and the antifeminist condemnation both in a serious vein in moralist authors and in humorously obscene works of entertainment, such as the *comedia latina.* With the development of bourgeois literature in the thirteenth century, poems against women seem to proliferate even more, becoming, at the same time, increasingly obscene and crude, as, for example, in the second part of the *Roman de la Rose.* The ambiguous social category of widowhood fares particularly badly, with male fear of vidual sexuality apparent throughout antifeminist literature, so that widows are portrayed almost exclusively in a negative light.

The one genre where widows do tend to be favorably treated is in the stylized debates discussing the relative advantages and disadvantages of sexual relations with women of various conditions, generally classified as virgin, married woman, widow, and nun. The comparative accessibility and sexual ardor of each group was a popular question and is related to other love debates, such as the advantages of a cleric versus a chevalier as lover, or the choice between two or more lovers of differing but equal merit. In these debates, widows are often praised as the best lovers because of their sexual expertise and ease of access.

Probably the single most widespread tale concerning widows is that of the faithless Matron of Ephesus (or *Vidua*), which had a tremendous vogue both in ancient and medieval folk literature, and is still alive in modern oral folklore. In the first century A.D., the story of the widow was already very popular, and versions of it existed in the ancient Orient, from China to India. In the Middle Ages, an eleventh-century collection, the *Romulus Nilantii,* an adaptation of the tale from Petronius's *Satyri-*

con, became the height of popularity with countless manuscripts and early printed versions throughout France, Germany, Italy, and England. The *Romulus* was probably the ultimate partial source for many versions of the story of the widow, including Marie's *Fables,* and other Isopets, Gautier Le Leu's *La Veuve,* and *fabliaux* tales and novelle (see Arden in this volume). The story continued to spread through Western Europe during the Renaissance, with the widow continuing as a stock figure until at least La Fontaine's *la jeune veuve.*

The tale of the widow, stressing the inconstancy of women's emotions and the effects of the deprivation of sex on them, concerns a woman who mourns inconsolably day and night at her husband's grave. Soon, however, she allows herself to be seduced by a guard watching over a hanged man. The body is stolen while the guard is dallying with her, and rather than lose her lover, she offers to substitute her husband's corpse on the gallows. In some earlier versions, the widow is depicted as only human, her only sin being preferring a live lover to a dead husband. In the *Satyricon,* for example, the role of the widow's maid becomes very important in this respect. While the lady is at first inconsolable, it is the maid who has to persuade her to eat and drink a little, with the author adding "now you know what temptations assail poor human nature after a hearty meal." The maid represesents the earthier, naturalistic approach to life, with her exhortation to the widow to begin her life anew and enjoy its pleasures as long as possible. However, in the more misogynist versions, the growing tendency is to portray the widow as totally faithless and depraved, with her depravity symbolized by her willing mutilation of the corpse in order to make it correspond to that of the hanged man. This can range from ripping out all its hair with her hands, knocking out its teeth, or wounding it, to decapitating it, or cutting off its ears or genitals.

In some later medieval tales, the emphasis on ghoulish details is replaced by an ever more insistently obscene description of the widow's uncontrolled sexuality. In *De celle qui se fist foutre sur la fosse de son mari* (Montaiglon-Raynaud 1867, 3:118–22) 'the woman who got herself fucked on top of her husband's grave' (a title so offensive that it was never printed in full until recent editions), a woman makes a tremendous show of a *grant duel,* pulling her hair, saying she will never leave her husband's grave. A *chevalier estraigne* comes by with his squire, with whom he wagers that he can seduce her. He goes up to the grieving widow and tells her that he is in even greater grief because he has accidentally killed his beautiful mistress by too much sex. At this the widow becomes so excited that she immediately lifts her robe, and has him demonstrate his skills right there, hence the title of the tale.

Another extremely obscene tale is Gautier Le Leu's *La Veuve*, whose characterization has been shown to be related to both the *vieille* in the *Roman de la Rose* and to Chaucer's Wife of Bath. Both Gautier's heroine and the Wife are represented as widows, with overdeveloped sexual appetites, who are already eager for remarriage at the funeral of their husbands. *La Veuve* begins with the standard description of the widow's excessive lament, but then goes to a detailed and violently obscene description of her immediate search for a new husband. She loudly proclaims to everyone that she hates old men but is rich enough to buy herself a young husband. However, when she does find one, she soon realizes that even he is unable to satisfy her excessive sexual demands. Similarly, the fourteenth "joy" in the *Quinze Joyes de Marriage* is an obscene portrayal of a widow who remarries and makes her husband's life miserable with her excessive sexual demands.[5]

Another vastly influential work in the depiction of widows is *De Vetula* (Klopsch 1967; Robathan 1968), which figures among the number of pseudo-Ovidian works produced in medieval Latin in the twelfth and thirteenth centuries. Along with the *PA* it seems to be the primary literary source for the *LBA*. The work, a thirteenth-century anonymous pseudoautobiography of Ovid, perhaps produced in France, enjoyed widespread influence, judging by the surviving thirty-nine manuscripts. In book 1 of the vast compilation, devoted to erotic material, the author discusses the comparative advantages of the *virgo, nupta,* and *vidua*. He does not give a preference for one category, but concludes that the lover should try to succeed with whichever one he can. However, Ovid, the pseudoautobiographical narrator, is shown to fail with a virgin and succeed with a widow, the latter the same woman twenty years later.

Among the many other manifestations of the medieval stereotype of the widow I can make only brief mention here, to illustrate not only the pervasiveness of the central motif across languages but also even the constancy of its subtopics, such as, for example, the first sight by the lover of the beautiful young widow dressed in black, or the figure of the confidante who urges the woman to shed her widow's weeds. The excessive preoccupation with the widow's potentially uncontrollable sexuality is most succinctly expressed in the *Testament de l'âne* (Montaiglon and Raynaud 1877, 3:215), a mock testament in which an ass named

Baudoin (a stock fabliau name for 'donkey/penis') leaves various parts of his body to appropriate classes of society, such as unmarried girls, various ranks of clerics, and, among them, widows, to whom he leaves his *priapumque . . . una cum testiculis* 'phallus, along with his testicles.'

The Wife of Bath, one of only three secular women depicted in the *Canterbury Tales,* fits the stereotype of the oversexed widow, from her gap teeth to her overdressing. When, in her lay sermon, she preaches on scriptural opinion regarding sex and marriage, she deliberately subverts the Church's antifeminist authority, ascribing its origin to frustrated clerics. The Wife's autonomy, sexual and economic, depends on the land and property she controls, but, ironically, she has gained it through her sexuality, having been three times widowed and having retained the property of all her husbands. The forty-year-old Wife's dishonesty at her third husband's grave compares to that of the *Matron,* as she spends her time looking at Johnny's legs, whom she then marries one month later.[6]

In Chaucer's *Troilus and Cryseida* (2:16,32), a young woman much closer to Endrina's age than to that of the Wife of Bath also speaks of the advantages of widowhood, while it is her uncle, Pandarus, who plays the role of go-between, who tries to get her to get rid of her widow's habit and take advantage of the sexual adventure that has come her way. Cf. the same *topos* put into the mouth of Trotaconventos in *M-E* (762a,c): *Qué provecho vos tiene' vestir esse negro paño . . . / Señora, dexad duelo e fazed el cabo de año* [What good does it do for you to wear that black cloth . . . Lady, cast off your mourning clothes and make the end of the year of mourning]. (All quotes and translations are from Ruiz 1972.)

In the *Decameron,* Boccaccio presents several widows who do not remarry, among them only one sexually chaste one (*Dec.* 8.4), a young widow who lives with her brothers. The others all have lovers, or amuse themselves making fun of potential lovers. In one happy account (*Dec.* 2.2) a youth chances upon a young widow with a *corpo bellisimo.* She is awaiting her lover, but when he does not appear, she propositions the youth instead and they spend the whole night in amorous pursuits. In *Dec.* 8.7, a young student falls in love at first sight with a beautiful widow dressed in black.

> Davanti agli occhi si paro questa Elena, vestita di nero si come le nostre vedove vanno, piena di tanta belleza, al suo giudicio, e di tanta piacevolezza quanta alcuna altra ne gli fosse mai paruta vedere . . .

[Before his eyes there appeared this Elena, dressed in black as our widows do, filled with more beauty, in his opinion, and with more charm, than any woman he had ever seen.]

However, the widow only leads the inexperienced student on, leaving him to stand outside all night in the snow, while she is cavorting with her lover, but he gets his revenge by leaving her to "burn" in the nude on top of a tower in mid-July.

The most eloquent and tragically sympathetic account of a widow in Boccaccio is the story (*Dec.* 4.7) of the young widow whose father is negligent in arranging a new marriage for her, so that she takes it upon herself to find a suitable lover. When the affair is discovered, she offers to her father a long, naturalistic plea, excusing her behavior on the basis of her youth and previous sexual experience.

Widows are one of Boccaccio's favorite subjects in a number of other works as well. In his *Corbaccio,* another fictitious autobiography, the object of "Boccaccio's" passion is an overripe widow, who is physically repulsive but still sexual, and dressed in black like a crow, in whom are found every feminine vice ever imagined by misogynist writers. The work's autobiography as well as its antifeminism have generally been taken seriously, but its stridently exaggerated clichés suggest that it is making fun of the misogynist genre. Other depictions of widows in Boccaccio include that of *Criseida,* like Endrina, *giovane bella, vaga e lieta,/ vedova, ricca, nobile ed amata,* in his *Filostrato* (*Dec.* 2.69.1–3), and the important love debate in the *Filocolo* (*Dec.* 4.51.2) about whom a youth should prefer, the *pulcella,* the *maritata,* or the *vedova.* Unlike in *De Vetula,* the author declares his clear predilection for the widow, who because of her experience, is better at sex, a conclusion that follows the influential *De amori libri tres* of Andreas.[7]

Folk genres, such as the proverb, convey identical stereotypes about widows. In his *Refranero,* Correas plays with the concept of sensual widows dressed in black by listing all the things in which black is best: *carnero negro* 'black mutton,' *gallina negra* 'black hen,' *vino negro* 'black wine,' and *viuda negra* 'widow in black.' Other typical proverbs include: *viudas de ogaño/largas tocas y anda el rabo* 'widows nowadays, long skirts and moving their tail'; *boca besada no pierde ventura* 'a kissed mouth loses no fortune'; *la biuda rica haze que llora y repica* 'rich widows pretend to cry while they're itching to do it'; *las tocas negras y los pensamientos verdes* 'black habits and green [i.e., dirty] thoughts';

viuda es, que no le faltará marido 'she is a widow who doesn't want for a husband.'[8]

Two Italian lyrics illustrate two popular reactions to the sexual longings of young widows. One is that of sympathetic understanding, in the form of a lament put into the mouths of the young women themselves, asking others to have pity on them (Singleton 1936, nos. 58 and 60; Bruscagli 1986, 280–82):

> No' sián pur tenere d'anni,
> e abbián giovin il core . . .
> vorrem esser maritate . . .
> e pur siam de carne e d'ossa

> [We are tender in years and have youthful hearts . . . we want to be married . . . as we are but of flesh and blood.]

Another lyric takes the more customary "verbal voyeristic" view, describing widows' sex lives with leering double entendres. The widows come to "doctors" with the complaint that they have no peace because of a fire *nelle rene* 'in their kidneys'; the doctors propose an ointment in their *matrice* 'womb' and bed rest, to be administered by a servant who will also provide other restoratives, such as a *zucca* 'pumpkin' or a *melone* (cf., here, *Don Melón*'s name); (see Vasvari 1988 on phallic cucurbits). Obscene carnivalesque songs about widows proliferate so much in Renaissance Italy that, in one song, the widows themselves race to defend their honor, complaining that they always appear as stock characters in the company of such disreputable types as *turchi, diavoli o romiti* 'turks, devils, or pilgrims' (Singleton 1936, 298–99; Bruscagli 1986, 165–66).

These widows are at least better treated by the poet than the unfortunate Spanish widow who, out of despair, is forced to resort to vegetal autoeroticism while fantasizing about a certain *fray Lucas* (Alzieu et al. 1975):

> Tu, rábano piadoso, en este día
> visopija serás en mi trabajo;
> serás lugarteniente de un carajo,
> mi marido serás, legumbre mía . . .

[You {my} merciful radish, will today be my vice-penis in my task, you'll be lieutenant to a cock, you'll be my husband, my legume.]

The tradition of widows as particularly fair game may have diminished today but is far from extinguished in popular culture, as we can see by the final examples. The first is a Galician lyric, collected at the end of the last century, in which a man assures a *viudiña* that no one will ever find out about the tryst he proposes because in a harvested "vineyard" no one could think to look for grapes (Braga 1886, 239).

Ai, viudiña, dame creto
que ninguen ch'o ha de saber
que n-a viña vendimiada
ninguén pode ir á escoller.

[Oh, little widow, believe me {that} no one has to know, in a harvested vine orchard, no one can go picking fruit.]

The lusty widow is also well and alive in contemporary carnival songs in Spain, although these were long forbidden under the Franco regime. One example of many is the carnival verse collected in 1976 in Cádiz ("Los pegotes del capitán Trueno," in Paz Pasamar 1987, 160–63).

Quería cierta viuda
de mirada misteriosa
que matara unos ratones
con mi espada prodigiosa.
Cuando cogí el instrumento
para hacerle aquel trabajo
me dijo muy zalamera
"tócame un poco más abajo."

[A certain widow / with a mysterious gaze / wanted me to "kill" some "mice" / with my enormous sword. / When I took a hold of my "tool" / She said to me very coyly / "Touch me a little lower" (*Ratones* has the same connotation as other little furry animals, as, for example, in English 'pussy.')]

Compare also the contemporary Mexican joke, centered on the double entendre *paloma/pájaro* 'bird/phallus.'[9]

"Viudas loçanas y gordillas" in the "Libro de Buen Amor"

Within the *LBA*, widows are depicted four times in addition to the *M-E* episode; in two brief failed love adventures (1315–20, 1321–31) which follow one upon another, and in the long invective against death. The first two are like skeletal versions of parts of the *M-E* that, in spite of their extreme brevity, can shed light on the longer episode.[10] In the first, Trotaconventos recommends a *viuda loçana, muy rica e bien moça e con mucha ufana* 'a merry widow, very rich and still young and full of noble pride' to the lonely protagonist, a description that could also exactly fit Endrina. The description of the widow as *loçana* 'full of sexual vigor, lascivious' is highly suggestive.[11] Nor is there any doubt about what kind of courtship the bawd is trying to arrange when the Archpriest laments that, for all her efforts, *non pudo traba(ja)r, atar, nin dar nudo* (1320b) '[she] was not able to seize hold of her, tie her, or fasten the knot'—all terms with established sexual connotations, with their denotative meaning belonging to the semantic field of witchcraft (spell binding).[12]

The initial half of the adventure with the second widow (1321–31) is a *parodia sacra,* where religious terms are transposed to the erotic level, as already briefly pointed out by Zahareas (1965, 31). The Archpriest catches sight of the widow while she is praying very devoutly in church (perhaps for the soul of her deceased husband?). He, in turn, "prays" to Trotaconventos to have "pity" on him, as if she were the Virgin Mary, and ask that she *andudiesse por mi passos de caridad.* Couching the request for sexual favors in the language of the poor and the hungry begging for alms from charitable Christian ladies is a well-established game (cf. the "starving" *pobre* who begs in an imitation of the litany of streetbeggars that the ladies give him a *limosna* 'alms' of *carne cruda y caliente / que es propio manjar de hombre* 'warm raw meat / which is appropriate food for men' in Alzieu et al. 1975, no. 96).

The remainder of the episode of the second widow takes a new direction. Trotaconventos comes back from her initial visit with the lady buoyed with news of likely success, once again expressed in a bawdy subversion of a proverb: *el que al lobo enbía, ¡alafé! carne espera.*[13] She tries to convince the lady that it would be wiser to take on the Archpriest as a lover rather than rush into a hasty second marriage.

Apparently following the same line of spurious logic, the suitor himself then sends the lady a singularly inappropriate poem on the theme of the *tortolilla en el regno de Rodas,* by which he wants to convince her to imitate the turtledove and remain a widow, but, of course, not in order to continue in chaste mourning as the turtledove tradition would demand, but to be available for him.[14]

In a third passage pertaining to widows, the long invective against death, "Juan Ruiz" describes how friends and family have no grief for a dead man but only want to bury him as soon as possible and steal his riches. He points out that widows do not feel much grief for the departed's soul even during the thirty days of obligatory masses and that if they are young, rich, or good looking they will immediately remarry, either a richer man or a *moço más valiente* (1542c), who will satisfy them sexually.[15] It is evident from the foregoing analysis that in these three passages concerning widows, the one mention of the tradition of the chaste widow via the ludicrous turtledove lyric is to subvert it. The sustained emphasis is on both the Archpriest and his bawd considering widows as promising targets for their designs. Some of the very same ideas, expressed in virtually identical terms, appear in *M-E.*

From the initial description of Endrina walking down the plaza, a Miss "*N'y touche,*" who is enjoying the attention she is getting, the *M-E* episode is highly charged with eroticism. When, after Endrina's rebuff to him in the *plaza,* the protagonist Don Melón divulges to Trotaconventos her name, by way of a reassuring reply the old bawd launches into a concatenation of obscene subversions of traditional proverbs, all to the effect that he need not worry about the outcome of his suit because, since the young woman is a widow, she already knows what sex is all about and will certainly want more. Compare here Pitas Payas's *muger moça,* who, although not a widow, suffers from the same problem of having been introduced to sex and now having to do without it. Thus, when her husband goes off on a two-year business trip, during which (477d) *faziasele a la dona un mes año entero* 'each month was like a year for his lady,' it leaves her with no choice but to take a lover, and she virtually tells her husband as much on his return.

Trotaconventos begins by comparing Endrina to a pack animal who is used to "carrying" the weight of a man and so will easily be willing to take on another. Next she compares her to cold wax that is heated and "melted" by being "kneaded" with the fingers. She ends with the advice to her client, "remember, (712b) '*çivera en molino, quien ante viene ante muele,'* " usually rendered in English, without the milling metaphor, as 'first come, first served.' The context here recalls the Wife of Bath's "whose that first to mille comth, first grynt," where she implies that she is willing to accept the first lover who asks. The play is based on the pervasive traditional erotic reinterpretation of the interrelated semantic fields of milling, grinding, and the preparation of bread, where *molino* 'mill'/'vulva,' *moler* 'to mill'/'copulate,' *harina* 'flour'/'semen,' wordplay that is also the key to the episodes of the bakergirl Cruz *cruzada panadera* (st. 115–22) and to that of the *hijo del molinero* (st. 189–98).[16]

Throughout Trotaconventos's several subsequent visits to Endrina never once does the latter evoke chaste devotion to her deceased husband as a reason not to get involved with a new suitor, but only reasons such as fear of being deceived and fear of losing her reputation and even her property if she remarries too soon. From the very beginning she is only too eager to listen to the bawd's detailed praises of her client and is anxious to have his identity revealed. Although Trotaconventos cites the turtledove myth to Endrina, telling her that she is thin and sallow because she is (757ab) *viuda e mancebilla, / sola e sin compañero, como la tortolilla,* it is only to proceed to subvert all the moral values of the myth, assuring the young widow that one should mourn in sackcloth and in black for a bad husband only briefly, because it is only the natural desire of all to make sorrow brief and pleasure lengthy. Her use and abuse of the *tortolilla* is identical to that in the brief affair of the second unnamed widow, except that here the emphasis is on the unworthiness of all first husbands, while in the other it was on the danger of ending up with an unworthy second husband. In all these cases, Trotaconventos, representing the same voice of naturalism as the maid in the *Matron of Ephesus* story in the *Satyricon,* is counseling widows precisely that faithlessness of which tradition has always accused them. The bawd's lesson is also that lovers freely chosen are to be preferred to husbands. But this is advice that can only be given to widows, the only class of women who are potentially able to exercise such freedom of choice.

When Trotaconventos reports to Don Melón on her initial meeting with Endrina, she describes a woman in sexual heat. Endrina goes pale, her lips tremble, and her eyes light up, and she insists on hearing over and over again about her suitor, all the while touching Trotaconventos affectionately. The bawd assures Melón that this means she has her prey bagged, but demands some payment before proceeding, once again referring to Endrina in vulgar alimentary-erotic terms (815d): *si buen manjar quieres pagat bien el escote* 'if you want a good meal, pay up well for your share.'[17]

On her second visit, Trotaconventos greets Endrina with (828) *Véovos bien loçana, bien gordilla, fermosa* 'I see you are good and spry, nice and plump, and pretty.' This is, of course, to mark the contrast that thoughts of love have improved the lady's earlier sallow turtledove mooning. However, the implications of *gordilla* 'plump' refer to far more than of youthful good health, because the term is traditionally associated with women, and especially widows, who are *loçana*. The two terms will also be paired in *La Lozana andaluza*, where the heroine *Lozana* is also described as beautiful, *gordilla*, and robust (Allaigre n.d, 125). Compare also the popular anecdote about a man who wanted to buy a mule, where both *gorda* and *andadora* are suggestive.[18]

Un señor pidió a un corredor le hiciese haber una buena mula. El corredor preguntó: "¿De qué condición la quiere vuestra merced?" Respondió: "Hacedme haber una mula viuda." Maravillóse el corredor de tal necedad. Replicó el caballero, diciendo: "Hermano, si la mula es viuda, tendrá tres condiciones muy buenas, que las viudas tienen: gordas, comedoras y andadoras."

[A man asked a broker to get a good mule for him. The latter asked him: "What kind of mule would you like, my lord?" The man replied: "Get me a widowed mule." The broker marveled at such a silly comment. The man countered, saying: "Brother, if the mule is widowed, it'll have three very good characteristics, which widows have: that they are plump, have good appetites, and run around."]

The chubby widow formula is also used very cleverly in an English ballad, "The widow that keeps the Cock Inn" (Sola Pinto and Rodway 1957, 269–70), where the narrator, a traveling salesman who knows all the inns and their mistresses, in the refrain of each of eight strophes extolls the superiority of:

the plump little widow,
the gay little widow,
the spirited widow that keeps the Cock Inn

where he manages to pun on the name of the inn she manages and on her particular "in[n]-keeping" abilities.

Trotaconventos next tries to elicit Endrina's sympathy by describing in detail how her lover is pining away for love of her, but, again, some of her proverbial descriptions are highly suspect, for example, (835b) *quien si non el mesquino sienbra en el arena* 'who but the witless man sows his seed in sand?' (and cf. [170b] *sembré avena loca ribera de Henares* 'I'll sow wild oats along the shore of the Henares,' "the poor sucker is wasting his time," at the end of another failed adventure), an echo of Genesis 38:8–10, where Onan refused God's wish that he impregnate his brother's wife and instead *semen fundebat in terram*. The erotic exploitation of the Biblical phrase can be traced at least to *Si linguis angelicis* in the Carmina Burana, where a man is debating whether he should get involved with a beloved, ambiguously said to be named Rose, or a *rose* 'flower/pudendum' (Whicher 1949, 51).

By this second visit of Trotaconventos, Endrina loses all self-control, and the more she talks the more she becomes inflamed (st. 856), finally even adopting some of the bawd's own language. She quickly admits that she is burning up and that it is only fear of being deceived and the potential loss of face and the lack of a trysting place that keep her from acceding immediately to (839c) *el trebejo*. Corominas, who, in verse (1609b) *en cama, solaz, trebejo, plazenteras e rientes* 'in bed, a comfort, a sport, affable, and full of laughter' sees no excessive obscenity in *trebejo*, glosses it as *'retozo, jugueteo'* (cf. Willis's superior 'a sport'). Actually, the term is quite vulgar, as in (560b) *el trebejo dueña non lo quiere en otra aljaba* 'no woman wants a chess piece to be put in another's pouch' where *aljaba* means 'pouch'/'vulva.' Endrina has to be just as aware of the connotation of the word as another lady, who at least plays harder to get (*y aun porque lo reciba es muy rogada, / con ser ella quien huelga, / él quien trabaja* 'and she lets herself be begged for her favors, even though she has only to rest and he does all the work' [Alzieu et al. 1975, no. 39]; cf., in no. 75, the much more obscene *trabaja y porfía, /más de noche que de día* 'works and tussles, more at night than during the day').

Endrina admits she is ready for *el trebejo* right after Trotaconventos's suggestion (837cd): *descobrid vuestra llaga, si non, así morredes; / el fuego encobierto vos mata e penades* 'uncover your wound, if not, you will die this way; the hidden fire is killing you and you suffer.' Now, this is either ridiculously inflated language about a *llaga* 'love suffering' coming from the mouth of an old whore, or, even more hilariously, it suggests a more literal uncovering of the lady's *llaga* 'the everlasting wound, vagina' as a cure for her illness.[19] Consciously or not, Endrina immediately echoes the word, foregrounded in rhyme (847b), when she begs for guidance on her plight, adding ludicrously that the old woman should not be bashful about her advice. (Cf. the same play on *llaga* in many sacred parodies, in the *Celestina* [Costa Fontes 1985, 33], and in a *romance* [Alzieu et al. 1975, no. 140] about *una hermosa viuda* who laments her lonely fate at great length, but suddenly decides "Why, I'm crazy, the world is full of mil Juanes who can give me what I need": *a quien desde hoy encomiendo / la cura de aquesta llaga / pues es necedad morirme / de vergonzosa o de casta* 'to whom I entrust from today the curing of this wound, as it's silly for me to die shy and chaste.')

Trotaconventos invites Endrina to visit her, dressed only in a *pellote* 'a kind of undergarment,' to *jugar a la pella* 'play ball' and to partake of a *merienda* 'snack' consisting exclusively of a selection of phallic and testicular fruits, which I have already discussed elsewhere.[20] She promises, appropriately (861d), *jugaredes e folgaredes e darvos he ¡ay, qué nueces!* 'you'll play, you'll have fun, and I'll give you, oh, such nuts!' Although the final rape scene is missing, having been ripped out either by a lascivious or an overprudish reader, we get a suggestive preplay of the whole event.[21] Endrina is waiting inside the old bawd's *tienda,* in a state of suggestive deshabillé; Melón, like a devilish big, bad, hot, wind, or, alternately, dog in heat, bangs at the door, practically breaking it down; the bawd, just before she conveniently exits the scene, shouts at him that he hasn't put a single *clavo* 'nail' into that door, furnished by another, the abbot of San Pablo. The dense suggestiveness of words expressed and implied, *pellote, huerta, viento, quebrantar la puerta,* and *clavo,* are inescapable.[22] When the deed is done, Endrina blames the old woman, who rightly replies(878c): "don't blame me, you got what you deserved." Both of them know that, since Endrina had not been abducted, she was responsible for her downfall and that legally no rape had occurred (Brundage 1978, 65,69). Moreover, throughout the negotiations about the whole affair Endrina had been complicit in the game of linguistic deflection used as a cover. Nor are we to put any more faith in the author's final disclaimer of responsibility for the *villanía* of the episode, in which he blames it all on his sources.[23] In fact, by borrowing from both folklore and literary traditions of erotic language, subverted proverbs, and tales of lascivious widows, the author has made his already bawdy main literary source, the *PA,* twice as long, twice as bawdy, and at least twice as funny.

In the foregoing analysis of the three briefer episodes and the major *M-E* section, in which widows feature prominently, I did not discuss the one additional mention of widows, which initially may seem rather unimportant in comparison. In the long digression against sins, the protagonist accuses a personified *Don Amor* of the sin of pride. As I have discussed elsewhere (Vasvari 1985), the Archpriest talks about pride rather as just another variant of *luxuria,* accusing *Amor* of causing men to rape women (231cd): *forçar muchas mugeres casadas e esposas, / virgenes e solteras, viudas e religiosas* 'raping countless women, betrothed and married, virgins and spinsters, widows, and nuns.' Here, widows are obviously not foregrounded, but are merely part of that familiar catalog of women in the debates about the sexual merits of each group.[24] Variants of the syntagma can be traced from erotic *zéjels* through crudely obscene manipulations in Golden Age poetry. Particularly striking is the early example that warns women against libidinous clerics (Frenk 1978, 320).

> D'aquel fraire flaco y centrino,
> guardaos, dueñas, d'él, qu'es un malino.
> Ni dexa moça ni casada,
> beata, monja ençerrada
> que d'él no á sido tentada,
> y ést'es su ofiçio de contino...

> [Girls, watch out for that scrawny and melancholy friar, there are no unmarried girls, married women, pious ones, or claustered nuns that he hasn't tried it with, and that's his constant occupation...]

Another lyric devotes one strophe each to the *doncella, casada, viuda, beata, monja,* and then goes back to the *soltera,* giving the advantages of each. While the *doncella* is beautiful, the *beata* does not demand money, and the *casada* does not have to be watched over, the widow is praised in the following terms (Alonso and Blecua 1969, no. 210).

> el amor de la viuda
> por mi casa y puerta acuda,
> que no hay peligro ni duda,
> si la pica sólo un cardo...

[the widow's passion comes to my door, there is no danger or doubt,
if even just a thistle pricks her . . .]

The same, very obscene Golden Age verse discussed in the *parodia sacra*
of the second widow who is reduced to practicing autoeroticism combines the erotic motif of the *pobre* begging alms for his "*niño*" with the
catalog of women. After saying that married women are to be preferred
to virgins, because the former *tienen hecho el camino* 'have the road
already opened up,' while with *doncellas . . . es dificultosa la entrada*
'virgins . . . entry is difficult.' The poet turns his plea directly to widows:

Viudas de gallardo brío,
si a compasión os movéis,
por vuestra vida me deis,
en que envuelve un niño mío,
que se me muere de frío
y a ratos se me desmaya.
Metedle bajo la saya,
si queréis que calor cobre.

[Widows of graceful vigor, if you are moved to compassion, for your
life give me something to wrap a baby of mine, who is dying of cold
and at times faints. Put him under your skirt, if you want him to get
back his color.]

To the basic catalog based on social categories, *solteras, casadas,
viudas, monjas,* can be added additional ones, based on physical attributes. The praise of *dueñas chicas* 'small women' (1606–17) is within
this same tradition (cf. Alzieu et al. 1975, no. 95), where *la chiquita*
'small woman' is preferred to the *gorda* 'plump' and the *flaca* 'skinny.'
Perhaps the most ridiculously extended catalog is in a poem that figures
in one manuscript with the appropriate title *Los gustos del fraile.* The
priapic *fraile* in question, speaking in the first person, declares his taste
for all women, devoting a strophe each to the praise of *tuertas, bobas,
corcovadas, neqras, blancas, viudas, romas, flacas, cojas, rameras, her-
mosas,* and *feas* 'squint-eyed, silly ones, hunchbacked, dark ones,
scrawny, lame, prostitutes, beautiful and ugly' (Alzieu et al. 1975, 183–
84; cf. *LBA* 257c: *luego quieres pecar con qualquier que tú veas*).

If, as Gilman suggested (1983, 252), the *LBA* can be understood as an immensely complex and subtle gloss of the (perverted) quote from Aristotle (71), *el mundo por dos cosas trabaja: la primera / por aver mantenencia, la otra cosa era / por aver juntamiento con fembra plazentera* 'the whole world turns on only two things: the first is to find sustenance, the other thing is to couple with a pleasing female' [my translation], then widows are but another category of women, only "more so" because, based on their reputation, they offer a slightly fairer probability of success. It is, then, not by chance that the first-person protagonist fails miserably in most of the love adventures but succeeds with the widow Endrina. Tradition demands that it be so.

Whatever the historical reality of the changing situation of widows in various periods in the Middle Ages, their depiction in literary as well as oral sources remains constant. As surely as doctors always kill, tailors and millers always rob, and millers, sailors, tinkers, and tailors are lustful, so widows are both faithless and have an overdeveloped sexual appetite. The one counter lyrical tradition in Spanish, of the tender image of the disconsolate widow, the turtledove *que está viuda y con dolor* 'who is widowed and full of sorrows' is specifically rejected by the bawd Trotaconventos, who displaces it with the traditional erotic motif of the "merry widow" or *viuda alegre y gorda*. There is, in short, little in the depiction of widows to support established views that Endrina's widowhood is meant to depict "realistically" medieval Spanish women's moral rectitude or to signal the author's moral intent in the episode, and by extension, in the whole work. Rather, Endrina as widow is merely a necessary example in the possible types of *fembra plazentera* (71d). Endrina's widowhood, rather than supporting the supposed "originality" and didactic intent of the presumed author of the *LBA,* provides further evidence for the work's indebtedness to oral culture at the same time that it places it more firmly in the erotic literary tradition of medieval Latin *comedia,* and vernacular genres, such as the fabliau, the *questioni d'amore,* and what Bec (1977) dubbed the *antilyrique.*

NOTES

I want to thank the National Endowment for the Humanities for a grant for the 1988–89 academic year, and the Office of the Dean of Humanities, SUNY, Stony Brook, which supported the preparation of this essay.

1. Lida de Malkiel also sought explanations for the names of both Endrina and Melón in traditional proverbs. On the basis of "que también la doncella es como endrina, que apenas la han tocado / cuando el dedo lo dejan señalado," she saw Endrina's name as a symbol of delicate feminine honor, an interpretation for which she had to disregard that Endrina was not a *donçella*. Had she examined proverbs about widows, she would have had more difficulty in defending Endrina's virtue.

2. See Ransom (1985, chap. 2) on the tradition of the widowed turtledove as a symbol of fidelity. In Spanish, the best known version of the theme is the romance *Fonte Frida,* reproduced in Torner 1962 (90–91), along with several other variants, which may substitute the *torcaza* or *palomita* for the *tórtola/ tortorilla/tortolica.* The lyric also appears embedded in the separation scene between Roboán and Nobleza in the *Caballero Cifar* (Dutton and Walker 1963, 44):

vivré sola syn plazer como
la tórtola quando enbiuda,
que no sabe catar otro
marido ni posa en ramo verde,
mas en el más seco que falla

In the *M-E,* Trotaconventos will anticipate the later rejection of the theme by Góngora in his "Guarda corderos zagala" (Góngora y Argote 1932, n. 87):

Tortorilla gemidora
depuesto el casto desdén,
tálamo hizo segundo
los ramos de aquel ciprés.

Quevedo will go even further in ridiculing the turtledove by turning her into another stock female character, the drunken *comadre* (Quevedo 1971, 3:282):

como tórtola viüda
quedé, pero no sin ramo,
pues en el de una taberna
estuve arrullando tragos.

Here the *rama seca* 'dry branch' on which the turtledove traditionally cries for her dead husband becomes the *ramo* 'branch,' the sign signaling a tavern and/or whorehouse (from where *ramera*/prostitute) on which the drunken widow takes support.

For an Italian version of the turtledove theme, see Cocchiara 1951, 15:

La tortora che ha perso la compagna
Fa una vita molto dolorosa;
Va in un fiumicello e vi si bagna,
E beve di quell' acqua torbidosa;
Cogli altri uccelli non ci si accompagna,
Negli alberi, fioriti non si posa;

Si bagna l'ale e si percuote il petto.

Ha perso la compagna.

3. On the social status of widows, see Huizinga 1954, 57–58. On medieval mysogyny, see Bloch 1987 for a discussion of antifeminism in general, but many of the most virulent works concern widows.

4. For a list of medieval poems for and against women, see Meyer 1877 and 1886.

5. On the theme of the faithless widow in general, see Grisebach 1889; Ure 1956; Schwarzbaum 1979, 394–417; Blumstein 1977, chap. 5; on Marie, see Beyerle 1971; Runte 1983; see Muscatine 1967 on Gautier; Livingston 1951 on Gautier and later French versions; Schwarzbaum 1979 and 1983, 71–74 for medieval Hebrew. I have not been able to see Gerhards 1961 or Huber 1989.

6. On the Wife of Bath, see Muscatine 1967; Garbathy 1968; Amsler 1987. Important in the depiction of rich widows such as the Wife and Endrina is that, between the twelfth and fourteenth centuries, widows increasingly began to have the right to inherit property and to manage their affairs, including lawsuits, on their own (MacFarlane 1979, 131–35).

7. For a brilliant analysis of *Dec.* 4.7, see Almansi 1975. On the *Corbaccio,* see Bruni 1974; for a little known poem by Boccaccio on the *pulzella* versus *vedova* debate, see Ferreri 1970.

8. See these proverbs in Correas 1967; Horozco 1986. Cf. also *Tres días ha que murió / la viuda casarse quiere . . .* (Frenk 1978, 159). For examples from other languages, see Thiselton-Dyer 1906, chap. 19.

9. La paloma es el pájaro de la paz.

El casado no tiene paz en el pájaro.

La soltera no conoce la paz (y se supone que ni el pájaro).

La viuda no puede vivir en paz sin el pájaro.

El viejo mantiene el pájaro en paz.

Y la vieja, por fin, vive en paz, sin el pájaro.

[The *paloma* is the bird of peace. Married men have no peace in their *pájaro*. Unmarried girls don't know what peace is (nor, it is to be hoped, what a *pájaro* is). Widows can't live in peace without a *pájaro*. Old men keep their *pájaro* in peace, and old women, finally, live in peace without a *pájaro*.]

10. These two brief episodes have been considered intercalations of the so-called 1343 version, so that the introductory stanza (1315–18) of the first episode would have originally introduced the very lengthy adventure with the nun Garoza. On the two-redaction theory, see Willis 1974, 215 n. 2; Marmo 1983, 17 nn. 12 and 13. My own view is that the *LBA* is a text of accretion that likely existed in a plurality of versions, although not necessarily in only two. These two pieces about *viudas* seem so closely related to the tone of Endrina as widow that it is difficult to see them as anything but earlier, less developed versions, even if

they may have found their way into a later manuscript. Whatever the number of versions, a view that is untenable is Corominas's (Ruiz 1967: n. to 1315–18) assertion that "Juan Ruiz" added these and other adventures that ended badly because "era prudente cargar la parte moral de su libro" while he was supposedly in prison. The biographical fallacy aside, someone in prison would hardly add two episodes full of bawdy double entendres, the second one a *parodia sacra.* Much more likely, as Willis proposed (1974), the author, responding to the tastes of his audience, increased the bawdy love adventures.

11. *Loçano* is one of the author's favorite adjectives, most often applied to women, appearing as an adjective twenty times referring to women, eleven times to men, and once as a noun, *loçania* 'sexual vigor,' as, e.g., in the obscene *parodia sacra* of the Canonical Hours, *vas a rezar la nona con la dueña loçana* (383a). In later works, too, the adjective is much more frequently applied to females. Cf. the Golden Age verse about two men who take turns with one woman. After tiring out both of them, *aun le quedaba brío y lozanía;* 'she still had vigor and sexual energy' (Alzieu et al. 1978, no. 37.8). The *Lozana andaluza*'s name has the same connotation as the proverb *La mujer mucho loçana / darse quiere a vida vana* 'women full of sexual vigor want a foolish life' (see Allaigre n.d., 122–25, 129 for other, unambiguous examples). Willis's frequent translation (1972) of *loçana* as 'lively' is too gentle, as is Corominas's (Ruiz 1967, 1318a) gloss '*garrida, gallarda.*'

12. For all citations and translations from the *LBA,* see Ruiz 1972; however, in the semantic context of 1321b, I find *trabar* more convincing than his *trabajar* (in a recent comment on this essay, Prof. Willis agrees that *trabar* is to be preferred). On witchcraft as a donor field for erotic terminology, see Herrero 1986, 143–44. *Travar* 'bind, unite' also has this sense in the poem about the phallic *caldero* 'tinker' who wants to *trabar* 'bang' with his *ferramen* 'tool' (Alzieu et al. 1975, no. 81.8).

13. Cf. English *(bit/piece of) meat/pork/mutton* 'vulva, woman, prostitute'; French *viande* 'meat'/'woman, prostitute,' *manger de la chair crue* 'eat raw meat'/ 'copulate.' An exact analogue of Trotaconventos's subverted proverb appears in Alzieu et al. 1975, no. 61, where a woman is giving instructions to a clumsy lover on how to proceed: *que si va sin carne el lobo / haréis que de vos me ría* 'if the wolf ends up without any meat, you'll cause me to laugh at you.'

14. Corominas (Ruiz 1967, n. to 1328–29) assumes that this is one of the places where the author forgot to put in the promised verses, or that they were later removed. He thinks that 1329abc, where the turtledove asks women if they aren't afraid to remarry, is actually a self-reproach the young widow's heart makes to her for having considered the Archpriest's proposal, which causes her to go off and marry someone to whom she was already promised. This argument is not very convincing both because this kind of internal monologue has no role in the work and because turtledoves of tradition never compare a potential lover

versus a husband but are only able to talk of fidelity to a dead husband. The Archpriest's verses to the lady play with this tradition by having the *tortolilla* counsel her not to remarry, implying, however, that having a lover would not constitute faithlessness.

15. Like *loçano (–a)*, *valiente* is never used with its simple denotative meaning of 'strong, physically graceful,' but always connotes sexual vigor, as in 189a: *porque forzó la dueña el su señor valiente* (237b); see also 373c, 987b. Cf. Vasvari 1985, 166–67 and 1989, n. 12 and the documentation cited there, which shows that this connotation goes back to Latin. Cf. also in English, where the OED gives 'erection' as one meaning of *valiant*. Willis's translation of 1542c as 'lustier youth' carries just the right flavor.

16. Cf. (472b) *mujer, molino e huerta siempre quieren el uso* 'a woman, a mill, and an orchard require constant use,' and the proverb *las dos hermanas que al molino van, como son bonitas, luego las molerán* 'the two girls who go to the mill, since they're pretty, they'll get ground.' For many other examples and extensive documentation, see Vasvari 1983 and 1989.

17. Cf. variants of the same proverb in (944d), where the Archpriest uses the same vulgarism at the death of a girl with whom he did succeed. Cf. also 983c and 992a, where it is the Archpriest who is the sexual prey to the *serrana* Gadea de Río Frío.

18. Collected in the sixteenth century by Melchor de Santa Cruz de Dueñas in his *Floresta española,* a collection of *géneros chicos,* such as jokes, anecdotes, and proverbs from oral tradition, grouped according to classes or categories of people. The chapter on widows (1947, 177) includes seven items.

19. The vulva is often seen as a "wound"—prosaically as the "everlasting wound," or more poetically as the "delicious or sweet wound" (H. von K. 1912, 78).

20. See Vasvari 1988, 17–18; to which add further Alzieu et al. 1975, no. 131 *(piñones)*, no. 81 *(avellan[it]as).*

21. The audience knew what to expect from the scene if they were familiar with the genre of the *comedia latina.* Cf. the *Facetus,* very similar to the *Pamphilus,* where it is explained why rape is the socially approved etiquette in such situations (Goddard 1977, 45).

Let the youth employ force although she strenuously resists, for if he should stop, the girl would grieve. A woman expects to be conquered in the fight rather than, like a whore, endure the crime willingly. Only in the stews [i.e., whorehouses] do women, who willingly sell themselves to anyone for a price, seek out intercourse.

22. On *clavo,* see Vasvari 1983; on *pellote,* see Vasvari 1988. On the theme of the door, especially the closed door locked to the lover in erotic poetry, see Copley 1981; cf. also st. 1519; Gulstad 1979, 74 on Calisto threatening to have his servants chop down the door, and many references in Alzieu et al. 1975 and

elsewhere. On wind as a phallic image, see Morales Blouin 1981, 56; on the concept of man's libidinous winds, with the phallus and testicles as containers or vehicles for winds of desire, see Cadden 1984, 157. This is the same *viento hombrón* with his *espada caliente* that still pursues Lorca's gypsy girl Preciosa in the *Romancero gitano*.

23. The disclaimer of responsibility for bawdy is a topos in its own right. Cf. the author's very similar words in blaming Aristóteles for what he actually then takes as the leitmotif of the whole work (71c): *aver juntamiento con fembra olazentera*. Cf. also Boccaccio, who claims that people have wrongly blamed him for using words like *salciccia* and *mortar and pestle*, when he had, in fact, built a whole story around the sexual double entendres surrounding the borrowing of a mortar and the act of grinding.

24. The erotic catalog of women is prevalent also in other languages (cf. the obscene suggestiveness of no. 85 in Singleton 1936, directed to *pulzelle e maritate e a vedove velate*). The tradition remains alive in oral culture, as in the following riddle (which, however, does neglect widows).

Adivinanza:
señoras y señoritas
casadas y solteritas
se las meten estiradas
y las sacan arrugadas
[las medias]

(Jiménez 1983, 63)

(Riddle: women and young ladies / married women and unmarried girls / put it on/in extended and take it off/out all wrinkled / [stockings].)

BIBLIOGRAPHY

Allaigre, Claude. *Le "Retrato de la Loçana andaluza" de Francisco Delicado.* Publié avec le concours du ministère des universités, n.d.

Almansi, Guido. *The Writer as Liar: Narrative Technique in the Decameron.* London: Routledge and Kegan Paul, 1975.

Alonso, Dámaso, and J. M. Blecua. *Antología de la poesía española: Lírica de tipo tradicional.* Madrid: Gredos, 1969.

Alzieu, Pierre, Robert Jammes, Yvan Lissorgues, eds. *Léxico del marginalismo del Siglo de Oro.* Toulouse: France-Ibérie Recherche, Université Toulouse-Le Mirail, 1975.

Amsler, Mark. "The Wife of Bath and Women's Power." *Assays* 4 (1987): 67–83.

Bec, Pierre. *La lyrique franaise au moyen âge.* Paris: Picard, 1977.

Beyerle, Dieter von. "Marie de France und die Witwe von Ephesus." *Romanische Jahrbuch* 22 (1971): 84–100.

Bloch, J. Howard. "Medieval Misogyny." *Representations* 20 (1987): 1–24.

Blumstein, Andrée Kohn. *Misogyny and Idealization in the Courtly Romance.* Bonn: Bouvier Verlag, 1977.

Braga, Théophile. *Cancionero popular gallego.* Madrid: Ricardo Fe, 1886.

Brundage, James A. "Rape and Marriage in the Medieval Canon Law." *Revue de droit canonique* 28 (1978): 62–75.

Bruni, Francesco. "Dal 'De Vetula' al 'Corbaccio.' *Medioevo Romanzo* 1 (1974): 161–216.

Bruscagli, Riccardo, ed. *Trionfi e canti carnascialeschi toscani del rinascimiento.* 2 vols. Rome: Salerno Editrice, 1986.

Cadden, Joan. "It Takes All Kinds: Sexuality and Gender Differences in Hildegard of Bingen's Book of Compound Medicine." *Traditio* 40 (1984): 149–74.

Cirot, Georges. "L'Episode de Doña Endrina dans le *LBA.*" *Bulletin Hispanique* 45 (1943): 139–56.

Cocchiara, Guiseppe. *Il linguaggio della poesia popolare.* Palermo: Palumbo, 1951.

Copley, Frank O. *Exclusus amator: A Study in Latin Love Poetry.* Chico: Scholars Press, 1981.

Correas, Gonzalo. *Vocabulario de refranes y frases proverbiales* [1627]. Ed. Louis Combet. Bordeaux: Institut d'Etudes Ibériques et Ibéro-Américaines de l'Université de Bordeaux, 1967.

Costa Fontes, Manuel da. "Celestina's 'Hilado' and Related Symbols: A Supplement." *Celestinesca* 9 (1985): 33–38.

Dutton, Brian, and Roger Walker. "*El Libro del Caballero Zifar* y la lirica castellana." *Filología* 9 (1963): 53–67.

Ferraresi, Alicia. *De amor y poesía en la edad media: Prólogo a Juan Ruiz.* Mexico City: Colegio de México, 1976.

Ferreri, Rosario. "Una Risposta di Antonio Pucci Al Boccaccio." *Romance Notes* 12 (1970): 189–91.

Frenk [Alatorre], Margit. *Estudios sobre lírica antigua.* Madrid: Castalia, 1978.

Garbathy, Thomas J. "Chaucer's Weaving Wife." *Journal of American Folklore* 81 (1968): 342–46.

Gerhards, Gisela. *Das Bild der Witwe in der deutschen Literatur des Mittelalters.* Ph.D. diss., University of Bonn, 1961.

Gilman, Stephen. "Quatrain 449 of the *LBA.*" *Corónica* 4 (1976): 67–71.

———. "Doña Endrina in Mourning." In *Homenaje a José Manuel Blecua: Obrecido por sus Discípulos y amigos,* ed. José Angel Blesa Lalinde, 247–55. Madrid: Gredos, 1983.

Goddard, Alison. The *Facetus* or The Art of Courtly Living." *Allegorica* 2 (1977): 27–57.

Góngora y Argole, Luis. *Obras completas.* Ed. Juan Millé Jiménez and Isabel Millé Jiménez. Madrid: Aguilar, 1932.

Grisebach, Eduard. *Die Wanderung der Novelle von der treulosen Witwe durch die Weltliteratur.* Berlin: F. und P. Lehmann, 1889.

Gulstad, Daniel E. "Melibea's Demise: The Death of Courtly Love." *Corónica* 7 (1979): 71–79.

Hart, Thomas R. *La alegoría en el* Libro de Buen Amor. Madrid: Revista de Occidente, 1959.

Herrero, Javier. "The Stubborn Text: Calisto's Toothache and Melibea's Girdle." In *Literature Among Discourses: The Spanish Golden Age,* ed. Wlad Godzich and Nicholas Spadaccini, 132–47. Minneapolis: University of Minnesota Press, 1986.

Horozco, Sebastian de. *Teatro universal de proverbios.* Ed. José Luis Alonso Hernández. Salamanca: Ediciones Universidad de Salamanca, 1986.

Huber, Gerlinde. *Das Motiv der 'Witwe von Ephesus' in lateinischen Texten der Antike und des Mittelalters.* Tübingen: Günter Narr Verlag, 1989.

Huizinga, Johan. *The Waning of the Middle Ages.* New York: Doubleday, 1954.

H. von K. "Die Nomenklatur der Vulva." *Anthropoeia* 9 (1912): 76–81.

Jímenez, A. *Picardía mexicana.* 83d ed. Mexico City: Mexicanos Unidos, 1983.

Klopsch, P. *Pseudo-Ovidian "De Vetula."* Leiden: E. J. Brill, 1967.

Lázaro Carreter, Fernando. "Los amores de don Melón y doña Endrina." *Arbor* 62, no. 18 (1951): 210–36.

Lecoy, Félix. *Recherches sur le "Libro de Buen Amor" de Juan Ruiz, Archiprêtre de Hita.* Reproduced with bibliographical essay by A. D. Deyermond. Farnborough: Gregg, 1974.

Lida de Malkiel, María Rosa. "Notas para la interpretación, influencia, fuentes y texto del *Libro de Buen Amor.*" *Revista de Filología Hispánica* 2 (1940): 105–50.

Livingston, Charles H. *Le Jongleur Gautier Le Leu: Étude sur les fabliaux.* Cambridge, Mass.: Harvard University Press, 1951.

MacFarlane, Alan. *The Origins of English Individualism.* New York: Cambridge Unversity Press, 1979.

Marmo, Vittorio. *Dalle fonti alle forme: Studi sul Libro de Buen Amor.* Naples: Liguori, 1983.

Meyer, Paul. "Plaidoyer en faveur des femmes." *Romania* 6 (1877): 409–503.

———. "La bonté des femmes." *Romania* 15 (1886): 315–21.

Montaiglon, Anatole de, and Gaston Raynaud. *Recueil général et complet des fabliaux des XIIIe et XIVe siècles.* Paris: Librairie des Bibliophiles, 1877.

Morales Blouin, Egla. *El ciervo y la fuente: Mito y folklore del agua en la lírica tradicional.* Madrid: Studia Humanitatis, Porrúa Turranzas, 1981.

Muscatine, Charles M. "The Wife of Bath and Gautier's *La Veuve.*" In *Romance Studies in Memory of Edward Billingsham,* ed. Urban T. Holmes, 109–14. Hayward: Cal State College Publications, 1967.

Paz Pasamar, Jorge Antonio. *La temática de las coplas del carnaval.* Cádiz: Cátedra Adolfo de Castro, Fundación Municipal de Cultura, 1987.

Quevedo, Francisco de. *Obra poética.* 4 vols. Ed. José Manuel Blecua. Madrid: Castalia, 1971.

Rico, Francisco. "Sobre el origen de la autobiografía en el *Libro de Buen Amor.*" *Anuario de estudios medievales* 4 (1967): 301–25.

Robathan, D. M. *The Pseudo-Ovidian "De Vetula."* Amsterdam: Adolf H. Hakkert, 1968.

Ruiz, Juan. *Libro de Buen Amor.* Ed. Juan Corominas. Madrid: Gredos, 1967.

———. *Libro de Buen Amor,* ed. Raymond S. Willis. Princeton: Princeton University Press, 1972.

Runte, Hans R. "'Alfred's Book,' Marie de France, and the Matron of Ephesus." *Romance Philology* 36 (1983): 556–64.

Santa Cruz de Dueñas, Melchor de. *Floresta española.* Mexico City: Espasa-Calpe, 1947.

Schwarzbaum, Haim. *The Mishle Shu'alim (Fox Fables) of Rabbi Berechiah Ha-Nakdan: A Study in Comparative Folklore and Fable Lore.* Kiron: Institute for Jewish and Arabic Folklore Research, 1979.

———. "International Folklore Motifs in Joseph Ibn Zabara's 'Sepher Sha'shu'im.'" *Folklore Research Center Studies* 7 (1983): 55–82.

Singleton, Charles. *I canti carnavaleschi.* Bari: Laterza, 1936.

Sola Pinto, Vivian de, and Allan Edwin Rodway, eds. *The Common Muse: An Anthology of Popular British Ballad Poetry, 15th– 20th Centuries.* London: Chatto and Windus, 1957.

Spitzer, Leo. "Zur Auffassung der Kunst des Arcipreste von Hita." *Zeitschrift für Romanische Philologie* 54 (1934): 237–70.

Thiselton-Dyer, T. F. *Folklore of Women.* London: Elliot-Stock, 1906. Reprint. Detroit: Singing Tree Press, 1968.

Torner, Eduardo M. *Lírica hispánica.* Madrid: Castalia, 1962.

Ure, Peter. "The Widow of Ephesus: Some Reflections on an International Comic Theme." *Durham University Journal* 49, n.s. 28 (1956): 1–19.

Vasvari, Louise O. "La semiologia de la connotación: Lectura polisémica de Cruz cruzada panadera." *Nueva Revista de Filología Hispánica* 32 (1983): 299–344.

———. "La digresión sobre los pecados mortales en el *Libro de Buen Amor.*" *Nueva Revista de Filología Hispánica* 34 (1985): 156–80.

———. "Vegetal-Genital Onomastics in the *Libro de Buen Amor.*" *Romance Philology* 42 (1988): 1–29.

———. "The Miller's Millstones: Erotic Popular Tradition in the *Libro de Buen Amor.*" State University of New York at Stony Brook, 1989, Typescript.

———. "The Tale of *L'usignolo (Dec.* V,4): Popular Tradition and Pornographic Parody." State University of New York at Stony Brook, 1989, Typescript.

———. " 'Pornithological' Riddle and Visual Pun: Middle English *I have a gentil cok.* State University of New York at Stony Brook, 1989, Typescript.

Whicher, George F., trans. *The Goliard Poets: Medieval Latin Songs and Satires.* New York: New Directions, 1949.

Willis, Raymond S. "Thirteen Years: Seedbed of Riddles in the *Libro de Buen Amor.*" *Kentucky Romance Quarterly* 21 (1974): 215–27.

Zahareas, Anthony. *The Art of Juan Ruiz.* Madrid: Estudios de Literatura Española, 1965.

Chapter 12

The Widow in Hispanic Balladry: *Fonte Frida*

Philip O. Gericke

Fonte Frida.

Fonte frida, fonte frida,	Fount of freshness! fount of freshness!
fonte frida y con amor,	Fount of freshness and of love!
do todas las auezicas	Where the little birds of spring-time
van tomar consolación,	Seek for comfort as they rove;
si no es la tortolica	All except the widow'd turtle—
qu'está biuda y con dolor;	Widow'd, sorrowing turtle-dove.
por allí fuera passar	There the nightingale, the traitor
el traydor del ruyseñor;	Linger'd on his giddy way;
las palabras que le dize	And these words of hidden treachery
llenas son de traycíón:	To the dove I heard him say:
Si tú quisiesses, señora,	"I will be thy servant, lady!
yo sería tu servidor.	I will ne'er thy love betray!
Vete d'ay, enemigo,	"Off! false-hearted!—vile deceiver!
malo, falso, engañador,	Leave me, nor insult me so:
que ni poso en ramo verde,	Dwell I, then, midst gaudy flowrets?
ni en prado que tenga flor:	Perch I on the verdant bough?
que si el agua hallo clara,	Even the waters of the fountain
turbia la beuía yo;	Drink I dark and troubled now.
que no quiero hauer marido,	Never will I think of marriage—
	Never break the widow-vow.

porque hijos no haya, no;	Had I children they would grieve me,
no quiero plazer con ellos,	They would wean me from my woe:
ni menos consolación.	
Déxame, triste enemigo,	Leave me, false one!—thoughtless traitor!
malo, falso, mal traydor,	Base one!—vain one!—sad one—go!
que no quiero ser tu amiga,	I can never, never love thee—
ni casar contigo, no.	I will never wed thee—no!"

This ballad, deservedly well known and appreciated in the Hispanic world for its beauty, poignancy, and emotional force, is unusual in several respects. It is the only poem in the entire corpus of old Spanish ballads to feature, as protagonists, characters from the animal kingdom endowed with human attributes in the manner of the bestiaries and Oriental apologues. It is also one of only a very few that deal with widows, and the only one to treat the ideal of a conjugal fidelity so powerful that it transcends the death of the spouse.

The version transcribed here is one of four that were printed in the sixteenth century. As is the case with most traditional ballads, its composition and oral dissemination must have antedated its printing (in the *Cancionero General* of 1511) by many years. It is by far the best known of the four sixteenth-century versions, and the preferred choice of anthologists since Wolf and Hofmann's classic collection, *Primavera y flor de romances*. It will serve us well as our study example, although it is only fitting to point out, in passing, that other versions of the ballad have merit as well. The fine rendition into English, which conveys both the beauty and the sense of the original as faithfully as any translation can be expected to do, is by Sir John Bowring. The ballad has inspired numerous other English versions, including those of such well-known figures as James Gibson, W. J. Entwistle, and George Umphrey.[1]

The story is a simple one, but its elaborate symbolism (derived in part from exegetical tradition, in part from the bestiaries, and in part from courtly poetry) is the product of several centuries of evolution. Birds gather at the cool fountain, a source of consolation in the text and in Biblical exegesis but suggestive also of love, fertility, and sensuality in secular works. Only the widowed turtledove stands apart, refusing to seek solace or renewal. The nightingale offers to be her lover (*servidor* 'servant' = courtly lover), but the turtledove angrily rebukes him in a tirade of unflattering epithets. She will not be consoled, and rejects not only the offer of friendship (love) but also the notion of remarriage, lest her interlocutor should happen to be entertaining such an idea. The text does not specify the sort of "treachery" that the turtledove is imputing to the nightingale (reinforced by the narrative voice of the poet, l. 7), although other versions of the poem make clear that her fury stems from being asked to betray the cherished memory of her late husband.[2]

Spanish Ballads

A few brief observations of a general nature on Hispanic balladry might provide a useful and helpful prelude to further discussion of *Fonte Frida*. Spain has been called, with some justification, "the land of the ballad,"[3] for its rich ballad tradition extends in an unbroken line from the fourteenth century (if not earlier) down to the present day. Kept alive on the Iberian Peninsula through a deep-rooted oral tradition and carried to all parts of the globe by the exiled Sephardim and by the colonizers of the New World, the ballad today constitutes a unique window on a multisecular cultural heritage.

A good number of the early ballads had their origins in epic poetry. As the popularity of the longer narratives waned, some of their more memorable passages were rescued from oblivion by the jongleurs and gained new life in oral tradition, surviving there until the first printed collections of the early sixteenth century. At the same time, ballad poets began to exploit a wide variety of material of a different nature—newsworthy events of the turbulent political climate surrounding Peter I of Castile (ruled 1350–69), for instance, and memorable moments in the ongoing efforts to recapture Granada from the Moors—as well as the matter of other literary traditions (Carolingian, Breton). Finally, there are numerous ballads that derive from none of the aforementioned sources, and are often grouped together for convenience's sake under such rubrics as "novelesque and lyric" ballads. These may have antecedents in folklore, in popular lyrics, or in literary works too remote from the ballads derived from them to permit identifying them as sources. *Fonte Frida* belongs to this latter category; its poet drew from a store of motifs that, by the fifteenth century, were widely known in both exegetical and courtly literature. The courtly treatment is not without interest, as the solitary turtledove is readily converted into a symbol of a lover pining for her absent beloved. However, it is the exegetical vein (with its emphasis on chaste widowhood) that is reflected in our study example, and is central to our concerns.

Portrayals of Women in Old Spanish Ballads

Predictably, ballads derived from or based on epic material tend to revolve around the lives and deeds of royalty and the upper nobility, to the near exclusion of the other classes. There are no nonnoble protagonists of either sex, and few memorable secondary figures either. Ballads derived from other sources feature a somewhat broader range of social strata, but the tendency there as well is for the characters to be of noble birth.

In light of this significant limitation, the range and diversity that characterize the portrayals of women in the ballads are all the more remarkable. Women are prominent figures in the historical ballads, especially when compared to their epic antecedents, as Lucy A. Sponsler (1975, 41) has pointed out. Their roles may be stereotypical to the extent that they are reflective in some way or the other of their relationship to men—whether mother, wife, lover, or daughter—but the spectrum of shadings with which their characters are drawn is rich. The range extends from the heroic valor of Doña Sancha in the Fernán González ballads to the wanton treachery of Urraca (the *femina mente dira* of the Zamora cycle) or to the righteous indignation of the outraged Jimena in the ballads dealing with the youth of the Cid. The ballads based on the Lara epic bring two magnificently limned female characters—the stalwart, long-suffering Sancha and the petulantly vindictive Lambra—into conflict with one another. And these are only the most memorable of the female characters in one ballad type; there are numerous others in the Carolingian, historical, novelesque, and lyric ballads as well.

As we will see presently, the role of the widow in medieval society differs from that of other women in one important respect. The widow must fend for herself, without the protection of her father or her husband; it is thus expected and understood that she may display a degree of assertiveness that would be unbecoming in some of the other roles. In the ballad, assertiveness in a strong female character is not typically viewed as a positive trait, especially when directed at a husband or father; for every woman who rises up against the husband who has wronged her (*Blancaflor y Filomena*, e.g., derived from the story of Procne, Philomela, and Tereus), there is one who accepts her fate with resignation, as in the chilling *Retraída está la infanta,* in which the countess (an ideal wife and mother) dies at the hands of her husband, Count Alarcos, on the king's orders so that the count will be free to marry the king's daughter.[4] Women who assert themselves sexually are often portrayed in an especially unfavorable light: the lady in *Estase la gentil dama* brazenly offers herself to a shepherd, but is unable to seduce him despite extolling, at some length, the hidden charms she has to share with him; the *serrana* ['mountain woman'] *de la Vera,* who kills her lovers after taking her pleasure with them, is depicted as a wild animal who bounds down the mountain in desperate pursuit of one such lover (more fortunate than most) who managed to steal away from her while she slept.

> Y en esto la vi venir,
> bramando como una fiera,
> saltando de canto en canto,
> brincando de peña en peña.
>
> (Díaz Roig 1985, 268)

> [And then I saw her coming,
> bellowing like a wild animal,
> jumping from rock to rock,
> leaping from cliff to cliff.]

By law and custom, adultresses were treated harshly in Spanish society; ballads tend to portray them negatively and/or punish them severely for their indiscretions. The queen in *Landarico,* for instance, is unattractively portrayed as a conspirator to murder and as a usurper of a masculine role. At the ballad's beginning, she inadvertently reveals to her husband, the king, that she has a lover. She tells her lover, who (finding no solution) can only wring his hands and rue the day they met. The queen castigates him for his pusillanimity:

> —Calla, calla, Landarico,
> calla, hombre apocado;
> déjame tú hacer a mí,
> que yo lo habré remediado.
>
> (Díaz Roig 1985, 264)

[Shut up, shut up, Landarico,
shut up, you wimp of a man;
you just leave it to me,
I'll fix it all up.]

She proceeds to arrange for the king to be killed and then mourns him loudly while thinking of "something else" the while.

An even better known old ballad, *Blancaniña*, illustrates the difference between Spanish ballad treatment of the adultress and that of the French *fabliau* from which it derives: in the Spanish ballad, the adultress (whose husband returns unexpectedly while she is entertaining a lover) tries to explain away telltale evidence, but finally acknowledges her guilt and asks her husband to kill her; in the *fabliau* she saucily turns her husband's interrogations around and convinces the old fool of her innocence.[5]

One common denominator in the portrayal of women, then, seems to be that they are characterized most favorably when they conform to societal norms in the fulfillment of their expected roles. Men (fathers, husbands) are responsible for women's honor; only in their absence or incapacitation is a woman entitled to stand up for herself. Jimena does, in *Día era de los Reyes:* the Cid has killed her father and now torments and threatens her. With neither father nor husband to protect her, she (not unlike a widow) must take her own case to the king, and does (although her proposed solution—to ask the king to give her the Cid in marriage—may be as perplexing to the modern reader as it was to the king). So, too, does the young lady in *Rico Franco,* who astutely borrows her abductor's knife on a pretext and kills him with it (thus avenging the death of her parents and brothers). Like them, the widowed turtledove must look to her own resources as she fends off the unwelcome advances of her suitor, and she does so assertively.

The Widow in Medieval Spanish Society and Literature

The rights and duties of a widow vary in medieval Hispanic society according to local *fueros* (codes of law). Heath Dillard (1976) notes the myriad problems connected with widowhood, but reminds us at the same time of the widow's special status as an independent woman. In some areas, she will lose this "independence of property and person which she has gained as a widow" (Dillard 1976, 84) if she goes to live with a relative or remarries.[6] In no case would it make sense for a widow to remarry beneath the station of her first husband, and remarriage carried with it the additional risk of having to give up the children of her first marriage to her late husband's family. It is reasonable to assume that there were more disincentives for widows than for widowers, for whom many of the disadvantages of remarriage did not apply.

The most famous widow in all of medieval Spanish literature is Doña Endrina, protagonist of one of the central episodes of the *Libro de buen amor* of Juan Ruiz, Archpriest of Hita (composed ca. 1330–43). The episode is based on the *Pamphilus*, but, in his reworking of his model, Juan Ruiz introduces substantial modifications into the character of Doña Endrina. Among the most important of these is her widowhood. Theodore L. Kassier has focused on this aspect of the episode, pointing out the many ways in which Doña Endrina's situation accurately reflects the conditions faced by widows in society: the ban on remarriage for a year, the risk of loss of status through marriage to a man of lesser station, and her vulnerability to litigation against her estate (sometimes by adversaries whose power was intimidating, making it difficult to obtain good legal representation). It is no surprise to find that Juan Ruiz (connoisseur of bestiaries that he was) is familiar with the story of the turtledove and makes apt use of the motif in this episode:[7] his male protagonist's go-between pursues her campaign to seduce the widow by likening her to the mourning bird (an unhealthy condition for which the go-between will be only too happy to provide a remedy):

> "Así estades, fija, biuda e mançebilla,
> sola e sin conpañero como la tortolilla:
> d'eso creo que estades amarilla e magrilla:
> do son todas mugeres, nunca mengua renzilla."
>
> (Ruiz 1974, St. 757)

> [So, my daughter, you are a widow and still young, all alone
> and without a companion, like the little turtledove: I believe
> that is why you are sallow and a bit thin; where there are only
> women, there is never a lull in the squabbling.]
>
> (Ruiz 1972, 202)

The go-between goes on to suggest that the widow needs a man around the house to set things right, and that she knows just the man. This episode may well mark the first time in medieval literature that the motif of the turtledove is used as a negative example (and not without tongue-in-cheek humor), to support the argument that a widow should end her mourning and get on with her life. It is an excellent example of Juan Ruiz' skill at having his characters subvert their texts by interpreting them to suit their own purposes and not necessarily as they were "meant" to be interpreted.

Fonte Frida

Against this backdrop, we can now return to *Fonte Frida,* to examine its motifs, symbolism, and significance in greater detail. The solitary, mournful voice of the turtledove was celebrated poetically as early as Virgil ("nec gemere aeria cessabit turtur ab ulmo," *Eclogue* I, 59) and the Song of Songs ("Vox turturis audita est in terra nostra," 2:12). How she came to represent chaste widowhood and the symbols and motifs associated with that representation warrant further attention.[8] It was not uncommon for naturalists of pre-Christian antiquity to assign human qualities to animals. Aristotle underscores the conjugal fidelity of the turtledove as well as the ringdove; Pliny the Elder mentions only the dove (*columba*) in his natural history, but remarks that neither partner would leave the nest after the death of the spouse: "Nisi coelebs aut uidua, nidum non relinquit" (see Bataillon 1953, 293). Aelianus (2d century A.D.) speaks of the monogamous practices of the turtledove and the ringdove, but asserts that chaste widowhood is a characteristic of the raven, and it is the raven (and not the turtledove) who comes to symbolize chaste widowhood in the earliest medieval bestiary, the Greek *Physiologus*.

The turtledove's passage from monogamous spouse to chaste widow comes about in patristic commentary on Creation. The transition is a logical one, as fidelity to the memory of the deceased husband is the highest form of monogamy (and continence) according to the newly emerging Christian feminine ethos. Thus, hexaemeral literature (which looks upon the exemplary virtues of the animal kingdom as one of the wonders of creation) is wont to hold up the turtledove as a paragon to be emulated by Christian womanhood.

The possibilities for figural interpretation were not lost on the early commentators either. The turtledove could stand for the Church, whose spouse (Christ) has been taken from her and crucified; she (like the Church) will take no other, but wait to be reunited in the next world. Later bestiaries, such as the Waldensian, equate the turtledove with the soul, which can lose its mate (Christ) through sin, and she also provides an excellent model of the lonely, repentant soul for the mystics.[9]

Representation of chaste widowhood falls naturally to the turtledove in light of the attributes ascribed to her; but what of the nightingale as the roguish suitor who would distract her from her mourning? As Asensio (1957, 249–51) points out, this is not the plaintive Philomena of Ovid (and, later, of the Renaissance) mourning her tragic loss. The nightingale (*ruiseñor,* a masculine noun in Spanish) is Theocritus' "messenger of spring," the bird of the May song, the happy celebrant of times of renewal. Asensio explores his growing reputation as a rogue: he is portrayed as a false friend in Brunetto Latini, and as an untrustworthy adviser of lovers in the *Cancionero de Baena.* Alfonso Alvarez de Villasandino, for instance (cantiga 11), rails against Love and against his messenger, the nightingale, whom he calls a "gabby liar" (*parlero mentidor,* Asensio 1957, 251). The significance of this portrayal, I believe, is crucial for an understanding of the turtledove's reaction to the nightingale in this version of *Fonte Frida;* there will be more to say on the matter in my concluding remarks.

The dialogue between the two birds recalls yet another traditional literary form: the *pastorela* (French *pastourelle*). In these, a knight encounters a peasant girl in an idealized country setting. They converse; he attempts seduction, and is usually rejected politely. The *serranillas* of the Marquis of Santillana (1398–1458) are the best known examples of serious *pastorelas* in the literature of medieval Spain; earlier, Juan Ruiz had parodied the genre in the *cantigas de serrana* included in his *Libro de buen amor* (1330–43).

Scholars have remarked on other symbolic elements and their elaboration. To demonstrate her rejection of the pleasures of the world, the turtledove refuses to perch on a green branch. This motif is attested in two twelfth-century examples adduced by Bataillon (1953, 295–96): St. Bernard of Clairvaux's *Sermones super Cantica* and the *Bestiary* of Philippe de Thaün. The motif is subsequently embellished in two ways: in one, the negative action of eschewing the green branch is converted to its positive converse, and the turtledove is represented as not shunning the green but rather seeking the dry branch in subsequent literary manifestations and iconography (Bataillon 1953, 297–99; Groos, 1968, 635–39; Gericke, 1979, 41). In another, the *Fonte Frida* poet (in a use of *amplificatio* typical of ballad style) expands the concept, having the bird reject not only the green branch but also the meadow in flower:

Rest not I on verdant branches,
Flower-strewn meadows now I shun.[10]

The refusal of the bird to drink clear water, either seeking muddied water or muddying it herself before drinking it, is another of the motifs that comes to be associated with the topos. It is traceable to Boncompagno of Florence, in his thirteenth-century *Rota Veneris*.

Otherwise I will do as the turtledove who loses her spouse ...; no more does she sit on the green branch, but on a dry one cries constantly with a mournful voice, and disturbs the clear water when she wants to drink...[11]

Interestingly enough, the motif is taken up by other Spanish ballads in which it symbolizes not mourning but penance. Ballads that deal with the sins and repentance of King Roderick, the last of the Goths, have the vanquished king wandering the earth in search of forgiveness. In some versions in modern oral tradition, his confessor orders him to travel barefoot to Rome as a condition of absolution, drinking no wine but only the muddy water he finds on his way: "and if you don't find any muddy, muddy it yourself."[12]

Apparently, none of the sixteenth-century versions of *Fonte Frida* has survived intact in modern oral tradition. Several of its motifs have, however, and are widely attested in the Hispanic world. Besides the example of King Roderick just mentioned, Luis Monguió has drawn attention to a simile based on the turtledove ("... like the loving turtledove / who lost her consort...") in a poem by the Gauchesque poet Bartolomé Hidalgo; Asensio (1957, 275–76) has published a Sanabrian version of the famous May song ("Por mayo era, por mayo") that has reminiscences of *Fonte Frida;* there are others in a ballad based on the death of Prince John sung in the Canary Islands published by Diego Catalán (1969, 2:396); and Sandra Robertson has studied the confluence of motifs in *Fonte Frida* and the *Ballad of the Prisoner*. Some version of the ballad spread to Portugal, where it was still being sung in the second half of the sixteenth century (see Asensio 1957, 273), and Leite de Vasconcellos gives examples of its persistence in modern Portuguese popular song, including this lovely fragment (1906, 33):

Eu sou como a triste rola
Quando os seus amores perde:

Anda de ramo em ramo,
Nem agoa clara bebe!

[I'm like the sad nightingale
When she loses her love:
She goes from branch to branch,
And doesn't drink clear water!]

Conclusions

Generally, Spanish traditional ballads reflect the values of the society
within which they are composed and preserved through oral tradition;
this is a premise that I think no one would dispute today. A ballad may
even begin its traditional life grounded in an event of immediate relevance (say, a political dispute) and come to be modified through the
workings of tradition over time to reflect broader societal concerns.
Menéndez Pidal (1953, 1:310–11) has shown such a transformation in
the case of a ballad on King Ferdinand IV, *Valasme nuestra señora.* The
difficulty is that some ballads are more clearly reflective of such values
and concerns, whereas in others it is extremely difficult to detect any
reference to a uniquely Hispanic ethos.

Fonte Frida, I think, finds itself at a considerable remove from any
direct, immediate, or specific reference to widowhood in Spanish society
of the fifteenth century. It is most readily seen to reflect the more universal medieval ideal (externally imposed, one could add) of conjugal chastity and fidelity beyond death—an ideal that not even St. Paul was willing
to prescribe for women and that never seems to have applied to men
anywhere.[13] Even so, it is tempting to seek an explanation of the turtledove's fury in something peculiar to the Hispanic frame of reference:
surely her protest is excessive, not only for the immediate context but
for the dialogue's generic antecedent, the *pastorela,* as well?

Two explanations make sense. One could argue that the turtledove
(sincere in her mourning, to be sure, but also aware of the privileged
social status conferred upon her by her widowhood) is irate over the
prospect of being subject (again) to the control of a man. As intriguing
as this hypothesis is, a careful reading of the text leaves us without
grounds to pursue it further. Indeed, other versions of the poem reinforce
the thought that the widow's only concern is for the memory of the
deceased: the version of the British Museum *cancionero,* for instance,
concludes thus:

Vayaste de ay, cruel,
malo, falso, engañador;
a quien tan suia me hizo
no le haría trayción.

(Asensio 1957, 245)

[Go away, you cruel,
bad, false deceiver;
I'll not betray the one
who made me such a part of him.]

Another possibility is that the nightingale is to be viewed as an unworthy suitor whose temerity provokes the lady's ire. No basis for the nightingale's inferiority on social grounds is apparent in the ballad, which makes no mention of wealth or status. Nor are there any apparent violations of ethical or moral strictures, as the nightingale comports himself most circumspectly and tenders his offer to "serve" in the courtliest of terms.

The solution must be sought, I think, in a strictly literary context, but one not readily accessible to twentieth-century readers. My earlier discussion of the nightingale stressed his literary reputation as harbinger of spring, but also as rogue, roué, false friend, and counselor of lovers; this aspect of his characterization was well established by the fifteenth century, as Asensio has shown (1957, 249–51). The notion that a rake such as that would be so presumptuous as to offer himself in the stead of the (legendarily monogamous) deceased is what moves the widow to a paroxysm of righteous wrath.

It is not sufficient to explain the widow's fury as simply her response to the offer of a new relationship, for, if that were the case, a simple "no, thank you" would have sufficed (or—thinking again of proper context—the elegant refusal of a peasant girl in a typical *pastourelle* would have been most appropriate). To appreciate the full import of the ballad's message, one must understand the symbolic significance not only of the turledove but of her suitor as well. Only then does the strident tone make sense.

Fonte Frida, then, combines the simple eloquence of the traditional Spanish ballad with a complex symbolism drawn from venerable literary and exegetical traditions. I continue to believe (as I did in 1979) that it came to life originally at the hands of a poet of uncommon cultural formation. It is thoroughly Hispanic in its expression and shows the effects of oral tradition in its style, but its symbolic content would have struck a responsive chord almost anywhere in medieval Europe. In its exaltation of chaste widowhood, it expresses an ideal that may well have borne no relationship at all to contemporary reality or to the values of a particular people.

NOTES

1. For the sixteenth-century texts and bibliographical information, see Asensio 1957, 245–46. A discussion of the relative merits of the several versions can be found in Gericke 1979. Bowring's translation is most accessible in Bryant 1973, 214–15 (an excellent source for texts and discussions of Spanish ballads in English translation). Among reliable studies of early ballads written with an English-speaking audience in mind, those of Smith (1964) and Foster (1972) stand out.

I am grateful to Prof. Marjorie E. Ratcliffe for a copy of her 1988 MLA paper, "La viuda en la legislación medieval española," and to Prof. Theodore L. Kassier for a copy of his 1988 MLA paper, "The Widow Doña Endrina," together with another paper, "Widows in the *Cantigas de Santa Maria*," and helpful bibliographical references.

2. Cf. the British Museum version's concluding lines: "A quien tan suya me hizo, / no le haría traición" [I would not betray one who made me such a part of him]. (Spanish text from Asensio 1957, 245.) Here and elsewhere, unless otherwise noted, the English translations are mine.

3. In Spanish, *el país del romancero*. Individual ballads are called *romances*, while the term *romancero* may refer to a specific collection of ballads or to the entire ballad corpus. The poems so designated, of course, bear no relationship to the long prose narratives called romances in English. Ballads may vary considerably in length, though few are longer than 200 lines. Almost all are written in eight-syllable lines, with assonance rhyme in the odd-numbered lines and no rhyme in the even-numbered ones. Some scholars view the ballad line as consisting of two hemistichs of eight syllables each, separated by a fixed caesura, for a total of sixteen syllables. The long line recalls the origins of the ballad in epic poetry, which (though anisosyllabic) features a line of fourteen to sixteen syllables with moveable caesura. For our purposes, the distinction is not crucial.

4. These texts may be consulted in any of a number of fine Old Spanish ballad anthologies, such as those of Smith (1964) or Díaz Roig (1985).

5. For a study of this ballad and the *fabliau*, see Entwistle 1939.

6. See also Dillard 1987.

7. See Vasvari in this volume.

8. Among scholars who have traced the circuitous path of the turtledove as symbol of chaste widowhood from the Song of Songs through the Middle Ages and beyond, the masterful complementary studies of Marcel Bataillon (1953) and Eugenio Asensio (1957), each a model of its type, are most pertinent for students of *Fonte Frida*. Arthur B. Groos, Jr. (1968) gives an extensive list of patristic sources and an illuminating discussion of the motif in Middle High German. My 1979 study devotes some attention to the two traditions—the exegetical and the courtly—in sixteenth century versions of *Fonte Frida*.

9. Clearly, the Waldensian text's concern is not with the turtledove as a symbol of widowhood. The loss is more akin to the absence that is central to the courtly tradition than it is to the finality of death, and the text takes pains to point out that it is not involuntary: "Mas alcun non po perdre Dio, si el non vol" [But no one can lose God if he doesn't want to] (Borghi Cedrini 1976, 34–36).

10. The translation here is George Umphrey's (Bryant 1973, 215). Bowring reverses the order of the elements in the interest of retaining his assonance rhyme.

11. Purkart's edition of the Latin text of the Strassburg incunabulum reads as follows:

Alioquin facia*m* sicut turtur que suu*m* p*er*didit maritum . . . Illa quid postea no*n* sedet i*n* ramo viridi sed gemit i*n* sicco voce flebili iugiter, et aqua*m* clara*m* turbat cu*m* appetit bibere. . . . (Boncompagno of Florence 1975, 58–59).

12. See, for example, Menéndez Pidal 1957, 66, version 14h (collected in 1905). I am indebted to Flor Salazar for much valuable information concerning this motif.

13. Certainly not with regard to medieval Castile and Leon, where (as Marjorie Ratcliffe has pointed out) the majority of widowers remarried but widows did not. See Ratcliffe 1988.

BIBLIOGRAPHY

Asensio, Eugenio. "*Fonte Frida* o Encuentro del Romance con la canción de Mayo." In *Poetica y Realidad en el Cancionero Peninsular de la Edad Media*, 241–77. Madrid: Editorial Gredos, 1957.

Bataillon, Marcel. "La Tortolica de *Fontefrida* y del *Cantico Espiritual*." *Nueva Revista de Filología Hispánica* 7 (1953): 291–306.

Boncompagno of Florence. *Rota Veneris*. Ed. Josef Purkart. New York: Delmar, 1975.

Borghi Cedrini, Luciana. *Appunti per la Lettura de un Bestiario Medievale: Il Bestiaro Valdese*. Turin: G. Giappichelli, 1976.

Bryant, Shasta M. *The Spanish Ballad in English*. Lexington: The University Press of Kentucky, 1973.

Catalán, Diego, ed. *La Flor de la Marañuela: Romancero General de las Islas Canarias.* 2 vols. Madrid: Cátedra-Seminario Menéndez Pidal/Editorial Gredos, 1969.

Díaz Roig, Mercedes, ed. *El Romancero Viejo.* Madrid: Cátedra, 1985.

Dillard, Heath. "Women in Reconquest Castile." In *Women and Medieval Society,* ed. Susan Mosher Stuard, 71–94. Philadelphia: University of Pennsylvania Press, 1976.

———. *Daughters of the Reconquest.* Cambridge: Cambridge University Press, 1987.

Entwistle, W. J. "*Blancaniña.*" *Revista de Filología Española* 1 (1939): 159–64.

Foster, David William. *The Early Spanish Ballad.* New York: Twayne, 1972.

Gericke, Philip O. "The Turtledove in Four Sixteenth-Century Versions of *Fontefrida.*" In *El Romancero Hoy: Historia, Comparatismo, Bibliografía Crítica,* ed. Diego Catalán, Samuel G. Armistead, and Antonio Sánchez Romeralo, 37–45. Madrid: Cátedra-Seminario Menéndez Pidal/Editorial Gredos, 1979.

Groos, Arthur B., Jr. "'Sigune auf der Linde' and the Turtledove in *Parzival.*" *Journal of English and Germanic Philology* 67 (1968): 631–46.

Kassier, Theodore L. "The Widow Doña Endrina." Paper presented at the 1988 meeting of the Modern Language Association.

Leite de Vasconcellos, J. "A Rola Viuva na Poesia Popular Portuguesa." *Modern Language Notes* 21 (1906): 33.

Menéndez Pidal, Ramón. *Romancero Hispánico: Teoría e Historia.* 2 vols. Madrid: Espasa-Calpe, 1953.

———. ed. *Romancero Tradicional de las Lenguas Hispánicas,* vol 1. Madrid: Seminario Menéndez Pidal/Editorial Gredos, 1957.

Monguió, Luis. "Un Rastro del Romance de Fontefrida, en la Poesía Gauchesca." *Revista Iberoamericana* 10 (1945–46): 283–85.

Ratcliffe, Marjorie. "La viuda en la jurisprudencia medieval española" (Abstract). *La Corónica* 17 (1988): 131–32.

Robertson, Sandra. "The Limits of Narrative Structure: One Aspect in the Study of 'El Prisionero.'" In *El Romancero Hoy: Poética,* ed. Diego Catalán, Samuel G. Armistead, and Antonio Sánchez Romeralo, 313–18. Madrid: Cátedra-Seminario Menéndez Pidal/Editorial Gredos, 1979.

Ruiz, Juan, Arcipreste de Hita. *Libro de buen amor.* Ed. Jacques Joset. Madrid: Espasa-Calpe, 1974.

———. Edited with English paraphrase by Raymond S. Willis. Princeton: Princeton University Press, 1972.

Smith, C. Colin, ed. *Spanish Ballads.* Oxford: Pergamon Press, 1964.

Sponsler, Lucy A. *Women in Medieval Epic and Lyric Traditions.* Lexington: The University Press of Kentucky, 1975.

Wolf, Ferdinand, and Konrad Hofmann. *Primavera y Flor de Romances.* 2 vols. Berlin: Asher, 1856.

Chapter 13

Grief, Widowhood, and Women's Sexuality in Medieval French Literature

Heather M. Arden

The most common image of widows in medieval French literature is the recently bereaved woman, intensely grieving yet easily consoled. These widows are members of a long tradition—they first appeared in Indian and Greek literature—but in the context of medieval France, they also reflect contemporary cultural and religious assumptions. That widows are much more common than widowers in this literature; that they share certain responses to sexuality; and that their male antagonists, and authors, show toward them a deeply felt hostility, sometimes mixed with admiration, are all factors that indicate conflicting psychological impulses and cultural values for medieval writers.

Widowhood in the Middle Ages could be a time of increased freedom and, also, social power for a woman. Many women married men much older than they, and they were thus often widowed quite young. Furthermore, since a woman who lived beyond the childbearing years was less threatened by the violence that often killed men, especially noblemen, she stood a good chance of living to an old age (and thus becoming one of the "old wives" whose accumulated experience is deprecated in the expression, "old wives' tales"). Although younger widows were often left with children to raise, many seemed to enjoy the independence of widowhood and chose not to remarry.[1] Indeed, if she remained chaste, Christian teaching elevated the widow to a position of respect and influence. In sum, the favorable situation that Judith M. Bennett describes for English widows in "Widows in Brigstock" was probably true for French widows also.[2]

One example of how widowhood gave medieval women the opportunity to live an active, productive life is the remarkable Christine de Pizan (1365–1430?), who, at the age of twenty-five, was left a widow with small children. Despite her youth, she never remarried, in part because of her lifelong grief over the loss of her husband. In her writings, we have an unusual record of a real widow's feelings, especially in the ballads that express her sadness and feelings of loss after the death of her husband and in her partly autobiographical work, *L'Avision Christine.*[3] Christine's widowhood, although accompanied by economic and legal difficulties, undoubtedly helped make it possible for her to write an enormous number of literary, historical, and moral works (more than thirty major works in thirty years).

Medieval French literature, however, does not reflect this social reality for the most part. In nonepic narrative, we find a number of works that present the recently bereaved widow, but these works, more or less closely related to the "Widow of Ephesus" fable, use the image of the grieving widow to expose the untrustworthiness, variability, and emotional instability of women. In a less direct way, these stories also suggest that a widow is simply another lecherous female who thinks only of finding a new outlet for her sexual needs. Despite their manifest grief, recently bereaved widows in medieval French literature soon begin thinking of getting a new man. When these widows remarry, they do so only to provide a legal sanction for their sexual desires. The fourteenth-century writer, Jean Lefevre, argued that widows would voluntarily "soy sous le mascle soubmettre" 'to submit/place themselves under the male' (1861, 25), if it were not for their fear of conception. Widows fear pregnancy so much that they resort to witchcraft and potions in order to abort (31). Therefore, they may find it simpler to cover their lechery with a new husband, like that "literary personification of rampant 'femininity' or carnality," the Wife of Bath (Robertson 1962, 321).

The motif of the grieving but easily consoled widow will be analyzed in this essay as an archetypal embodiment of deeply rooted male attitudes toward women and female sexuality. Six representative examples from fable, fabliau, lai, and romance will be examined. These stories—three versions of the "Widow of Ephesus" fable; two fabliaux about newly bereaved widows, "Celle qui se fist foutre sur la fosse de son mari" and "La Veuve"; and the sections of Chrétien de Troyes's *Yvain* that involve the widow, Laudine—share the narrative elements of the story of a widow who appears to be excessively aggrieved by her husband's death but who quickly accepts the first opportunity to take up with a new man.[4] All six stories, despite many differences of incident and character, portray these two characteristics of the widow: her excessive grief and her haste in accepting a new man. In addition, the three "Widow of Ephesus" stories add a secondary motif, that of the mistreatment of the dead husband's body, a motif that appears to be a symbolic restatement of the first one, that of the wife's infidelity to her husband. That is, the basic "widow" tale in European literature is defined by the infidelity of a new widow to her husband, and the "Widow of Ephesus" motif (the addition of an episode involving the husband's body) is a subcategory of it. This will be clearer after a closer look at the six stories.

Both of these essential components—great grief and easy acceptance of "consolation"—show many variants when realized in particular stories. The three major variables in the passages dealing with the widow's mourning are the amount of detail with which it is described, whether it is sincere or feigned, and whether there is an audience of friends and relatives. All of the stories indicate the widow's great grief, but the amount of description runs from two succinct lines in Marie de France's fable (1987): "Sa femme demeine grant dolur / Sur sa tumbe e nuit e jur" [His wife mourned him most woefully / Over his grave both night and day; ll. 3–4],[5] to hundreds of lines in Chrétien's *Yvain*. Despite these differences, certain "mourning motifs" recur in the stories, motifs that include ceaseless and vociferous wailing, remaining on the tomb, wanting to die, refusing to listen to friends or relatives, and manifesting physical signs of grief, such as twisting hands, tearing hair and clothes, and fainting.

When reading the mourning ballads of Christine de Pizan, it is striking to find many of the same motifs expressed by a real widow. The beginning of Ballad 6, for example, pours out a series of modified nouns expressing her extreme grief.

Deuil engoisseux, rage desmesuree,
Grief desespoir, plein de forsennement,
Langour sans fin, vie maleuree
Pleine de plour, d'engoisse et de tourment. . . .

[Anguished grief, unlimited pain, bitter despair full of madness, unending sadness, unhappy life full of weeping, anguish, and torment; 1886, ll. 1–4.]

The cumulative effect suggests an unbearable intensity of grief, such that we seem to be hearing the wailing of the fictional widows. Furthermore Christine often expresses the same desire as they to die and join the dead husband, as in Ballad 8: her mourning is so great "qu'il me fait desirer / Morir briefment" [that it makes me want / to die soon; 1886, ll. 9–10; see also ballads 5, 6, 9, and 17]. Finally, we find the motifs, as in the narratives, of grief that is too great for words, of sorrow that will last all her life, of a refusal to ever be consoled or comforted, of others' wonder at her continued grieving. Although Christine by no means fits the image of the easily consoled widow (the second element in the paradigm mentioned above)—the ballads were composed over a period of ten years and her sorrow lasted all her life—the expression of her grief takes many of the same forms as that of the fictional widows.

This raises the question of the relationship of culturally sanctioned modes for the expression of mourning to literary manifestations of grief. "She knew well the way to mourn" ("elle en a le molle trové" [*molle:* manner or mode]), we are told by the narrator of one version of "Celle qui se fist foutre" (Lacy 1967, 103).[6] We cannot simply conclude that medieval tales that describe the way widows grieve were being "realistic," since the medieval conception of realism is so different from the modern. It is also possible that life imitated art in forms of mourning, as it did in other areas (this is especially true of courtly culture). Thus, Christine's literary mourning was modeled on her socially influenced experience of grief, which was perhaps in turn influenced by literary traditions of the grieving widow. The question of the relation of literary models of mourning to social forms could certainly be explored further.[7]

Like Christine's expression of grief, that of most fictional widows appears to be sincere, a circumstance that supports the official moral of many of the tales that women are variable and unstable. That is, if the widow truly loves her husband, her emotional instability, as revealed in her acceptance of another man, is indeed amazing. However, at least one tale, "Celle qui si fist foutre," suggests that the wife's grief is "laid on," and that, consequently, she is in fact guilty of hypocrisy and lechery, not instability, although that is still given as the interpretation of her behavior in the moral to the tale. The problem may result from the poet's desire to attribute contradictory vices to his female character—both hypocrisy and emotional instability.

The second major component in the grieving/consoled widow stories concerns the way in which the wife's infidelity is realized. Again, three types of variants are found. These regard whether the shift in her affections is motivated or abrupt, who initiates the new love affair, and whether a new union is formed. Each category is, of course, capable of many further variations in details, as we shall see when we look at the six stories.

The first group of stories to be discussed are forms of what is called the "Widow of Ephesus" motif. Many medieval versions exist of the "Widow of Ephesus" story, which has been called "perhaps the most popular of all stories" (Joseph Jacobs, quoted in Runte 1974, xlviii). Although many studies of fables have discussed it and some have suggested ways to break it into constituent motifs (see Runte 1974, l–li), the fable's significance for understanding medieval attitudes specifically toward widows has not been examined. Yet the fable's popularity suggests that it did, indeed, hold a special meaning for medieval as well as classical storytellers.

Three manuscripts of the fable collection called the *Isopet* I (Bastin 1929–30, 333–36) contain a representative version of the basic tale: a worthy man (*preudons*), seemingly happily married, dies; his wife shows great grief by refusing to move from the tomb and by asking only to die there. A thirsty knight guarding a hanged robber nearby goes to ask her for something to drink when her lamentations make him aware of her presence. He finds her attractive, pursues her (in between three trips to check on the body he is supposed to be guarding), and seems to win her love. When, on the third return to his post, he discovers that the corpse is missing, the distraught knight runs to the widow with his problem, for he is threatened with the same fate if he lets the hanged body get away. She suggests substituting her husband's body. He does as she suggests, then marries her for having saved his life.

The moral of the story is typically misogynistic: this is a cautionary tale for husbands; wives quickly forget their husbands; the same thing could happen to the second one; finally, a woman living alone deceives both the living and the dead. The storyteller's view of the widow is conflicted: she is both very attractive and morally repulsive. She is offered to the husbands in the audience as a striking representation of the variability, the instability of women, for it seems to be her variability that explains her infidelity to her husband. We will see, however, by examining other versions of the story, that this moral is an inversion of the more fundamental medieval view of widows—and of women generally—that their sexual appetite explains their variability, rather than the other way around. The unspoken question that the fable raises is whether widows easily accept another man because they are variable, or whether their desire for another man makes them appear to be variable. In other words, are they variable simply because they are female?

One of the important retellings of the story of the easily consoled widow is found in the many medieval versions of *The Seven Sages of Rome*. In this frame story, seven wise men tell stories to disprove those of the evil stepmother who is trying to persuade her husband, the emperor, to put his son (her stepson) to death. One of the wise men's stories is usually a version of the "Widow of Ephesus," such as the one given in the Seven Sages' story entitled *Li Ystoire de la male marastre* [The Story of the Evil Stepmother]. While the core of the story remains the same, the *Seven Sages* version differs from the *Isopet* fable through the addition of episodes at the beginning and end: an introductory scene explains the husband's death as a result of his remorse for having accidentally nicked his wife with his knife, and a lengthy conclusion shows the widow hanging and wounding the body of her dead husband, with little or no help from the recently amorous knight, who then insults or kills the unhappy widow (see the chart of variants in Runte 1974, li). Both of these episodes appear to reinforce the misogynistic message of the story: it is because of his love for her that the husband dies (after accidentally wounding her), but she does not hesitate to willingly mistreat his body—cutting the head, breaking teeth, cutting the side, even castrating it—in order to please her new lover. The *Seven Sages* stories, although they recognize the widow's attractiveness, stress her moral repulsiveness more emphatically.

A less misogynistic version of the standard tale, Marie de France's twenty-fifth fable, reduces the reprehensible faithlessness of the widow in a number of ways. To the core story of the excessively grieving widow who falls in love, on her husband's grave, with another man to whom she gives her husband's body in order to save his life, Marie appears to have added elements that play down the misogynistic point of view by suggesting a courtly affair of the heart.[8] First, Marie conveys the widow's relationship to her husband in two quick references that cast him in the role of the shadowy husband of courtly poetry and narrative: in the beginning we learn simply that *un humme* ('a man') has died and been buried; at the end the widow refers to him simply as *mun barun* ('my husband'). There is no indication of the husband's worthiness, as in most other versions. Second, the soldier of the standard version has become *uns chevaliers* (although an unscrupulous one—he decides to seduce the widow *after* he gets in trouble, thus decreasing her guilt by increasing his own), and he speaks to her *cuintement* (that is, in an elegant and courtly way). Then, in a wonderful example of her power of concision, Marie conveys the widow's response in three lines that encapsulate the course of a courtly love relationship: "La prude femme l'*esguarda;* / grant *joie* fist, si *otria* / qu'ele fera sa volenté" [The worthy lady *looked* him through; / She felt great *joy,* and she vowed (*granted*) to do / Whatever he might wish or want; Marie de France 1987, ll. 23–25; italics added]. In addition to conveying the immediacy of her response, these lines point to its courtliness: it is through the eyes that courtly love (*fin' amors*) moves to the heart, that the lady "sees" the man as deserving of love, and that subsequently she experiences and then bestows (*otrier*) that courtly *joie* the poets celebrate.

It is perhaps the courtly point of view that leads the widow, in the moral she draws, to stress the life-affirming value of her act: "Deliverer deit hum par le mort / Le vif dunt l'em ad cunfort" [One ought to use the dead to free / The living, who can comfort be; ll. 35–36]. In the author's moral, Marie does not refer to women's variability, but to the little faith that the dead can expect from the living: this moral extends to *li mund* [everyone] rather than just to women. Marie has thus managed to indicate a respect for the widow as courtly beloved in a tale that was one of the outstanding medieval examples of women's lack of courtly virtues.

Although these three versions of the tale of the easily consoled widow differ greatly in detail, they can be seen to represent the same "functions" in a two-move story (see Propp 1975). That is, in the "Widow of Ephesus" fables, the same functions, or underlying events, occur twice: in the first "move" (Ia), the body of a dead husband is buried, this causes anguish in his wife, she is approached by a second man, she betrays her husband with him; in the second "move" (Ib), the body of a dead wrong-doer is removed, this causes anguish in the second man (the guard), the widow is approached by the second man, she mistreats her husband's body because of him. Schematically, the two parts of the story reveal this pattern:

Ia The Husband Betrayed	Ib The Dead Man Betrayed
M1 placed in grave	M3 displaced from gibbet
W anguished	M2 anguished

M2 approaches W   M2 approaches W
W betrays M1   W betrays M1

(W the widow; M1 the husband; M2 the lover; M3 the hanged man)

Thus, the four functions of the "Widow of Ephesus" story are: movement of a dead body (placed or displaced), anguish in a person concerned with the dead body, appeal by a living man to the widow, and betrayal of the dead husband. The double story explores the two significant components of the first man's identity: he is a husband and he is dead; in Ia the wife betrays her marital feelings, in Ib, her duty to the dead. But rather than two distinct betrayals, the pattern of underlying functions suggests that the second part of the story is a restatement of the first, that the mistreatment of her husband's body reenacts the widow's betrayal of their marriage. This conclusion is further supported by the fact that, while the first part of the story is found without the second, as we shall see, the second part is never found without the first. That is, there are no cases of a widow who mistreats her husband's body without first having formed an amorous attachment with another man, nor are there any cases of a woman betraying in this way anyone but her dead husband. Therefore, it appears that the motif of erotic betrayal is the model for the motif of disrespect to the dead.

It has generally been accepted by scholars that the moral of these stories, the variability of women, is really what they are about. For example, the eminent medievalist, Paul Zumthor, accepted the fabliau, "Celle qui se fist foutre," as a "dénonciation plaisante des perfidies féminines" (1954, 256). Norris Lacy, in a note to his edition of "Celle...," argued that "the seduction is only a consequence and a visible sign of [the widow's] inconstancy, which is itself the real point of the fabliau" (1967, 119). However, it has not been recognized that we are, in effect, dealing with three possible forms of perfidy or inconstancy: the widow's infidelity to her husband, her emotional instability in quickly forgetting her grief, and her disrespect to the dead. In any case, all of these inconstancies can be seen as springing from the widow's sexual needs. Joseph Bédier is one of the few scholars to have argued that women's supposed perfidy or inconstancy is really another form of their lechery. He sees fabliau widows as "affolées du besoin de jouir, comme la hideuse Matrone d'Ephèse du XIIIe siècle" (1925, 324). The three stories to be discussed next, in which the grieving widow motif is

found without the motif of disrespect to the dead husband's body, supports Bédier's assumption by pointing to an underlying view of women's
sexuality as the cause of their other vices.

One of the most popular fabliaux, "Celle qui se fist foutre sur la fosse
de son mari," has been classed as a variant of the "Widow of Ephesus"
motif (Lacy 1967, 8) because, although the story lacks the hanging of the
dead body, the grieving widow is made love to on her husband's grave.
The presence of the husband's body at his widow's "comforting" is
enough, it seems, to tie the story to the "Widow of Ephesus" tales. The
fabliau, which shares with the other easily consoled widow stories a
description of the extreme grief of the widow, relates how a rich man's
widow mourns him in all the prescribed ways: exaggerated wailing,
remaining on the tomb night and day, physical injury to herself, wanting
to die, and refusing the comfort of relatives. It is of interest that a number
of lines describing the widow's grief appear to be variants of lines in
Chrétien's *Yvain*.[9] This borrowing suggests that medieval authors saw
Laudine as an example of the easily consoled widow. But this is the only
similarity between the two heroines. The widow of "Celle..." proves
to be either remarkably naive or outstandingly lustful, for when a passing
squire reveals that he has killed the woman he loved by screwing her,
she, who wants to die, asks him to do the same for her! She soon realizes,
however, when she nearly dies of pleasure, that the squire will pass away
before his new "victim" does. The scandalous change in the widow's
behavior makes the author feel justified in drawing out the usual moral
on the variability and untrustworthiness of women.[10]

In the "Widow of Ephesus" and similar stories, the grief-stricken
widow is approached by a willing man, while in other stories the widow
herself sets out to find a new man. In the fabliau, "La Veuve," for
example, Gautier Le Leu combines motifs from the "Widow of Ephesus"
story with a satiric portrait of a powerful woman acting on her own
sexual behalf.[11] Like the Widow of Ephesus, the widow of the fabliau
shows great grief at her husband's death, even to the point of wanting
to jump into the grave after him. She is quickly persuaded, however, to
think of taking another husband. With her new independence and wealth
("je sui riche femme à force," 'I am a powerfully rich woman'; Le Leu
1877, 206), she decides to be her own marriage broker in order to find
a husband to her taste. Her enormous sexual appetite is described canni-
balistically: her sex wants to eat "char crue" ('raw flesh'; 201); it is also
described as an illness in her loins to be cured by a stick (with two

meanings?). She is so frantic to find a new husband that she hates her children because they might discourage a suitor. In a long monologue to a woman friend, she debates which man she should take as her next husband: she wants to find a young, vigorous one: "Suer, je n'ai cure de vielhart" [Sister, I'm not interested in an old one; 208]. Her unfortunate second husband is soon worn out by her sexual demands. When she complains of his lack of interest, the new husband replies that he cannot do it all the time, and that she is killing him. (Is the author suggesting that her first husband's purported indifference was, in reality, sexual exhaustion and that was why he passed away?) Cursing himself for having taken a "vielh femme a enfans" [an old woman with children; 211], as though that accounts for his problem, the new husband beats his wife soundly—behavior that gets him pardoned by his wife.

The narrator's ironic moral is that a man should treat his wife gently because she is "desous et vos desore" [she is on the bottom and you on top; 213], but the example of the husband's aggressive behavior may have been the more pointed moral for medieval husbands. These conflicting lessons—gentleness and aggression—suggest feelings of anxiety and fear in the narrator faced with what he sees as the dangerous power of female sexuality. Of course the stories of lecherous widows reflect the medieval male writer's view of all women as inherently lecherous. But the widow's situation differs from the unfaithful wife of medieval narrative in two ways—her expression of her animalistic sexuality is not opposed or frustrated by a husband and she has the means to satisfy her needs. This may help explain why widows appear so much less frequently in medieval narrative than wives, and why authors much preferred the narrative possibilities of the unfaithful wife—who proves there must be fifty ways to deceive a husband—rather than of the widow, who can express her sexual desires more overtly.

Elements of the easily consoled widow tale are also found in that quintessentially courtly romance, Chrétien de Troyes's *Le Chevalier au Lion (Yvain)*. The widow's first appearance shows her extreme grief for her dead husband, whom she wants to follow to the tomb: Laudine's demonstration of mourning includes all the variables described above. Her grief, which Chrétien spends 300 lines describing, is so great that thrice the author declares it to be indescribable (1971, 1174–76). Yet within a day she will have accepted the idea of marrying another man. A comparison of Laudine with the other widows, however, shows that

Chrétien is working toward other narrative purposes. Laudine is not simply another Widow of Ephesus.

The fact that her husband's killer will be the man who consoles Laudine for the loss adds the ironic conflict of love and hate that appealed to Chrétien (see the conflict of love and hate in Yvain and Gauvain's duel at the end of the romance). This conflict enhances Yvain's "feat" in winning the widow but also makes her remarriage more shocking. Despite the enormous obstacles, however, the love-stricken Yvain does not despair, for he believes that "fame a plus de cent corages" [a woman has more than a hundred states of mind; 1440]. Yvain is expressing the moral of the fables we have studied, a circumstance that suggests that he is taking the point of view of the lover in the fables. In fact, we see Laudine largely through his eyes—it is he who witnesses for us her grief and her beauty. Chrétien may be suggesting that Yvain, at this stage in his development, still holds simplistic and derogatory views of women, and that his evolution in the romance will bring him to a wiser understanding of Laudine and all women.

Cast in the role of the easily consoled widow, Laudine plays her part by changing her mind quickly (with a little help from her skillful chambermaid, as in Petronius's fable of the Widow of Ephesus), when she realizes that she will be getting a better—stronger and younger?—husband. After clearing Yvain in her mind of any wrongdoing, she becomes enamored of him in a kind of spontaneous combustion: "par li meismes s'alume" [she catches on fire by herself; 1779]. Since Arthur is not coming to challenge her for a week or so, it is her desire for Yvain, rather than her legitimate concern for the defense of her fountain, that explains her great impatience to have Yvain in her presence that night, or the next day at the latest ("Quand le porrons nos avoir?" 'When can we have him?' she asks her chambermaid; 1822). Her request for counsel from her cowardly barons is a formality to legitimate the choice that this widow has already made of a new husband.

Yet the subtle emotional stages that Chrétien shows his heroine passing through makes us see her change of heart as natural and sympathetic. Chrétien's interest in motivation contrasts with the misogynistic abruptness of other stories of easily consoled widows. In addition to the exploration of her thoughts and feelings, the romance shows Laudine to be a more admirable and more complex character than the typical widow. For all her feudal need of a warrior-husband, Laudine manages her fief well in his absence and is so strong willed that she has to be tricked into taking him back. Thus, Chrétien's charming, gentle mockery of his widow is far from Gautier Le Leu's coarse satire. The courtly writer has woven into his plot traditional motifs that suggest a recognition of the strong erotic needs and the independent mind of a wealthy widow, while ironically showing the limitations of his hero's, and society's, misconceptions about widows.

Thus, in contradiction to the realities of many widows' lives, the widow is portrayed in medieval French literature as an excessively grieving woman who nonetheless betrays her recently dead husband by quickly accepting a new lover or husband. Although most storytellers offer these narratives as examples of women's variability, arguments can be offered to support the hypothesis that this reputed variability, or emotional changeability, is another form of, and a result of, how medieval men viewed women's sexuality.

The most striking evidence is the abruptness and inappropriateness with which widows are shown accepting (or propositioning) a potential lover, an abruptness that suggests a sexual appetite that even great grief cannot diminish. Scholars who have considered the abruptness of the widow's change of heart to be a narrative defect are missing the point the author is making, that women change suddenly and without reason. But is the changeableness of widows really the cause of their behavior, or a symptom? The explanation by variability is an avoidance of an explanation, for by claiming that women change continuously, medieval writers were denying women a stable identity—they were defining women as an absence, a lack that may have been a less disturbing transmutation of the underlying view of women as a negative force because of their very femaleness. That is, if chastity is positive and sexuality negative, variability is a way of saying that women always move from the positive to the negative state (their variability is, finally, not random). This may be a reflection of the frustration inherent in men's possessiveness toward their wives, their need to determine and fix their behavior, but if this is part of the reason for the view that women are variable, it is also tied into medieval men's view of the uncontrollable and threatening nature of women's sexuality.

Other evidence to suggest that these narratives are, in reality, talking about female sexuality is found in the fact that the only person betrayed by unstable women are their husbands. Thus it is primarily sexual relationships with which the storytellers are concerned. This is further indicated by the storytellers pointing their tales specifically to husbands rather than to men in general. It is husbands who have the most to fear from women's uncontrollable sexuality. The presence of a sexual motive can also be seen in the stories in which infidelity occurs without disrespect to the dead husband's body, but not vice versa. Finally, some storytellers, such as Gautier Le Leu, directly express a view of female sexuality as animalistic and uncontrollable. It is, therefore, probable that other poets held the same views even though they did not express them so overtly.

Finally, the attitude toward female sexuality that we find in the stories of easily consoled widows is consistent with the medieval belief that, while sexuality is an inherently sinful force to be distrusted and restrained, female sexuality is even more dangerous than the male—more forceful, more irrational, less restrainable. For this reason, even in the sacrament of marriage, women were seen as led by their animalistic sexuality to betray their marriage vows, and in their mourning to betray both their marriage vows and their duty to the dead. While the Church saw it as preferable that widows not remarry, since to do so would indicate a reprehensible interest in sexual activity, medieval writers of narrative evidently saw widows as unable to choose chastity or even a period of fidelity to their dead spouse.[12] Thus, theologians and writers in the Middle Ages forced on women the destructive belief that, though their sexual needs were greater than men's, they must show more sexual restraint than men. For these reasons we cannot accept the medieval storytellers' contention that their widows are offered as examples of women's variability—instead we must look beneath this polite surface to examine medieval men's attitudes toward, and fears of, women's sexuality.

NOTES

1. This is indicated by such sources as the Parisian tax roles; see Labarge 1986, 151.

2. Bennett's essay is reprinted in this volume (chap. 3).

3. See, in particular, her *Cent Ballades*, nos. 5 to 20. Dulac's essay in this volume also deals with Christine's widowhood (see chap. 10).

4. Many other versions of the story are found in medieval French literature. A particularly misogynistic one is given by Matheolus in the *Lamentations* (see

Matheolus 1905, 42–44; see also Lacy 1967, 44–46). This version, as well as most of the others, such as Eustache Deschamps's retelling (1878–1903, 9:131–33), show only minor variations from the stories studied here.

5. The translations are those of Spiegel.

6. The Wife of Bath also suggests that she knows the conventional forms of grieving: "Whan that my fourthe housbonde was on beere, / I weep algate, and made sory cheere, / As wyves mooten, for it is usage . . ." (Chaucer 1933, 587–89), but in reality she wept little, for she already had her eye on her next mate.

7. Donald Maddox has demonstrated a revealing parallel between the social conventions relative to the proper way to die, moral literature on the subject, and drama in his analysis of Maître Pathelin's parody of a dying man in *La Farce de Maître Pathelin* (Maddox 1984, chap. 5).

8. See the intelligent analysis of Marie de France's possible changes in the Matron of Ephesus motif in Runte 1983.

9. Compare, in particular, l. 24 and ll. 37–38 of "Celle . . ." with l. 1174 and ll. 1251–52 of *Yvain.*

10. See Norris Lacy's criticism of "Celle . . ." (1967). "If this account of the widow has a serious flaw, it must be the implausibility of such a sudden and extreme change" (37).

11. A similar situation is found in the farce, "La Veuve" (1939).

12. James A. Brundage's monumental work, *Law, Sex, and Christian Society in Medieval Europe* (1987), gives many examples of medieval man's attitude toward female sexuality; see 350, 427–28, 548, and 591. On widows' remarrying, see 97–98, 142, and 477–78.

BIBLIOGRAPHY

Bastin, Julia, ed. "D'un homme et de sa femme." In *Recueil général des Isopets,* 2:333–36. Paris: Champion, 1929–30.

Bédier, Joseph. *Les fabliaux: Études de littérature populaire et d'histoire littéraire du moyen âge.* 4th ed. Paris: E. Champion, 1925.

Bennett, Judith M. "Public Power and Authority in the Medieval English Countryside." In *Women and Power in the Middle Ages,* ed. Mary Erler and Maryann Kowaleski, 18–36. Athens, Ga.: University of Georgia Press, 1988.

Brundage, James A. *Law, Sex, and Christian Society in Medieval Europe.* Chicago: University of Chicago Press, 1987.

"Celle qui se fist foutre sur la fosse de son mari." In *Nouveau recueil complet des fabliaux,* ed. Willem Noomen and Nico Van Den Boogaard, 3:400–403. Assen: Van Gorcum, 1983.

Chaucer, Geoffrey. *The Works of Geoffrey Chaucer.* Ed. F. N. Robinson. Boston: Houghton Mifflin, 1933.

Chrétien de Troyes. *Le chevalier au lion (Yvain)*. Paris: Honoré Champion, 1971.

Christine de Pisan. *Oeuvres poétiques*. Ed. Maurice Roy. 3 vols. Paris: Firmin Didot, 1886.

Deschamps, Eustache. *Li miroir de mariage*. Vol. 9 of *Oeuvres d'Eustache Deschamps*. Ed. Gaston Raynaud. Paris: Firmin Didot, 1878–1903.

Labarge, Margaret Wade. *A Small Sound of the Trumpet: Women in Medieval Life*. Boston: Beacon Press, 1986.

Lacy, Norris J. "*La Femme au Tombeau:* Anonymous Fabliau of the Thirteenth Century." Ph. D. diss., Indiana University, 1967.

Lefevre, Jean. *La Vieille*. Ed. Hippolyte Cocheris. Paris: Auguste Aubry, 1861.

Le Leu, Gautier. "La Veuve." In *Recueil général des fabliaux des XIIIe et XIVe siècles,* ed. Anatole de Montaiglon and Gaston Raynaud, 2:197–214. Paris: Librairie des Bibliophiles, 1877.

Maddox, Donald. *The Semiotics of Deceit: The Pathelin Era*. Lewisburg, Pa.: Bucknell University Press, 1984.

Marie de France. "De la femme ki fist pendre sun mari." In *Fables*, ed. and trans. Harriet Spiegel, 92–95. Toronto: University of Toronto Press, 1987.

Matheolus. *Les lamentations de Matheolus et le livre de leesce*. Trans. Jehan Le Fevre. Paris: Emile Bouillon, 1905.

Propp, Vladimir. *Morphology of the Folktale*. 2nd ed. Ed. Louis A. Wagner. Austin: University of Texas Press, 1975.

Robertson, D. W., Jr. *A Preface to Chaucer: Studies in Medieval Perspectives*. Princeton: Princeton University Press, 1962.

Runte, Hans. "'Alfred's Book,' Marie de France, and the Matron of Ephesus." *Romance Philology* 36, no. 4 (May, 1983): 556–64.

———, ed. *Li Ystoire de la Male Marastre: Version M of the Roman des Sept Sages de Rome*. Tübingen: Max Niemeyer, 1974.

"La Veuve." In *Six farces normandes du recueil La Vallière*, ed. E. Philipot, 153–86. Rennes: Plihon, 1939.

Zumthor, Paul. *Histoire littéraire de la France médiévale*. Paris: Presses Universitaires de France, 1954.

Chapter 14

The Widow as Heroine: The Fifteenth-Century Catalan Chivalresque Novel *Curial e Güelfa*

Montserrat Piera and Donna M. Rogers

Curial e Güelfa, a Catalan chivalresque novel of the mid–fifteenth century, has a young widow named Güelfa as its protagonist. Güelfa is wealthy, powerful, independent, attractive, and strong willed. She is a noblewoman who wields great influence over others, suffers the trials and tribulations of love, and eventually finds happiness, albeit at the cost of great emotional and financial distress.

Curial e Güelfa is a work of interest to scholars for a variety of reasons. Its plot, as chivalresque novels go, is unusually realistic; its characters, situations, and locations are remarkably true to life. Although its author and exact date of composition are unknown,[1] it is clearly a work of transition, looking back for inspiration to an earlier period, the age of chivalry, yet, at the same time, looking forward to the Renaissance, to the "rebirth" or at least rekindling of interest in Classical ideals and forms, to a greater awareness of and interest in the individual.

Of immediate concern in this essay is the character of Güelfa as widow. We shall approach this character by examining the status, both financial and emotional, of medieval widows in general, and of the Catalan widow in particular. We will use both a historical and a literary perspective.

In her recent book, *A Small Sound of the Trumpet: Women in Medieval Life,* Margaret Wade Labarge described the pattern of life for many medieval women.

The young girl or infant was in the same state of legal powerlessness as her brother, but her upbringing was mainly devoted to inculcating

321

the feminine ideal of passivity and submissiveness to her parents and a future husband, whoever he might be. Her marriage, often at a very young age, meant total domination by her husband and, for all practical purposes, the extinguishing of her legal rights during the term of the marriage. Despite this, she was also supposed to be competent and resourceful in running the household once she was married, since its material comfort and maintenance was primarily her responsibility. Finally widowhood, if she had any resources, opened to a woman the possibility of the exercise of personal power. She regained her legal personality, was entitled to a certain share of her husband's holdings and, for the first time in her life, could make independent decisions. Widowhood could be perilous, with the danger of violence and intimidation being used to overturn legal rights, but its possibilities for action seem to have exhilarated many medieval women, and the challenges brought forth quick responses. Because men tended to marry somewhat later and usually preferred younger partners, even when they themselves had reached middle age, the widow, especially of a third or fourth marriage, might well be quite a young woman.... It is a tribute to the flexibility of medieval women that such a number managed to reconcile successfully the contradictory attributes they were admonished to display at different periods of their lives. (27–28)

While not all medieval women's lives conformed to this pattern (religious women, for example, had very different experiences), for those women who did marry it appears to have been common throughout most of Europe and through much of the Middle Ages. Labarge's study deals chiefly with northern Europe, as does Angela M. Lucas' *Women in the Middle Ages;* nevertheless, studies of medieval Spanish women's lives document a similar pattern.[2]

When we attempt to discover the circumstances of medieval widows, we find a number of general characteristics in these women's lives and in their society's view of them. In Spain, the law codes uniformly mandated a year of mourning upon the death of a husband (Díez 1983, 111; Mitre 1983, 81; Pérez de Tudela 1983, 71; Vigil 1986, 196; Voltes and Voltes 1986, 153–54). Exceptions were rare, and then only in extreme situations: an example is the proclamation at the Cortes de Valladolid in 1351 that the year of mourning (during which remarriage was not permitted) was to be reduced to six months, due to the high mortality during the Black Death, and the usual penalties for infringement were eliminated. This law was promulgated again in 1400 and in 1401. Upon her husband's death, a widow could inherit part or all of his estate, although this was by no means assured. A widow could be named as executrix of her husband's will, responsible for ensuring that the funeral and burial were carried out according to the testator's wishes, and that his estate was disposed of according to his instructions. She could have been given responsibility for the education of their children, or the administration or usufruct of the estate until the heir came of age.

The state of widowhood could bring with it a series of conflicts or contradictions: a woman who during her marriage had shouldered the responsibility for running a large household might find that the usufruct or administration of that household had passed to someone else; conversely, a widow unused to such responsibilities during marriage might find herself saddled with them at her husband's death. She might have little or no say in the education of her minor children. And society had high expectations of widows: widows were often expected to shut themselves away from any kind of public life for the year of mourning (and sometimes indefinitely); to devote themselves to good works; to dress simply, without adornment of any kind. The widow's inheritance was sometimes conditional upon her remaining chaste (i.e., unmarried) indefinitely after her husband's death (Díez 1983, 111; Vinyoles et al. 1984, 32). Yet a widow's family might pressure her to remarry, especially if money was tight and they had to support the widow and her children.

It was generally considered to be unsuitable for aristocratic women to practice any kind of profession, even though they could inherit substantial wealth. The money brought them a certain degree of independence, but did not necessarily give them the freedom to do whatever they wanted. The situation of the Catalonian widow was, in some respects, different from that of other Spanish widows. Catalonia, an important sea power and a flourishing merchant society during the Middle Ages, was wealthier than other parts of medieval Iberia. That prosperity seems to have provided its widows with additional legal security (Voltes and Voltes 1986, 154). Upon her husband's death, a widow was entitled to the return of her dowry plus the *escreix,* a contribution paid by the husband that could equal half of the dowry. During the official year of mourning, a widow had the right to be maintained by the husband's estate, a right known as the *any de plor.* This provided her with food, clothing, and shelter, and was limited only by the resources of the deceased. Every widow was entitled to the *any de plor* unless she held the usufruct of her husband's estate or claimed the *tenuta,* which granted her control over and administration of his estate until her dowry plus *escreix* had been paid. Her remarriage before the end of the year of mourning would forfeit her *any de plor* rights (Vinyoles et al. 1984, 30–31).

In a study of men's and women's wills made in Barcelona from 1350 to 1410, Vinyoles et al. find that, among marriages with children, the widow was left without any legacy or inheritance whatsoever in only 8 percent of the wills. In most cases, she was part heir (or legatee) or usufructuary. In Catalonia, too, however, some testators specified that their widows could lose all or part of their inheritance if they were to remarry. It is striking that, of the 75 wills made by married men (out of a total corpus of 200 wills), only one left an unconditional legacy to the widow.

According to Vinyoles' research, many widows maintained strong ties to their husband's and their own families, especially the latter in the case of childless marriages (1984, 34–35). Another contemporary source would seem to support that claim: private letters written by widows themselves. In the *Epistolari del segle XV* (1926), a collection of fifteenth-century Catalan letters, there are several written by widows: one from a widow to her brother, two from widows to their brothers-in-law, and one from a widow to her late husband's creditors. The three family letters provide glimpses into the daily affairs of these widows. In a letter to her brother, Blanquina de Claret asks after his family's health and informs him about the status of some household repairs (*Epistolari* 1926, 55–56). She also asks him to forward to her some money so that she can pay three men, whom she mentions by name (possibly apprentices?).

In another letter, Avinyent Cugullada writes to her brother-in-law about family matters, specifically the arrangements for the marriage of her daughters (*Epistolari* 1926, 70–72). He has proposed a match with a young Barcelona merchant and will provide the couple with a house in Barcelona. She is agreeable to whatever arrangements he wishes to make. She also mentions several times that her daughters regard him as their father, since they have no other.

In the third family letter written by a widow, a woman named Pressaguera writes to her brother-in-law asking for news about the family's health (*Epistolari* 1926, 118–19). She specifically asks after her brother-in-law, his sons and daughters, and her own sons. She then inquires about news of her brother and pregnant sister-in-law. She is clearly anxious, since she has arranged for the bearer of the letter to wait for a reply.

Another letter of interest is from "Beatriu de Maldà, vídua de Pere de Cardona," to her late husband's creditors (*Epistolari* 1926, 98–99). She is, in fact, advising them of his death and arranging for her representative to visit them in a fortnight's time to settle his affairs. Her son is the heir, and she is attempting, on his behalf, to execute her husband's wishes. This is further attested to by the fact that the representative she is sending was a trusted intimate of the deceased.

The letters collected in the *Epistolari* depict widows who are managing households, overseeing repairs, and administering estates. They are concerned with their children's welfare and that of their close relatives. The writers' sentiments are clear and direct across five centuries: Beatriu de Maldà refers to herself as "posada en gran tribulació," "trista e dolorosa" upon the recent death of her husband. Pressaguera writes for news of family members "ab gran desig" and assures her brother-in-law that she would be with them if she could. Avinent Cugullada assures her brother-in-law that his nieces miss him and think of him as a father. Blanquina de Claret's letter seems strangely lacking in the affectionate salutations and commendations so frequent in the other family letters in the collection; it is, however, a brisk, businesslike epistle that contains interesting details of her home-improvement project and some family matters.

Another source of information about medieval Catalan widows is the fourth treatise of Francesc Eiximenis's *Libre de les dones* (1981, chaps. 95–100). It was probably written about 1388, some six decades before *Curial e Güelfa;* nevertheless, Eiximenis's observations about the proper comportment of widows and their place in his society are illuminating and seem to conform to the models presented in the other sources we have consulted.

Eiximenis, a Franciscan, refers repeatedly to Biblical and patristic authorities to elaborate his view of the widow's role in society. He maintains that widowhood is an honorable and desirable state, since widows have been chosen by God to serve Him (1981, 145). God places women in that state to test their patience and prudence (153). Widowhood brings great blessings and benefits to women: freedom from worldly cares and "tota aquella misèria que la persona en matrimoni passa"

(145). Not only are widows under God's special protection, they are also to receive charitable support from their society, and a double reward in heaven.

Eiximenis continues, stating that women should welcome widowhood because it brings freedom to serve God and freedom from the tyranny of men (146–47). Widows should devote their lives to prayer, and their prayers are better and wiser than those of married women, since they have renounced the desires of the flesh and escaped the continual fear that wives have of their husbands (147). Eiximenis feels strongly that widows should not remarry; if, however, they are in danger of falling into the sin of lust by committing adultery, they should remarry, because a man makes a better mate than the devil (148).

As part of his exhortation that widows should dress modestly and humbly in black, Eiximenis gets a bit sidetracked in an interesting diatribe against the dress and behavior of some widows of his time:

> Oh! What would St. Jerome say now if he could see our widows wearing hats in the Castilian style, with painted faces and wide shifts, tight over the arms, wearing dresses cut as delicately as those of married women? They wear black only to make themselves appear paler, not out of grief; they attend tournaments and jousts; they pass time at the window, joking and laughing in front of everyone, and they display their venality to whoever wants them or gives them the most. In their houses little or no work is done; rather, they go from their bed to the table, and from the table to the window to joke with everybody, and such are the paternosters and masses for the soul of their dead husband.
>
> Oh! You who desire such a woman, listen to the requiem she offers for her dead husband, for such a one will she make for you when you are in your grave! Leave her your money, taking it from the poor and from your own family, and she will enjoy it with another if she can, when the worms are eating you, and you will not find her saying so much as a pious paternoster for you. Oh fool, oh madman or worse! You see that you have made your testament to the devil, and your wretched soul will remain in grief and misery for a long time to come. . . . (1981, 148–49; our translation)

Eiximenis's treatise on widows is fairly repetitive, as he elaborates on his theme: widows should not remarry, and in support of this he cites canon law; they should withdraw from public life and dedicate themselves to a life of religious devotion (152). He does mention the *any de plor,* in a jibe against widows who can barely wait out the year of mourning before getting married again (152). Eiximenis concludes by assuring the good widow of God's mercy and grace, and that she will be "honrada e . . . coronada en glòria" (153).

Although the information we have about medieval Catalan widows from these wills and letters, as well as from the *Libre de les dones* paints an incomplete picture of the lives and circumstances of these women, it does provide us with a perspective from which to view the widow who is the heroine of the novel, *Curial e Güelfa.*

As *Curial e Güelfa* is not very well known outside the world of Catalan letters, a short synopsis of the plot is in order at this point. The novel is divided into three books. The first tells how Curial, a young man of humble birth, joins the household of the Marquis of Montferrat, whose sister is the beautiful young widow, Güelfa. Güelfa falls in love with Curial and decides to sponsor his knightly education and training. Curial sets out to learn and to prove himself as a knight, and his travels take him to Austria, where he saves the life and honor of a beautiful duchess who has been falsely accused of adultery. As a reward for his intervention, Curial is offered the duchess's beautiful sister Lachesis as his bride, but he refuses her, remembering his love for and responsibility to Güelfa. Güelfa hears of Lachesis's beauty and fears that Curial will succumb to her charms, yet, although they have a brief flirtation, such is not the case. Curial remains true to Güelfa and returns to Montferrat having made a good beginning to his career as a knight.

The second book tells of how Curial sets out to make his name in the world; he has many adventures and is victorious at numerous tournaments. He meets Lachesis again and their mutual attraction is renewed. Güelfa's jealousy is also rekindled and fanned by the gossip of two old men of the court who are envious of Curial; she decides to cease her support of Curial and turns him away when he returns to Montferrat to beg for her favor. Curial, thus rejected, goes to seek the hand of Lachesis in marriage. She, however, weary of waiting for Curial to return her love, has become engaged to the Duke of Orleans. Curial goes back yet again to Montferrat to plead with Güelfa one more time: her refusal is more adamant than ever, and this time she swears an oath that she will forgive Curial only if the entire French court meets with the king and queen in attendance, and they and all true lovers present beg her for mercy in Curial's name.

In the third book, bereft of Güelfa's love and the trappings of the comfortable life to which he had grown accustomed, Curial sets out on a pilgrimage to the Holy Land. On his way back to Italy, he is captured by Moors and sold into slavery in Tripoli, although word reaches Italy and Catalonia that he is dead. Even as a slave, Curial remains handsome and accomplished, and his owner's daughter, a young woman named Camar, falls in love with him. Eventually, she kills herself out of love for Curial, preferring to die rather than to marry the king who has asked for her hand. Upon her death she leaves Curial a huge fortune, which will ultimately buy his freedom and allow him to return to Montferrat. Curial's trials are not yet over, however; Güelfa still refuses to speak to him, even though she is overwhelmed with joy at his safe return. Disillusioned, Curial goes to France, where he leads a dissolute life, frittering away all his time and money on pursuits of the flesh. It takes the intervention of Bacchus himself, appearing to Curial in a dream, to persuade Curial not to squander his erudition and knightly qualities in such a life. Curial then goes into battle to defend Christendom against the Turks, and under the protection of St. George, slays the strongest and most fearsome of all the Turkish warriors. His fame and fortune now at their pinnacle, Curial attends the gathering of the French court at Le Puy and wins the tournament held there; Güelfa has been summoned to attend with her brother and his wife. The king and queen have learned of Güelfa's vow, and, for love of Curial, they and the court assembled there beg her for mercy on his behalf. She accepts Curial as her husband, and the lovers are finally united.

The early years of Güelfa's and Curial's lives are sketched out in a very cursory manner, although we later come to know their most intimate thoughts and feelings. Güelfa's first marriage and widowhood are told in a few lines: she was thirteen when the lord of Milan, a young and noble knight, heard of her beauty and asked for her hand; after long negotiations the marriage was made. Güelfa's husband loved her a great deal, as did his vassals, for her wisdom and discretion. Before they had been married two years, however, Güelfa's husband fell ill with a fever. On his deathbed, "in the presence of all his barons, he made his will and testament decreeing that Güelfa, with or without a husband, should be the Lady of Milan, and that after her the city should pass to whomever she wished; and while he was still alive he made his vassals swear to observe his will" (Gustà 1986, 25; Waley 1982, 3).[3]

The few details the reader is given about Güelfa's husband's will are interesting in light of the wills studied by Vinyoles et al. The novel takes care to record, for example, that Güelfa's husband specifically declared in his will that her inheritance would not in any way be affected should she choose to remarry. (Indeed, Güelfa's husband imposed no conditions on her inheritance whatsoever, a circumstance reflected in only one will of the sample group [Vinyoles et al. 1984, 32].) In addition, he made no attempt to name an heir from his own family, which could occur when the marriage had produced no children (Vinyoles et al. 1984, 34).[4] The circumstances surrounding Güelfa's widowhood thus immediately place her remarriage on the agenda. Indeed, the text begins to show positively how desirable remarriage is for the widow, a point that we will develop further.

After the death of her husband, Güelfa returns to her brother's house. He is fearful that someone might take advantage of her, as she is young, wealthy, and beautiful, and offers her his protection. We have seen that widows often maintained strong ties to their own families, especially after childless marriages, and that is certainly true in Güelfa's case.

When Curial and Güelfa meet, they are clearly destined for each other; the beautiful, wealthy, young widow at loose ends in her brother's house, and the handsome, erudite, young page, whose nobility of spirit is far greater than that of his social class. As the passage describing Güelfa's choice of Curial relates:

> Güelfa, who was young and tender and lacked nothing save only a husband, knew herself to be pretty and much praised and rich and favoured by Fortune, admired and courted by many, and idle. But she saw that her brother had no thought of finding a husband for her, and she did not think it was seemly to ask him for one herself. Nevertheless, she could not resist the natural instincts of the body, which continually troubled her and goaded her without ceasing. She thought to herself that if it so happened that she came to love secretly some excellent young man, as long as nobody was aware of it, this would not be a shameful thing, and that a thousand and more other ladies had done this before her; and that even if some people might guess from signs what they did not know in fact, they would not dare to gossip about so great a lady as she was. And so she allowed her eyes to consider carefully all the young men in her brother's household. Since she was not concerned with blood or wealth, Curial particularly pleased her, above all the rest; and seeing that he was very refined in

his person and noble of heart, and very wise for his years, she thought that, if he had the means, he would become a very worthy man. So she decided to help him (Gustà 1986, 26; Waley 1982, 4).

Thus does Güelfa set her sights on Curial. She begins to spend a great deal of time in his company and quickly falls in love with him.

The quoted passage tells us that Güelfa's motivation for pursuing Curial is sexual desire; we know that she is a widow, that she has had a happy marriage, albeit a brief one, and presumably she has experienced sexual fulfillment with her husband. Now, as a young, attractive, unmarried woman, she decides to seek out a young man to satisfy her appetites. Yet Güelfa then decides to keep her patronage secret from Curial for a time, and even after she reveals to him that she is the one supplying him with money, she does not try to consummate her love for him. Indeed, she says to her steward Melchior, "... my intention is to make him a man, but I do not intend to give him my love but rather to work to make him worthy and valorous by giving him to understand that I love him" (Gustà 1986, 30; Waley 1982, 8).

While physical desire is at the root of Güelfa's passion for Curial, she chooses to dominate him through her superior wealth and social position rather than to yield to him sexually. Her authority over Curial is clearly gratifying to her. This must be why Güelfa takes the trouble to mold and train Curial when she could simply choose from among many potential, and more appropriate, suitors. (She did not fall in love with him at first sight, as the courtly tradition would require; rather, she chose him from among the young men of her brother's household because he was beautiful and intelligent.)

It is thus Güelfa's widowhood and Curial's lack of money and social position that form the dynamic of the relationship between the two. Güelfa, a widow of high social standing, is free to use her wealth as she sees fit and to set whatever terms she wishes for making her own match. Had she not been a widow, she would not have been able to decide for herself how to spend her money (men administer her fortune, but they do not control it) and she would not have possessed the financial means to carry out her sponsorship of Curial. And widowhood is what gives Güelfa her independence; she is subservient to no man. Even her brother can only advise her; he does not control her actions. Widowhood also frees Güelfa from some of the behavioral restrictions imposed by society: for example, she may travel freely and she may be alone with a man without necessarily blemishing her reputation (behavior that would not be condoned in a young, unmarried woman). Yet widowhood is also portrayed in the text as a means toward an end. The text tells us, "Güelfa lacked nothing save only a husband" (Gustà 1986, 26; Waley 1982, 4). Thus Güelfa's youth, beauty, wealth, social position, and capacity for independent action will all ultimately collaborate in the project of restoring Güelfa to the married state. The story will end when Güelfa, whose resources have been exhausted in her quest for Curial's advancement, recognizes her own need for a sponsor and marries the man she had previously supported.

It is important to reiterate that, had Güelfa chosen a lover from her own social class, she could never have controlled him so completely as she controlled Curial. One of the factors that allows Güelfa to dominate and control Curial as she does surely is the class difference between them. Güelfa is obviously conscious of this, just as she is conscious of the fact that what Curial really needs to be worthy of her love is money of his own. These are clearly fifteenth-century values, although the novel is set in the thirteenth century. With the acquisition of wealth not tied to estates and family succession, anyone could rise in social status. Indeed, the merchants of the middle class were powerful members of the society of the time, and in many cases they controlled vast amounts of wealth. The anonymous author of *Curial e Güelfa* reflects important changes in European society with his depiction of a hero who rises above his lowly birth to attain sufficient social status to marry a wealthy aristocrat. Similarly, the idea of an aristocratic woman marrying a man born to a station so far below her own may herald the acceptance of a new social order. And the fact that Güelfa is in no way discouraged from remarrying (indeed, she is portrayed in the text as incomplete until she makes the decision to marry again) indicates that the medieval ideal of chaste widowhood, so strongly supported by Eiximenis little more than a half-century earlier (and upheld in the wills of many medieval Catalan men), may have been challenged by values of greater relevance to the material life of prosperous Catalonia.[5]

There remains to be considered another facet to the control Güelfa exerts over Curial. The author has constructed an elaborate symbolic correspondence within the novel between Güelfa and another character who supposedly decides Curial's eventual fate: Fortune. Fortune is mentioned at the very beginning of the novel, as are her opposites, the "Infortunis" or Misfortunes. She is not really a character at this point, but her introduction at the start, even before we meet Curial or Güelfa, demonstrates her importance to the story. Indeed, the exact words used at her first appearance are repeated at the end of the novel, as if to make absolutely certain that we understand her significance. We are told that those who are loved by Fortune will triumph after infinite misfortunes (Waley 1982, 1; "... alguns *amats de la Fortuna aprés d'infinits infortunis,* sien arribats al port per ells desijat..." [Gustà 1986, 23]). Then, after Curial has risen to the pinnacle of his achievements, we are reminded that he, "favoured by Fortune after infinite misfortunes... won in a single day a wife and a principality" (Waley 1982, 284–85; "... *favorit de la Fortuna aprés d'infinits infortunis...* obtengué principat e muller" [Gustà 1986, 336]).

The first appearance of Fortune as a character in the story of Curial and Güelfa comes toward the end of the second book, when she turns her back on Curial.

> Until that day, Fortune had showed Curial a cheerful and smiling face, although she had been many times pressed and indeed importuned by false, wicked Envy, who always accompanies her. Now she decided to harm Curial with all her power so as to test him and his virtue more than she had been able to do before. Whereas she had formerly granted, freely and generously, all the good things and the prosperity he could desire, it was now her will to harm him, and indeed she was to harm him with all her might and knowledge, as much as she could. (Gustà 1986, 215; Waley 1982, 170)

In this episode, Fortune calls upon the gods to aid and abet her persecution of Curial. She enlists the help of Juno, Neptune, and Pluto; with their support she sends Envy to keep company with Ansaldo and Ambrosio, the two meddling old courtiers, and the Misfortunes to remain with Curial. These actions are mirrored immediately by Ansaldo and Ambrosio, who run to Güelfa with more gossip about Curial and Lachesis, and by Güelfa herself, who vows that unless Curial can meet her impossible challenge, she will never speak to him again.

Just as Fortune has smiled on Curial up to this point, so has Güelfa favored him with her love and support. When Fortune turns her back on Curial, so does Güelfa. This is not mere coincidence. Güelfa directs Curial as if she herself were Fortune, who dominates the lives of those under her influence. Each of them blames Curial's ingratitude for her change of heart. The author's association of Güelfa with Fortune, however, is not a casual one. It provides a structure by means of which the reader can understand the nature and extent of Güelfa's power and how capriciously she uses it.

The human Güelfa and the mythological Fortune have many characteristics in common. The figure of Fortune already had a very long tradition by the time of *Curial e Güelfa*'s composition. In Roman mythology, Fortune was depicted as a goddess whose "changeability was regarded as typifying the fickle unreliability of women" (Pitkin 1984, 138). She was also linked with "*virtus,* human manly energy or capability capable of confronting Fortuna's power" (139).

By the Middle Ages, Fortune had evolved from the personification of capriciousness to that of inexorability; she was no longer open to human influence through supplication. In this sense, the Fortune reflected by Güelfa is closer to the medieval image than to the Roman one. Güelfa is cruel; once she makes a decision, even the most piteous of Curial's supplications cannot make her change her mind.

The parallelism between Güelfa and Fortune becomes obvious again in the third book, when Fortune decides to stop persecuting Curial and to restore him to her favor. This scene, however, follows one in which Güelfa listens, secretly pleased, to a soldier praising Curial's deeds. Here, the change in Güelfa's attitude toward Curial seems to determine that the mythological Fortune will cease her torment of Curial, and not the reverse. It appears that Güelfa is the one who really turns the wheel.

The suggestion that Güelfa is capable of making decisions binding not only on Curial, a member of a lower social class than her own, but also on so powerful a figure as the mythological Fortune, points in the direction of a woman who enjoys extensive authority in her society.[6] This is certainly an unusual circumstance for the Middle Ages, and in order to account for it, we must again return to the fact that the heroine of the novel is a widow. On her own as a result of her husband's death, she has acquired not only her husband's wealth, but also much of his "manly" status as well. As Erler and Kowaleski point out (1988), married women labored under the most severe handicaps during the Middle Ages because their husbands, as heads of households, held the fullest rights. Yet as widows, these same women enjoyed many rights and participated actively in the public community, for *they* were now the heads of the household (3). Thus the allusion to Fortune appears to be a literary pretext for elaborating on the character who truly controls Curial's life:

Güelfa, the widow. The author is very consistent in this use of the motif of Fortune.

Yet Güelfa does not actually turn the wheel throughout the novel. At a certain point, she begins to lose her authority. This theme is developed on a mythological level when, immediately before Fortune and Güelfa restore Curial to their favor, he has a dream-vision in which the Roman god Bacchus appears to him, admonishing him to abandon his profligate life-style. In the dream, Hercules appears with Bacchus, a significant detail when we recall the Renaissance theme of the struggle between Fortune and Hercules. Hercules, a symbol of heroic masculinity, fought mightily against the inexorability of Fortune. This appearance of Hercules is a premonition of Curial's forthcoming victory over Güelfa. On the level of their love relationship, Güelfa's loss of authority can be attributed to Curial's evolution and growing maturity; he has become more able in his struggle against his misfortunes.

This leads us to consider the Renaissance transformation of the figure of Fortune. In the Renaissance model, it was more difficult for Fortune to influence the course of human life at maturity.

> The power of external forces over us is greatest when the self is still undeveloped, in childhood and youth. It recedes as the self awakens, strengthens, and becomes autonomous; it is forced to give way before the striving of man's cultural and intellectual energy. Thus, it is *virtus* . . . that ultimately conquer[s] the opposing powers of the heavens, as manhood is fully achieved. (Pitkin 1984, 142–43)

Güelfa must give way before Curial, for he has grown up and become a man with his own resources, a knight admired by all for his courage and strength. He has been transformed into a wealthy man and, more importantly, a perfect knight; he now controls his own destiny.

In the Renaissance concept of Fortune, it is possible for people to overcome the inevitability of Fortune. Curial accomplishes this on the strength of his own *virtus*. That his *virtus* is being tested is made explicit at Fortuna's first appearance, when she sends the Misfortunes to accompany him, saying:

> I shall see whether he can feel gratitude, for he takes for granted that all the prosperity and the good things that he has had and possesses have come to him through his own merit, not giving thanks to

the giver, nor does he think that he could ever be without them. If he bears with equal heart both myself and you [the Misfortunes], I shall know his virtue, for even if he has much to do in enduring good things and knowing how to behave in prosperity, nevertheless it is misfortunes which demonstrate the virtue of men. (Gustà 1986, 215; Waley 1982, 170)

By means of his success in the process of chivalric perfection, he succeeds in overcoming Güelfa's domination of him. Güelfa set in motion her own downfall when she set forth her plan to transform Curial into a perfect knight. Although ultimately she derives some benefit from the transformation in that she marries this personification of the ideal knight whom she has created to fulfill all her desires, at the same time she loses the last of the special abilities that her widowhood has conferred upon her.

The concept of transformation is an important key that can help us understand the complex character of Güelfa. One of her most striking characteristics is her fidelity to Curial, yet, at the same time, she seems fickle and changeable in her attitude toward him. She is remarkably constant in her love for him over a period of many years; she never even considers another lover, which is somewhat unusual in view of the carnal appetites that supposedly underlie her choice of Curial as a lover in the first place. On the other hand, she acts on whim, offering Curial her favor and then withholding it capriciously. She plays the role of the *belle dame sans merci* convincingly, but is it her true nature?

The phenomenon of transformation or metamorphosis can explain the seeming contradictions in the character of Güelfa; as the protagonist of the novel, she undergoes a series of changes. She is just a child when she first appears (she is thirteen when mentioned next). She is married and widowed; she acquires wealth and authority; she returns to her brother's home and meets Curial, who will be at the heart of all the subsequent changes in her.

We have mentioned the constancy of Güelfa's love for Curial; despite the trials she sets for him, despite her rejection of him that sends him into exile, she continues to love him. But Güelfa's love changes throughout the course of the novel, as her circumstances and even her very character change. Indeed, it is these changes, or metamorphoses, that ultimately lead to the resolution of the conflicts in the relationship of the two lovers.

The author makes explicit the idea of metamorphosis in the third book of *Curial e Güelfa,* during Fortune's name-dropping tirade against the gods who refuse to help her persecute Curial. She begs Venus's mother Dione to come to her assistance, reminding Dione of the favorable destiny she, Fortune, has bestowed upon her and her daughter. Fortune enumerates the many exploits of Venus, culminating in her transformation of "the women of Cyprus into cows, and a stone image into a noble and most beautiful woman" (Gustà 1986, 256; Waley 1982, 207). These are references to book 10 of the *Metamorphoses,* where Ovid tells the story of the wicked Propoetides of Cyprus, who indulged in human sacrifice. Venus, deeply offended, turned them into cattle. The legend that immediately follows that of the Propoetides, both here and in the *Metamorphoses,* is that of Pygmalion.

There are obvious parallels between the story of Curial and Güelfa and the mythical tale of Pygmalion. According to Ovid, Pygmalion was a sculptor who lived in Cyprus. He had witnessed the wickedness of some of the girls who lived there, and resolved to remain celibate rather than take such a woman to be his wife. He sculpted a beautiful ivory statue, in the form of a woman, and fell in love with his own work of art. His creation was so beautiful and so lifelike that, at times when he touched it, even he could not believe that it was not alive. In his obsession he began to talk to her, bring her gifts, caress her, kiss her; he imagined that she returned his caresses and his love. During the festival of Venus he made offerings to the goddess of love and asked that she provide him with a wife just like his beautiful ivory statue. Venus knew that he was in love with the statue itself and brought the ivory woman to life under his touch. She returned Pygmalion's love, and Venus herself witnessed their marriage. The story ends with the birth of their daughter, Paphos, nine months later and we assume that they lived happily ever after.

There are some similarities in the two stories of love. In each tale, a person lonely for love sets out to create a worthy recipient for that love. In each case, once the creation has taken shape, has been formed and perfected, the creator finds that he or she cannot have what he or she really wants.

In the Pygmalion story, the sculptor has created his image of the perfect woman, but his creation is lifeless. Güelfa has created in Curial her ideal knight and lover; so long as he is dependent on her, however, he has no life of his own. In each case, some external force, invoked or occasioned by the creator, brings the creation to life: for Pygmalion's ideal woman, it is Venus, the goddess of love, for whose intervention

Pygmalion prayed. For Curial, it is more complex: on one level, the force is Fortune, reflecting Güelfa. Güelfa has brought about Curial's captivity by her rejection of him, and has thereby been instrumental in Curial's acquisition of wealth, which will free him from her control. Fortune takes the credit for this, but realizes that she cannot complete the metamorphosis without Venus's help; therefore, Fortune herself goes to the temple of Venus in Cyprus and prays for the goddess's help in turning her wheel (Gustà 1986, 308–10; Waley 1982, 257–58). The external force that ultimately brings both creations to life is Venus.

This vivification, this metamorphosis, is the pivotal point in the relationship of Güelfa and Curial in the novel, as it clearly is in the Pygmalion myth, too. The lovers have moved from an abnormal situation, an unnatural relationship in each case, to a normal situation or natural relationship: from dissatisfaction to satisfaction through the metamorphosis of both creator and creation. Perhaps the unhappiness of the creators stems from their attempted usurpation of creative power that does not rightfully belong to them as mortal beings, but to a divine creator (God or goddess).

The structural progression of both the Pygmalion myth and the story of Curial and Güelfa can be summarized as:

1. dissatisfaction,
2. creation of a being to satisfy one's needs,
3. inability of the creation to satisfy,
4. metamorphosis in creator,
5. metamorphosis in creation, and
6. satisfaction.

In the novel, Güelfa's dissatisfaction with her lot begins after she has already undergone several important changes in her young life: she has been married and left a widow, a circumstance that empowers her to undertake the shaping of Curial's destiny, to create for herself a perfect knight and perfect mate. Her condition as a widow provides her with everything she needs to be happy, except one thing: again we refer to the novel's declaration that "Güelfa . . . lacked nothing save only a husband" (Gustà 1986, 26; Waley 1982, 4).

In this state of dissatisfaction, Güelfa chooses a young page in her brother's household as a likely candidate for her sponsorship. We have already described the conflicts embedded in Güelfa's patronage of Curial from the beginning—their class differences, his poverty—and from a purely practical point of view, she would have received more immediate gratification from a more suitable young man. Perhaps she was disillusioned, like Pygmalion, with the choices available to her. In any event, Güelfa, in her state of dissatisfaction, has chosen the clay from which she will form her creation. She has chosen carefully: Curial is already perceived to be honest and loyal, attractive, and reasonably well educated, particularly so for a servant. Güelfa embarks on her project, and lavishes all the resources of her wealth on outfitting Curial and training him to be a knight.

Once her creation has been shaped and refined to her taste, Güelfa discovers to her dismay that he is pleasing to other women as well: a beautiful, young, German noblewoman named Lachesis falls in love with Curial while he is away from Güelfa. Curiously, Lachesis herself is the only one who defends the relationship of Curial and Güelfa.

> . . . if Curial is loved by Güelfa I am glad, and I am grateful to her, for Güelfa caused him to rise and has made him a man, and has placed him and maintains him in the position and estate he enjoys. So who can reproach Curial if he loves Güelfa? Indeed, let who will blame him, I do not, especially as I know Güelfa to be one of the most honourable ladies in the world. Humanity and virtue have moved her to give him advancement on account of his merits. I have never heard anyone, wise or foolish, speak dishonourably of them. (Gustà 1986, 190; Waley 1982, 147)

Lachesis's role in the novel is an interesting one: she is the third corner of a love triangle, the rival for Curial's affections who brings to the surface Güelfa's jealousy and insecurity about Curial's love for her. Lachesis's very name indicates that she is part of the grand design for Güelfa's relationship with Curial: Lachesis was one of the three mythical Fates, sisters who spun, measured, and cut the threads of human lives. The author is anxious for us not to miss the connection. Early on, we learn that Lachesis's sister, the Duchess of Austria, whose honor Curial has restored, is named Clotho (Gustà 1986, 56; Waley 1982, 31). A little later the picture is completed, when Melchior says to Curial: "that damsel may have the name of Lachesis, but she is surely Atropos, and in time you will discover this" (Gustà 1986, 61; Waley 1982, 36). Lachesis's role as Fate is to decide the destiny of each man, by determining the length of his lot of thread. The novel's Lachesis is not the ultimate arbiter of the fate of Curial and Güelfa, but she has an important part in the playing out of that destiny. Our Lachesis is necessary to the evolution of both Güelfa as creator and Curial as her creation: she is one of the reasons for Curial's failure to satisfy his creator/protectress. He is on the verge of falling in love with Lachesis and accepting her father's offer of his daughter in marriage when he is reminded of his obligations to Güelfa; things will never be quite the same between the two of them, however, because, although Curial has returned to Güelfa, he has taken his first, hesitant step as a man, toward emotional independence of Güelfa.

At this point, Güelfa's creation is clearly unable to satisfy her needs: Curial's life away from her has little to do with her own daily life. She thrills to his exploits vicariously, she fears for his life in his knightly battles and fears for her own heart when she hears of Curial's friendship with Lachesis. But he is not yet a knight, and has not attained the social standing that would allow their relationship to be fulfilled. It has not turned out as she had hoped and they have reached something of an impasse. The malicious gossip of the two old men wounds Güelfa: she believes that Curial has abandoned her for Lachesis and she decides to withdraw her financial support of him. She justifies this change by telling herself that her transformation of Curial is complete: "Curial was now rich and in high favour, and what she had intended to do was now accomplished" (Gustà 1986, 218; Waley 1982, 173). This is not really the case, however, and there will be repercussions from Güelfa's change of heart and her decision to alter the dynamics of their relationship.

This, then, is the moment of Güelfa's metamorphosis: she has begun something that she is unwilling to finish, and by turning her back on Curial and sending him away, she sets in motion a chain of events that will ultimately resolve the conflicts in their relationship. By rejecting Curial, she makes both herself and him miserable; even Lachesis gives up on Curial and marries the duke of Orleans, who has long loved her and whose proposal she has put off, hoping to win Curial. Güelfa's metamorphosis is motivated by baser instincts, by her insecurities and her belief in the old men's gossip. She refuses to heed either her companion, Festa, or the abbess, who are her real friends and who try to tell her the truth about Curial's devotion to her. Similarly, she ignores the advice of her faithful steward, Melchior de Pando, and rebuffs Curial's attempts to see her and speak with her. Her repudiation of him is complete.

Güelfa's metamorphosis, her change of heart, brings about a reaction of change on the part of Curial. What she has done for him has been external, even superficial, since his qualities of honesty and gentility were always within him, even before she took him as her protégé. Her sponsorship of him, however, has introduced him to the life he was spiritually, if not socially, born to. Since he no longer enjoys Güelfa's patronage, he must fend for himself and so he goes off to sea. Thus begins the series of adventures that bring about the final metamorphosis of Curial: his captivity in North Africa, his acquisition of wealth, and his triumphant return to favor at the court of the king of France. The change in Güelfa (creator) produces a change in Curial (creation), a reaction to her action. These changes in Curial's position and wealth complement his natural nobility of spirit and knightly qualities, and all these characteristics in combination permit Curial to succeed in the final trial Güelfa sets for him: her insistence that the king and queen and the entire French court beg her to forgive Curial. This they do, and Güelfa finally capitulates.

The transformations are complete: both creator and creation have undergone metamorphosis. Güelfa has lost the control she once had over her creation, as he has become empowered by circumstances external to that control, although she is the one who set them in motion. Pygmalion's creation, brought to life by Venus, was no longer the statue he had given shape to: she had taken on a life of her own. Güelfa's ideal knight, whom she guided and formed, has ultimately gained his independence from her; in so doing, he has gained what she has lost.

In sum, although the novel is called *Curial e Güelfa,* Güelfa is, in fact, the work's true protagonist. Not solely an inspiration for her knight, as in the Provençal tradition and in other novels of chivalry, she effects a control over her knight that is more "real" than conventional. Güelfa is a widow and, as we have seen, this contributes to the dynamic of her relationship with Curial. Widowhood is what allows Güelfa to behave as an independent woman. She is aware of her special capacities as a widow and she takes advantage of them. She devises a plan to create a man who fulfills her needs and desires and, after she creates him, she determines the course of his life by casting herself in the role of a capricious and inexorable Fortune. Nevertheless, Güelfa does not remain in such a position of authority forever. The novel makes clear that while the perquisites of widowhood may enhance a woman's ability to make decisions binding on others, this is an extraordinary and temporary circumstance. Moreover, the work strongly suggests that the effects of widowhood may be best employed in the pursuit of a new husband. Güelfa, we learn, has used her special capacities as a widow to develop an ideal person who can restore to her the perfect state for a woman in her society: marriage.

It is interesting to note, finally, that Güelfa's decision to remarry is a voluntary one. Thus, the novel ultimately gives us a *woman* who freely and willfully chooses to restore the traditional, male-favoring balance of control and authority to her society.

NOTES

1. For a full discussion of the date of composition and authorship of *Curial e Güelfa*, see Espadaler 1984. It is generally agreed that the novel shares the basic premise of its plot with Antoine de la Sale's *Le petit Jehan de Saintré* (1456), but the similarities are quite superficial and definitely do not extend to characterization.

2. See, for example: Mitre Fernández 1983; Pérez de Tudela y Velasco 1983; Vigil 1986 (while she does not deal specifically with the Middle Ages, Vigil does refer to medieval sources as well as sixteenth- and seventeenth-century ones; because the novel under study dates from the mid-fifteenth century, we feel the material is relevant); Voltes and Voltes 1986.

3. This and all other quotations from *Curial e Güelfa* are taken from the English translation by Waley; the page number from the Catalan edition by Gustà is also given.

4. Vinyoles et al. also mention one will in which a wife made her husband swear, within the document, that he would fulfill her wishes to the letter (1984, 34). This echoes Güelfa's husband's insistence before he dies that his vassals swear to uphold his will.

5. Duby argues that, within the feudal system, the royal obligation to protect widows and orphans led to efforts on the part of medieval society to reinstate widows within the boundaries of conjugality—i.e., to find husbands or families for them (1988, 122). Yet there were other reasons for encouraging widows—especially wealthy widows—to remarry. See Hanawalt in this volume.

6. See Rosaldo 1974 for further discussion of this concept of authority.

BIBLIOGRAPHY

Díez de Salazar, Luis Miguel. "La mujer vasco-navarra en la normativa jurídica (S. XII–XIV)." In *Actas de las II jornadas de investigación interdisciplinaria: Las mujeres medievales y su ámbito jurídico,* ed. Cristina Segura Graiño,

95–114. Madrid: Seminario de Estudios de la Mujer, Universidad Autónoma de Madrid, 1983.

Duby, Georges. *Mâle Moyen Age.* N.p.: Nouvelle Bibliothèque Scientifique, Flammarion, 1988.

Eiximenis, Francesc. *Lo libre de les dones.* 2 vols. Ed. Frank Naccarato. Barcelona: Curial Edicions Catalanes, 1981.

Epistolari del segle XV: Recull de cartes privades. Ed. Francesc Martorell i Trabal. Els Nostres Clàssics, no. 9. Barcelona: Editorial Barcino, 1926.

Erler, Mary, and Maryanne Kowaleski, eds. *Women and Power in the Middle Ages.* Athens, Ga.: University of Georgia Press, 1988.

Espadaler, Anton. *Una reina per a Curial.* Barcelona: Quaderns Crema, 1984.

Gustà, Marina, ed. *Curial e Güelfa.* 2d ed. Barcelona: Edicions 62 i "la Caixa," 1986.

Labarge, Margaret Wade. *A Small Sound of the Trumpet: Women in Medieval Life.* Boston: Beacon Press, 1986.

Lucas, Angela M. *Women in the Middle Ages: Religion, Marriage, and Letters.* Brighton: Harvester Press, 1983.

Mitre Fernández, Emilio. "Mujer, matrimonio y vida marital en las Cortes Castellano-leonesas de la Baja Edad Media." In *Actas de las II jornadas de investigación interdisciplinaria: Las mujeres medievales y su ámbito jurídico,* ed. Cristina Segura Graiño, 79–86. Madrid: Seminario de Estudios de la Mujer, Universidad Autónoma de Madrid, 1983.

Ovid. *Metamorphoses.* 4th ed. Ed. William Anderson. Leipzig: Teubner, 1988.

Pérez de Tudela y Velasco, María Isabel. "La mujer castellano-leonesa del pleno medioevo: Perfiles literarios, estatuto jurídico y situación económica." In *Actas de las II jornadas de investigación interdisciplinaria: Las mujeres medievales y su ámbito jurídico,* ed. Cristina Segura Graiño, 57–77. Madrid: Seminario de Estudios de la Mujer, Universidad Autónoma de Madrid, 1983.

Pitkin, Hanna F. *Fortune is a Woman.* Los Angeles: University of California Press, 1984.

Rosaldo, Michelle. "Women, Culture, and Society: A Theoretical Overview." In *Women, Culture, and Society,* ed. Michelle Rosaldo and Louise Lamphere, 17–42. Stanford: Stanford University Press, 1974.

Vigil, Mariló. *La vida de las mujeres en los siglos XVI y XVII.* Madrid: Siglo XXI de España Editores, 1986.

Vinyoles, Teresa María, and Equip Broida. "La viudez, ¿triste o feliz estado?" In *Actas de las III jornadas de investigación interdisciplinaria: Las mujeres en las ciudades medievales,* ed. Cristina Segura Graiño, 27–41. Madrid: Seminario de Estudios de la Mujer, Universidad Autónoma de Madrid, 1984.

Voltes, María José, and Pedro Voltes. *Las mujeres en la historia de España.* Barcelona: Planeta, 1986.

Waley, Pamela, trans. *Curial and Guelfa.* London: Allen and Unwin, 1982.

The Contributors

Heather M. Arden is professor of Medieval French Literature and Language and Women's Studies at the University of Cincinnati. She is the author of *Fool's Plays: A Study of Satire in the Scottie* (Cambridge University Press, 1980), of *The Romance of the Rose* (Twayne, 1987), and of articles on women in medieval French literature.

Judith M. Bennett is associate professor of History at the University of North Carolina, Chapel Hill. In addition to her book, *Women in the Medieval English Countryside: Gender and Household in Brigstock before the Plague* (Oxford University Press, 1987), she has published articles in such journals as the *Journal of Interdisciplinary History, Signs: A Journal of Women in Culture and Society, Feminist Studies,* and *Gender and History.* A coeditor of *Sisters and Workers in the Middle Ages* (University of Chicago Press, 1989), she is now working on a study of women in the English brewing industry, ca. 1200–1700.

James A. Brundage is Ahmanson-Murphy Professor of History at the University of Kansas. He is the author of numerous books on medieval history, including *The Crusades; The Chronicle of Henry of Livonia; Medieval Canon Law and the Crusader;* and, most recently, *Law, Sex, and Christian Society in Medieval Europe* (University of Chicago Press, 1987).

Ann Morton Crabb teaches history at Virginia Commonwealth University. She is the author of *A Renaissance Widow and Her Family: The Strozzi of Florence* and has presented papers on marriage and motherhood in fifteenth-century Florence.

Liliane Dulac is *Maître des conférences de langue et littérature médiévales* at the Université Paul Valéry, Montpellier, France. Her publications include *Christine de Pizan et le malheur des "vrais amans"* and numerous other studies of the medieval French writer. She is preparing *Autour de Christine de Pizan,* a collection of essays by diverse hands (with Bernard Ribémont).

Clara Estow is associate professor and chair of the Department of Hispanic Studies at the University of Massachusetts, Boston. She is the author of *Pedro el Cruel de Castilla, 1350–1369.* She has also written numerous articles on medieval and modern Spanish literature and history.

Thelma Fenster is associate professor of French and director of the Medieval Studies Program at Fordham University. She has translated Christine de Pizan's *Book of the Duke of True Lovers* (lyric poetry by N. Margolis; Persea, 1991), of which she has also completed a new edition. Her other new Christine editions/translations appear in *Poems of Cupid: Christine de Pizan's "Epistre au dieu d'Amours" and "Dit de la Rose"; Thomas Hoccleve's "The Letter of Cupid"; with George Sewell's "The Proclamation of Cupid"* (with Mary Erler; Brill, 1990).

Philip O. Gericke is professor of Spanish at the University of California, Riverside. His writings on medieval Spanish literature have included studies on epic and ballad poetry, the *Libro de Buen Amor,* and such fifteenth-century works as the *Vençimiento del Mundo,* the *Invencionario,* and the *Laberinto de Fortuna.* He is currently preparing an edition of the *Invencionario.*

Barbara A. Hanawalt is professor of History at the University of Minnesota. She is the author of *Crime in East Anglia in the Fourteenth Century: Norfolk Gaol Delivery Rolls, 1307–1316* (Norfolk Record Society, vol. 44); *Crime and Conflict in English Communities, 1300–1348* (Harvard University Press, 1979); *The Ties that Bound: Peasant Families in Medieval England* (Oxford University Press, 1986); and of numerous articles on women and families in medieval England. She is also editor of and contributor to *Women and Work in Preindustrial Europe* (Indiana University Press, 1986).

Louise Mirrer is professor of Spanish and Comparative Literature at Fordham University and visiting professor of Spanish at the University of California, Los Angeles. She is the author of *The Language of Evaluation: A Sociolinguistic Approach to the Story of Pedro el Cruel in Ballad and Chronicle* (Purdue University Monographs in Romance Languages, John Benjamins, 1986), as well as articles on medieval Spanish language and literature. She is currently writing a book on women and "others" (Jews and Muslims) in medieval Castilian literature.

Harry A. Miskimin is professor of History at Yale University, former chairman of the Department, and director of Graduate Studies in Economic History. He is the author of *Money, Prices, and Foreign Exchange in Fourteenth-Century France* (Yale University Press, 1963); *The Economy of Early Renaissance Europe, 1300–1460* (Prentice-Hall, 1969); *The Economy of Later Renaissance Europe, 1460–1600* (Cambridge University Press, 1977); *Money and Power in Fifteenth-Century France* (Yale University Press, 1984); and coeditor of *The Medieval City* (Yale University Press, 1977). He has written numerous articles on medieval and Renaissance French economic history and is general editor of the Cambridge University series, The Economic Civilization of Europe.

Linda E. Mitchell is assistant professor of history at Alfred University and holds the Ph.D. from Indiana University. She is presently working on a book based on her dissertation on thirteenth-century noble widows.

Montserrat Piera is assistant professor at Temple University. She has presented papers on Catalan literature at the Medieval Institute of Western Michigan University, the Kentucky Foreign Language Conference, and the Canadian Association of Hispanists. She recently finished her dissertation, which studies the generic transformations in *Curial e Güelfa.*

Donna M. Rogers is assistant professor of Hispanic Languages and Literatures at Pennsylvania State University and visiting professor at Queen's University (Kingston, Ontario). Her research interests include medieval Catalan and Castilian literature and Romance historical linguistics. She is currently at work on a critical edition of Francesc Eiximenis's *Regiment de la cosa pública.*

Joel T. Rosenthal is professor of History at SUNY–Stony Brook. He is the author of *The Estates and Finances of Richard, Duke of York* (University of Nebraska Press, 1965); *The Training of an Elite Group: English Bishops in the Fifteenth Century* (American Philosophical Society Transactions, 1970); *The Purchase of Paradise* (Routledge and Kegan Paul, 1972); *Angles, Angels, and Conquerors* (Random House, 1973); *Nobles and the Noble Life* (Barnes and Noble, 1976); *Anglo-Saxon History: An Annotated Bibliography, 450–1066* (AMS Press, 1985); as well as editor of several books. He has also written numerous articles on medieval English history.

Cheryl Tallan recently received the M.A. in Interdisciplinary Studies from York University, Ontario. She compiled a bibliography, "Medieval Jewish Women in History, Law, Literature, and Art," which appeared in the *Medieval Feminist Newsletter.* Her article, "Medieval Jewish Widows: Their Control of Resources," appeared in *Jewish History 5,* no. 1 (1991). She has presented papers on medieval Jewish widows for the Association for Jewish Studies, the International Congress on Medieval Studies, and the World Congress of Jewish studies.

Louise O. Vasvari is professor of Comparative Literature and Linguistics at SUNY-Stony Brook. She has been an NEH Fellow and is the author of two books on Juan de Mena as well as numerous articles on Romance literatures, translation theory, and linguistics. She is currently at work on a book on popular culture and literary culture in the *Libro de Buen Amor.*

Index